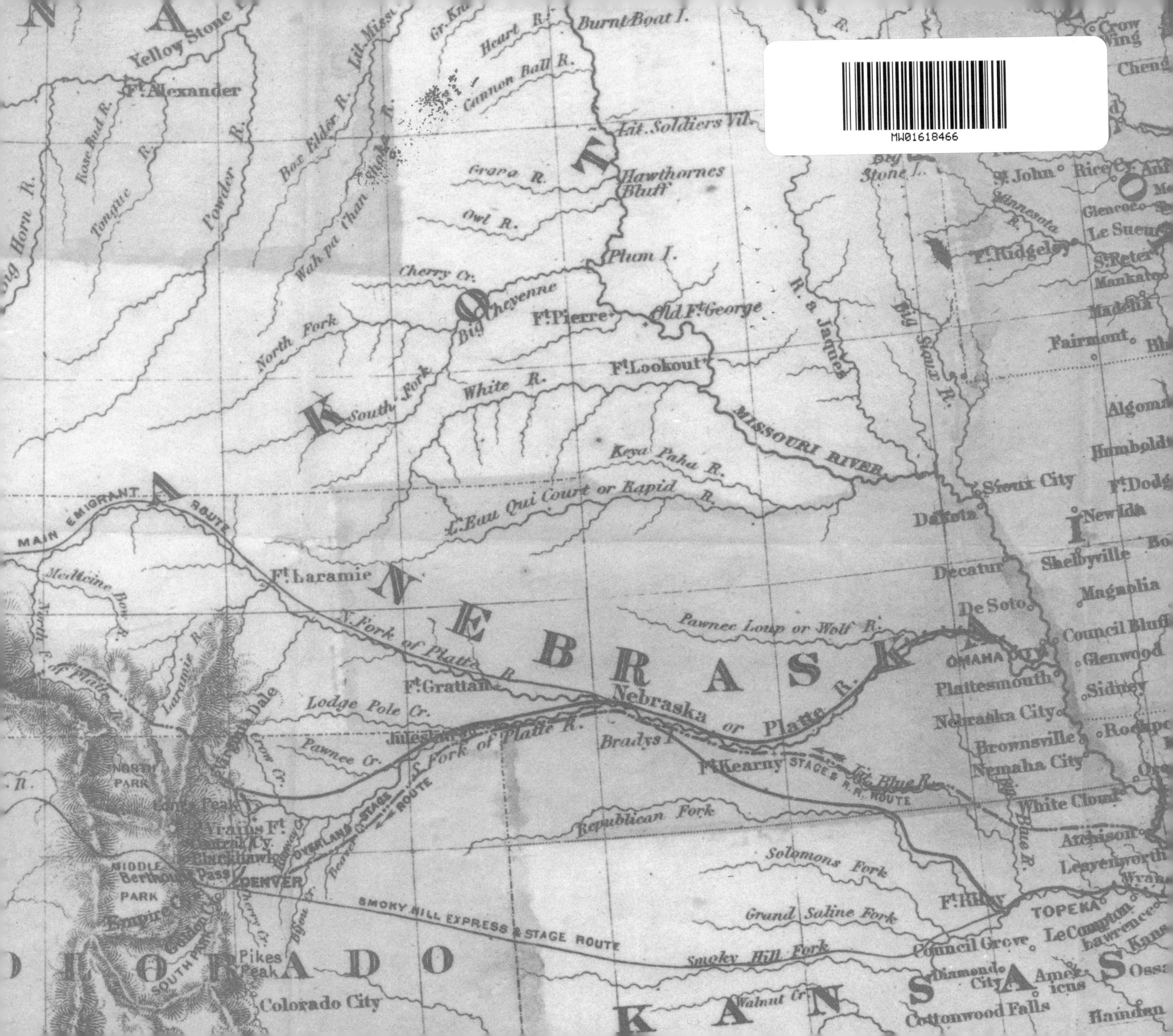

Yellow Stone
Ft. Alexander
Rose Bud R.
Tongue R.
Powder R.
Box Elder R.
Lit. Missi
Heart R.
Burnt Boat I.
Cannon Ball R.
Lit. Soldiers Vil.
Hawthornes Bluff
Grand R.
Owl R.
Plum I.
Wah pa Chan
Cherry Cr.
Big Cheyenne
Ft. Pierre
Old Ft. George
North Fork
South Fork
White R.
Ft. Lookout
R. a Jaques
Big Sioux R.
Big Stone L.
St. John
Rice Cr.
Minnesota R.
Glencoe
Le Sueur
Ft. Ridgeley
St. Peter
Mankato
Madelia
Fairmont
Algoma
Humboldt
Ft. Dodge
MISSOURI RIVER
Keya Paha R.
L. Eau Qui Court or Rapid R.
Sioux City
Dakota
New Ida
Shelbyville
Decatur
Magnolia
De Soto
Council Bluffs
Glenwood
OMAHA CITY
Plattesmouth
Sidney
Nebraska City
Rockport
Brownsville
Nemaha City
White Cloud
Atchison
Leavenworth
MAIN EMIGRANT ROUTE
Ft. Laramie
Medicine Bow R.
North F. of Platte R.
Laramie R.
N. Fork of Platte R.
Pawnee Loup or Wolf R.
N E B R A S K A
Ft. Grattan
Nebraska or Platte R.
Lodge Pole Cr.
Julesburg
S. Fork of Platte R.
Bradys I.
Ft. Kearny
STAGE & R.R. ROUTE
Lit. Blue R.
Pawnee Cr.
Crow Cr.
NORTH PARK
Vrains Ft.
Black Hawk
OVERLAND STAGE ROUTE
Beaver Cr.
Republican Fork
Solomons Fork
MIDDLE PARK
Berthoud Pass
DENVER
Empire City
Golden City
Cherry Cr.
Bijou Cr.
SMOKY HILL EXPRESS & STAGE ROUTE
Grand Saline Fork
Ft. Riley
TOPEKA
Lecompton
Lawrence
Council Grove
Smoky Hill Fork
Pikes Peak
SOUTH PARK
Colorado City
Diamond City
Americus
Cottonwood Falls
Walnut Cr.
K A N S A S

The Anatomy of Nature

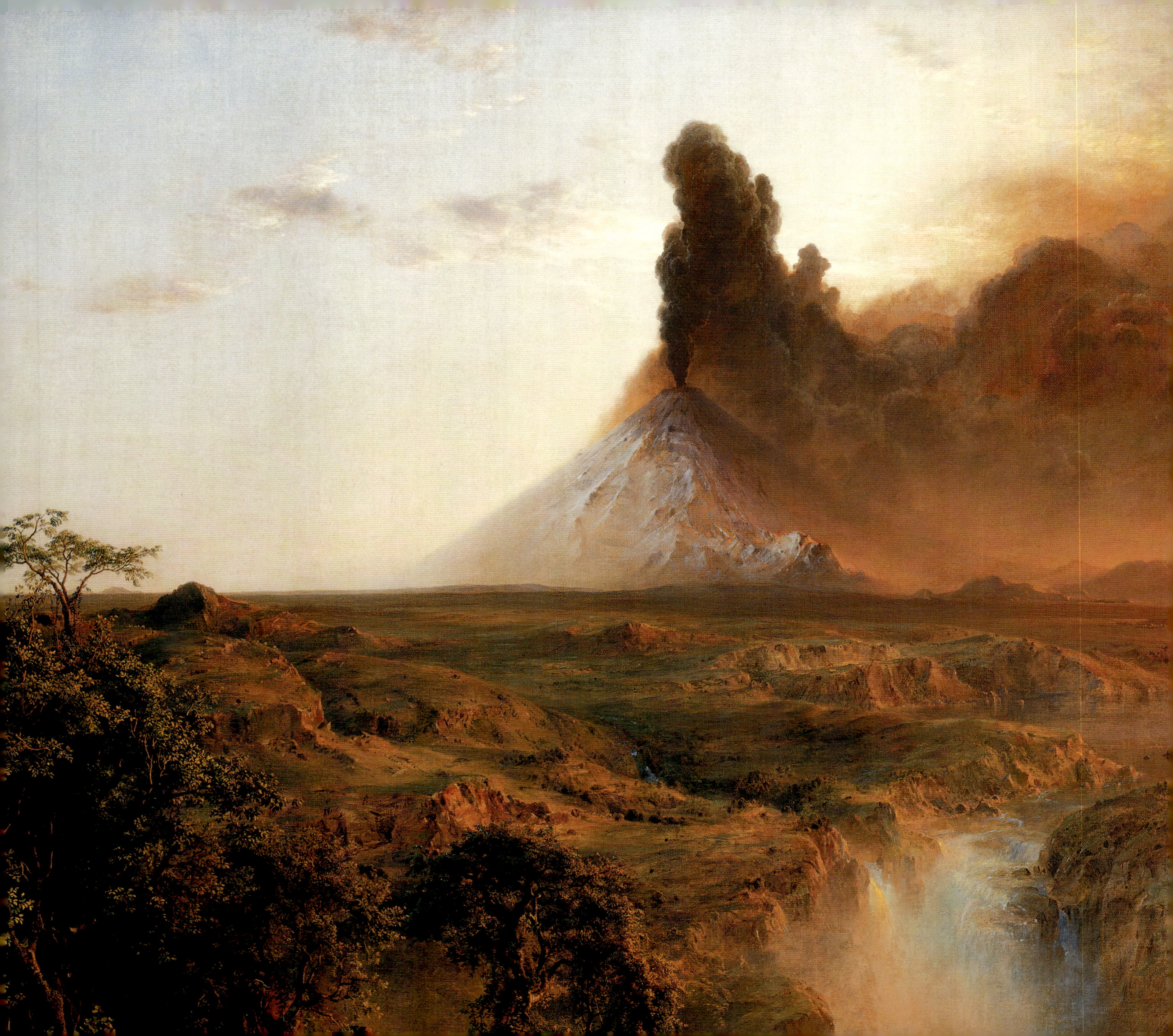

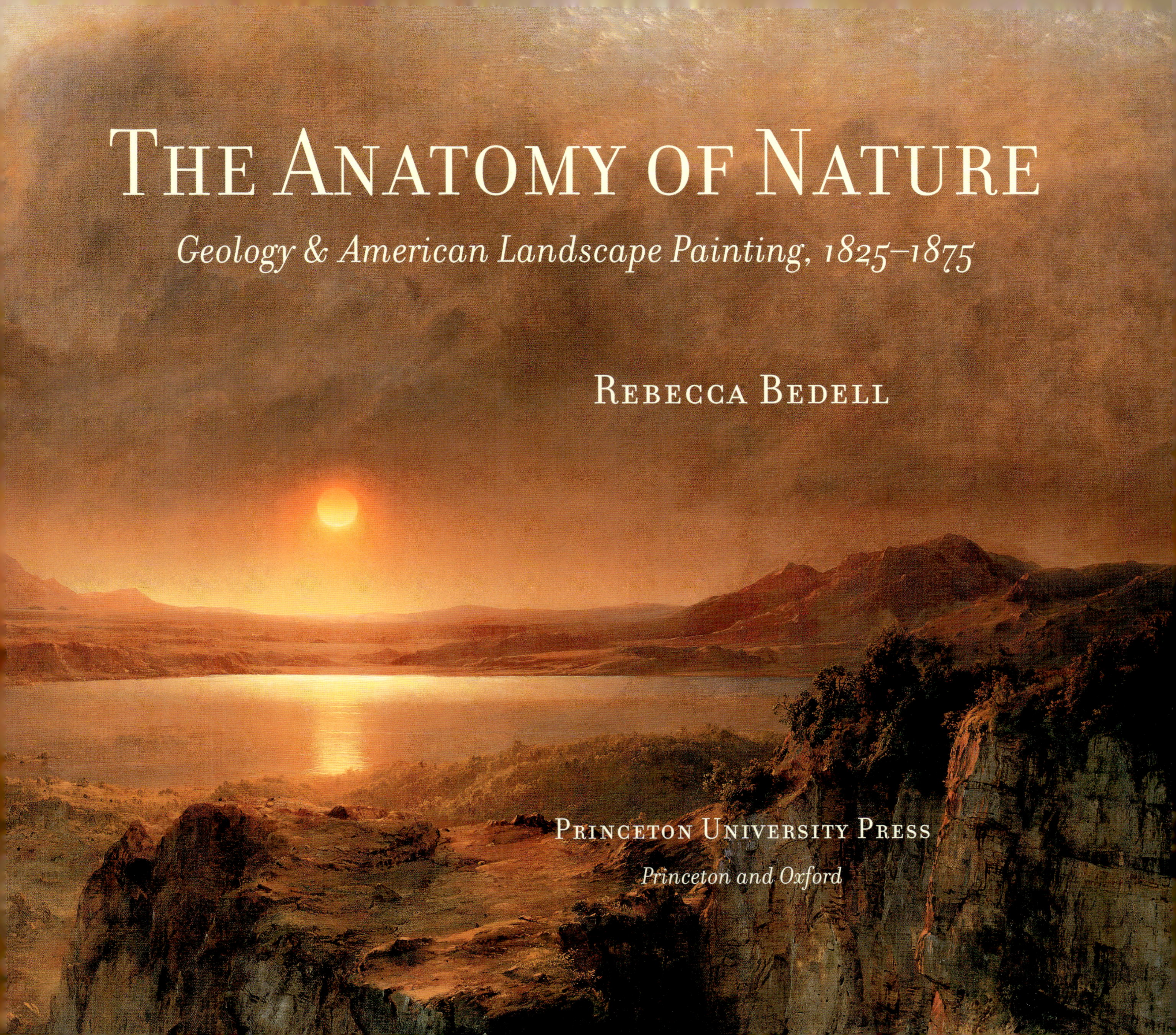

The Anatomy of Nature

Geology & American Landscape Painting, 1825–1875

Rebecca Bedell

Princeton University Press
Princeton and Oxford

Cover: Thomas Moran, *The Grand Canyon of the Yellowstone*, 1872 (detail of Fig. 71)
Binding: Thomas Cole's fossil and rock collection (detail of Fig. 5)
Endpapers: Map of the Territories and Pacific States. Engraving by J. H. Goldthwait, 1865. From Samuel Bowles, *Across the Continent* (S. Bowles and Company, 1869)
Frontispiece: Frederic Church, *Cotopaxi*, 1862 (detail of Fig. 41)

Published by Princeton University Press
41 William Street, Princeton, New Jersey 08540
In the United Kingdom:
Princeton University Press
3 Market Place, Woodstock, Oxfordshire OX20 1SY
www.pup.princeton.edu

Publication of this book has been made possible in part by grants from the Millard Meiss Publication Fund of the College Art Association of America and the Wellesley College Faculty Awards Program through the Mildred McAfee Horton Fund.

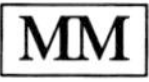

Printed in Hong Kong
10 9 8 7 6 5 4 3 2 1

Library of Congress Cataloging-in-Publication Data

Bedell, Rebecca Bailey.
The anatomy of nature: geology & American landscape painting, 1825–1875 / Rebecca Bedell, p. cm.
Includes bibliographical references and index.
ISBN 0-691-07463-1 (alk. paper)
1. Landscape painting, American. 2. Landscape painting—19th century—United States. 3. Geology in art. I. Title.

ND1351.5 .B43 2001
758'.1'097309034—dc21 00-068691

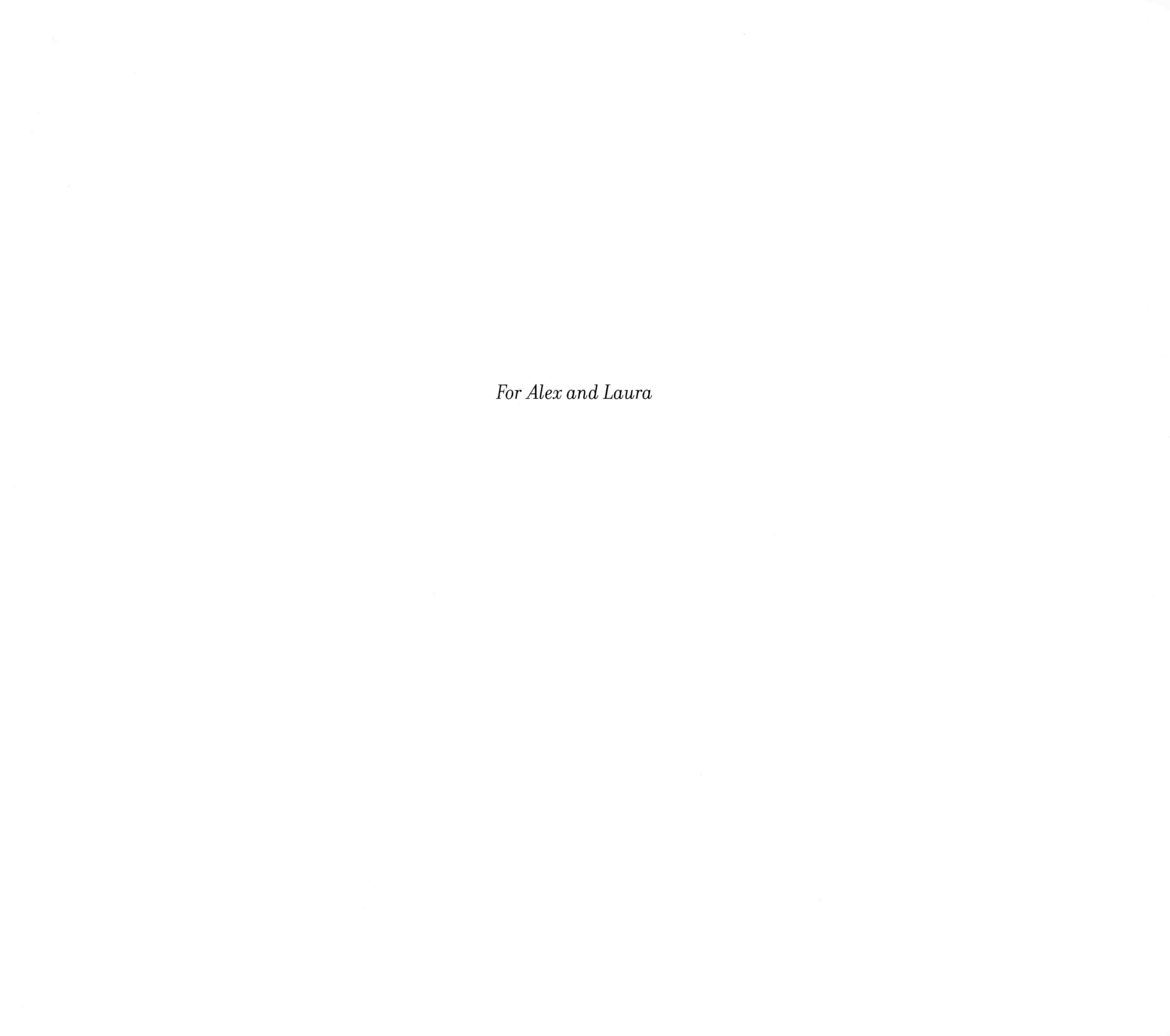

For Alex and Laura

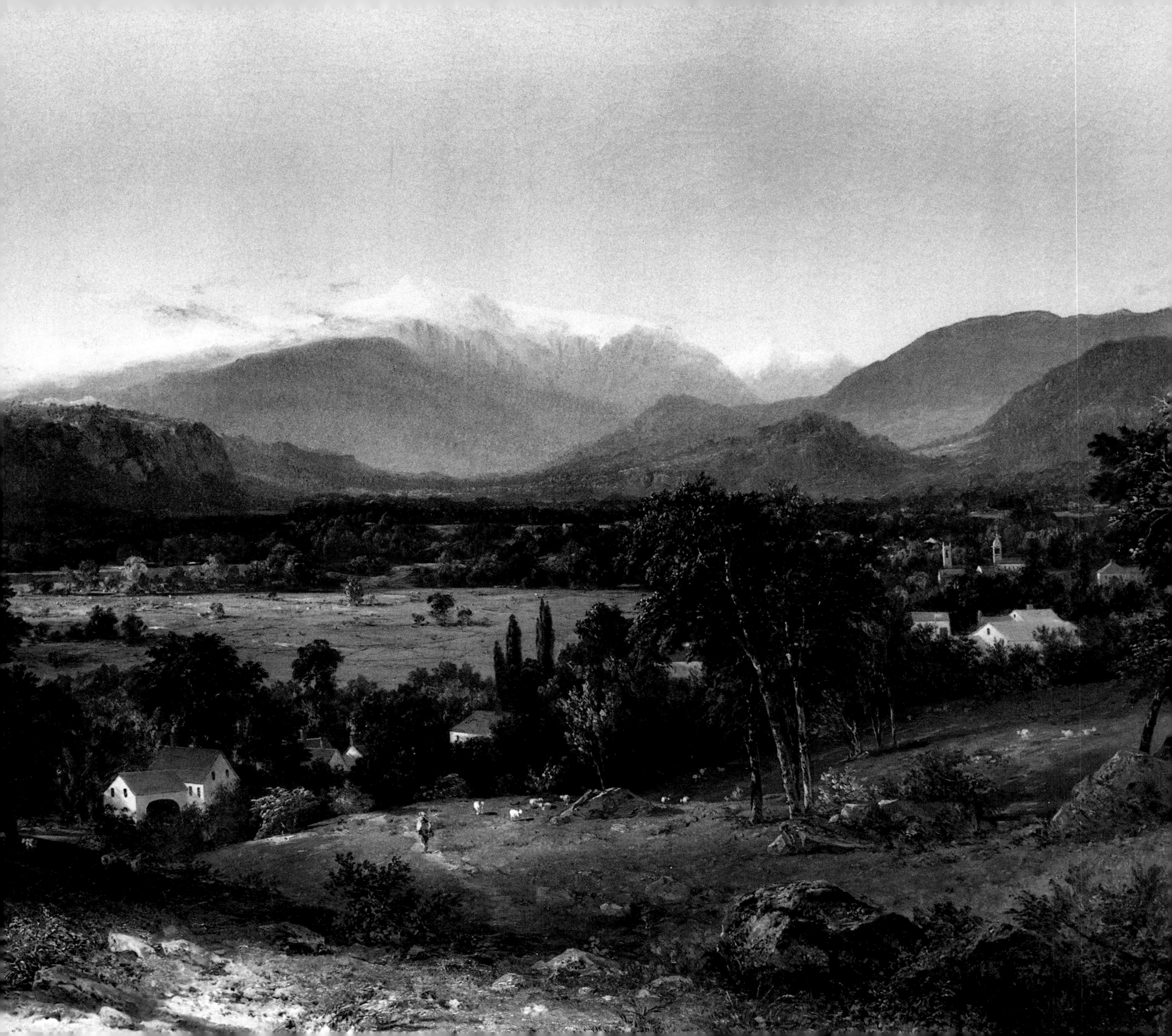

Contents

Opposite: Detail of Fig. 45

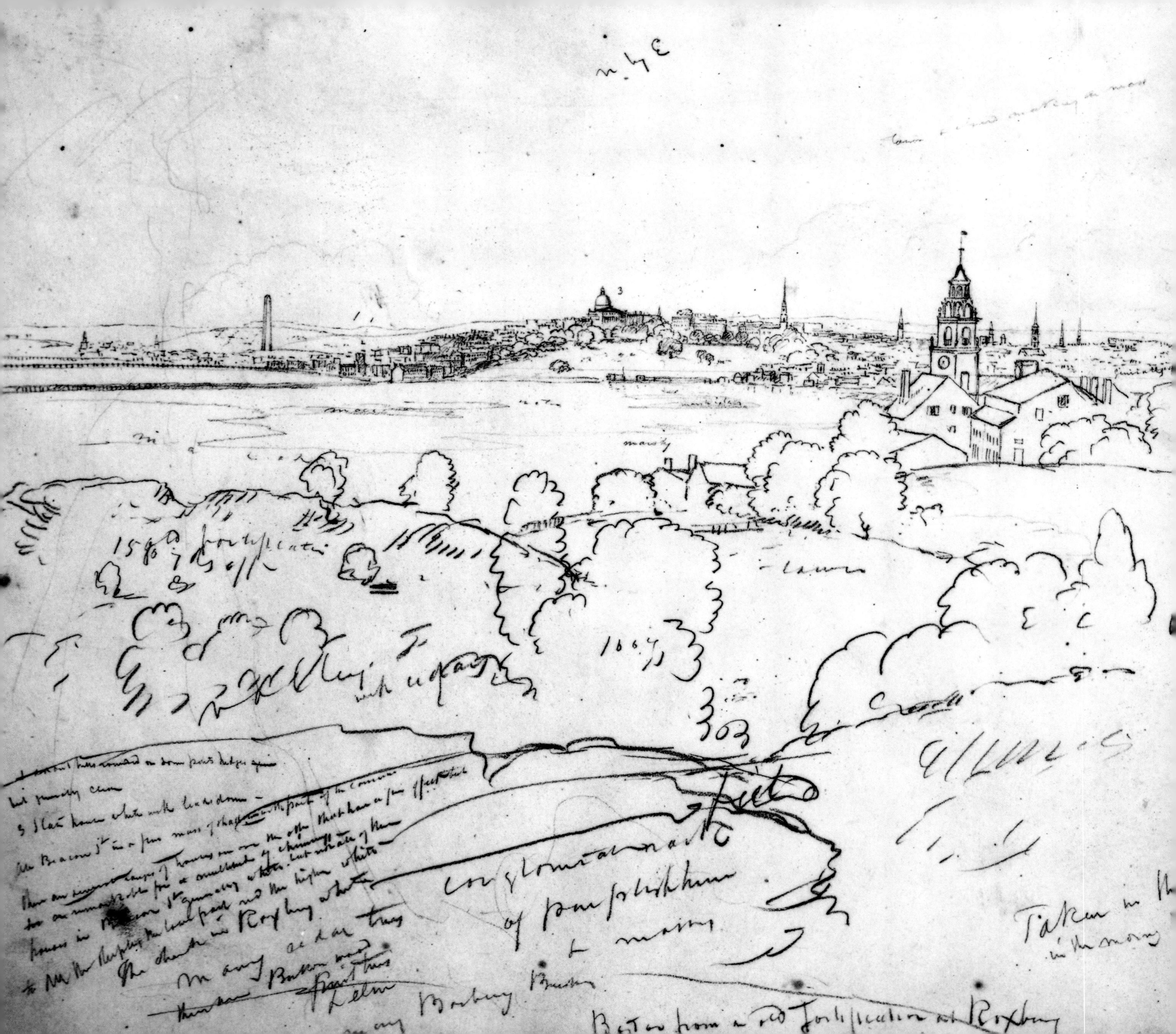
marsh
lawn
conglomerate rock

Preface

IN THE SPRING of 1872 Thomas Moran was struggling to complete his huge canvas *The Grand Canyon of the Yellowstone.* He needed help, and he wrote for it — not to a fellow artist nor a professional art critic, but to the geologist Ferdinand Hayden with whom he had traveled in the Yellowstone region the previous summer. "[Y]our judgment of the truths of the picture," Moran told him, are "of far greater value to me than that of any other man in the country."

American landscape painters and geologists then stood on common ground. We now tend to consign art and science to separate epistemologies, regarding them as distinctive pursuits, with completely different methodologies directed toward completely different ends. Yet in the middle decades of the nineteenth century, a strikingly different model of the relationship between art and science prevailed in both popular perception and in practice.

In the United States between 1825 and 1875, geology and landscape painting were closely allied pursuits. Both disciplines, it was pointed out at the time, were rooted in a careful observation of the natural world, and both were dedicated to illuminating the diversity and order of God's creation. Moreover, both geologists and landscape painters were self-conscious participants in the antebellum enterprise of nation-building. With a perception of their compatible methods and aims, geologists and landscape painters were able to collaborate in numerous social endeavors: promoting patriotism, spreading scientific knowledge, teaching moral lessons, inspiring religious awe, encouraging westward expansion, and fostering tourism. This rich, complicated, and productive relationship is the focus of this book.

The book had its genesis in the early 1980s when, as a graduate student, I read Barbara Novak's *Nature and Culture* (1980). In her provocative chapter "The Geological Timetable: Rocks," she summarizes some of the major geological controversies of the nineteenth century and offers evidence of American artists' interest in them. Finishing the chapter I found myself, as I believe Novak intended, left with more questions than answers. Who was caught up in the geological enthusiasms of the period, and why? What was the nature of the relationship between artists and geologists? How did the artists'

Opposite: Detail of Fig. 6

engagement with the science shape the way they perceived and painted nature? And these were just the initial questions.

For answers, I looked to the published writings and unpublished papers of the era's geologists and artists, as well as the writings of the artists' friends, patrons, and critics. I have also drawn heavily on the newspapers and periodicals of the day, with their extensive treatment of both science and art, and on contemporary travel literature and art criticism. At the core of the book are the works of art themselves. Trying to understand better why they look the way they do, how they were perceived, and how they functioned in their time has been a major goal.

In pursuing this interdisciplinary study, I have drawn extensively on the work of colleagues in art history, the history of science, and American cultural history. The intersections of art and science have been a major topic of discussion in academic circles during the last two decades, and several scholars have paid particular attention to the relationship between geology and art. Focusing on European scientific illustration, Martin Rudwick's writings, including *Scenes from Deep Time: Early Pictorial Illustrations of the Prehistoric World* (1992) have explored the emergence and development of a visual language for geological science in the nineteenth century—a language of columnar sections and imaginative re-creations of bygone epochs, all shaped by the theories preoccupying geologists at the time of their creation. Charlotte Klonk, in *Science and the Perception of Nature* (1996), has argued that "phenomenalism" (the notion that the inquiring observer should approach nature "merely descriptively" or without preconceived theories) provided a discursive structure that shaped both British science and British landscape painting at the beginning of the nineteenth century. Timothy Mitchell, in *Art and Science in German Landscape Painting, 1770–1840* (1993), has discussed how the "progressive rewriting of the earth's history" at the turn of the nineteenth century informed the works of German Romantic landscape painters from J. A. Koch to Caspar D. Friedrich. Scholars of American art also have been working in this field. Elizabeth Childs, Kenneth Haltman, Franklin Kelly, Katherine Manthorne, Ellwood C. Parry III, William Truettner, and Virginia Wagner, among others, have offered insightful accounts of how particular geological theories have informed works by individual American artists. Their works are gratefully cited in the main text. *The Anatomy of Nature* is, however, the first book to focus on the relationship between geology and landscape painting in the United States.

The book is organized to illuminate the varied ways and the varied venues in which art and science intersected in the mid-nineteenth century. The introduction describes geology's widespread popular appeal in the pre–Civil War era and examines the religious, economic, recreational, intellectual, and nationalistic factors that underlay it. Each of the six subsequent chapters focuses on a different artist chosen to emphasize a different facet of the geology-landscape alliance. These six were certainly not the only mid-century American landscape painters involved with geology. William Trost Richards, Jasper Cropsey, William Keith, Albert Bierstadt, Gilbert Munger, James Hope, Russell Smith, and dozens of others could be added to or substituted for the six discussed here. While I hate to omit any of them, I think that the works of the included artists exemplify well the varied forms, meanings, and functions that geologically informed landscapes assumed at mid-century.

The chapters progress in a roughly chronological order, beginning with a consideration of Thomas Cole's work of the 1820s and 1830s. Launching his career when landscape was just gaining a following in the United States, Cole argued for the study of geology as a way to bolster the status of his chosen genre. Through his study of the science, he aligned his interests with those of his wealthy and powerful patrons and developed an expressive vocabulary of landscape elements, which he used to underscore his paintings' moral themes. His friend Asher Durand, working from the later 1840s into the 1860s, drew on geology's revelations to create some of the most powerful, acutely observed rock studies of the nineteenth century. They embody his meditations on mortality and his allegiance to the philosophical paradigm of the microcosm, while belonging firmly within the developing therapeutic culture of the era. He posited the contemplation of nature studies as a restorative exercise, an antidote to the hectic pace and materialistic tenor of his times.

Cole's pupil Frederic Church, whose mammoth landscapes toured the country in the 1850s and 1860s, collaborated with scientists in educating the populace about the natural world while simultaneously underscoring the nationalist ideology of the era and encouraging a Christianized perception of nature. John F. Kensett joined geologists in promoting the development of American landscape tourism. At a time when many of the best-selling guidebooks and travelogues were written by geologists, and geologizing was one of the pleasures pursued on wilderness vacations, Kensett crafted his pictures to allude to and accommodate this mode of apprehending the world. William Stanley Haseltine's paintings of *The Rocks at Nahant*, dating from the 1860s, became intertwined with definitions of social status in antebellum New England, as well as with the transcendental geology of Louis Agassiz. Thomas Moran, in the 1870s, participated in several geological surveys of the American West, and through his works promoted the surveys' discoveries and helped to both imaginatively and practically open the western lands to settlement and other forms of economic exploitation.

Unifying these six artists (and the six chapters) is their shared interest in the intersection of geology and religion. These men were not drawn to all aspects of geology—Darwin's materialist science, for example, held few attractions for them. At a time when many geologists, including Darwin, were fighting to liberate their science from revealed religion, these artists staunchly maintained their allegiance to the older, conservative geology, a geology that found evidence of God's shaping hand in the fabric of the earth, a geology that could draw moral and spiritual lessons from stones. This is the geology that the painters drew upon and gave expression to in their art. But it was a geology that was doomed to extinction. In some ways this book is the story of the artists' valiant yet ultimately futile effort to preserve the unity of God and nature.

Acknowledgments

I HAVE BEEN WORKING on this book for so long and I owe so many thanks to so many people that it is hard to know where to begin. The good part is, looking back, I realize how blessed I have been in the many friendships and kindnesses that have sustained me as I've worked on this project. Yet I also approach this task with trepidation knowing that I'm sure to omit some of those many people who have helped. Please, if you don't see your name here, know that I'll remember it tomorrow and curse myself for leaving it out.

At Princeton University Press, it was my pleasure to work with Patricia Fidler, Curtis Scott, Nancy Grubb, Ken Wong, Devra Kupor, Sarah Henry, and Kate Zanzucchi; they guided me graciously and expertly through this process. Sally Hayden copyedited the manuscript, Susan Marsh provided the elegant design, and Kathleen Friello prepared the index. Color reproductions were made possible by generous grants from the Millard Meiss Publication Fund of the College Art Association and the Wellesley College Faculty Awards Program through the Mildred McAfee Horton Fund.

At Yale, my thesis advisor Jules Prown encouraged this project from its inception and has given me far more than the title for the book. Bryan Wolf's brilliant and abundantly creative interpretations of American painting have also been an inspiration to me.

When I was working on my thesis, I was able to spend two wonderful years at the National Museum of American Art, where Lois Fink and her colleagues created an ideal environment for intellectual camaraderie. William H. Truettner, my advisor for those years, and Alan Wallach, then a senior fellow at the NMAA, have been extraordinary friends, colleagues, and candid critics of my work. They have also provided me with the example of their splendid scholarship.

Marc Simpson, David Brigham, and J. Gray Sweeney offered valuable advice on the manuscript, and Ellwood C. Parry III has generously shared his expertise on Thomas Cole.

For help with geological queries, I am very grateful to the following geologists: my old friend Philip Moss; Maria Nadakavukaren Waller and Margaret Thompson in Wellesley's geology department; E-an Zen, Nicholas Ratcliffe, and their colleagues at the U.S. Geological Survey, Reston, Virginia; and Ellis Yochelson and Anita Harris of the Museum of Natural History, Smithsonian Institution.

I owe special thanks to my friends and colleagues in the Wellesley art department — every single one of them — who nudged and cajoled and asked at least once a week, "When are you going to finish that book?" Many of them read parts of the manuscript, offered valuable advice all the way through the process, and generally helped out in ways large and small. I am especially indebted to Andrew Warren for his photographs and to Peter Fergusson, Alice Friedman, Miranda Marvin, Patricia Berman, Jay Oles, John Rhodes, and James F. O'Gorman for their sage advice and comments on the text. My generous friend Jay Panetta from the music department was always willing to advise, encourage, and comment on drafts. As my undergraduate advisor, James O'Gorman set me off on the path that led to this book. He has been unfailingly supportive ever since, and has earned my heartfelt gratitude.

My good friends Jennifer Danly, Sarah Cohen, Wendy Greenhouse, Janet Headley, Susan Danly, Janet Dwyer Schiavoni, Erica Hirshler, and Rebecca Zurier have read, listened, supported, sent information, and offered good advice of all sorts. Janet Headley especially has been practically a partner in this project, wading through many drafts over the years. Without her I might have given up.

My family — my brothers, Matthew and John; my stepson, David Steinbergh; my mother, Jeanne F. Bedell; my father, Frank C. Bedell, and his wife, Lois Bedell — have helped me in more ways than I can list here. My daughter, Laura, and my husband, Alex, have been the best reasons I could think of to finish, and I dedicate the book to them.

The Anatomy of Nature

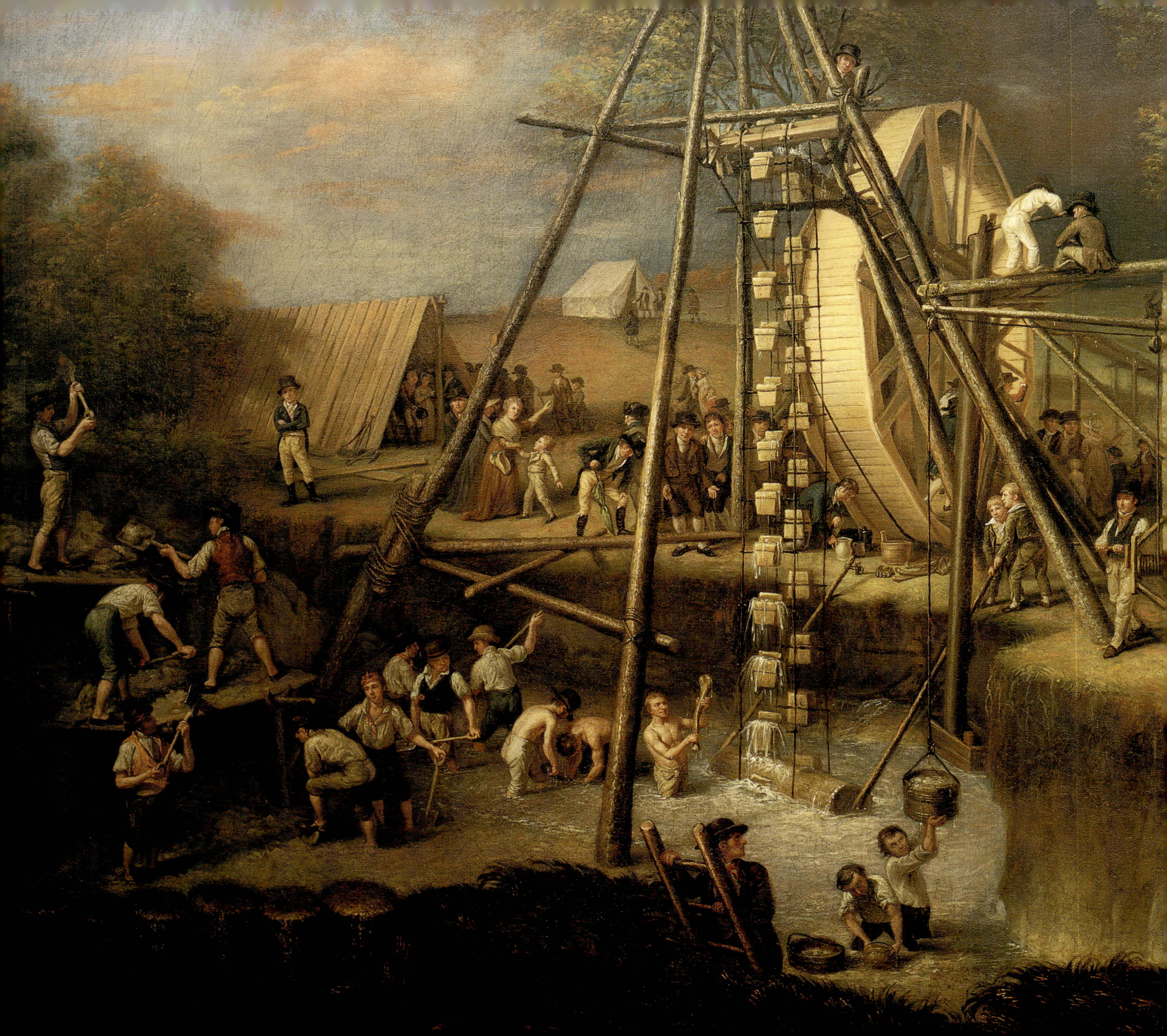

Introduction

The Popularity of Geology

Geology reigned through much of the nineteenth century as America's most "fashionable" science. Between 1820 and 1870, men and women across the country avidly pursued an interest in the field. They pushed their way into crowded lecture halls to hear talks by prominent geologists; they bought geological textbooks, and they scoured the countryside for specimens to fill their mineral cabinets. Joining potted palms and china shepherdesses in many American parlors, these mineral cabinets served not only as objects of adornment but also as signs of social respectability and intellectual engagement.

This enthusiasm for geology developed gradually. In the first two decades of the century, the discipline attracted few adherents. In 1817 a commentator for the *North American Review* remarked, "A few only among us have learned to love stones. . . . there is perhaps as much indifference towards . . . [the] science as there is ignorance of it."[1] But by the 1830s the situation had changed dramatically. In 1834 a writer for the *Knickerbocker* commented that geology "is, indeed, the fashionable science of the day; and may be said to form a necessary part of practical and ornamental education."[2] In 1835 the *New England Magazine* noted that Bostonians had gone "geologically mad," and in 1841 the *American Journal of Science* happily reported that "lectures upon geology are demanded and given in all our larger towns; and the wonders of this science form the theme of discussion in the drawing-rooms of taste and fashion."[3] Geology retained its popular appeal until about the last quarter of the century, when increasing specialization and professionalization made the science less accessible to the average citizen.

The popularity of geology was not a uniquely American phenomenon. Like many facets of American culture in the nineteenth century, the enthusiasm for geology was an imported phenomenon. In Germany, France, and especially in England, the science had been in vogue since the late eighteenth century, several decades before it became popular in the United States.[4] Not until it received the sanction of taste and fashion in Europe did it win general acceptance on this side of the Atlantic.

In the United States, as well as in Europe, the interest in geology was part of a wider fascination with natural history in

Opposite: Detail of Fig. 1

general.[5] The nineteenth century saw the blossoming of many of the natural sciences, including geology, botany, zoology, and meteorology. All of these sciences had their partisans. Zoology and meteorology were often recommended as pastimes for their recreational and intellectual benefits, while botany was widely touted as a healthy, genteel pursuit, particularly suitable for women. As young disciplines, these sciences offered special advantages to the beginning student. With relatively little in the way of accumulated facts and established doctrines to be memorized and digested, they could be quickly and easily comprehended by the beginner. Also, with so much work to be done in these fields, even the amateur could hope to make significant contributions and participate in important national, even international scientific endeavors.

Although botany, zoology, and meteorology had their attractions, geology held a special place in the natural history pantheon. It differed from the other sciences in being both historical and highly controversial. At the time, it was the only one of the natural sciences that dealt with the "history of nature rather than its order."[6] While botanists and zoologists were concerned primarily with collecting, labeling, and classifying specimens, geologists were delving into such inflammatory questions as the age of the earth and its history since creation.

Nineteenth-century writers, evaluating the appeal that geology held for their era, identified many reasons for its popularity: economic, recreational, intellectual, nationalistic, and, above all, religious. It offered the opportunity, as one nineteenth-century scientist said, "to become acquainted with the ideas of God Himself."[7] Geology, according to the *North American Review*, "opens to us the great book of nature, where we may read the eternal truths of creation, those 'sermons in stones' which were written by the finger of the Almighty, and which bear indisputable proofs of His wisdom, power, and omnipresence."[8]

In the late eighteenth and early nineteenth centuries, geologists placed their science in the service of religion.[9] They searched for proofs of order and design in the geologic record and tried to furnish scientific evidence for the biblical account of creation. In those years clergy and scientists established a harmonious working relationship. Numerous theologians became students of geology, while geologists published and lectured extensively on the connections between their science and natural religion. The Reverend William Buckland's *Geology and Mineralogy Considered with Reference to Natural Theology* (1836), Benjamin Silliman's *The Consistency of the Discoveries of Modern Geology with the Sacred History of the Creation and the Deluge* (1837), and Edward Hitchcock's *The Religion of Geology and its Connected Sciences* (1851) are just a few of the nineteenth-century publications that offered geologic testimony to the power and wisdom of God.

As the decades passed, however, the relationship between the two disciplines became increasingly stormy. Mounting geologic evidence indicated that the pages of the Bible and the strata of the earth offered differing versions of the world's history. When geologists began to question such long-accepted notions as the six days of creation, the universality of the Deluge, and the permanency of species, theologians were placed in an awkward position. Some accommodated the new scientific discoveries by liberalizing their interpretation of the Bible, as, for instance, by reading the six days of creation metaphorically as six geologic periods rather than actual days. Other clergy, unable to reconcile their religious beliefs with the new discoveries and theories, abandoned the field or became hostile toward it, denouncing it as heretical and irreligious.[10] This controversial side of geology may have offended the more pious members of the public and dampened their interest in the science. In general, however, the controversies seem only to have enhanced the subject's popular appeal.

In addition to its religious implications, geology was a rewarding intellectual pursuit. The nineteenth century was a period of great foment in geology, a period when long-held notions about the earth were overthrown. Charles Lyell (1797–1875), one of the era's most prominent geologists, described the revolutionary nature of nineteenth-century geology:

> Never, perhaps, did any science, with the exception of astronomy, unfold, in an equally brief period, so many novel and unexpected truths, and overturn so many preconceived opinions. The senses had for ages declared the earth to be at rest, until the astronomer taught that it was carried through space with inconceivable rapidity. In like manner was the surface of the planet regarded as having remained unaltered since the creation, until the geologists proved that it had been the theatre of reiterated change and was still the subject of slow but neverending fluctuations.[11]

In the space of a few decades, geologists expanded the age of the earth from six thousand years to tens of millions of years and began slowly to recreate its ancient history. Paleontologists populated those vast centuries with towering lizards, woolly mammoths, and flying reptiles. In 1836 a writer for the *North American Review* marvelled at the revelations of geology: "The world has a history written on its strata; a history so interesting, that the most splendid fictions of the human imagination sink into insignificance when compared with it."[12]

In his autobiography, Henry Adams remarked, somewhat facetiously, that geology "suited idle minds as well as though it were history."[13] Like history, geology offered its students the opportunity to travel through time and explore bygone epochs. As a writer for the *Knickerbocker* commented in 1862, it allowed one to "shake hands with centuries across the great abyss of time."[14]

In the United States the enthusiasm for geology also carried a nationalistic component. Americans had long suffered from an inferiority complex about their continent. It had been stigmatized as "The New World," a savage place devoid of historical associations and bereft of intellectual and aesthetic stimuli. In geology and in the geologic features of the American landscape many found answers to these accusations. The United States, they discovered, "had the equivalent of a cultural past in its natural phenomena."[15] Fitz Hugh Ludlow (author and friend of the painter Albert Bierstadt) explained, "We go out of our way to lavish raptures upon the temples of Yucatan, . . . the Sphinx, and the Cave of Elephanta, while through our own mountain fastness and trackless plains exist ruins of architecture and statuary not one whit behind the foreign remains of forty centuries in power of execution, and far vaster in respect to age and size."[16]

In the great falls of Niagara and in the sculptured towers

and ravines of the Southwest, Americans found substitutes for the castles and cathedrals of Europe. They could take pride in the sublimity, vastness, and beauty of their country's natural wonders. "Why," asked *Scribner's Monthly*, "should we waste ourselves in unpatriotic wonderments over the gorge of the Tamina or the Via Mala, when nature has furnished us with the Grand Canyon of the Yellowstone, in which the famed Swiss ravines would be but a crevice or a wrinkle?"[17]

Americans had no need to be ashamed of their country's physical appearance, nor, geologists told them, need they tolerate the epithet "New World." In his *Geological Sketches* of 1866, Louis Agassiz (1807–1873) included an essay entitled "America the Old World." Arguing that North America was the "first-born among the Continents," he wrote, "America, so far as her physical history is concerned, has been falsely denominated the *New World*. Hers was the first dry land lifted out of the waters, hers the first shore washed by the ocean that enveloped all the earth beside; and while Europe was represented only by islands rising here and there above the sea, America already stretched in an unbroken line of land from Nova Scotia to the Far West."[18]

The English geologist Charles Lyell, after his 1841–42 trip to the United States, noted how ironic it was that "we must turn to the *New World* if we wish to see in perfection the oldest monuments of the earth's history."[19] At a time of intense cultural nationalism when Americans defined their identity largely in relation to the land they had settled, these revelations of the antiquity and geological magnificence of their country did much to boost patriotic pride.

Geology's attractions were not limited to its religious, intellectual, and nationalistic aspects. It was also an amusing outdoor pastime often touted for its recreational benefits. To the health-conscious, geological fieldtrips provided opportunities to "invigorate the body" and "tranquilize the mind."[20] It was even suggested that votaries of geology enjoyed "longer life than those attached to other pursuits."[21] Geology shared its healthful aspects with the other natural sciences. As one writer noted, "everyone who has anything of the naturalist about him, leaves his books and the narrow enclosure of his study, and goes forth into the open fields of nature."[22] Physically invigorating, intellectually stimulating, and morally uplifting, geology offered just the sort of wholesome occupation approved of by Victorian society.

To the pragmatically inclined, the study of geology also provided practical economic benefits. Here in the United States, with vast tracts of territory still unexplored and unexploited, an intrepid entrepreneur armed with appropriate geologic knowledge could hope to earn a healthy return on his intellectual investment. Untold geologic riches were waiting to be tapped by those with the right information. This was one case in which knowledge could literally be turned into gold—or diamonds or coal or zinc. At least a few of those who packed the lecture halls to hear learned discourses on geology must have arrived with visions of nuggets dancing in their heads.

In explaining why geology was the first of the natural sciences to be embraced by the American public, the nineteenth-century paleontologist Jules Marcou remarked, "People in general, and agriculturalists in particular, soon showed an eager desire to know the resources of the soils, the rocks, and the mines."[23]

Nineteenth-century American geologists were well aware of their countrymen's utilitarian biases. When they sought to justify their work to the public (and to the legislatures that so often funded it), they consistently stressed the discipline's economic aspects. When Thomas Cole's patron George Featherstonhaugh submitted his report on the geology of the Arkansas Territory to Congress in 1835, he noted, "This inquiry is of deep interest to this country, not simply as one which leads us into a field of philosophical research, highly favorable to the enlargement of intellectual powers, but as pregnant with utility to the business pursuits of life, enabling us to apply the fruits of their long and rich experience to the immediate development of the mineral resources of this country."[24] A few years later, in defending the work of the New York Geological Survey to the state legislature, one of its members pointed out that the survey's work not only enriched the state's coffers by uncovering buried geologic resources, but also saved the public thousands of dollars "which for twenty years previously had been annually squandered in trials for coal in rocks below the carboniferous series."[25] Whatever their own reasons for pursuing the science (which tended to be more intellectual than otherwise), geologists clearly felt compelled to market their work by reference to its pecuniary possibilities.

Geology's appeal, if one accepts the assertions made in numerous nineteenth-century periodicals, cut across social and economic boundaries. In 1842 the *American Journal of Science* remarked, "Geology is not confined to the learned. Popular lectures upon this science are now demanded in many of our cities, towns, and villages, and with the aid of diagrams and specimens, the subject is rendered intelligible and instructive to large and attentive audiences."[26] That same year, when Charles Lyell delivered a series of public lectures in Boston, New York, and Philadelphia, the audiences were supposedly composed of as many as three thousand "persons of both sexes, of every station in society, from the most affluent and eminent in the various professions to the humblest mechanics, all observing the utmost decorum."[27] Louis Agassiz, professor of geology at Harvard University, confidently expected his volumes on the natural history of North America to be "read by operatives, by fishermen, by farmers, quite as extensively as by the students in our colleges or by the learned professions."[28] In Great Britain during this same period, the cultivation of geology and the other natural sciences was recognized as "a mechanism for 'the social legitimization of marginal men,'" a way for them to climb the social ladder into the new intellectual class.[29] In the United States, scientific study certainly enabled some humbly born men such as John Muir and Ferdinand Hayden to rise to prominence. Yet, despite these specific instances and the many testimonials to geology's widespread appeal, in practice most amateur practitioners of the science in the United States, especially in the early decades of the nineteenth century, were probably drawn from the upper classes. The pursuit of geology required, in addition to scientific curiosity and access to books and journals, the leisure time to master the literature and to geologize in the field.

Whatever the actual demographic composition of geological devotées, their ranks certainly included many artists, art critics, and art patrons. These men and women tended to move in elite social circles, the sort of circles in which the new science of geology was a prominent topic of conversation.[30] The chasm that later came to separate art and science had not yet opened, and geologists, writers, and artists, together with other eminent citizens, often rubbed elbows at such exclusive clubs as the Century Association in New York City and the Saturday Club in Boston.[31] Artists joined scientific societies (Frederic Church belonged to the American Geographical and Statistical Society in New York City), and geologists participated in artistic organizations.[32] Geologists Clarence King and James T. Gardner, for instance, were charter members of the American Association for the Advancement of Truth in Art, an organization of American Pre-Raphaelite painters. The result of this fraternization and free-flowing exchange of ideas was considerable cross-fertilization among the disciplines. Artists and writers found inspiration in geology, while geologists such as King and Muir often colored their scientific writings with descriptions of their spiritual and aesthetic responses to the landscape. Critics, especially the influential English writer John Ruskin and his American followers, applied their scientific knowledge to their evaluation of art, and patrons sought out works informed by the new sciences.

American artists were among the first of their countrymen to be attracted to geology. At least as early as the late eighteenth century, several decades before the science became popular with the general public, a handful of artists were pursuing an interest in the field. Charles Willson Peale (1741–1827) divided his interests almost equally between science and art, combining a career as a portraitist with a zestful pursuit of natural history subjects. In 1784 Peale established America's first popular museum of science and art and two years later won election to the American Philosophical Society, the oldest scientific organization in the United States.[33] In his museum Peale exhibited portraits of eminent Americans side by side with natural history specimens, finding nothing incongruous in the juxtaposition. In true Enlightenment fashion, his purpose in both instances was didactic. He intended both the scientific and artistic components of his museum to have the same effect on the visitor: to be morally uplifting and intellectually stimulating. The portraits of Revolutionary War heroes were to inspire the audience to feats of patriotism and self-sacrifice, while the specimens, classified and displayed according to Linnean principles, were to impress upon the viewer the exquisite variety and ultimate order of God's creation.

The scientific portion of the museum consisted largely of zoological specimens, but there was also a geological display. This exhibit was described by one of Peale's contemporaries:

> There was a mound of earth, considerably raised and covered with green turf, from which a number of trees ascended and branched out in different directions. On the declivity of this mound was a small thicket, and just below it an artificial pond; on the other side a number of large and small rocks of different kinds, collected from different parts of the world and represented [*sic*] the rude state in which they are generally found. At the foot of the mound were holes dug and earth thrown up, to show the different kinds of clay, ochre, coal, marl, etc. which he had collected from different parts; also, various ores and minerals.[34]

This, in the opinion of Charles Frondel of Harvard's Geologi-

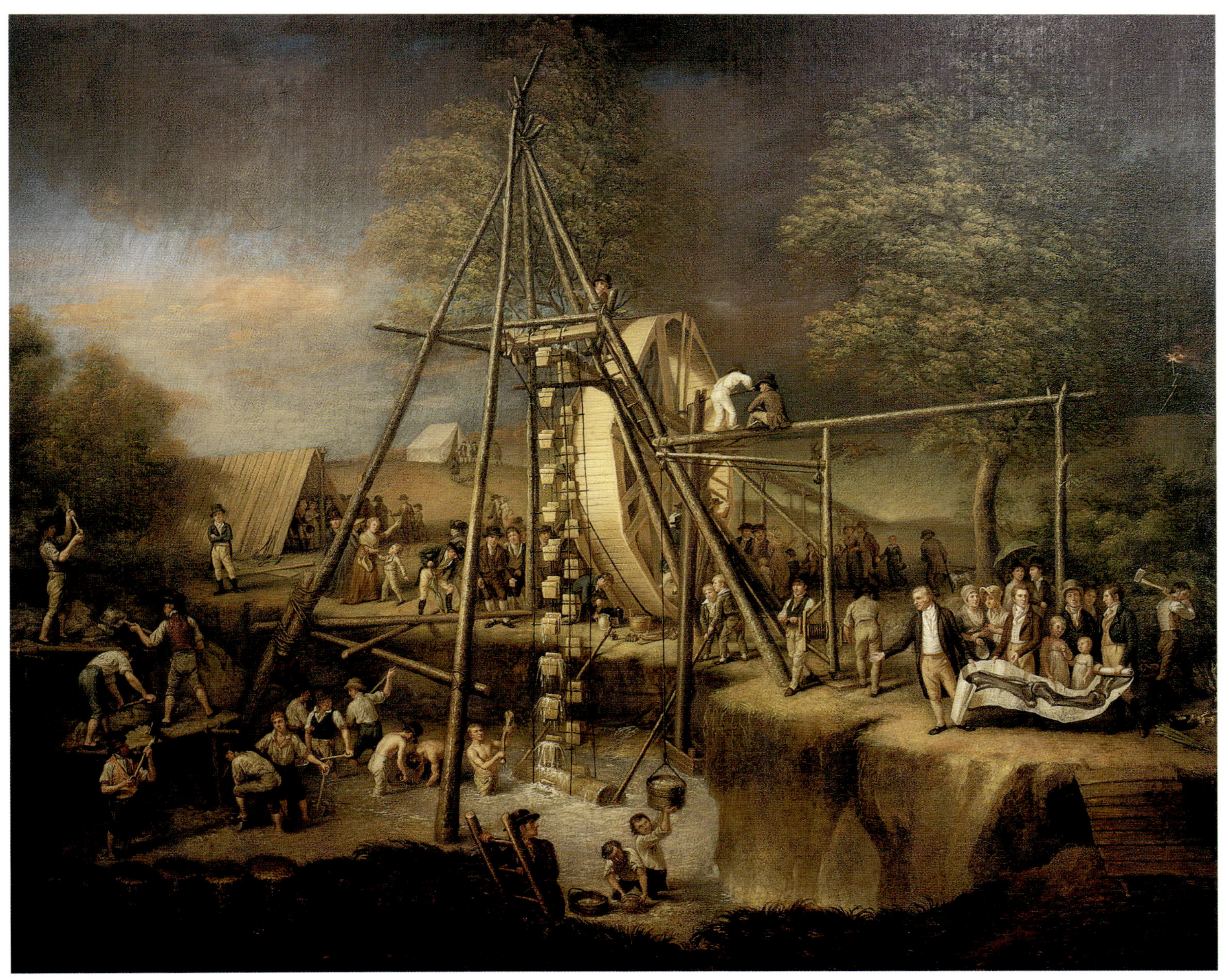

Fig. 1. Charles Willson Peale, *The Exhumation of the Mastodon*, 1806–8.
Oil on canvas, 50 x 62½ in. (127 x 58.8 cm). Maryland Historical Society, Baltimore

cal Museum, was "the first organized and effective display of minerals and geological materials" in this country.[35] Peale, in keeping with his desire to promote his museum as a public benefit, told his Board of Directors that this exhibit would be "highly usefull to America," in acquainting landowners, miners, and manufacturers with the resources lying beneath their feet.[36] So important did he consider this topic that he also sponsored public lectures on the subject.[37]

Peale was even more interested in fossils than he was in minerals. In the spring of 1801, when he heard that the gigantic bones of an unknown creature had been unearthed on a farm in Newburgh, New York, he hurried to the site. After negotiating with the owner for several days, he purchased the bones and the right to excavate for the remainder of the skeleton. That summer he undertook the formidable exhumation. To extract the bones from a waterlogged marl pit, he hired dozens of assistants and constructed a huge man-powered pump, eventually recovering the nearly complete skeleton of what he called "The Great American Incognitum," or mastodon.[38] This enterprise, according to the paleontologist John Ostrom, was the first truly scientific excavation for prehistoric mammals in North America, and the mastodon skeleton was the first nearly complete example of this creature collected anywhere in the world. It was also the first prehistoric skeleton of any kind to be reassembled in this country.[39]

To Peale and his contemporaries the mastodon was of even greater significance. Not only did it provide one of the missing links in the Great Chain of Being, but it also had patriotic implications.[40] In his authoritative treatise *Histoire Naturelle* (published in multiple volumes between 1749 and 1803), the Comte de Buffon argued that animal life had degenerated in the New World. American species, he claimed, were smaller and weaker than those in Europe. American scientists were particularly delighted with the mastodon skeleton because it proved that America could support creatures at least as large as those in the Old World.[41]

Peale commemorated his momentous discovery in his first history painting, *The Exhumation of the Mastodon* (fig. 1). Painted between 1806 and 1808, it shows the artist presiding over the excavation (fig. 2). Peale borrowed the pose for his own figure from the Apollo Belvedere, then one of the most highly regarded of classical sculptures.[42] Through this witty reference to the Greek god of light and knowledge, Peale identified himself as a man of the Enlightenment, a man of science, shedding light on the past, using his ingenuity to uncover long buried fragments of the earth's history. The event under Peale's direction is portrayed as a great collaborative enterprise uniting human intellect, technological ingenuity, and muscular power against the chaotic forces of nature, represented by the encroaching thunderstorm. The themes of the painting revolve around the pursuit of truth, the search for knowledge, and the willingness to persist in this quest in the face of great obstacles. The painting also underscores the place of men like Peale at the top of the Great Chain of Being.

Over a decade later, in one of his last paintings, *The Artist in His Museum* of 1822 (fig. 3), Peale portrayed himself in his dual role of artist-scientist.[43] He stands at the entrance to his museum, lifting a curtain to reveal long, ordered rows of cabinets and, directly behind him, a tantalizing glimpse of the mastodon. Beside him, on the floor and table, are the attri-

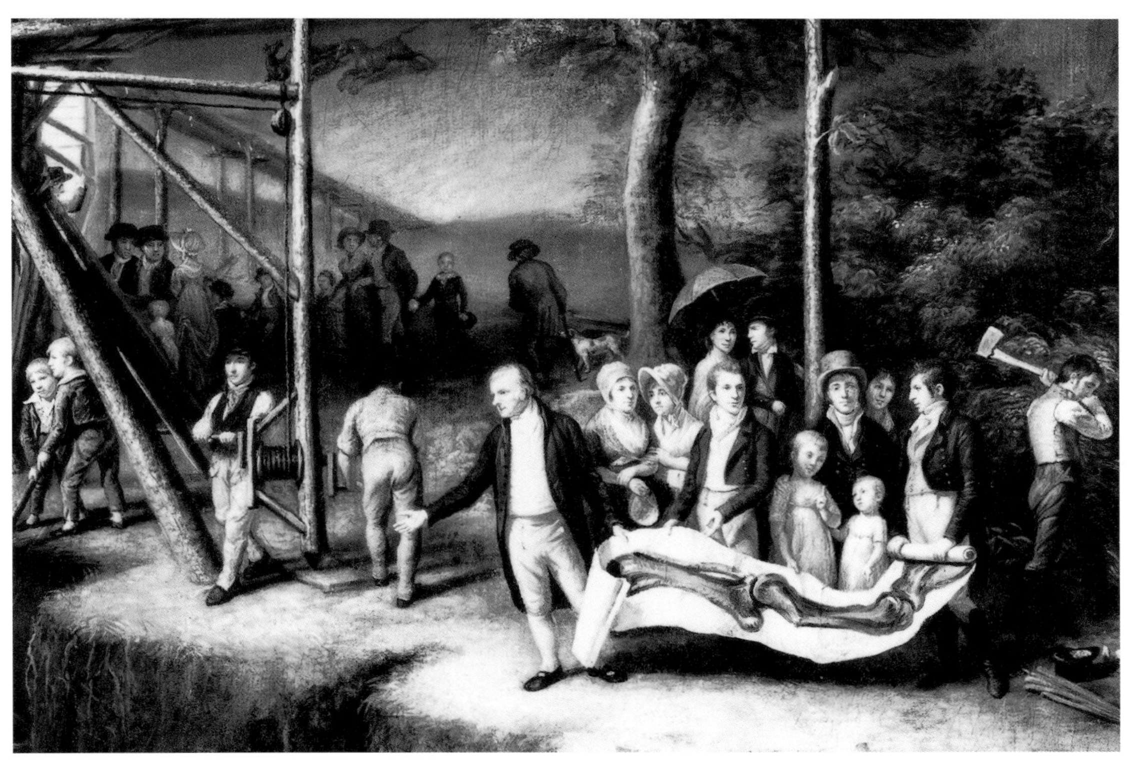

Fig. 2. Detail of Fig. 1

butes of his professions: a palette and brushes, the tools of a taxidermist, and a jumbled pile of fossilized bones. His role, as he defines it in the painting, is to transform the disorderly array of natural objects in the foreground — the dead turkey slumped over the toolbox and the skeletal fragments — through the application of his intellect, knowledge, and skill, into displays like those behind him that can reveal the underlying order and meanings of nature. The contrast between the varied, uneven lines and skewed forms of the foreground with the straight lines and clean perspective grid of the background visually underscores this theme. Once again Peale shows himself enlightening the public, metaphorically lifting the curtain of ignorance to open new vistas of knowledge.

Samuel F. B. Morse (1791–1872), American painter and inventor of the telegraph, also studied geology in his younger days. Between 1806 and 1810 he attended Yale College where he took classes taught by the most important American geologist of the era, Benjamin Silliman (1779–1864). In the years after his graduation, he and Silliman became close friends. They geologized together in the Berkshires and the Adirondacks, and in 1825 Morse painted the scientist's portrait (fig. 4).[44] In the painting, Silliman stands facing the viewer. He

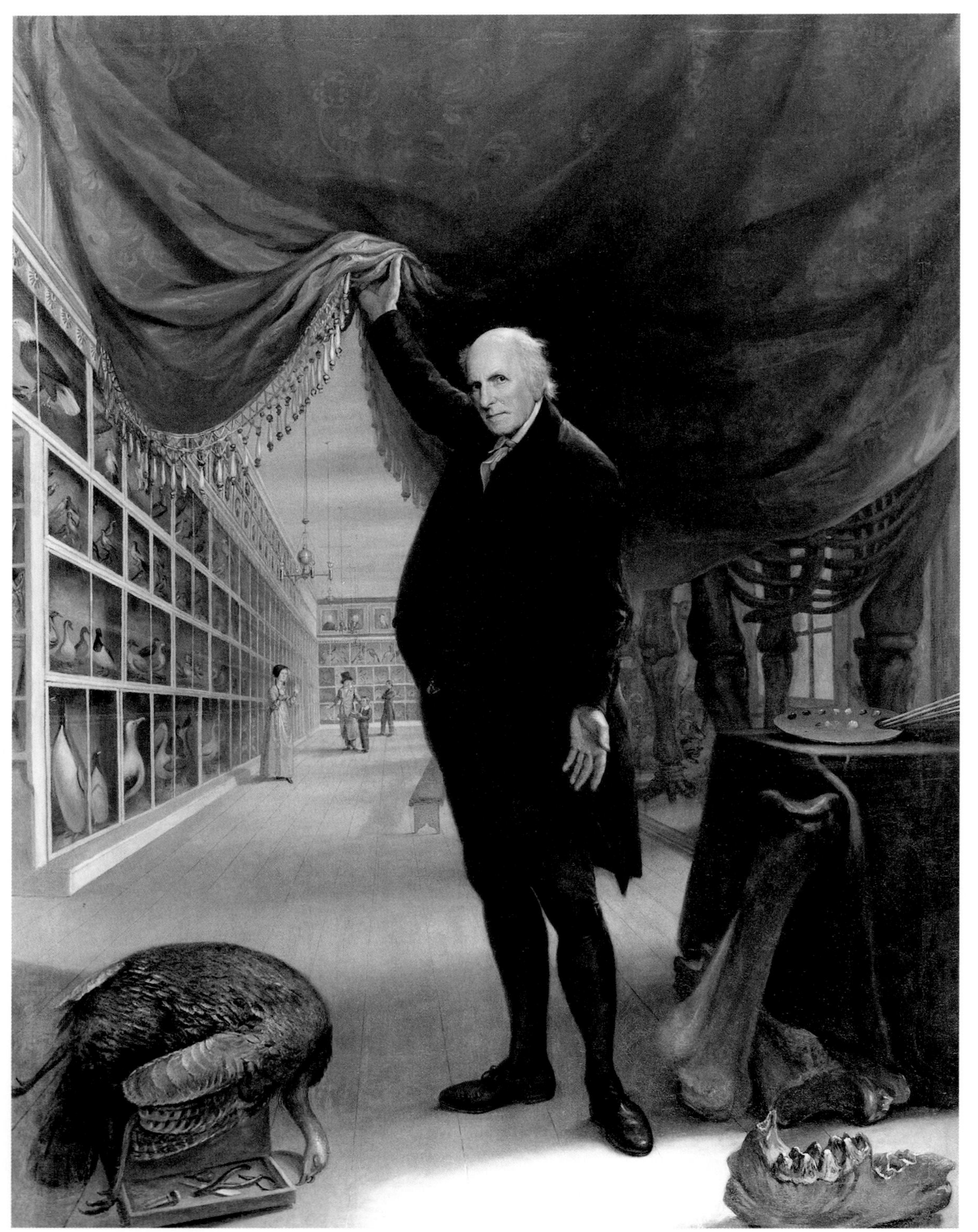

Fig. 3. Charles Willson Peale, *The Artist in His Museum*, 1822. Oil on canvas, 103 3/4 x 79 7/8 in. (263.5 x 202.9 cm). Pennsylvania Academy of the Fine Arts, Philadelphia. Gift of Mrs. Sarah Harrison (The Joseph Harrison Jr. Collection)

holds a mineral crystal in one hand; the other rests lightly on the lectern before him, as if he is pausing in the midst of a speech. Spread on the table in front of him is an array of geological specimens. Behind him, a heavy swath of maroon drapery has been drawn aside to reveal a view of West Rock, New Haven, Connecticut. Silliman had described the geology of this striking escarpment in a paper of 1806.[45]

The general composition of the Silliman portrait resembles standard pictures "of clergymen on the pulpit," a compositional similarity that may allude, Michael Quick has observed, to "Silliman's deeply personal religious beliefs and, in conjunction with the minerals, sum up Silliman's particular blend of science and religion."[46] Morse's contact with this devout scientist may have influenced his own interest in the relationship between geology and religion. In 1865, forty years after painting this portrait, Morse endowed a series of lectures at the Union Theological Seminary in New York City. The lectures were to explore the connections between religion and science, especially geology and geography.[47]

Morse and Peale were in the vanguard of American interest in geology, yet the impact of the science on their art was not extensive. As the popularity of geology escalated in the middle decades of the nineteenth century, so did artistic involvement in the discipline. By mid-century numerous American landscape painters, especially the artists of the Hudson River School, were studying the science and incorporating geological ideas into their art.[48] Thomas Cole, Asher Durand, Jasper Cropsey, Frederic Church, and William Trost Richards all read geological texts, and many of the painters were friendly with prominent geologists. Cole knew Benjamin Silliman. John La Farge

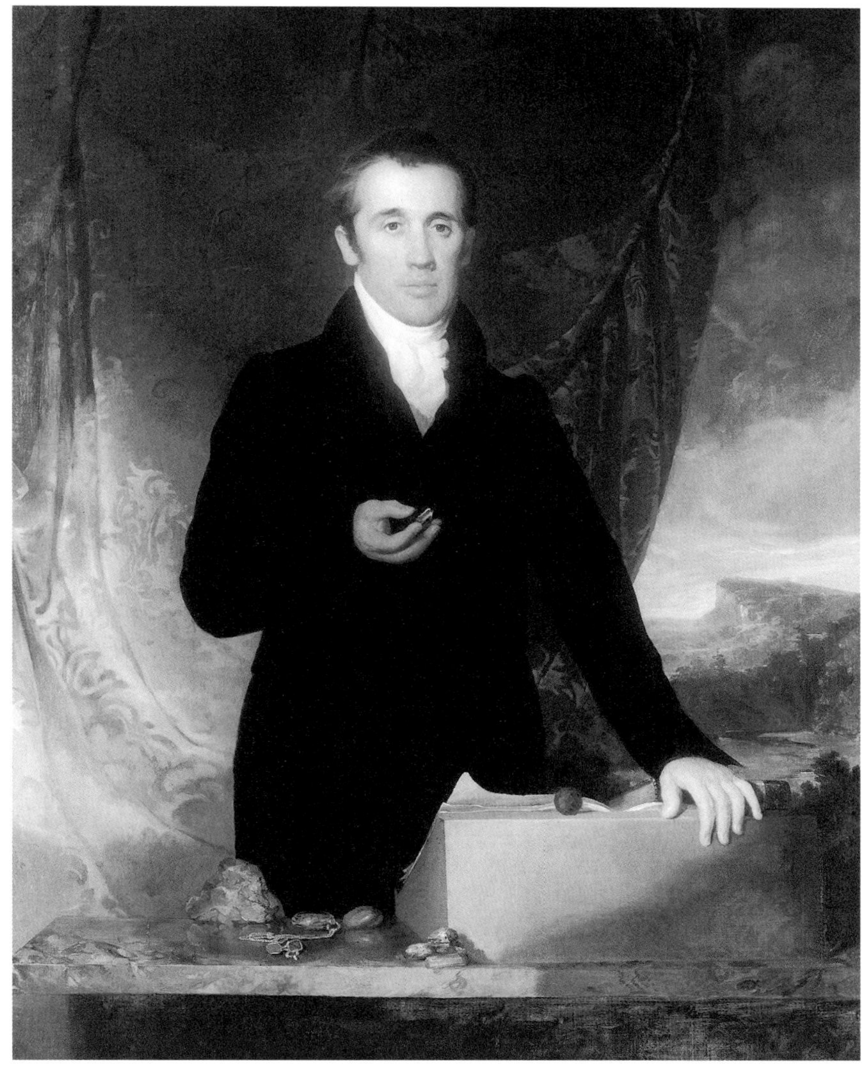

Fig. 4. Samuel F. B. Morse, *Benjamin Silliman*, 1825. Oil on canvas, 55 1/4 x 44 1/4 in. (140.2 x 112.4 cm). Yale University Art Gallery, New Haven, Connecticut. Gift of Bartlett Arkell, B.A. 1886, M.A. 1898, to Silliman College

was close to Clarence King. William James Stillman, John Kensett, and William Stanley Haseltine were acquainted with Louis Agassiz. A number of other artists learned about the science while serving on government-sponsored geological surveys. Thomas Moran, Sanford Gifford, William Keith, Albert Bierstadt, and a number of other artists and photographers participated in these expeditions. Through these and other means American landscape painters absorbed the geologic knowledge of the era. They went on to use that knowledge in multiple ways from shaping the content of their individual works of art to enhancing the status of their profession.

In 1767 America's preeminent portrait painter John Singleton Copley complained that "the people generally regard [painting] no more than any other useful trade, as they sometimes term it, like that of a Carpenter tailor or shew [*sic*] maker, not as one of the most noble Arts in the World."[49] By the early nineteenth century, artists were slowly climbing the rungs of the American social ladder, but art making was still widely regarded with suspicion as a distraction from more socially and economically useful tasks. Some even believed that art making could lead, through overindulgence in imaginative activities, to mental derangement. Science, on the other hand, was associated with rationality, practical endeavors, and factual knowledge.[50] By linking their work with a highly regarded science like geology, landscape painters could hope to endow their profession with at least a veneer of the factual, practical, and rational. In asserting, as many artists began to do in the second quarter of the nineteenth century, that a knowledge of the natural sciences was essential preparation for the pursuit of landscape art, they were establishing a firm intellectual and factual (rather than imaginative and subjective) foundation for their art. The realistic style that prevailed in American landscape painting in the middle decades of the nineteenth century, with its sharp focus, precisely described detail, and careful evocation of particular species of plants and types of rocks, likewise helped to align landscape painting with the much-admired methods of scientific observation and data collection.

For individual artists, their knowledge of geology came into play in diverse ways, shaping their perception of the land and offering them new interpretations of its features. Perception is an extraordinarily complex process. We "see" (that is, subject to attentive mental processing) only a small portion of what falls within our visual field. That small portion is determined by what psychologists call our "perceptual set." An interplay of physiological, psychological, and cultural factors primes us to focus our attention on particular aspects of our environment. Simply put, we see what we are looking for. In the mid-nineteenth century, geological theories deeply affected the "perceptual set" of many American landscape painters. To an eighteenth-century landscape artist steeped in the conventions of the picturesque and scanning the natural world for scenes resembling paintings by Claude Lorrain, a field strewn with small boulders would probably have passed unnoticed; but to nineteenth-century artists such as William Stanley Haseltine and William Trost Richards familiar with Louis Agassiz's ice-age theory, that same site became of great interest — a place full of evidences that a great glacier once passed over the land. Such theories not only led artists to focus their attention on sites and formations that had gone unremarked by earlier generations of American painters, but they also endowed natural topography with new layers of meaning that the artists were able to deploy in manifold ways to enhance and convey the narrative and thematic content of their art.

These "meanings" drawn from geological science, it is important to note, were unstable. Because geology was far from a static science in the nineteenth century — indeed was bubbling with controversy and divisiveness — artists who drew on it were on shifting ground. The same rock that Thomas Cole might interpret in the 1820s, through the lens of current geological theory, as a remnant of the biblical flood, could appear to William Stanley Haseltine, forty years later, as a relic left by an ice-age glacier.

Many of the artists discussed in this book saw themselves as joining hands with scientists in the grand project of describing and explaining the natural world. They went into the field to investigate nature's exterior aspects, they interpreted what they saw, and they reported their observations. Through their paintings, they brought new sites, new discoveries, and new interpretations to the attention of the public, catering to their audience's great appetite for empirical knowledge and their thirst for the novel and wondrous. Yet (like many scientists of the era) their ambitions extended far beyond the presentation of newly discovered natural facts or even the revelation of new theories about the workings of the natural world. They sought to use their scientifically informed canvases to, among other things, reveal the presence of the divine in nature, offer moral lessons, and promote patriotism.

The alliance between geology and landscape painting was shaped by and participated in the complex, shifting currents of nineteenth-century American society. It cannot be understood apart from other cultural developments of the time, including shifts in the social stratification of American society, the political and economic upheavals of the Jacksonian era, the explosive growth of public education, the rise of tourism, and the trauma of the Civil War. Investigating artistic use of geology brings into focus the ways that landscape painters sought to craft places for themselves in this world. Working in a society that valued production over consumption and communal contributions above self-fulfillment, they struggled to create respected, valued, and profitable positions for themselves, often defining their social roles to incorporate their contributions as educators, moralists, patriots, explorers, and facilitators of national expansion and economic development. In all of these ambitious undertakings, the artists' knowledge of geology played a part.

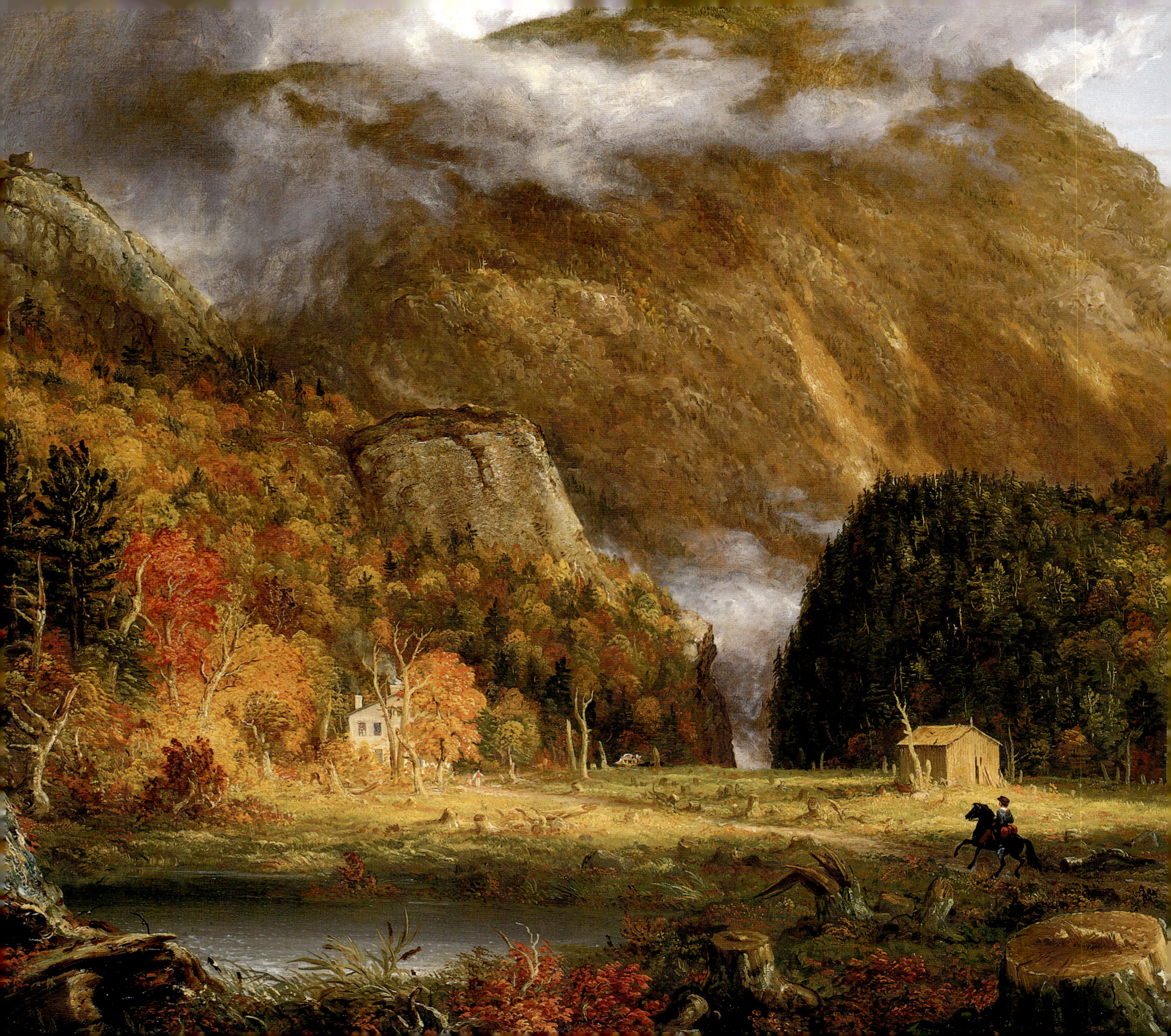

Chapter One

Thomas Cole and the Fashionable Science

In the collection of the Bronck Museum in Coxsackie, New York, is a battered wooden box the size and shape of a briefcase. It contains Thomas Cole's (1801–1848) mineral collection (fig. 5), one of the many bits of evidence we have of his interest in geology. Measuring about twenty by eighteen inches, the box holds an intriguing assortment of objects reminiscent of the curiosity cabinets of earlier eras. All of the items in the case are of mineral origin, yet some have been shaped and transformed by human hands. Fragments of limestone and quartz are mounted next to cameos, arrowheads, and a piece of mosaic work. This collection reveals much about Cole's attitude toward geology.

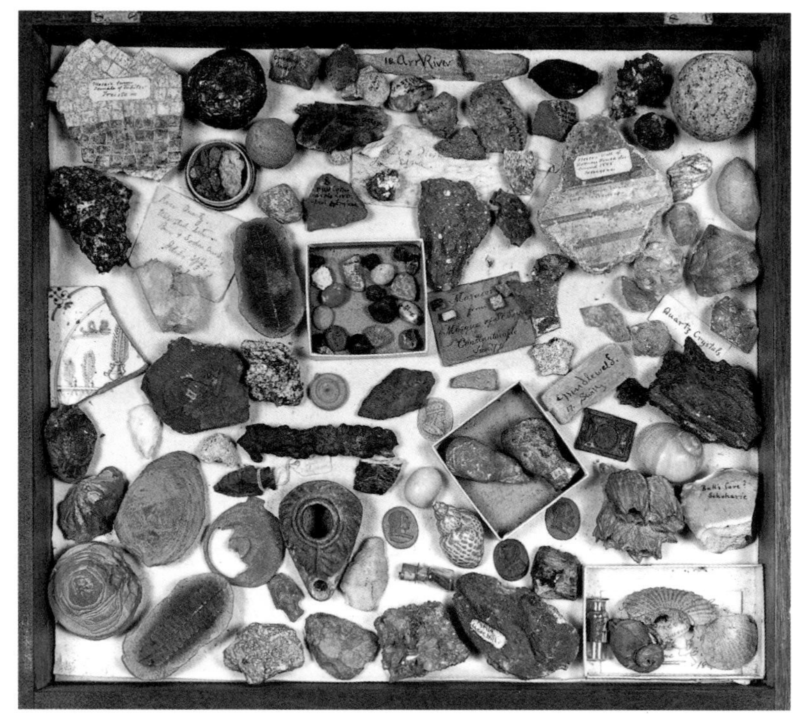

Fig. 5. Thomas Cole's fossil and rock collection. Bronck Museum, Greene County Historical Society, Coxsackie, New York. Gift of Edith Cole Silberstein

As his mineral cabinet suggests, Cole made no firm distinction between art and science, between human history and natural history. It was always, for him, the human implications of geological science that mattered. Just as the makers of the arrowheads and cameos took raw minerals and transformed them into useful objects, so too Thomas Cole sought, on an intellectual level, to do something useful with geological ideas, using them, for instance, to teach lessons about the human

Opposite: Detail of Fig. 25

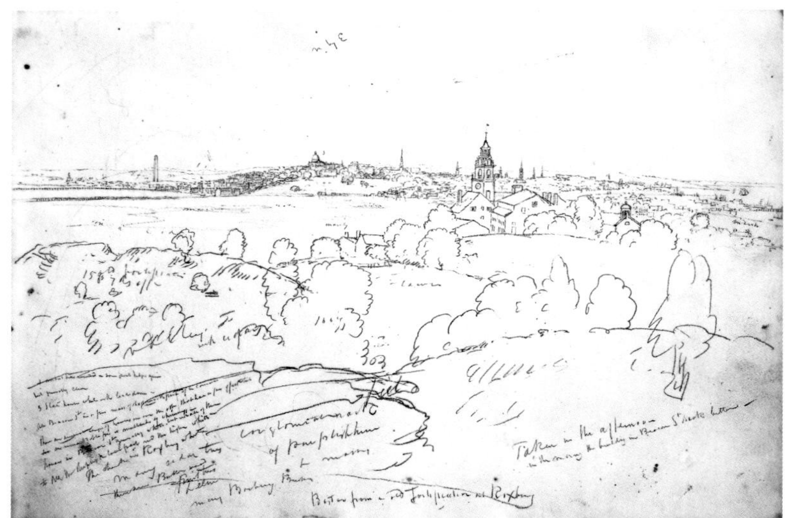

Fig. 6. Thomas Cole, *Sketch of Boston from an Old Fortification at Roxbury*, c. 1838. Pencil on paper, 8 7/8 x 13 1/2 in. (21.5 x 34.3 cm). The Detroit Institute of Arts. Founders Society Purchase, William H. Murphy Fund

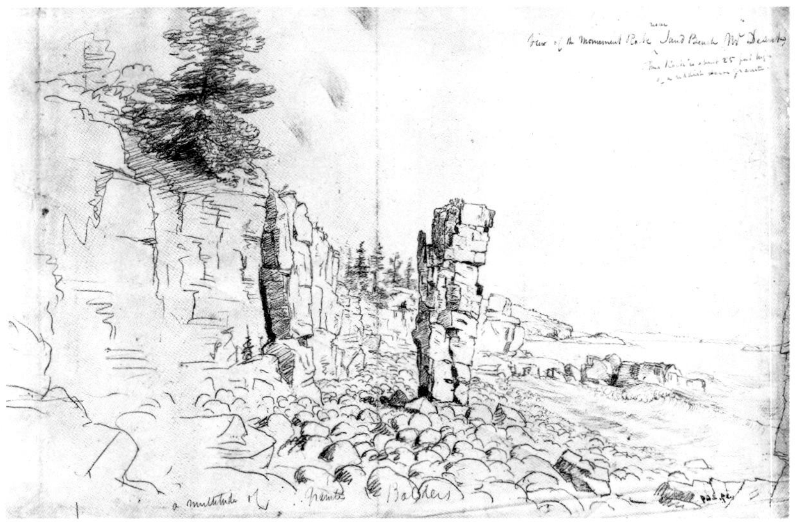

Fig. 7. Thomas Cole, *Sketch of Monument Rock near Sand Beach, Mount Desert*, August 1844. Pencil on paper, 9 3/4 x 16 in. (24.8 x 40.6 cm). The Detroit Institute of Arts. Founders Society Purchase, William H. Murphy Fund

condition. The ways Cole made use of geology in his life and in his art are the subject of this chapter.

COLE'S KNOWLEDGE OF GEOLOGY

Throughout his career, from the 1820s through the 1840s, Cole pursued an interest in geology. The evidence of his geological pursuits extends far beyond the mineral case. From his letters we know that he had begun fossil hunting with one of his friends as early as 1822.[1] He also kept abreast of the latest geological literature, reading books such as Ebenezer Emmons's geological survey of New York State (which he quotes in his journals) and J. L. Comstock's *Outlines of Geology*, a popular geology text which he kept on his personal bookshelf.[2]

Cole's familiarity with the field was furthered by personal contacts. Among his friends and acquaintances were a number of geologists including Benjamin Silliman, the leading American scientist of his era.[3] Silliman was a professor of geology and chemistry at Yale College; he was also among the first of his countrymen to urge American landscape painters to study geology. In an article written in 1830 he argued that, if they did so, the landforms in their paintings would "assume a verisimilitude, depending on physical laws."[4]

Cole seems to have agreed, at least to some extent, with

Silliman's advice, for his journals and sketchbooks include numerous testaments to his study of the science. During his many sketching trips through both the northeastern wilderness and Italian countryside, Cole filled his journals with observations on such things as the geological history of Niagara Falls, the effect of erosion on Kaaterskill Gorge, and the distinctive characteristics of the lavas of Aetna and Vesuvius.[5] In his journal entries Cole often reveals a sophisticated awareness of the ways that geological formations and geological forces shape the appearance of the countryside. For instance, on a trip through the Adirondacks in October 1835 he noted: "The country between Caldwell and Schroon is not very picturesque though rugged and often wild, but its formation is very remarkable. The mountains do not run in continuous chains as is generally the case but are insolated [isolated?] heaps of rocks scattered confusedly about. It is a Granitic Formation and one would be led to expect angular forms in the outlines of the mountains but they are generally lumpish, and all appear to have been rounded by the action of water."[6]

When Cole made drawings on these trips, he sometimes annotated them with geological references, a practice he followed more often in the latter part of his career. On his *Sketch of Boston from an Old Fortification at Roxbury* of about 1838 (fig. 6), he marked the foreground "conglomerate of purplish hue." On his *Sketch of Monument Rock near Sand Beach, Mount Desert* of 1844 (fig. 7), he noted that "the rock is about 25 feet high of a reddish worn [or warm?] granite." A foreground notation on the same drawing reads "a multitude of granite boulders." Cole's familiarity with geological nomenclature was such that he could use words like granite and conglomerate as a shorthand for himself. Back in his studio, looking over his sketches, these words could call up the appearance of a particular type of rock: the sparkling surfaces of granite or the rough, pebbly texture of a conglomerate.

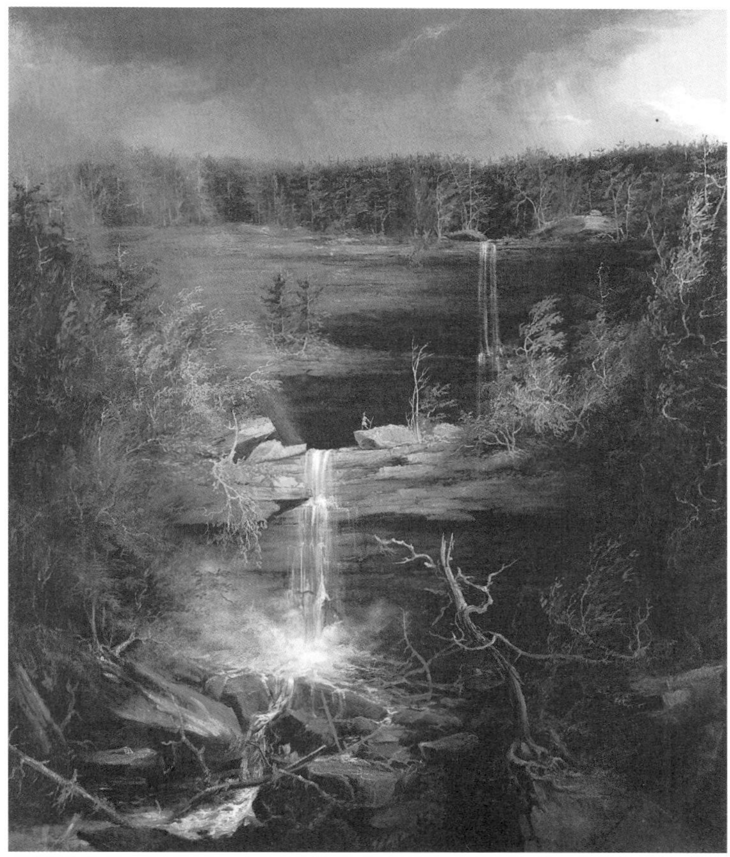

Fig. 8. Thomas Cole, *The Falls of Kaaterskill*, 1826. Oil on canvas, 43 x 36 in. (109.2 x 91.4 cm). The Warner Collection of Gulf States Paper Corporation, Tuscaloosa, Alabama

Yet, despite the keen interest in geological facts evidenced

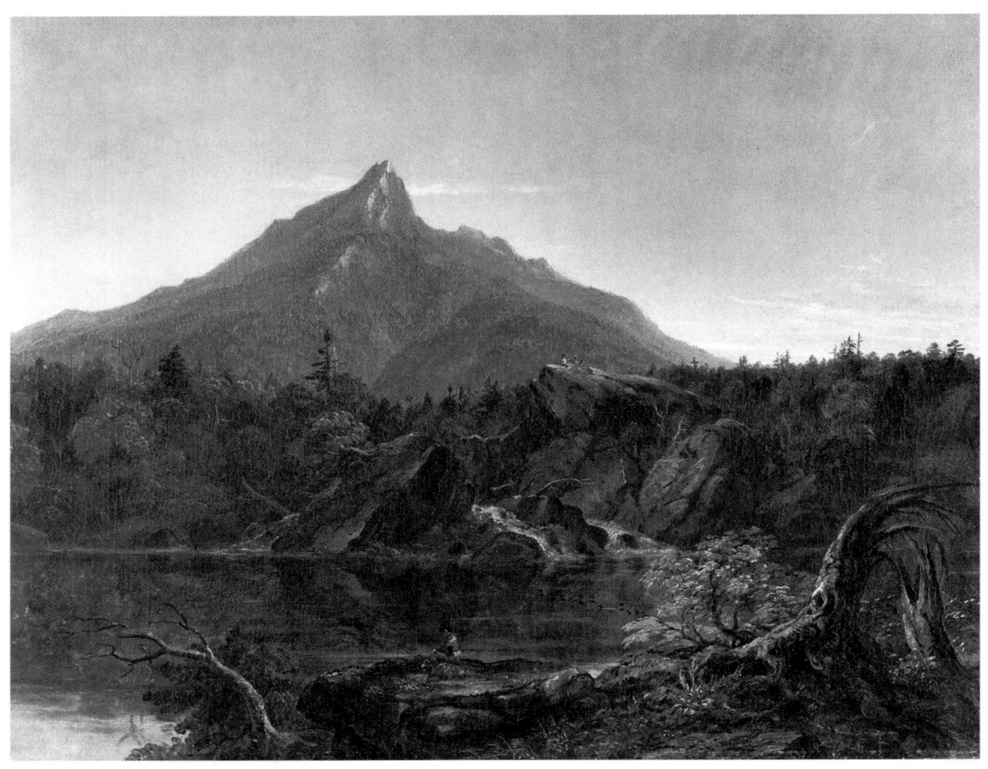

Fig. 9. Thomas Cole, *Corway [Chocorua] Peak, New Hampshire*, 1844. Oil on canvas, 18 x 24 in. (45.7 x 61 cm). Maier Museum of Art, Randolph-Macon Woman's College, Lynchburg, Virginia

Opposite: Fig. 10. Thomas Cole, *View of Schroon Mountain, Essex County, New York, after a Storm*, 1838. Oil on canvas, 39 3/8 x 33 in. (99.8 x 160.6 cm). The Cleveland Museum of Art. The Hinman B. Hurlbut Collection, 1335.1917

in his drawings and journals, Cole's finished paintings are not particularly notable for their geologic or topographic precision. It is true that in his paintings of specific sites, such as *The Falls of Kaaterskill* of 1826 (fig. 8) and *Corway [Chocorua] Peak, New Hampshire* of 1844 (fig. 9), he was usually faithful to the general geological character of the place represented. In these two images, painted nearly twenty years apart, he clearly differentiates the horizontal layering of the sedimentary formation at Kaaterskill Falls from the rugged granitic formations of New Hampshire's White Mountains. He tells us enough that we can sense the distinctive geological characters of the sites and perhaps jog our memories of the places if we have been there, but beyond that he does not seem to have felt bound by geological or topographical fact.

Instead, he often exaggerated the height and distorted the shape of the landforms in his views of American scenery, increasing the height of Kaaterskill Falls, for instance, or in the case of *View of Schroon Mountain, Essex County, New York, after a Storm* of 1838 (fig. 10), stretching the mountain up into the air, giving it a more strikingly pyramidal silhouette, and sharpening its peak. He also tended to paint his rocks with the same swirling strokes of pink, gray, and tan whether he was

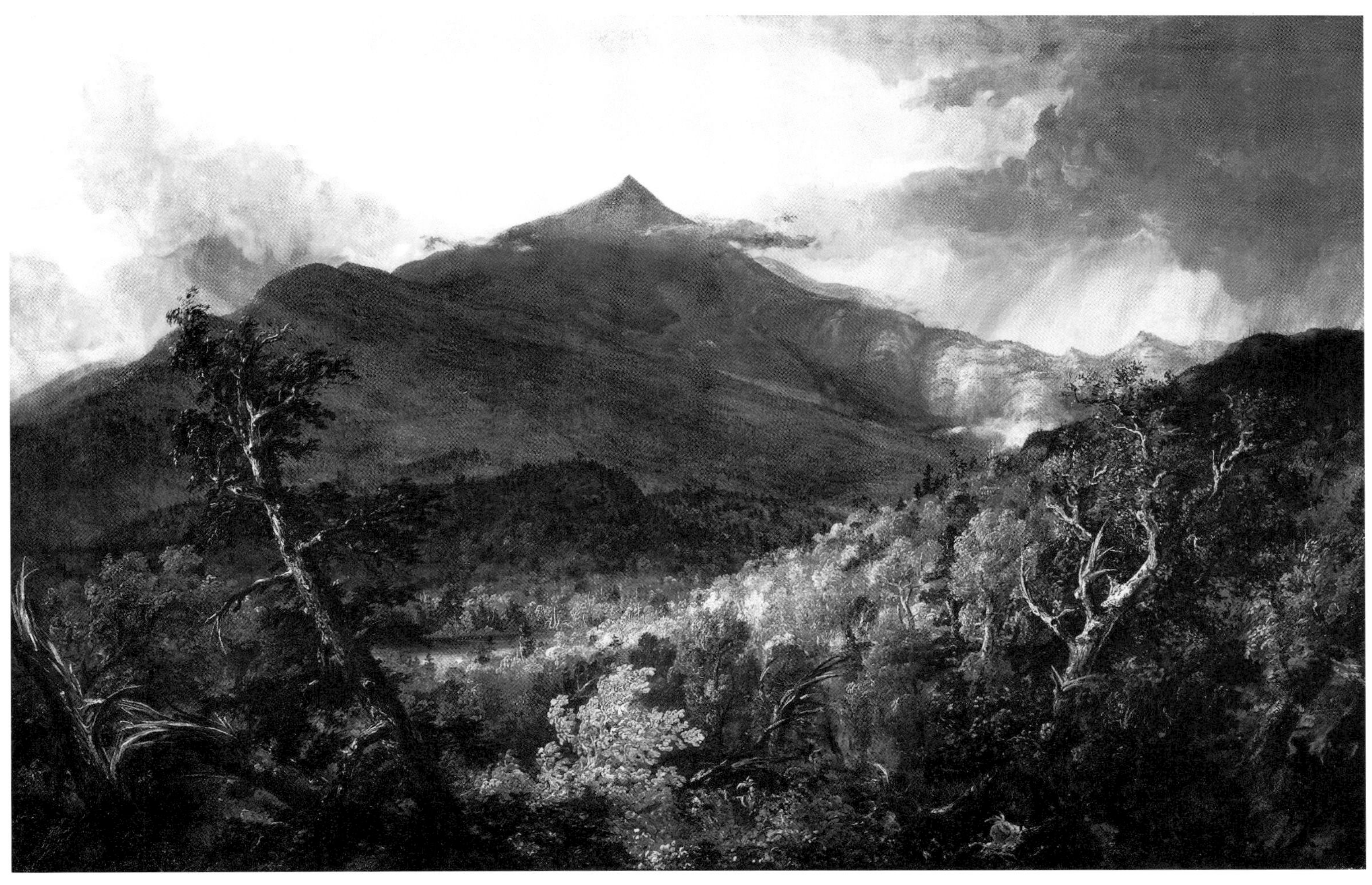

describing the granites of the White Mountains or the sedimentary formations of the Genesee region.

In his imaginary and allegorical landscapes he exercised even greater freedom in his handling of geological features, creating what are sometimes strikingly fanciful formations. In *The Expulsion from the Garden of Eden* of 1828 (fig. 11), for example, he joined a great gothic-shaped archway to a natural bridge in a conjunction that would never be found in nature, while in the *Voyage of Life: Youth* of 1840 (fig. 12) he created a highly improbable cluster of pointed peaks. These rocks do not refer to any place Cole encountered on his sketching forays, but rather to his conception of the fate awaiting human

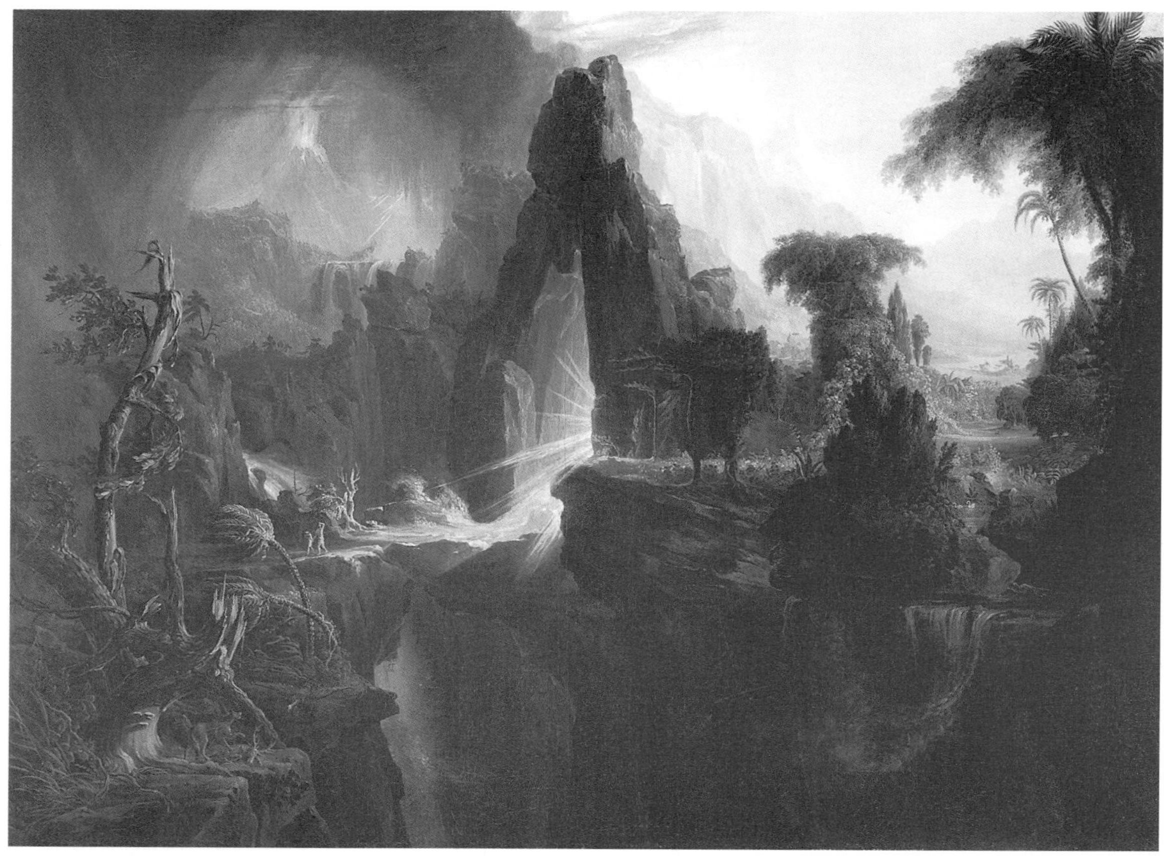

Fig. 11. Thomas Cole, *The Expulsion from the Garden of Eden*, 1828. Oil on canvas, 39 x 54 in. (99 x 137.2 cm). Museum of Fine Arts, Boston. Gift of Martha C. Karolik for the M. and M. Karolik Collection of American Paintings, 1815–1865, 47.1188

beings as they enter middle age. Traveling along the river of life, the young man in the painting is still surrounded by soft and verdant scenery, but the barren, unscaleable peaks in the background suggest the trials he will eventually encounter. As Cole's treatment of these landforms implies, he was usually less concerned with fidelity to natural fact than with symbolic and associative potential.

Cole's handling of the geological features in his paintings was wholly in keeping with his artistic philosophy. Deeply influenced by neoclassical art theory, especially the writings of Sir Joshua Reynolds, he believed that the painter should generalize his representations of the natural world rather than particularize them. In Reynolds's third discourse, delivered before the members of the Royal Academy in 1770, the eminent British artist disparaged the minute replication of natural details. "Nature," he said, "is not to be too closely copied . . . a mere copier of nature can never produce anything great. . . . The wish of the genuine painter must be more extensive: instead

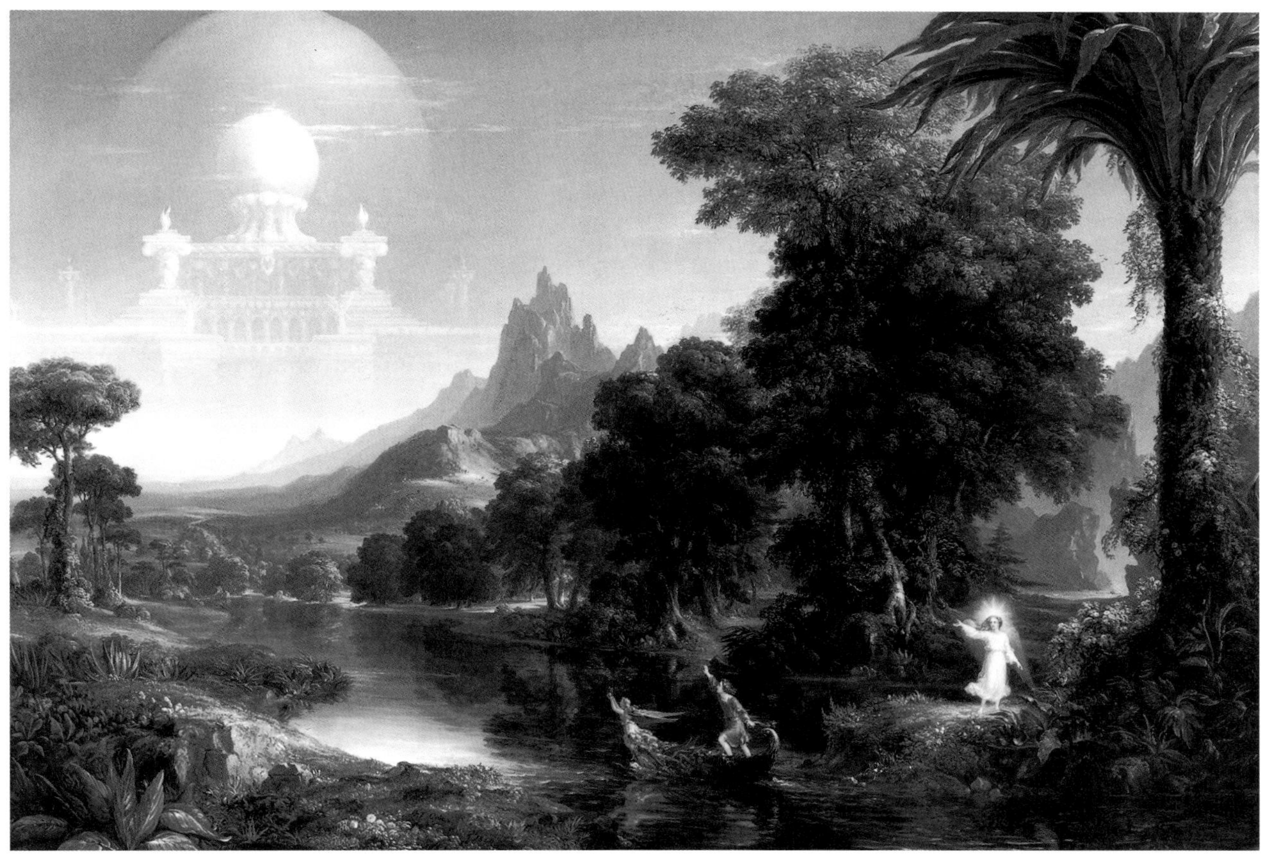

Fig. 12. Thomas Cole, *Voyage of Life: Youth*, 1840. Oil on canvas, 52 1/2 x 78 1/2 in. (133.4 x 199.4 cm). Munson-Williams-Proctor Arts Institute, Utica, New York, 55.106

of endeavoring to amuse mankind with the minute neatness of his imitations, he must endeavor to improve them by the grandeur of his ideas."[7] In keeping with Reynolds's advice, Cole believed that the landscape painter should study the natural world in all its specificity, but before transferring scenes to canvas, he should, as he told his friend Asher Durand, "wait for time to draw a veil over the common details, the unessential parts, which shall leave the great features, whether the beautiful or the sublime, dominant in the mind."[8] For Cole, the specificities of rocks and landforms seem often to have fallen into the category of "common details" and "unessential parts."

What then did geology mean to Cole? Why did he study the science? Certainly by the 1830s and 1840s he had come to regard the study of natural sciences, including geology, as essential preparation for landscape painters, familiarizing them with the subject of their art much as figure painters grounded their art in the study of human anatomy. In February of 1840 he wrote in his journal, "It is absolutely necessary that the painter have a minute I may say an anatomical knowledge of nature as well as a general one."[9]

The study of geology did more for Cole, however, than simply prepare him for the close observation of nature. In the course of his career, geology served him both artistically and socially. Artistically, he was able to draw upon his geological knowledge to invest his landscapes with narrative content and moral significance. Socially, his study of the science bolstered his claims to gentry status; it was knowledge that separated him from what his patron Philip Hone called "the vulgar and uneducated masses."[10] At a time when the vast majority of Americans were divided, as the historian Dixon Ryan Fox has pointed out, into two groups, gentry and commoners, it was very important to Cole, raised within the English class system, that he be identified with the former.[11] His study of geology—an intellectual attainment associated with the cultural elite—served him in this regard.

COLE'S PATRONS

In 1834 a writer for *Knickerbocker* magazine proclaimed, geology "is indeed the fashionable science of the day; and may be said to form a necessary part of practical and ornamental education."[12] Just how "fashionable" geology was at the time, just how "necessary" it was to the education of a gentleman, is indicated by the number of Cole's patrons who studied the science. In the 1820s and 1830s the majority of his most important patrons were involved with the science, some as amateurs, some as professionals. Most of these men were members of the old Federalist elite. This group was losing ground politically in the early nineteenth century and was turning increasingly to intellectual and cultural attainments to justify its elevated social position.[13] A knowledge of the natural sciences, including geology, was among the requisite attainments. On the founding of the Boston Athenaeum in 1807, the incorporators admonished their members, "Let men of leisure and opulence patronize the arts and sciences among us; let us love them, as intellectual men."[14]

Cole launched his career as a landscape painter in New York City in 1825. Among the first purchasers of his landscapes was the Connecticut landowner and Federalist Daniel Wadsworth (1771–1848), founder of the Wadsworth Athenaeum in Hartford.[15] Wadsworth was Benjamin Silliman's brother-in-law. He was also an amateur geologist and amateur artist whose sketches of geologic features were occasionally reproduced on the pages of the *American Journal of Science*, the major American scientific periodical of Cole's day, edited by Silliman.

Cole's relationship with Wadsworth was a close and affectionate one, especially in the mid-1820s when Wadsworth assumed a paternalistic attitude toward the young artist.[16] Cole visited Wadsworth at his estate, Monte Video, as well as at his Hartford house, and the two seemed to have shared many country walks together. Perhaps on these outings Wadsworth conveyed to Cole something of his enthusiasm for geology. At any rate, Wadsworth was one of the first wealthy aristocrats of Cole's acquaintance with an interest in the science. There were to be many others.

While Wadsworth was a scientific amateur, another of Cole's early patrons, the English-born George William Featherstonhaugh (1780–1866), was a serious professional geologist. A frequent contributor of papers to scientific societies both in the United States and in England, he also founded a scientific periodical, the short-lived *Monthly American Journal of Geology and Natural History,* that he intended to rival Silliman's *American Journal of Science.* In addition to this work, he authored several geological reports for the United States government.[17]

In November 1825, toward the very beginning of Cole's career, Featherstonhaugh made him an offer.[18] In the tradition of European aristocrats such as the Duke of Milan, patron of Leonardo da Vinci, Featherstonhaugh offered Cole a painting room for the winter at Featherston Park, his estate near Duanesburg, New York. In exchange for room and board Cole was to paint for Featherstonhaugh a number of pictures at the relatively low price of twenty or thirty dollars apiece. Cole gratefully accepted the offer but later looked back on this experience as one of the most mortifying of his life. Instead of treating Cole as a social and intellectual equal, Featherstonhaugh seems to have regarded the artist more as hired help, as a bought-and-paid-for symbol of his own aristocratic status. The Englishman, described by one of his fellow geologists as "selfish and disgustingly conceited," supposedly shunted Cole off to an unheated room during the day and tried to consign him to dinners with the children at night.[19] This treatment severely bruised Cole's ego. At the same time, it must have impressed upon him some sense of the relative social status of scientists and artists.

Moving back to New York City in early 1826, Cole met more congenial patrons, including the Baltimore merchant Robert Gilmor (1774–1848). In addition to his mercantile activities, Gilmor was an avid amateur geologist. He was a founding member of the American Geological Society and, along with Benjamin Silliman, was elected one of its vice presidents.[20] He also owned a library well stocked with geology books. Over fifty volumes on the subject lined his shelves, including "Silliman's Geological Lectures" and "Featherstonhaugh's Geological Report."[21]

One December day in 1827 Gilmor uncrated a box from Cole containing two pictures, *View of Corroway [Chocorua] Peak in New Hampshire—Sun Setting* (unlocated) and *Scene from "The Last of the Mohicans"* (fig. 13).[22] Gilmor quickly dashed off a letter to Cole informing him of their arrival and offering his critique of the images. He was, in general, pleased by the pictures, *but* he pointedly criticized Cole's handling of the geological features in *Scene from "The Last of the Mohicans."* "[T]he arrangement of your rocks," he told Cole, "is *artificial:* the rock falling against another on the opposite side of a deep ravine, is finely rendered, but strikes the eye as something forced, & not ordinarily seen in nature." He was also bothered by the large rock in the center of the composition. "The rock tottering on its pivot," he informed Cole, "is scarcely *balanced* enough. The spectator looks for it falling."[23]

As I will discuss later, I believe that Cole chose these geological formations for their dramatic and thematic potential—meanings that seem to have escaped Gilmor, at least upon his first acquaintance with the painting, when his scientifically trained eyes led him to judge the elements of the composition in terms of their fidelity to natural appearances rather than their symbolic associations. But what I want to suggest here is that criticism like this, indicating that his patrons were closely examining the geological formations in his paintings, must have spurred Cole to broaden and deepen his geological studies.

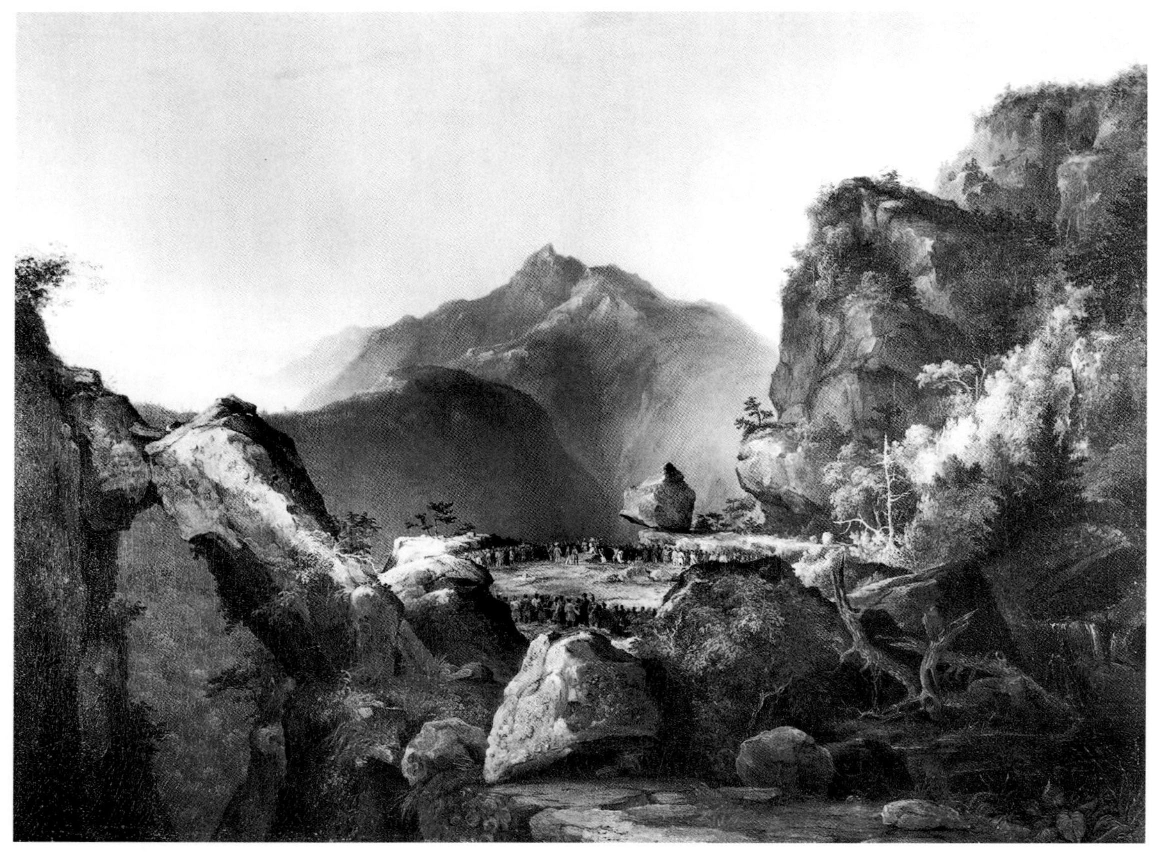

Fig. 13. Thomas Cole, *Scene from "The Last of the Mohicans": Cora Kneeling at the Feet of Tamenund*, 1827. Oil on canvas, 25 x 31 in. (63.5 x 78.7 cm). The New York State Historical Association, Cooperstown

And, in fact, in the following years his handling of geological features became increasingly naturalistic.

Gilmor fancied himself an informed connoisseur who could offer useful advice to a young artist. In Luman Reed (1785–1836) Cole found a patron with whom he enjoyed greater rapport, a patron who was at once more generous with his money and less stinting with his praise, a patron who looked up to Cole as an accomplished painter rather than down on him as a struggling young artist in need of help and guidance. Between 1833 and 1836 Reed commissioned ten works from Cole, including *The Course of Empire* series (figs. 18–24).

Reed, like so many New York gentlemen of the era, evinced an interest in geology. He owned forty volumes of Silliman's *American Journal of Science* and built a gallery in his New York house that included not only pictures by many of the leading American artists of the era but also cases of minerals.[24] Reed purchased his mineral collection from the Austrian consul general Baron von Lederer, just before the baron returned to

Europe.[25] This was one of the major private mineral collections in the United States, one well-known to practicing geologists in this country.[26]

By most standards of the day Luman Reed was a successful man, but his social position was rather different from that of Wadsworth, Featherstonhaugh, and Gilmor. The latter were born to wealth and social privilege; Luman Reed was a self-made man. He began his career as a store clerk, but by the age of forty-five he had amassed a fortune in the dry goods business and had turned the day-to-day operations of his company over to his associates so that he could spend the last years of his life cultivating the trappings of taste and fashion. For Reed, the collecting of art and the pursuit of science were his entrées to the fashionable world. In this regard, Baron von Lederer's mineral collection must have seemed to him an especially fortunate purchase, radiating both the intellectual aura of science and the mystique of European nobility.

THE USES OF GEOLOGY

Cole, like his patron Reed, was greatly concerned with his social status. And, as with Reed, his pursuit of geology seems to have been intertwined with his desire to distinguish himself from the masses. As Alan Wallach has pointed out, Cole was acutely aware of class distinctions, a concern that had its roots in his childhood in England.[27] He was born in the English Midlands, into the family of a relatively well-to-do textile manufacturer. But when Cole was still a boy his father's business failed. In the aftermath of this tragedy, he was forced to leave school and go to work as an engraver in a textile factory. This was a humiliating and terrifying experience for him. The horrors of the industrial workplace and the indignities of working next to what his friend and biographer Louis Noble called his "rude fellow operatives" left an indelible imprint on him.[28] For the rest of his life he was haunted, as Alan Wallach has said, by a "fear of sliding into the working class."[29] In his adult years, it was essential to his sense of self-worth that he be identified as a gentleman, as a member of the social and cultural elite. In this light we can read Cole's study of geology as part of his efforts to affirm his gentility. With so many of his aristocratic patrons involved in the science, he must have recognized, early in his career, the social utility of geological knowledge.

Cole's concern with rank and status embraced not only his place in the social world but also his place in the artistic world. Landscape painters, he felt, were not properly appreciated by the critical and academic establishments. Over and over again in his journals, letters, and lectures he lamented the relatively low position assigned to landscape painting in the academic hierarchy. (It was ranked below history painting, below portraiture, and only slightly above cattle pieces.)[30] He seems to have complained of this to his friend and fellow painter C. R. Leslie, who wrote to Cole from London in May 1835, "I quite agree with you that Landscape does not rank high enough in the scale of art as established by modern criticism."[31]

History painting was the most highly regarded of the genres, and throughout his career Cole was much at pains to elevate his landscapes to the level of history paintings (and himself to the status of history painter) by introducing epic, dramatic, and historical themes into his works. In this regard, geology was again of service to him, providing both associations and a storied past for his landscapes, and allowing him to teach moral lessons through the deployment of landscape elements. This does not mean that Cole's paintings are "about" geological ideas; he was an artist, not a scientist. But he drew on his knowledge of geological ideas and geological facts to help him convey the moral and religious themes of his works.

The geology embraced by Cole and his patrons was ideally suited to this task. At a time when many European geologists, including Cole's nemesis Featherstonhaugh, were insisting on an empirical approach to the science, emphasizing the mapping of strata and the classification of minerals, Cole and the majority of his patrons adhered to a more conservative and traditional geology.[32] Theirs was a patriotic and moralistic science, a science bound to revealed religion, a science, in short, designed to convey the sort of moral, spiritual, and historical lessons that Cole so loved to incorporate into his art. This science is epitomized in the person and writings of Benjamin Silliman.

Silliman was a member of the old Federalist elite from which so many of Cole's patrons were drawn.[33] The son of a general in the Continental army during the Revolutionary War, Silliman's social status was solidified by his marriage to Harriet Trumbull, daughter of Jonathan Trumbull, Federalist governor of Connecticut, and niece of the painter John Trumbull, president of the American Academy of Fine Arts. Silliman's social connections and political affiliations together with his intellectual attainments allowed him to move in the highest of American social circles. Few of Cole's patrons were unacquainted with him, even those with little interest in geology. A good example is Philip Hone, who purchased two of Cole's landscapes in the mid-1820s. A one-term mayor of New York City, ardent Whig, and acquaintance of a number of American presidents, Hone's interests extended beyond politics to embrace theater, literature, opera, history, and fine food and wine. In the several thousand pages of his diary, which Hone kept from 1828 to 1851, he expressed little interest in science, yet when Silliman arrived in New York in 1836 to offer a course of lectures on geology at Clinton Hall, Hone was in attendance.[34] And when Hone arrived in New Haven, Connecticut, for a Whig convention in 1840, Silliman escorted him and a number of his colleagues to Yale College for a quick glance at what Hone described as "the splendid mineralogical cabinet."[35] Cole was probably introduced to Silliman by either his early mentor John Trumbull or his patron Daniel Wadsworth. They became close enough that Cole visited Silliman at his home in New Haven and corresponded with him on a number of occasions.[36]

Silliman had much to recommend him to Cole beyond his social and political connections. He was also a pious Christian and committed patriot who placed his science in the service of God and country. He founded the *American Journal of Science* in 1818 to, as he said, "advance the interests of this rising empire, by exciting and concentrating original American efforts."[37] He hoped to further the economic development of his country by encouraging the discovery and exploitation of "those physical resources, which the bounty of God has given us."[38] Even more important (especially from Cole's point of view), he hoped to uncover the intersections between science and theology, between Genesis and geology. This concern is manifested in his *Geological Lectures*, published in 1820.[39] The

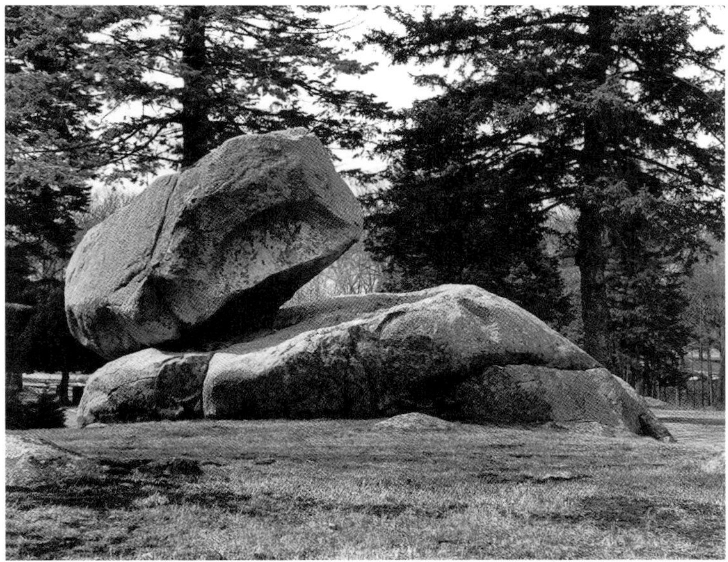

Fig. 14. Erratic boulder, Holliston, Massachusetts

book deals with many topics, but one to which Silliman devotes great attention is the geological evidence of the biblical Flood.

Silliman, along with many of his scientific contemporaries in the United States and Europe, believed that geological evidence of the Deluge was readily apparent around the globe. In the northeastern United States, great U-shaped valleys such as New Hampshire's Carrigain Notch and Crawford Notch were interpreted as thoroughfares excavated by the rushing waters of the Deluge. Great piles of unsorted rocks, sand, and gravel (such as those that make up Cape Cod) were seen as remains of the Flood. This so-called "diluvial drift" was identified as the deposits left by the receding waters of the Deluge. Of the various categories of diluvial drift, one received particular attention at the time: erratic boulders. Erratic boulders are rocks that have been deposited some distance from their place of origin. Some of them can be found in prominent positions on hillsides and mountaintops; these were referred to in Cole's day as "perched boulders." Other erratics were left stranded atop other rocks, some balanced so delicately that they can be rocked by the human hand (fig. 14); these were dubbed "rocking stones." All of these geological phenomena (the U-shaped valleys, the diluvial drift, the erratic boulders) are now attributed to the glacial action of past ice ages, but in Cole's day it was their associations with biblical history that captured people's imaginations.

COLE AND THE DELUGE

Cole was among those who became fascinated by these diluvial features, and in the 1820s and 1830s he incorporated them (particularly erratic boulders) into a number of his paintings.[40] They appear in both his allegorical-literary works, including *Scene from "The Last of the Mohicans"* (1827, figs. 13, 17) and *The Course of Empire* series (1833–36, figs. 18, 19, 21, 22, 23), and in his views of American scenery such as *A View of the Mountain Pass Called the Notch of the White Mountains (Crawford Notch)* (1839, fig. 25). Significantly, they do not appear in either of his paintings of the antediluvial world: *The Garden of Eden* (1828, Amon Carter Museum, Fort Worth, Texas) or *The Expulsion from the Garden of Eden* (1828, fig. 11).

Cole's interest in diluvial phenomena was probably stimulated by several different sources. He could certainly have heard about the geological proofs of the Deluge through his friends and patrons such as Silliman, Gilmor, and Wadsworth.

He could also have read about them in the scientific literature of the day. The *American Journal of Science*, for example, carried dozens of articles about erratic boulders, rocking stones, and diluvial drift.[41] By 1834 Cole could also have read of the connections between erratic boulders and the Deluge in his personal copy of Comstock's *Geology.* The book's central theme is the reconciliation of geology with revealed religion. In a long section devoted to the Flood, Comstock places great emphasis on diluvial boulders and drift: "The effects of that grand and awful cataclysm are still to be traced in every country, and in nearly every section of . . . the globe. Vast accumulations of rounded or waterworn pebbles, huge blocks of granite, and immense beds of sand and gravel are found in places where no causes now in operation ever could have placed them; and still that they have been moved is evident from the circumstances or places where they occur."[42]

Cole's sketchbooks from the 1820s and 1830s offer further evidence of his interest in diluvial phenomena. A number of them contain drawings of what appear to be rocking stones, perched boulders, and other unusually situated rocks. For example, in one sketch from 1831 a flat-topped, oblong boulder teeters atop a rocky ledge, and in another, a similarly shaped rock is precariously balanced on two rounded stones (fig. 15). That same year, Cole made still another drawing, which he labeled "Rock lying on the side of a mountain." This slight sketch of a boulder on a slope depicts the sort of geological phenomenon that was widely cited as evidence of the Flood.

Cole was almost certainly familiar with the biblical interpretation of these geological phenomena. He was without question fascinated by the Deluge itself. In 1825 he wrote a poem called "The Deluge: A Judgment," in which he described the fate of "the last sad victim of the rising flood."[43] A few years after completing this morbid verse, he made a sketch in his notebook that he inscribed "the Deluge." It depicts several

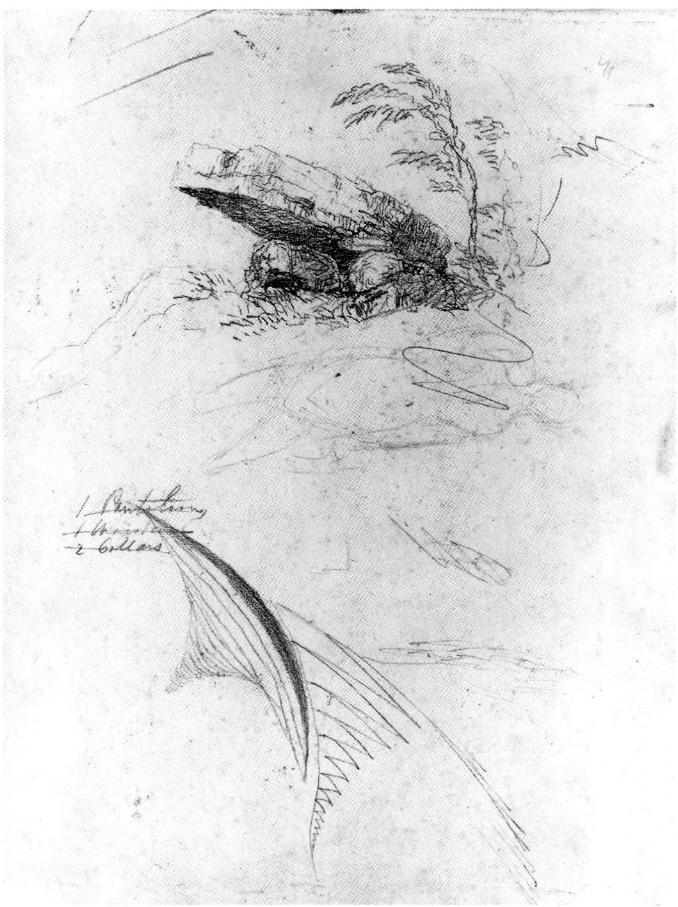

Fig. 15. Thomas Cole, *Drawing of Rocks*, 1831. Pencil on paper, 8 1/4 x 11 1/4 in. (21 x 28.5 cm). The Detroit Institute of Arts. Founders Society Purchase, William H. Murphy Fund

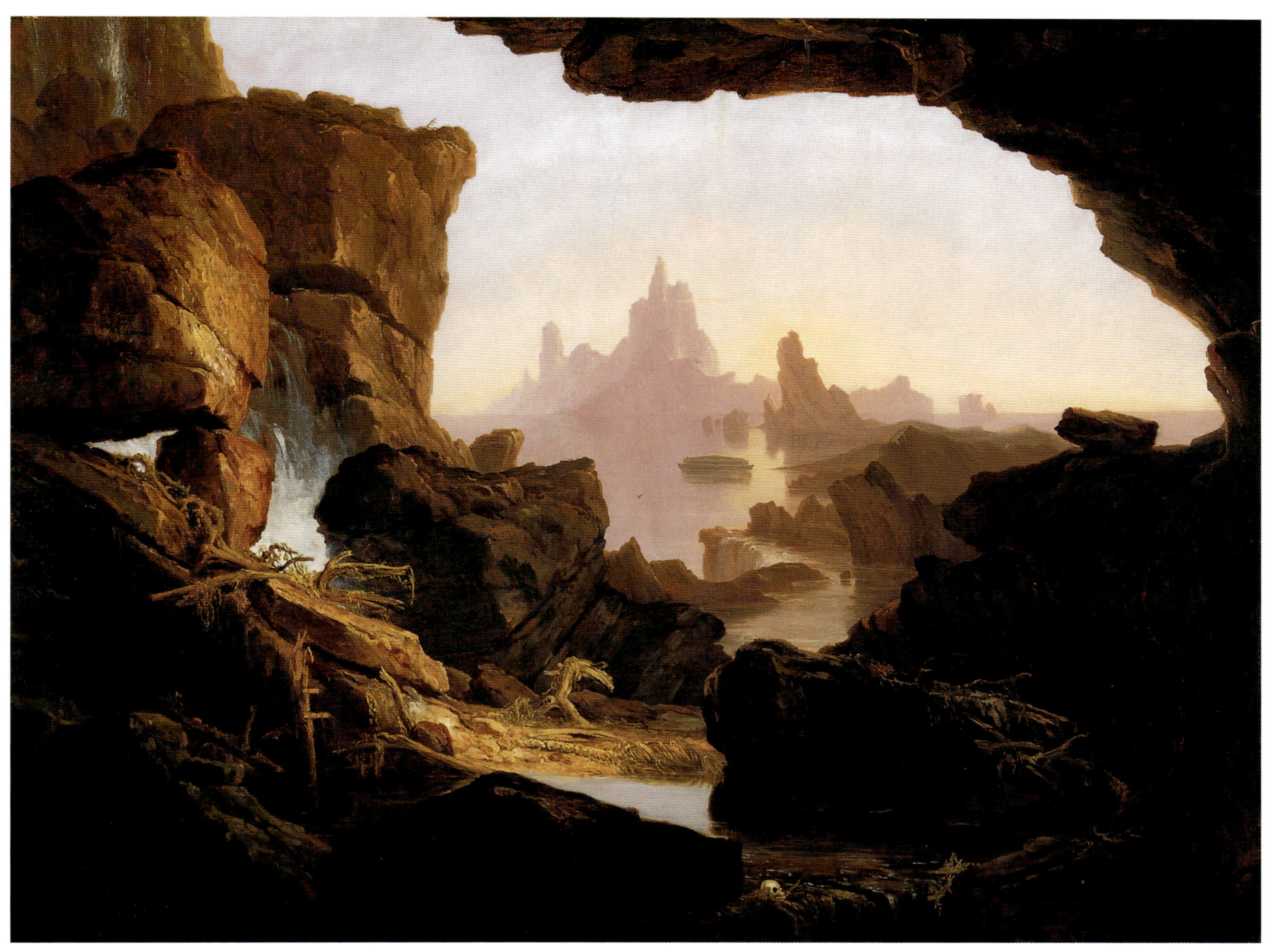

Fig. 16. Thomas Cole, *The Subsiding of the Waters of the Deluge*, 1829.
Oil on canvas, 36 x 48 in. (91.4 x 121.9 cm). Smithsonian American Art Museum, Washington, D.C.
Gift of Mrs. Katie Dean in memory of Minnibel S. and James Wallace Dean
and museum purchase through the Smithsonian Institution Collections Acquisitions Program

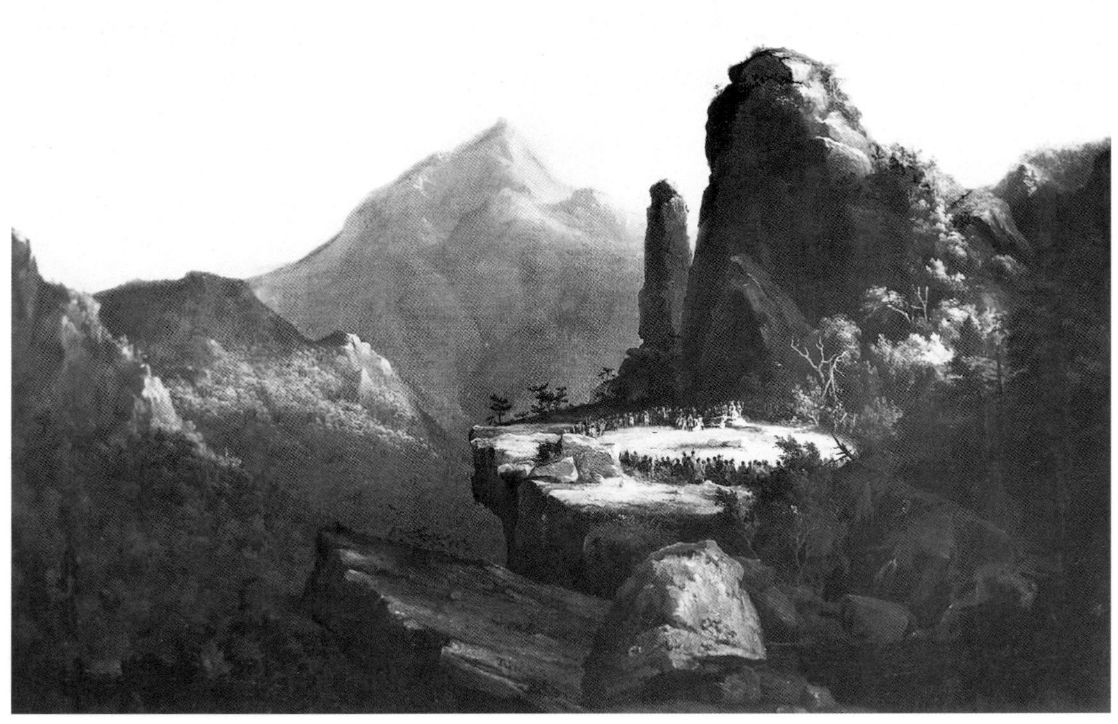

Fig. 17. Thomas Cole, *Scene from "The Last of the Mohicans": Cora Kneeling at the Feet of Tamenund*, 1827. Oil on canvas, 25 3/8 x 35 1/16 in. (64.4 x 89.1 cm). Wadsworth Atheneum, Hartford, Connecticut. Bequest of Alfred Smith

figures standing atop a conical mound of earth as torrents of water pour from the heavens and huge waves threaten to engulf them.

In the same notebook in which he made this sketch, Cole also listed potential subjects for future works.[44] On the list are two titles directly related to the Deluge: "First Rainbow after the Deluge" and "World after the Deluge." Sandwiched between these are two other subjects that may also have been intended as depictions of post-diluvial phenomena: "Rocks and trees heaped confusedly together as having been carried by the floods from the mountains" and "A picture in which nothing shall be but bare rocks and clouds — Rocks piled on rocks."

In 1829, at about the same time that he made this list, Cole produced a major painting of the Flood, *The Subsiding of the Waters of the Deluge* (fig. 16). From beneath a rocky overhang, the viewer looks out on a watery, yet peaceful world. The rains have finally ceased, and the golden light of dawn suffuses the scene. The ark is floating serenely in the distance, and the dove is skimming over the waters. Only the human skull and shattered ship mast in the foreground and the chaotic assemblage of rocks recall the nightmarish destruction of the previous days. Cole's inclusion of the jumbled masses of rocks in the foreground and boulders balanced on mountain peaks in the distance clearly indicate that he associated these geological features with the biblical Flood. This painting was purchased by Dr. David Hosack (1769–1835), a fashionable New York physician, accomplished botanist, and yet another of Cole's patrons with an interest in geology.[45]

For Cole, the Flood was a historical occurrence of profound moral and religious significance, and features such as erratic boulders were tangible proof that it had actually taken place. They attested to the credibility of the Bible, affirming its truths, and functioned as reminders of the power and potential wrath of God. Recognizing these associations allows us to better understand Cole's inclusion of these features in his landscape paintings.

Erratic boulders make their first appearance in Cole's art in his several versions of *Scene from "The Last of the Mohicans."* In the version that he painted for Daniel Wadsworth in 1827 (fig. 17), he set a rounded erratic atop a stone pillar. In a later version of that same year painted for Robert Gilmor (fig. 13), he perched a large angular boulder (perhaps a rocking stone) on a ledge in the middle ground of the painting.

While the boulder in the earlier version could be easily overlooked, the one in the second is much larger and more prominent compositionally. Its striking presence in the center of the canvas calls attention to the tiny figures beneath it, which might otherwise be overwhelmed by the landscape elements. The boulder also, by its precarious, threatening position overhanging and overshadowing the central figures, alludes to the nature of the unfolding human drama. In this scene, taken from James Fenimore Cooper's novel *The Last of the Mohicans*, Cora, the young white woman, is begging for mercy from Tamenund, the chief of the Delawares. Her pleas will be ignored, and in the ensuing action she will be killed along with Uncas, the last of the Mohicans.

In juxtaposing the diluvial boulder with this violent scene, Cole was perhaps intending to draw a parallel between the deaths of Cora and Uncas (who represented the last of his race), and the destruction of human life in the Deluge. This association between erratic boulders and human tragedy recurs in other of Cole's works. In each case the boulders are linked with the demise of a social unit: a race, a tribe, an empire, a family.

"THE COURSE OF EMPIRE"

In *The Course of Empire* series, commissioned by Luman Reed and painted between 1833 and 1836, Cole once again included an erratic boulder (fig. 20).[46] It appears perched on a ledge in the background of each of the five paintings that make up the series. As a striking topographic feature, the rock serves as a fixed reference point for the viewer, indicating the geographical continuity between the scenes.

The paintings trace the rise and fall of a civilization from *The Savage State* (fig. 18) to *The Pastoral State* (fig. 19) to *Consummation* (fig. 21), in which the empire reaches its peak, to *Destruction* (fig. 22) brought on by human weaknesses—greed, corruption, vanity, and vainglory. In the final painting, *Desolation* (fig. 23), the relics of empire are being slowly absorbed and reclaimed by nature.

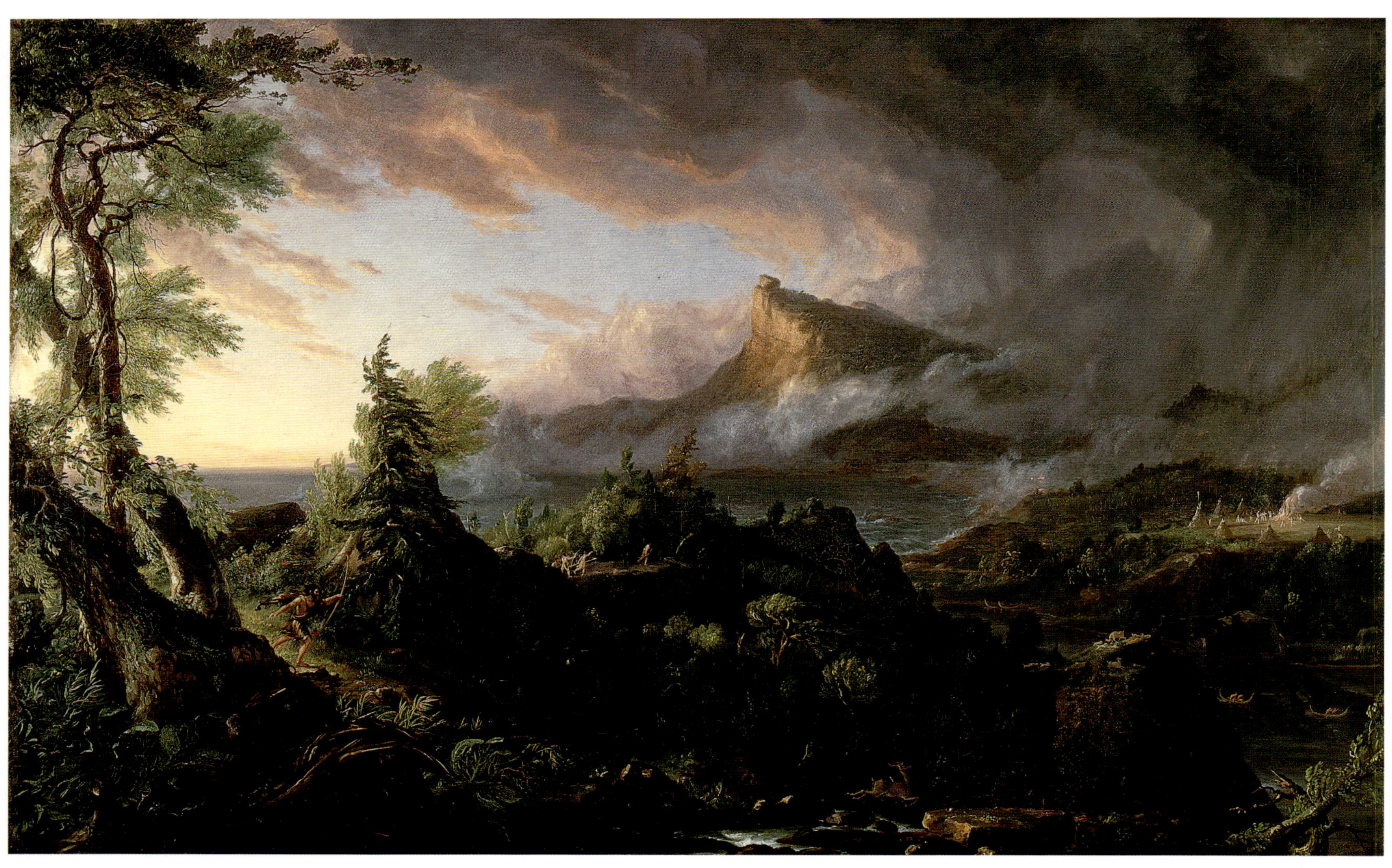

Fig. 18. Thomas Cole, *The Course of Empire: The Savage State*, 1834.
Oil on canvas, 39 ¼ x 63 ¼ in. (99.7 x 160.6 cm).
The New-York Historical Society, New York

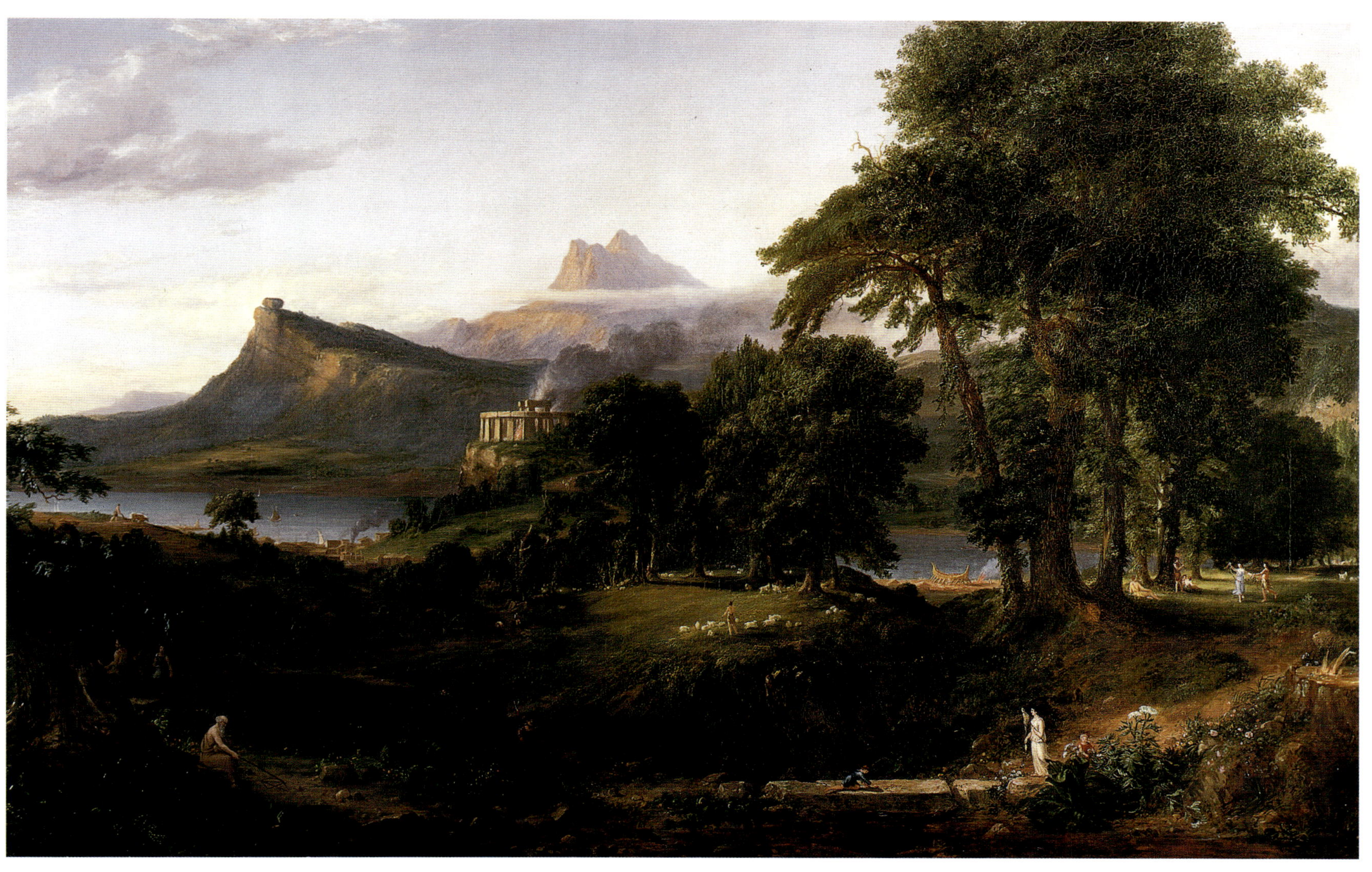

Fig. 19. Thomas Cole, *The Course of Empire: The Pastoral State*, 1834.
Oil on canvas, 39 ¼ x 63 ¼ in. (99.7 x 160.6 cm).
The New-York Historical Society, New York

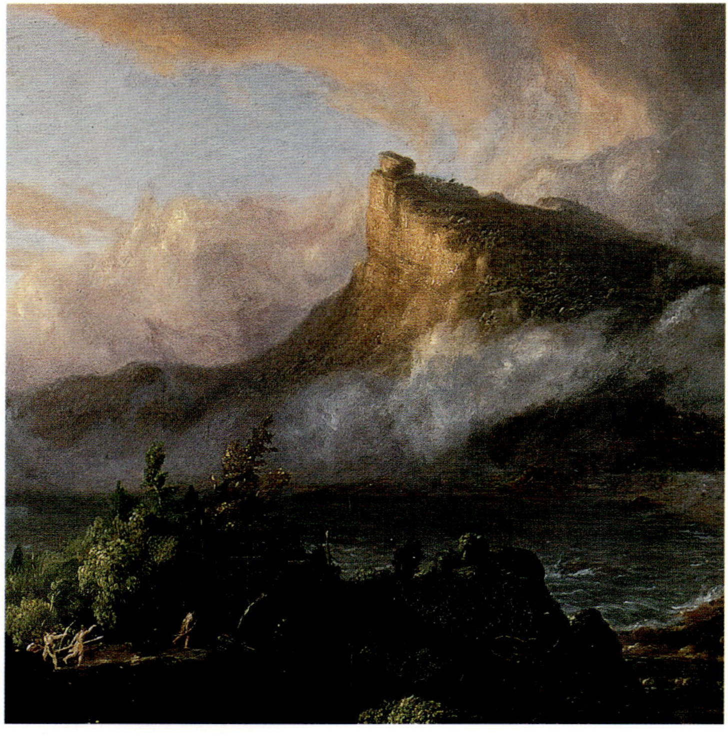

Fig. 20. Detail of Fig. 18

Cole intended the series to offer a pessimistic and moralistic lesson on the recurring cycles of human empire. It expressed his cyclical vision of history in which, as he explained it, "nations have risen from the savage state to that of power and glory, and then fallen to become extinct."[47] In this context we can interpret the boulder, sitting imperturbably above each scene, as a reference to the first civilization to pass through these stages: the civilization built by the offspring of Adam and Eve that fell into a moral degeneracy so appalling that God swept it away in the waters of the Flood.

By including the erratic boulder in *The Course of Empire* series, Cole naturalized the cycles of human empire. For just as many historians of the eighteenth and early nineteenth centuries viewed human history as a repetitive pattern of rises and declines, so many geologists of the period (including Benjamin Silliman) viewed the history of the earth as punctuated by cycles of creation and destruction.[48] Catastrophists, as geologists of this school were called, regarded the Deluge as the most recent geological cataclysm to reshape the surface of the earth, thus placing it at the intersection of human and natural history. Cole's boulder then refers both backwards to previous physical cycles of the planet's history and forward to the ensuing cycles of human history.

While *The Course of Empire* alludes to the sweeping panorama of human history, it also refers, as Angela Miller has convincingly argued, to a very specific historical moment —to the rise of Jacksonian Democracy (and, I would add, the triumph of the market revolution) in the United States in the 1830s.[49] Miller reads the series as a political allegory venting Cole's anti-Jackson sentiments. But perhaps the series expresses broader fears of which the election of Jackson was but a symptom.

It was painted during a time of dramatic social and economic upheaval when the nation was undergoing a painful transition from a traditional to a market economy. Perhaps nowhere in the United States in the 1830s were the evidences of the economic revolution more apparent than in New York (where Cole worked and many of his patrons lived). Sermons, newspaper editorials, political speeches, and private writings of that decade all comment on the city's emergence as a

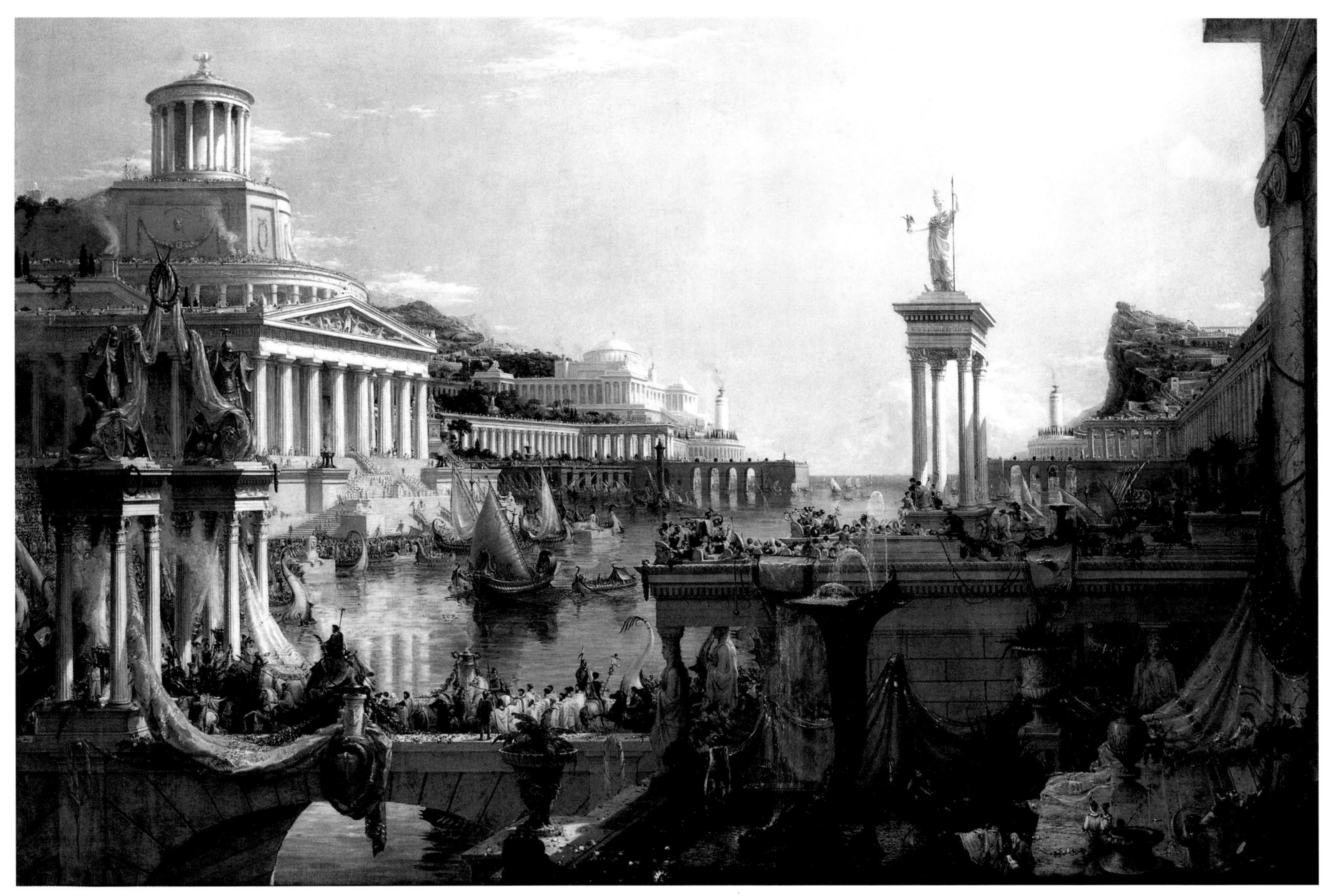

Fig. 21. Thomas Cole, *The Course of Empire: The Consummation of Empire*, 1835–36.
Oil on canvas, 51 1/4 x 76 in. (130.2 x 193 cm).
The New-York Historical Society, New York

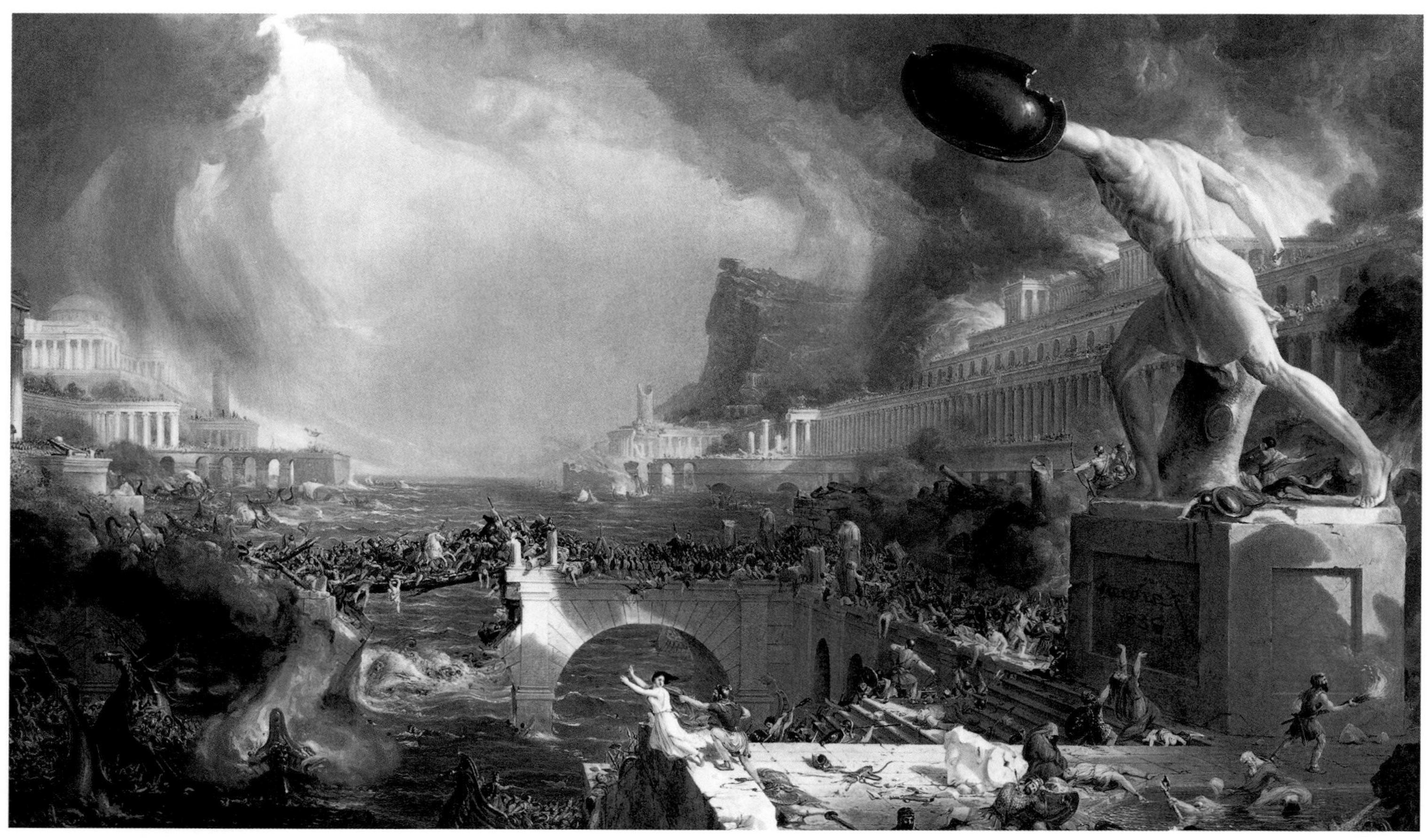

Fig. 22. Thomas Cole, *The Course of Empire: Destruction*, 1836.
Oil on canvas, 39 1/4 x 63 1/4 in. (84.5 x 160.6 cm).
The New-York Historical Society, New York

mercantile empire with its burgeoning trade, accumulating wealth, escalating competition, and growing individualism. Cole's decision to title his series *The Course of Empire* at the very moment when New York was becoming known as "the Empire City," reinforces the notion that Cole intended the series to offer topical social commentary. Likewise, the dramatic transformations of the site in the series' first three paintings from a wooded bay to a bustling port city seem to echo the dramatic transformation of New York during the years Cole worked there. While many New Yorkers took pride in these signs of economic robustness, there was at the same time a great unease about the materialistic tenor of the times, an unease shared by Cole and many of those who purchased his pictures.[50]

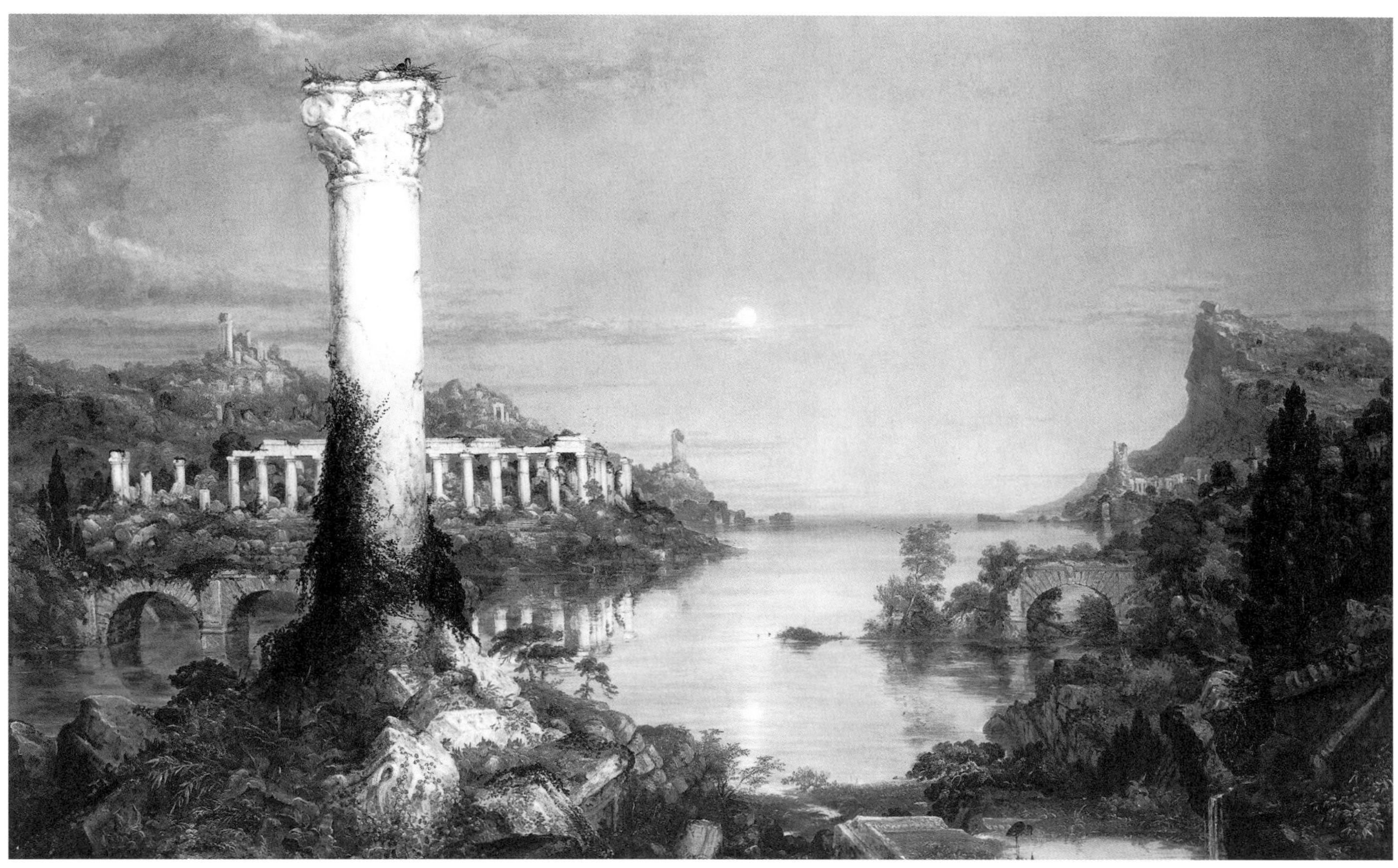

Fig. 23. Thomas Cole, *The Course of Empire: Desolation*, 1836.
Oil on canvas, 39 1/4 x 63 in. (99.7 x 160 cm).
The New-York Historical Society, New York

His patron Philip Hone, for example, a one-time mayor of New York City, fretted in his diary entries during the 1830s and 1840s about the evil effects of money on youth, recounting how the sons of his well-off friends (young men with no need to work for their living) were sinking into debauchery. Luman Reed, owner of *The Course of Empire*, was even more concerned about the potentially corrupting effects of wealth and luxury. According to one of his contemporaries, Reed was "opposed . . . to any outward show or display," and though possessed of a sizable fortune he refused to own a personal carriage, considering such a display too ostentatious and self-indulgent.[51] Moreover, it was to counter what he saw as the rampant acquisitiveness and moral degradation of his time

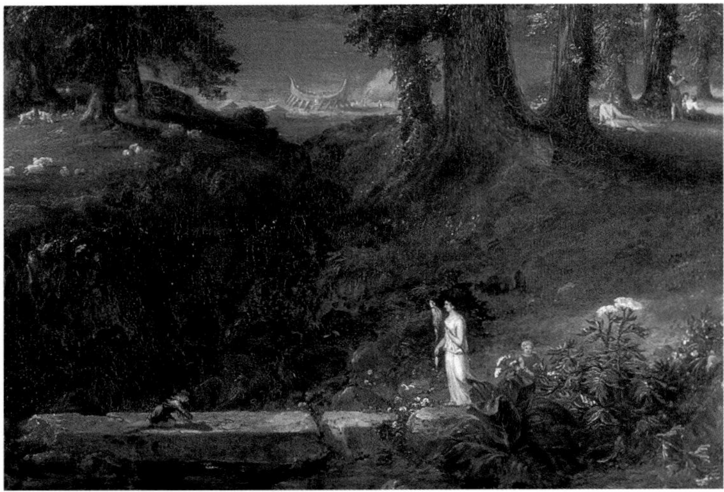

Fig. 24. Detail of Fig. 19

that Reed conceived of his picture gallery, of which *The Course of Empire* was the centerpiece, as "an instrument of moral reform."[52]

Cole's own fears about the materialistic bent of his times are clearly expressed in the series. In the second painting, the gently beautiful *Pastoral State*, he evokes the Jeffersonian ideal: a life of simplicity, of Republican virtue, lived close to the land. The painting recalls a way of life that, according to later scholars, "fostered family obligation" and "communal cooperation."[53] It depicts an age of homespun when women made the cloth for their families. Prominently situated in the right foreground, a white-robed woman crosses a small bridge, a spindle and distaff in her hands (fig. 24). Like so many images in the series, she has a dual identity. Within the long-ago-and-faraway setting of the picture, with its many allusions to classical antiquity, we can read her as Clotho, spinner of fate; but in terms of the painting's contemporary references, the figure reminds us that the painting depicts an age when the traditional, subsistence, home-based economy held sway.[54]

In the following canvas, *Consummation*, the empire has reached what Cole himself called "the state of luxury."[55] The brilliant noonday sun is glinting off the gilded statues of gods, reflecting from the gleaming marble facades of temples and palaces, and shimmering across the luxurious textiles draped over every available surface. These textiles, set against the image of the spindle and distaff in the previous painting, stand out as a significant detail, especially since they were painted by a man whose father had lost his fortune in the textile industry and who had spent some frightening months of his own youth toiling in a textile mill. These fabrics must have been for Cole a marker for the dark side of economic prosperity, just as the warriors and warships gathering in the harbor foreshadow the evil consequences of political and economic imperialism.

In *Consummation* Cole acknowledges both the advantages and the dangers of personal and national prosperity. Through his loving treatment of the art and architecture, he offers his admiration for the cultural achievements made possible by burgeoning commerce, yet, at the same time, he suggests the price to be paid for that prosperity—the desecration of nature, the temptations of luxurious idleness, and the potential repercussions of imperialism.

In the following canvas, *Destruction*, the city is sacked, pillaged, and burned. In describing the reasons for its fall, Cole explained that "luxury has weakened and debased."[56] He also appended to the series these words from Byron's *Childe Harold*:

"First freedom, and then glory; when that fails, / Wealth, vice, corruption."[57] These glosses, coupled with the many parallels between the civilization in the painting and the United States of Cole's day, convey the artist's fears that American society was sliding into the very sort of dissipation that led to the downfall of the empire in the picture, the sort of dissipation that had, in the more remote past, brought down God's wrath on Sodom and Gomorrah. The erratic boulder on the background cliff is an obvious reminder of the biblical cities' destruction in the Deluge, and it must have been intended by the artist to evoke for his viewers the dire consequences of moral failure. The entire series is a pictorial sermon urging Americans to turn from the self-absorbed pursuit of material gain and sensual indulgence and to re-embrace virtues of simplicity and frugality—before it is too late.

"CRAWFORD NOTCH"

In *A View of the Mountain Pass Called the Notch of the White Mountains (Crawford Notch)* of 1839 (fig. 25) erratic boulders (sitting atop the naked cliff on the left) are again associated with a scene of tragedy and destruction. At first glance this painting seems to offer a rather straightforward topographic depiction of a particular site in the White Mountains. Yet as John Sears has pointed out in *Sacred Places*, his book about American tourist sites, this spot abounded in frightful associations for the nineteenth-century viewer, associations in which geology played a part.[58] Crawford Notch was a place, it was argued at the time, where the effects of the Deluge were written clearly on the surface topography. The Notch itself was believed to have been excavated by the Flood, while the presence of erratic boulders high on the clifftops and mountainsides attested to the depth and ferocity of the torrential waters.[59] Not only did the landscape bear evidence of this great cataclysm of the past, but it was also the site of a much more recent tragedy known at the time as the Willey Disaster.

On the night of 28 August 1826, an avalanche of rocks and mud roared down one of the sloping walls of the Notch and buried alive Samuel Willey, his wife, their five children, and two hired men. The Willeys had experienced avalanches previously, and only two months earlier a rock slide had narrowly missed their home. Willey then constructed a shelter away from the house, and when they were awakened by the rumble of falling rocks on the night of 28 August, it was to this refuge that they fled—right into the path of the oncoming slide. Just before the avalanche reached the house, it changed course, leaving the building untouched. If the Willeys had stayed in their beds, they would have been spared.

On a visit to the site, in 1828, Cole found himself haunted by thoughts of the tragedy:

> The sight of that deserted dwelling the Willie [*sic*] House standing with a little patch of green in the midst [of] the dread wilderness of desolation called to mind the horrors of that night the 28th of August 1826 when these mountains were deluged and rocks and trees were hurled from high places down the steep channelled sides of the mountains. . . . A dreadful mystery hangs over the events of that night—We walked among the rocks and felt as though we were but as worms

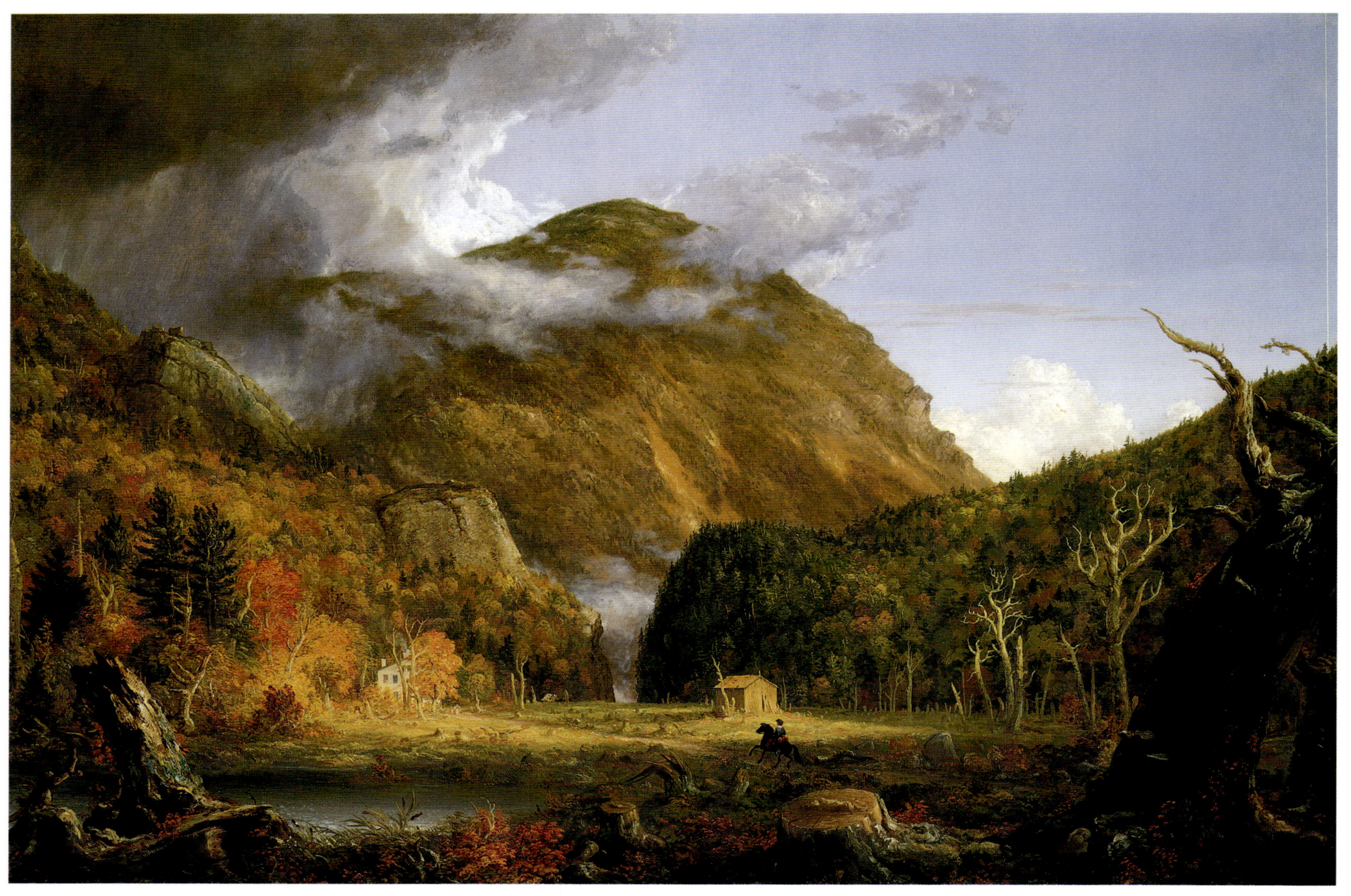

Fig. 25. Thomas Cole, *A View of the Mountain Pass Called the Notch of the White Mountains (Crawford Notch)*, 1839.
Oil on canvas, 40 x 61 ½ in. (101.6 x 156.2 cm).
National Gallery of Art, Washington, D.C. Andrew W. Mellon Fund

> insignificant and feeble for as worms a falling rock could crush us—We looked up at the pinnacles above us and measured ourselves as nothing.[60]

The Willey Disaster, as Sears has observed, posed to Cole's contemporaries an interpretive problem in terms of the divine meaning of the event. The problem was how to answer the question: Why were the Willeys destroyed? The diluvial associations of the spot naturally suggested divine retribution, and parallels between the Deluge and the Willey Disaster were drawn at the time. Benjamin Silliman, in a communication to the *American Journal of Science* in 1829, noted that the Willey catastrophe "enables one to form some feeble conception of the universal effects of the vindictive deluge which once swept every mountain and ravaged every plain and defile."[61] In this context, the Willey catastrophe can be interpreted as a warning, a reminder of the wages of sin.

But the question still remained: Why were the Willeys singled out for destruction? By every account they were a humble, upright, and industrious family. No hint of immorality, no taint of scandal ever touched them. They lived quietly, tending their small farm and catering to the needs of travelers who passed through the Notch. So in answering "Why the Willeys?" most interpreters were forced to fall back on the mysterious workings of God.

Cole's representation of the site is itself somewhat mysterious. It may be a topographic view of Crawford Notch as it appeared to Cole on his 1839 visit; on the other hand, it might be read in a different way. Comparing the painting to the drawing Cole made on the spot (fig. 26) reveals a close correspondence between the two. Even though Cole has shifted the point of view to the left in the painting, giving us a somewhat different perspective on the scene, the configuration of the topography (the shape of the notch and the mountains) is the same, as are the dead trees and the erratic boulders on the cliff. To that extent Cole remains true to what he saw on the spot.

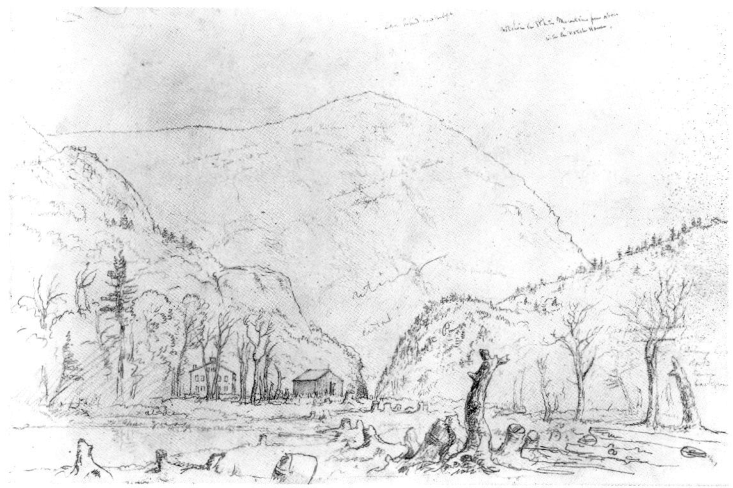

Fig. 26. Thomas Cole, *Notch in the White Mountains, From Above with the Notch House*, 1839. Pencil on paper, 11 1/8 x 16 7/8 in. (28.3 x 42.9 cm). The Art Museum, Princeton University, Princeton, New Jersey. Gift of Frank Jewett Mather Jr. Collection

Yet he has made enough changes and additions to the scene to suggest that this may not be a simple topographic view but rather a narrative picture, a reconstruction of the site in the hours before the Willey Disaster. This interpretation is indicated by a number of details. For example, the foliage has been returned to the trees around the house, and the dwelling is clearly occupied. Smoke curls from the chimney, and a man and child have emerged from the house to greet the approaching visitor. Goats graze beside the shed, and a stagecoach has just passed along the road.

In addition to these references to domestic felicity, there are intimations of the approaching tragedy. The horse in the foreground seems to be rearing back as if frightened, introducing a note of tension and apprehension into the scene. Huge, black storm clouds are unleashing torrents of rain on the mountain peaks as they did on the night of the disaster, while on the background mountain several diagonal streaks of loose swirling brown pigment suggest avalanches of mud and stone tumbling into the Notch. The dead trees add a spectral presence to the scene, their twisted, tormented branches evoking agonies of pain and death. Even the light alludes to the tragedy. A narrow band of golden light bathes the house and a section of the yard, demarking that slim zone of safety in which the Willeys might have found salvation.

But there is one detail of the picture that is not accounted for by this reading of the painting. If this is a historical view of the Notch on the eve of the Willey Disaster, why is the traveler given such prominence? Why is this figure one of the most conspicuous details in the painting? This anomalous horseman might be explained if we read the painting as referring not to the Willey Disaster alone but more particularly to Nathaniel Hawthorne's fictionalized account of the Willey Disaster — a short story entitled "The Ambitious Guest," which was included in his *Twice-Told Tales* of 1837.[62] Since Cole avidly sought out literary associations with the sites he painted, it seems likely that he would have known Hawthorne's tale. If Cole did intend the figure to refer to Hawthorne's story (and this is speculative) then the traveler is not a random tourist passing through the Notch, but the central figure in Hawthorne's short story — the ambitious guest himself.

Hawthorne's story takes place the evening of the disaster. The exemplary Willey family is seated around the fire basking in domestic bliss when a young man appears at their door seeking shelter for the night. They absorb him into their family circle and listen attentively as he spills out to them his hopes for the future, especially his desire for fame. As he speaks, the Willeys begin to feel stirrings of ambition in their own breasts. Mr. Willey dreams aloud of becoming a country squire. His daughter's thoughts turn to suitors, while the elderly grandmother begins to dwell on her approaching death. As her thoughts turn in that direction, an old superstition recurs to her: she remembers being told that if anything is amiss with a corpse it will not be able to rest easily in its grave. She then begs her family to hold a mirror over her face as she lies in her coffin so that she will be able to look at herself and see that all is right. It is at just this moment, when the Willeys' thoughts have been turned toward death, superstition, and ambition, that the avalanche claims their lives. The central irony of Hawthorne's story is that the young man so intent on winning earthly renown dies without leaving a trace, his presence unsuspected by those who sifted the slide for remains.

Cole's painting is clearly not a literal illustration of Hawthorne's story. The tale takes place entirely within the Willeys' abode, while Cole presents an exterior scene. Hawthorne's setting is nighttime, Cole's daytime. Hawthorne's young man is described as a pedestrian; Cole's is an equestrian. Yet these departures from the story are within the bounds of artistic license, adjustments made to the narrative to better suit Cole's own artistic gifts. By shifting the setting, he could play to his strength as a landscape painter; by changing the hours, he could avoid the difficulties of a nocturnal scene; and by placing the figure on horseback, Cole could give him a much more prominent place in the composition, in keeping with his central role in the story.

Hawthorne's tale, with its emphasis on ambition and its consequences, would probably have had strong personal resonance for Cole who felt that ambition was his own "master sin." According to his minister and biographer Louis Noble, Cole attributed "the most serious of [his own religious trials] to ambition. To win renown had been from his youth a ruling passion. In the light of religion that passion stood forth as his master sin. To vanquish it his most difficult labor."[63]

By alluding to Hawthorne's story in *A View of the Mountain Pass Called the Notch of the White Mountains*, Cole could embed a strong moral in the canvas, a moral much like that propounded in his *Course of Empire* series. In *The Course of Empire* it is pride and ambition (among other sins) that bring about the fall of the empire. Hawthorne's story points to the same lesson, the idea that pride and ambition precede a fall.

If this painting indeed contains an allusion to Hawthorne's story, then the sin of ambition may be the solution to the puzzle of the Willeys' demise. But this is a rich and complicated picture, and, through the details of the painting, Cole hints at another possible solution. Prominently displayed in the foreground of the picture are two stumps, their tops tilted toward us to display the marks of the axe.[64] At the time Cole painted this picture, he had become deeply disturbed by the devastation of the American wilderness. He lamented in his prose, poetry, and paintings the ravages that the axe was daily inflicting on American nature. Here he draws a connection between the violence man has wrought on nature and the violence nature has visited on man. In this context the Willey Disaster could be read as retribution for the desecration of what Cole's friend William Cullen Bryant called "God's first temples."[65]

In selecting Crawford Notch for his subject, Cole could rely on the site's rich scientific, historical, and literary associations to elevate his painting beyond the level of topographic art. These associations could carry the viewer's mind beyond the contemplation of this specific locale to ponder the moral implications of the scene: the frailties of humankind, the brevity of life, and the need to be constantly prepared for death. At the same time, the picture announced the ability of landscape to rival history painting in the complexity and profundity of its themes.

In *A View of the Mountain Pass Called the Notch of the White Mountains*, as in so many of Cole's landscapes, geological ideas are woven into a dense fabric of varied associations and meanings. Neither here nor in Cole's other works did geology provide the main motive for the painting. The lessons that he sought to teach were moral and religious, not scientific. Yet again and again he was able to draw upon geology to reinforce and bolster those lofty themes. At the same time, his geological knowledge helped him forge ties to his upper-crust patrons, aiding him in establishing himself in both his own eyes and in theirs as a "gentleman." In the end, geology was for Cole more than a merely "fashionable" science; it was an eminently useful one.

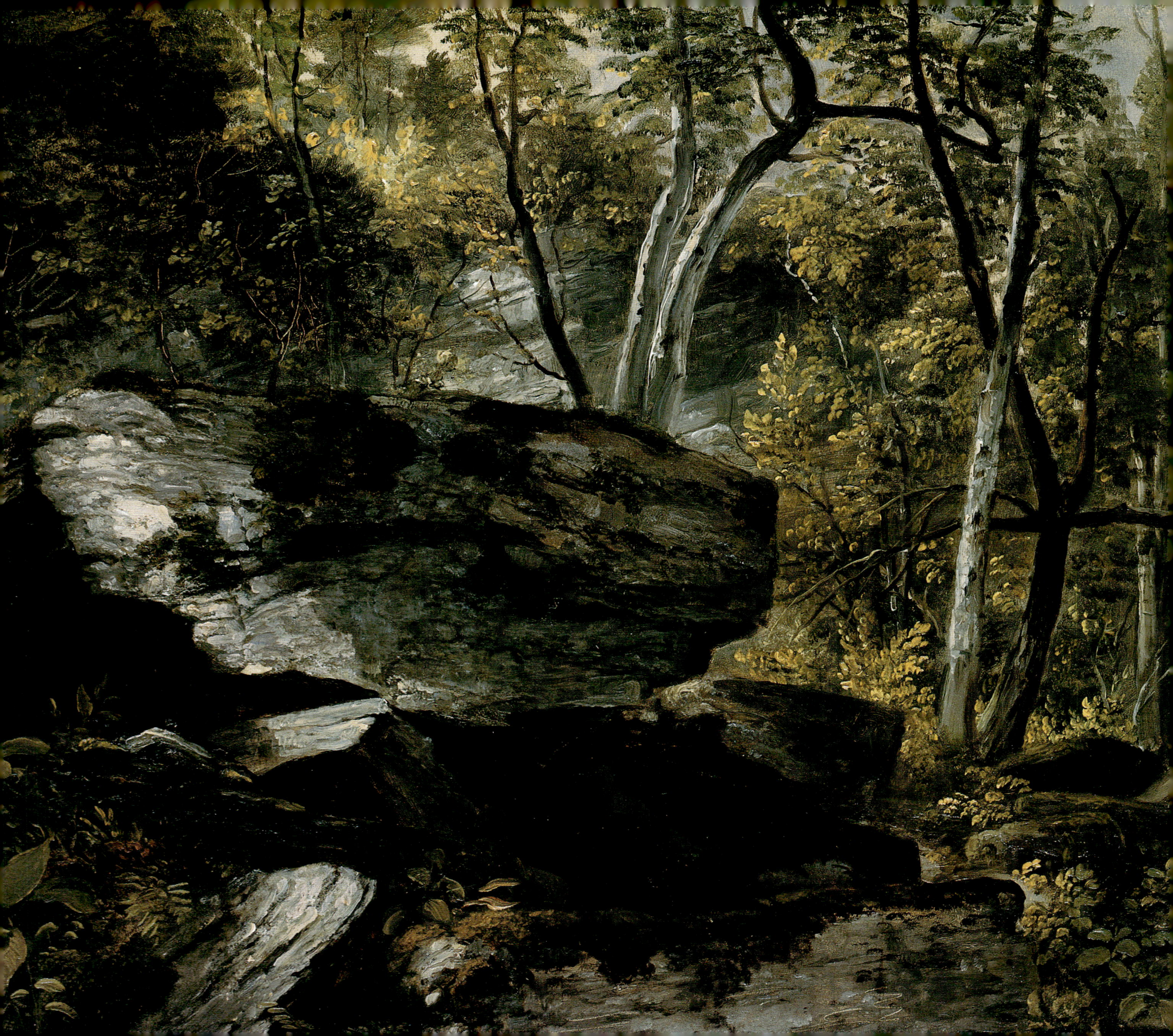

Chapter Two

Asher Durand and the Therapeutic Landscape

In late September of 1857, Asher Brown Durand (1796–1886), one of America's best known landscape painters, was working in the Catskill Mountains.[1] Rain had been falling for several days, confining him to his rented rooms in Palenville. To while away the hours he and his daughter Caroline read aloud to each other, not, as one might guess, from Dickens's novels or Byron's poems, but from Hugh Miller's *The Old Red Sandstone*, one of the most popular geology texts of the nineteenth century. According to Caroline, her father was so excited by Miller's revelations that he could hardly wait for the rain to let up so that he could rush down to a nearby creek, break open some of the sandstone on its banks, and see what it might reveal of the earth's history.[2]

Durand's enthusiasm for geology (shared with several of his children) gave rise to some of the most intensely observed geological studies produced in the nineteenth century (fig. 27, for example). These small canvases, most painted directly from nature in the 1850s and 1860s, depict rocky streambeds, mossy boulders, and shelving outcrops. Their small size and narrow compositional focus bear no relation, however, to the size of the ideas they address. These paintings embody Durand's meditations on mortality, his fundamental belief in the therapeutic power of nature, and his allegiance to the philosophical paradigm of the microcosm.

The title Durand gave to most of these paintings, *Study from Nature*, might suggest to readers versed in academic painting practice that he regarded them as mere painterly exercises, but this was not the case. As Eleanor Jones Harvey has demonstrated, the word "study," as used by Durand and his contemporaries, generally referred to plein air works "whose creation used the intellect, reflection, and aesthetic judgment."[3] These were works of art in their own right—finished, exhibitable, saleable works, much admired and eagerly collected in their day.

Durand proudly displayed his nature studies at the National Academy of Design and the American Art Union in New York, as well as other venues, where they drew considerable critical attention, almost all of it positive. An anonymous writer for *Literary World*, for example, reviewing the 1848 National Academy of Design exhibition, dismissed Durand's large entry *The*

Opposite: Detail of Fig. 31

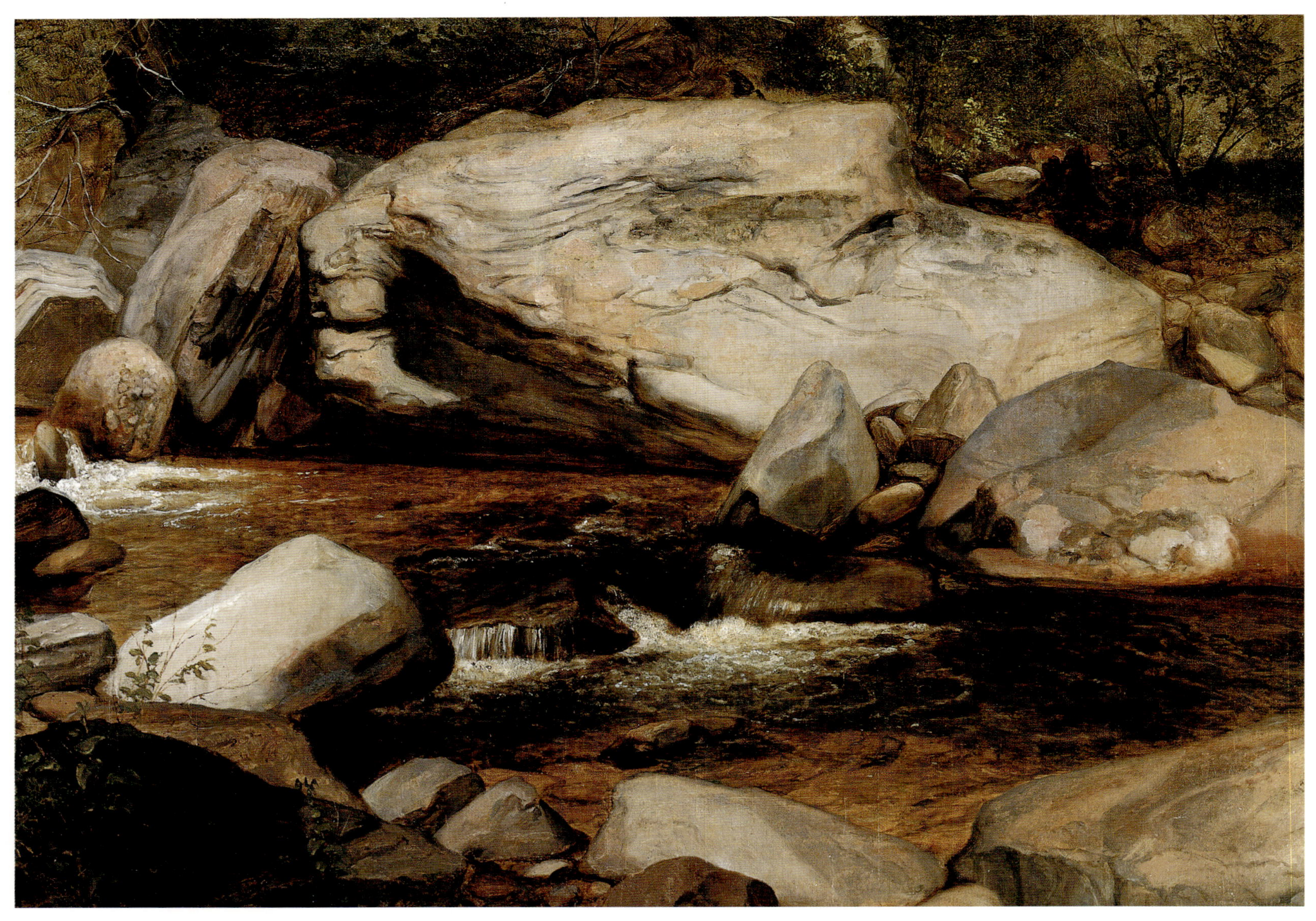

Fig. 27. Asher Durand, *Landscape: Creek and Rocks*, c. 1850s.
Oil on canvas, 16 15/16 x 24 in. (43 x 61 cm).
Pennsylvania Academy of the Fine Arts, Philadelphia. Gift of Charles Henry Hart

Fountain by saying, "Far better than this work of so much pretension is a little Study from Nature, which is all vigor and freshness."[4] Clarence Cook, art critic for the *New York Tribune*, found Durand "most enjoyable in his finished studies," adding that these works with their "minute and scientific study of natural forms . . . influenced many of the younger men [to turn] in this direction."[5]

As Cook's comment suggests, Durand's meticulously rendered views of rocky banks and riverbeds heralded a new direction for Hudson River School painting. His *Studies from Nature* — in their style, in their subject matter, in their philosophical underpinnings, and in the way they address the viewer — differ markedly from the paintings by Cole discussed in the previous chapter. Cole was one of Durand's closest friends and had a marked impact on his early landscapes. But in the later 1840s and early 1850s (after Cole's 1848 death), Durand's art moved away from the example set by his friend. He began to abandon the sort of grand allegorical canvases that had preoccupied Cole in favor of what were called at the time "simple, uncombined landscapes."[6] Increasingly he painted topographic views and characteristic bits of forest scenery rooted in his close observation of nature rather than in literary or historical sources. As Durand explained in 1855, landscape "will be great in proportion as it declares the glory of God, by representation of his works, and not those of man."[7] Furthermore, while Cole had advocated generalizing nature, Durand chose to particularize it. He shed Cole's broad painting techniques for a more highly finished style that allowed him to better express his keen regard for nature's specificities. His concern for natural detail is evident in paintings such as *Landscape: Creek and Rocks* (fig. 27) in which he carefully differentiated the round chunk of pebbly textured conglomerate on the far left from the slabs of small-grained sandstone beside it.[8]

JOHN RUSKIN AND THE TRUTHS OF NATURE

Durand's new interest in sandstone boulders, granite ledges, and humble bits of forest floor, his new attention to the specificities of rock type and plant species, and the new regard he and his contemporaries bestowed on the nature studies, all owe a debt to John Ruskin (1819–1900), the most influential art critic writing in English at mid-century.[9] By the mid-1840s Ruskin was usurping Sir Joshua Reynolds's place as prophet to America's landscape painters.

In Ruskin's writings, especially the five hefty volumes of *Modern Painters* (published between 1843 and 1860), Durand and many other American landscape painters found ideas that deeply affected both their attitudes toward their art and their practice of it.[10] Of great importance to American landscape painters (and to Durand's geological studies in particular) was Ruskin's conception of artistic truth. The English critic set himself firmly against the generalized depictions of nature advocated by Reynolds and embraced by Cole (see chapter 1). "Generalized!" Ruskin fumed, "As if it were possible to generalize things generically different. . . . It is just as impossible to generalize granite and slate, as it is to generalize a man and a cow. . . . a rock must be either one rock or another rock; it cannot be a general rock, or it is no rock."[11] Truth, he believed, resided not in some generalized Platonic ideal form, but in specific natural facts. For him, the universal was inherent in the particular; like William Blake he sought to find "a world in a grain of sand, / And a heaven in a wild flower."[12] Natural facts, to Ruskin's mind, were alive with spiritual meanings. Though these convictions would waver later in his life, at the time he wrote the first volume of *Modern Painters* he was convinced that the careful observation, contemplation, and depiction of natural forms was an avenue to spiritual truths.

This did not mean that Ruskin rejected idealization. He was not demanding that the artist replicate every rusty fissure of rock and every worm-eaten leaf he encountered. These were individual forms, not specific truths. Truth, as Ruskin was at pains to point out, resided not in individual forms, but in the characteristics of a species. While Reynolds may have believed in the existence of an ideal rock and an ideal tree, Ruskin believed in an ideal granite and an ideal oak. To create such forms, the artist needed to know the defining characteristics of each type of rock and species of plant he painted; he needed to know which aspects of their forms conveyed the most about their identities, their histories, and the ways they would grow or develop. Through the observation of such natural forms, artists would come to know the laws and lessons God had impressed on the natural world for our edification. These were the sorts of truths Ruskin believed artists ought to draw out in their works.

To aid landscape painters in their apprehension of nature, Ruskin laid out for them a course of study. At the core of his program was the close study and careful depiction of all aspects of the visible world. He urged young artists to focus their attention, not on the usual sublime vistas, but on a crumbling bank of earth, a single block of gneiss, or a bit of hedgerow (the sort of subjects Durand chose for his nature studies). "[G]o to Nature," the critic told them, "in all singleness of heart . . . having no other thought but how best to penetrate her meaning and remember her instruction, rejecting nothing, selecting nothing, and scorning nothing . . . and rejoicing always in the truth."[13]

To assist artists in their observations of nature, he also recommended the study of geology, botany, and meteorology. Likening these pursuits to the history painter's study of anatomy (as Cole was doing at about the same time), Ruskin argued that "every class of rock, earth, and cloud, must be known by the [landscape] painter, with geologic and meteorologic accuracy."[14] "For just," he commented, "as the highest historical painting is based on perfect knowledge of the workings of the human form and human mind so must the highest landscape painting be based on perfect cognizance of the form, functions, and system of every organic or definitely structured existence which it has to represent."[15]

Ruskin, an avid amateur geologist who had hoped in his youth to one day become president of the Royal Geological Society, argued that the geological features of the landscape were the most crucial to the landscape painter.[16] "Ground," he wrote, "is to the landscape painter what the naked body is to the historical. . . . Their [landscape painters'] results may be arrived at without knowledge of the interior mechanism, but for that very reason ignorance of them is the more disgraceful, and violation of them more unpardonable. They are in landscape the foundation of all other truths, [and] the most necessary."[17] To the landscape artist he issued the admonition: "Let him chisel his rocks faithfully."[18] Such words did much to encourage American landscape painters like Durand to study geology and to pay careful attention to the geological features they described in their art.

Durand later echoed Ruskin's advice in his own directives to the beginning landscape painter. These were offered in his famous "Letters on Landscape Painting," published in the *Crayon* (co-edited by his son John) in 1855. Like Ruskin, Durand encouraged the "truthful representation" of all aspects of the natural world with special attention to the characteristics of species.[19] "If your subject be a tree," he advised, "observe particularly wherein it differs from those of other species."[20] Also like Ruskin, he laid special stress on geological forms. He gave the artist license to subordinate or even omit various details of the observed world (one could, for example, "displace a tree . . . if disagreeable"). But, he warned, "the elevations and depressions of the earth's surface . . . may not be changed in the least perceptible degree, most especially the mountain and hill forms. On these God has set his signet, and Art may not remove it when the picture professes to represent the scene."[21]

HUGH MILLER'S MORALIZING, CHRISTIAN GEOLOGY

Durand's attitude toward the geological features of the landscape was affected not only by *Modern Painters*, but also by his readings in geology, particularly Hugh Miller's *The Old Red Sandstone*, which so absorbed him in the fall of 1857. Miller (1802–1856) probably played as prominent a role in shaping popular conceptions of geology at mid-century as Ruskin played in landscape art.[22] He even counted Ruskin among his admirers. This grizzled Scotsman began his working life as a laborer in a stone quarry, but eventually, by dint of hard work, an observant eye, and a lyrical prose style, became one of the century's foremost popularizers of geological science. His books sold an astounding number of copies on both sides of the Atlantic, with *The Old Red Sandstone* running through twenty editions before the century closed.

Those Americans (Durand among them) who snapped up Miller's volumes by the thousands were as captivated by his staunchly Christian creed and his self-help ethic as they were by his vivid and accessible prose. In *The Old Red Sandstone*, Miller preached the gospel of self-improvement and upward mobility. In his opening lines, he explicitly addressed his working-class readers: "My advice to young working men, desirous of bettering their circumstances, and adding to the amount of their enjoyment, is a very simple one. Do not seek happiness in what is mis-named pleasure; seek it rather in what is termed study. Keep your consciences clear, your curiosity fresh, and embrace every opportunity of cultivating your minds." Set aside political agitation and "occupy your leisure hours in making yourselves wiser men."[23] Study, he counsels, is both pleasurable and the best route to social esteem and political power.

Using the example of his own early years in the quarries, Miller showed how the meanest labor might be made enjoyable if turned to the pursuit of knowledge. His second day at work in the pits, he felt the aches in his arms and back disappear when he spied a newly exposed slab of sandstone, its surface rippled "like a bank of sand that had been left by the tide an hour before." He was soon discovering other wonders:

imprints of fish scales and fossilized shells in the blue limestone; large stones on a cliff top "rounded and waterworn as if they had been tossed about in the sea." How did these come to be? With so many of "Nature's riddles" before him, he had no time to think "of the unhappiness of a life of labor."[24]

In the quarries Miller found his life's work: deciphering the stories embedded in the rocks. Through his writings, such as *The Old Red Sandstone*, he sought to convey his discoveries to his readers. In one passage, he stood them before a seaside cliff. Pointing to the strata of which it was composed, he explained, "We may turn over these wonderful leaves one after one, like the leaves of a herbarium, and find the pictorial records of a former creation in every page."[25] Within the covers of his book, he brought these earlier epochs of the earth's history vividly alive for his readers. He turned them into explorers, accompanying him on journeys into a graphically imagined geological past. In one chapter, he set them in the prow of a ship "approaching the coastline of Europe during the Carboniferous era":[26] "Land, from the mast-head! land! land! —a low shore thickly covered with vegetation. Huge trees of wonderful form stand far out into the water. There seems no intervening beach. A thick hedge of reeds, tall as the masts of pinnaces, runs along the deeper bays, like the waterflags at the edge of a lake. . . . a sudden breeze stirs the hot air, and shakes the fronds of the giant ferns or the catkins of the reeds."[27]

Geology, as Hugh Miller presents it, is an adventure, a voyage of discovery, a thoroughly pleasurable pursuit. Yet he also meant it to be a stimulant to Christian faith. As a devout believer, he set himself firmly against the rising tide of geological materialism whose adherents sought to divorce the science from religion.

When Cole took up the study of geology in the early 1820s, it was still widely believed that the earth was approximately six thousand years old, formed, as the Archbishop Ussher of Ireland had calculated, on 26 October 4004 B.C.[28] Within this theologically defined chronological framework, Noah's Flood could easily appear as one of the most important geological events in the planet's past. By the 1830s, however, this view of the earth's history no longer seemed tenable. In that decade Charles Lyell, in his extraordinarily influential *Principles of Geology* (1830–33), argued compellingly for an earth of immense antiquity, a structurally dynamic earth whose surface had undergone slow but continual transformations since its origins in the almost incalculable depths of the past. It was so old that, in the famous words of another geologist, James Hutton, one could find "no vestige of a beginning, no prospect of an end."[29] How, though, could Christian believers reconcile this with the account of Creation in Genesis?

Not to worry, Miller told his readers. The Bible was never meant to be read as a scientific textbook. It is a revelation of God's nature and His expectations of humankind. Why would God keep Moses standing on the Mount while He recounted all the changes from the Paleozoic to the Pleistocene? He simply collapsed them into a metaphorical six days of Creation (corresponding to great geological epochs), while leaving a record of the planet's past in the rocks, which we may read at our leisure.

Having dealt to his satisfaction with the new geological timescale, Miller moved on to tackle "development" (the precursor theories to Darwinian evolution). Miller found the concept of human development from lower life forms morally and spiritually repugnant. The theory seemed to him to deny both the immortality of the human soul and the possibility of Redemption. He minced no words in dismissing it: "There is no progression. If fish rose into reptiles, it must have been by sudden transformation. . . . There is no getting rid of miracle in the case."[30] With other like-minded naturalists, he embraced the theory of special creations that saw God periodically intervening to wipe away one creation and begin anew with another cast of creatures. The geological record, Miller asserted, will "be found to testify of the Infinite Mind."[31]

In 1856 Miller died of a self-inflicted gunshot wound to the chest. At his death, the British theologian and mathematician Baden Powell tried to put to rest both Miller and what he considered the whole desperate enterprise of reconciling "the deductions of science with the language of Scripture." We should "be content," he argued, "to allow geology" to develop uninterruptedly without forcing its practitioners to continually make obeisance to religious beliefs.[32] Yet the immense popularity of Miller's books into the waning years of the century suggests the strength of popular resistance to the removal of God from nature.

DURAND AND THE MICROCOSM

All of Durand's readings and writings suggest that he aligned himself with Miller, not with Powell. Like Miller, he seems to have accepted the new geological timescale and the evolutionary character of the earth, while continuing to regard nature as God's second Holy Book. "The external appearance of this our dwelling place," he wrote, "is fraught with lessons of high and holy meaning, only surpassed by the light of Revelation."[33]

Durand's belief in the eloquence of natural forms could not help but inform his nature studies. To one who believed as he did, a careful study of a rock or a tree must of necessity be more than a painterly, visual exercise. It was an avenue to greater knowledge—of the construction of the world, of God's plan, of the sustaining lessons He had written in the stones and stems.

When Durand gazed on a granite outcropping, he saw much more than a coagulation of minerals or a composition of lights and darks. In his eyes, the stone was a work of God, a microcosm of creation, full of lessons for the attentive observer. In 1855 he wrote that "the imaginative artist," when looking on nature's forms, "comprehends the capabilities of the materials presented in all its relations to human sympathy . . . , and he reads the historic record which time has written on all things for our instruction, through all the stages of its silent transition, since the period when this verdant earth was a lifeless, molten chaos, 'void and without form.'"[34]

This mode of viewing nature deeply affected Durand's rock studies, including the beautiful *Landscape: Creek and Rocks* (fig. 27). In this intensely observed and carefully crafted work, Durand hints at the power of a quiet stream to significantly alter its surroundings over long periods of time. With a Ruskinian fidelity to geological detail, the painting focuses on a humble bit of nature: a group of waterworn boulders lying in a shallow stream. These pink-tinted sandstone rocks have been subtly sculpted by the running water. Their silhouettes have been softened and their surfaces smoothed. The stream has scooped out pockets in several of the rocks, and on the largest boulder has exposed a series of undulating bands — the bedding pattern of the stone.

This boulder with its prominent bedding is the focal point of the study. Not only is it the largest object in the painting, but the zigzag composition (rising from the lower right to the lower left, cutting back across the stream and then rising again toward the upper left corner) culminates in its light-suffused surface. Durand directs our attention to this spot where we may read the life history of the stone. In the well-lit bands we can trace, as Durand said, "all the stages of its silent transition." With the help of geologists like Hugh Miller, we can envision its formation millions of years ago in some forgotten sea or lake, and can imagine the geological upheavals that eventually brought it to rest in this peaceful woodland setting. In that rock we confront the vastness of geological time and through it are offered an experience of the sublime.

Moreover, because Durand gives us very little sense of scale in the picture, this bit of woodland stream appears as a miniature world of mountains and waterfalls, a miniaturized counterpart of Frederic Church's vast cosmic landscapes (discussed in the next chapter). It is a microcosm of creation, revealing the building up and wearing away of rock, the balanced forces of creation and destruction that are, according to God's plan, constantly shaping the surface of the planet.

To see the creek bed as a microcosm was to participate in what was for the nineteenth century a pervasive, even paradigmatic mode of thought. Although the notion of the microcosm dates back to ancient Greece, it had assumed a new form by the nineteenth century. From ancient times into the seventeenth century, the focus was on man as a microcosm, embodying in form and function all of God's laws. In the later eighteenth century, the concept broadened enormously. Not only man, but each individual natural form from a pebble to a planet was seen as a microcosm partaking of the same pattern and shaped by the same divine laws that animated the cosmos as a whole.

This view so saturated the thought of Durand's day that its influence can be felt in multiple fields, affecting everything from the writings of naturalists, such as Hugh Miller and Gideon Mantell (author of *Thoughts on a Pebble*, owned by the painter Jasper Cropsey), to the Romantic poetry of Blake and Tennyson, to the medical theories of men like George Henry Lewes, to the sermons of William Ellery Channing, to the philosophy of Emerson and Thoreau.[35] When Emerson declared that God "reappears with all his parts in every moss and cobweb," he revealed his allegiance to this microcosmic thought.[36] It even affected the popular pastimes of the era, such as the creation of bell jars — those tiny forests of mosses and lichens that graced so many Victorian parlors.

At a time when the dimensions and age of the universe seemed to be ever expanding and humans' place in it ever shrinking, microcosmic theory offered one way of coping with this immensity. It implied that to know well one part of creation was to come to know the whole, and it promised that a divine order underlay what might seem at times like a turbulent, chaotic world. One of the pleasures offered by Durand's studies like *Landscape: Creek and Rocks* is a sense of power and control arising from one's ability to take in at a glance this little world which synopsizes the natural laws governing God's creation. To understand these laws, Durand felt, was extremely important since our actions should be governed by our knowledge of them. We must, he once wrote (quoting William Cullen Bryant's "Forest Hymn"), "To the beautiful order of his works / Learn to conform the order of our lives."[37]

THE THERAPEUTIC LANDSCAPE

Durand's nature studies not only look quite different from Cole's grand allegories, they also address their viewers in a very different way. Under the influence of neoclassical theory, Cole conceived his large-scale exhibition pictures like *The Course of Empire* series as didactic works. The artist climbed the artistic equivalent of the pulpit or lectern and dispensed his lessons from on high. His aim was to instruct and improve the viewer. Durand's nature studies are much more personal and intimate in their address. Shedding the finger-wagging didacticism of Cole's work, they invite reflection and contemplation. They are meant to comfort and soothe, not improve. They are therapeutic paintings.

Durand believed firmly in the therapeutic value of nature studies. Both producing them and viewing them, he felt, was potentially a restorative activity, capable of soothing abraded psyches and lightening burdened souls. In his "Letters on Landscape Painting" he extolled nature study for "its influence on the mind and heart." In studying nature's forms, he wrote, "the intellect and the feelings become elevated and purified."[38]

In his own life, when he felt overwhelmed with cares, Durand turned to nature for solace. His son John recalled how his father, generally bound to New York City by his professional obligations, would go "into the country for rest and to console himself as usual for all kinds of trouble by studying and painting trees."[39] For those who could not indulge in a country visit, Durand recommended the next best thing: the contemplation of a landscape painting. "To the rich merchant and the capitalist," Durand wrote, landscape art could be "as an oasis in the desert." This was especially true, he felt, of those who had spent some of their early days amid pleasant landscape scenery. "Suppose such an one," he wrote,

> on his return home, after the completion of his daily drudgery—his dinner partaken, and himself disposed of in his favorite arm-chair, with one or more faithful landscapes before him, and making no greater effort than to look into the picture instead of on it, so as to perceive what it represents; in proportion as it is true and faithful, many a fair vision of forgotten days will animate the canvas, and lead him through the scene: pleasant reminiscences and grateful emotions will spring up at every step, and care and anxiety will retire far behind him.[40]

Nineteenth-century viewers seem to have responded in just this way to Durand's paintings. In 1844, for example, a critic for the *New Mirror* dropped by the artist's studio and found on his easel a large landscape painting, *The Solitary Oak*. "I sat down before it," he wrote, "and (to use a good word that is staled and blunted from over-using) it *absorbed* me. My soul went into it. . . . it seemed to me as if that landscape alone would be a retreat, a seclusion, a world by itself to retreat into from care or sad thoughts."[41]

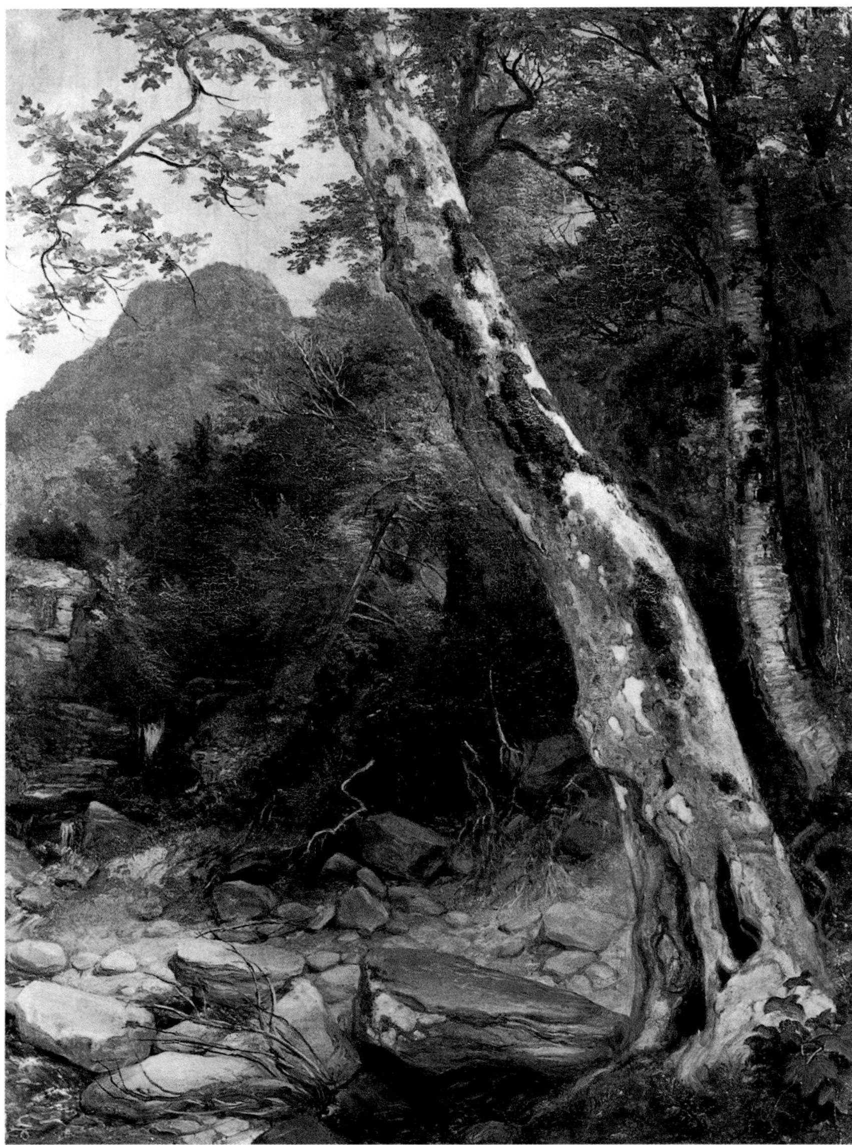

Fig. 28. Asher Durand, *The Sycamore, Kaaterskill Clove*, c. 1858. Oil on canvas, 24 x 17½ in. (61 x 44.5 cm). Yale University Art Gallery, New Haven, Connecticut. Gift of Mrs. Frederick F. Durand

The feeling of absorption was critical to the healing effects of Durand's art. As he explained, "That is a fine picture which at once takes possession of you — draws you into it — you traverse it — breathe its atmosphere . . . without thinking of its design or execution, effect or color."[42] "The less apparent the means and manner of the artist," he later wrote, "the more directly will his work appeal to the understanding and feelings."[43]

Durand designed many of his nature studies as well as most of his studio compositions to enhance this absorptive effect. Like *The Sycamore, Kaaterskill Clove* (c. 1858; fig. 28), most are framed on one side by the arching form of a tree or a rocky outcrop, while the other side opens up into what one critic called the "mellow and deep" distance.[44] Usually a diagonal path, like the rocky creek bed in the Yale study, draws one back into the landscape, toward the softly glowing light of the background; such light would have been widely recognized at the time as a symbol of the divine. As one wanders imaginatively through the landscape, the minutely rendered details of the trees and rocks invite one to pause and contemplate their forms, revelling in nature's diversity and beauty. At such moments, Durand wrote, "The reverent imagination ceases to exult in its own conscious power to change and recreate, while it contemplates the great miracle that is God's creation."[45]

When Durand envisioned the audience for such restorative landscape paintings as "rich merchants and capitalists," he was succinctly characterizing his own clientele. Though they were farflung geographically (ordering his paintings from as far away as New Orleans, St. Louis, and Chicago), ranged politically from Whigs to Republicans to Democrats, and embraced a wide variety of Protestant creeds, the majority were established professionals (lawyers, doctors, ministers) and entrepreneurial businessmen. They were men of energy, ambition, and enterprise, deeply involved in the endeavor of nation building, while making their fortunes in railroads, real-estate ventures, and steamship companies. The Vermont-born Mark Skinner (1813–1887), for example, left his native state as a young man in hopes of making his fortune in the new city of Chicago. He established himself there as a lawyer facilitating the booming real-estate market, did extremely well for himself, and eventually won election to the state legislature and a judgeship.[46] In the mid-1850s he commissioned from Durand a Vermont landscape, *Green Mountain Scenery, Stratton Gap* (1854, unlocated), which he desired "to revive in my memory continually the glorious scenery amidst which my childhood was spent & towards which my spirit yearns more & more as the years fade by."[47]

When Durand recommended to harried urban professionals like Mark Skinner a few hours of absorption in a sylvan landscape, he was prescribing what was then a common remedy for mental and physical ills of all sorts, most particularly for the corrupting and debilitating effects of city life. So deep and pervasive was this belief in the soothing and invigorating powers of nature that it contributed to a number of the most striking cultural developments of the mid-nineteenth century: the rise of the rural cemetery movement, the campaign for public parks, the launching of suburbia, and the development of seaside and mountaintop resorts.

In the 1840s and 1850s, when Durand was first producing his nature studies, the influential author and landscape gardener Andrew Jackson Downing (1815–1852) was extolling the virtues of closeness to nature in the form of country residences. "[A]ll sensible men," he wrote, "gladly escape, earlier or later, and partially or wholly, from the turmoil of cities."[48] While urban life induced vice, insanity, competition, corruption, greed, and a debilitating taste for luxury, life in a tasteful country home would breed stronger morals, heighten attachments to home and nation, and produce more equable temperaments. It would also have a softening religious influence since, in the country "one is constantly in the presence of God."[49] "We are scarcely aware," Downing wrote, "how much the mind is influenced and molded by the beautiful in nature around us; the elevating, tranquilizing, and we may add civilizing effects of the natural objects with which we are most familiar."[50]

So important did Downing consider contact with nature that for those unable to leave the city he advocated the construction of large-scale public parks where people of all classes could restore themselves after a wearying day. Strolling along curving landscaped paths, they would be invigorated by pure air and sunshine and refreshed by scents of grass and earth. Downing's ideas were later carried forward by Frederick Law Olmsted and Calvert Vaux, designers of Central Park in New York.

Even those so mentally impaired that they had to be confined to insane asylums could benefit, Downing and his contemporaries believed, from communion with nature. In 1842, the proprietors of the New York State Asylum in Utica approached Downing to design a landscaped park for their grounds that could aid the patients' recovery. Downing quickly complied with their request, writing in 1848, "Many a fine intellect, overtasked and wrecked in the too ardent pursuit of wealth or power, is fondly courted back to reason, and more quiet joys, by the dusky, cool walks of the asylum, where peace and rural beauty do not refuse to dwell."[51] Durand's paintings, though not addressed to the insane, partook of the same underlying philosophy and offered similar restorative benefits.

CONTEMPLATING MORTALITY

When Durand went to nature in search of solace, it seems often to have been the burden of mortality that he sought to lighten. The years Durand worked on his nature studies were troubled times for him. Death by then had become all too familiar; he had suffered the loss of many close friends, patrons, and family members. He had lost his two-year-old daughter Eliza in 1827 and her mother a few years later. His much-loved patron Luman Reed had died in 1836, his friend Cole in 1848, and his second wife, after a long illness, in 1857. His son John remembered how difficult the period from about 1848 to 1862 was for his father: "Productive as this period was, and professionally successful, my father cannot be said to have pursued the even tenor of his way. Domestic affliction, in the loss of his second wife in the last half of the year 1857, caused a blank in his life. Again, his health gave way, mainly on account of overwork. . . . moral and business turmoil . . . worried the artist and depressed him."[52] Turning sixty in 1856, his own mortality loomed before him. He was, wrote John, "fully aware that he had outlived his generation, and that he was getting old."[53]

From the 1840s onward, aging and death appear as themes in many of Durand's studio compositions. These include *An Old Man's Reminiscences* (1845, Albany Institute of History and Art), the unlocated *An Old Man's Lesson* (1846), and most obviously, *Landscape Scene from "Thanatopsis"* (1850, fig. 29), inspired by an eponymous poem by the artist's close friend William Cullen Bryant. One of the largest and most ambitious of Durand's works, *Thanatopsis* owes a debt to Cole in its allegorical construction and didactic content. The dark, shadowed right side of the canvas introduces the theme of death. The crumbling ruins of ancient civilizations frame a funeral taking place in a shadowy grove. A human skull lies gripped in the roots of a foreground tree. Yet set against this melancholy imagery, one finds, on the left, a river with its traditional associations with the river of life, winding out to the sea. There the heavens open, gilding the horizon with gold and silver light. This alluring horizon seems to offer the promise of immortality and union with the divine. As David Lawall has noted, the painting's imagery is calculated to "conduct the spectator out of the world of matter and into the presence of the supreme spiritual reality."[54]

Like *Thanatopsis*, many of Durand's rock studies seem to offer pictorial meditations on disintegration and death. Again and again they focus on hoary, weather-beaten, moss-covered, waterworn stone. The crumbling rocks speak of the passage of time and the essential fragility and transiency of all matter. In *Rocks and Trees in the Catskills* (fig. 30), for example, roots snake their way into the crevices of a rocky embankment, loosening and splintering the stone. Several limestone fragments lie at its base, their rounded contours and moss-covered surfaces testifying to their long exposure to the elements. The painting suggests the slow workings of nature, the transfor-

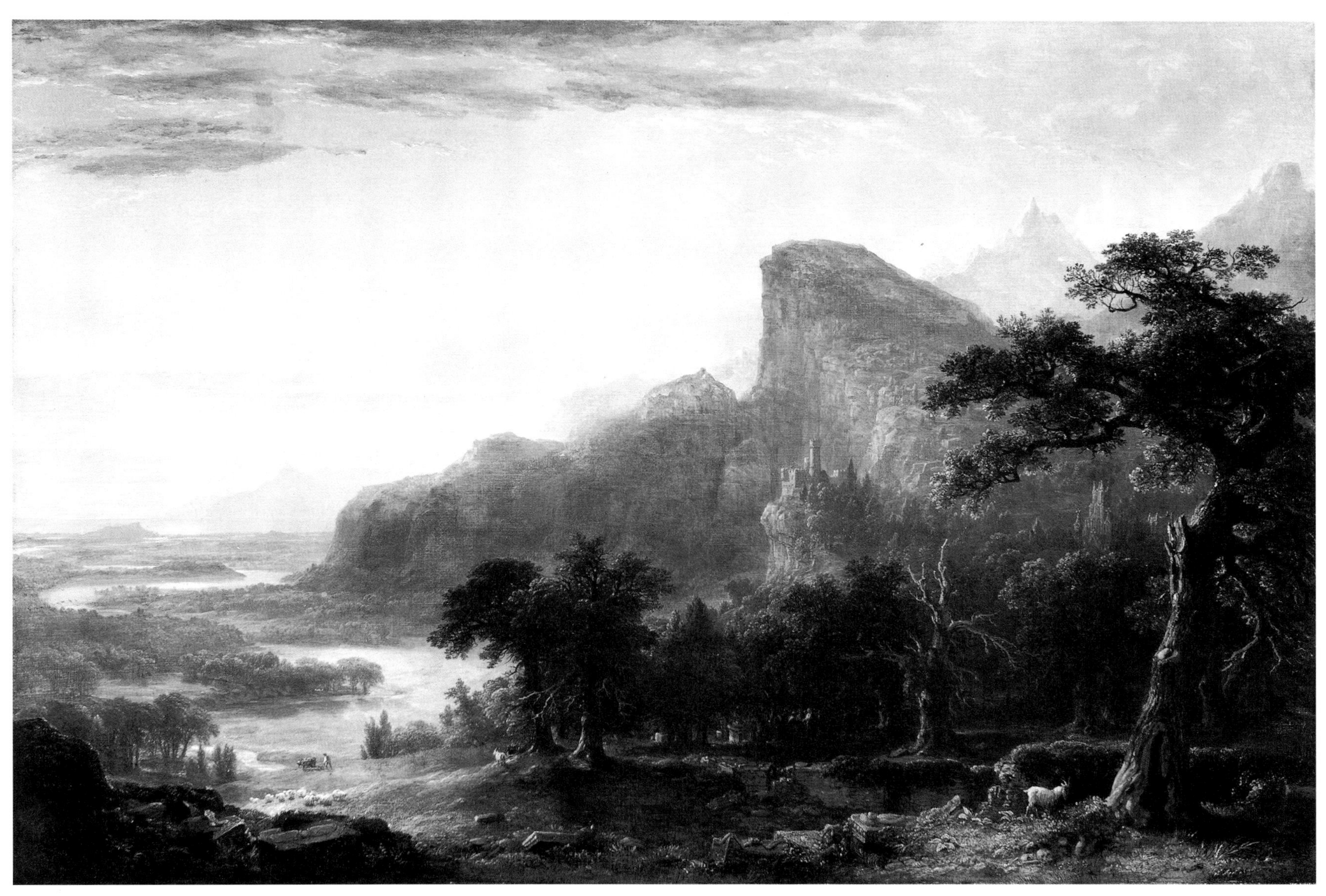

Fig. 29. Asher Durand, *Landscape Scene from "Thanatopsis,"* 1850.
Oil on canvas, 39 1/2 x 61 in. (100.3 x 154.9 cm).
The Metropolitan Museum of Art, New York. Gift of J. Pierpont Morgan, 1911. (11.156)

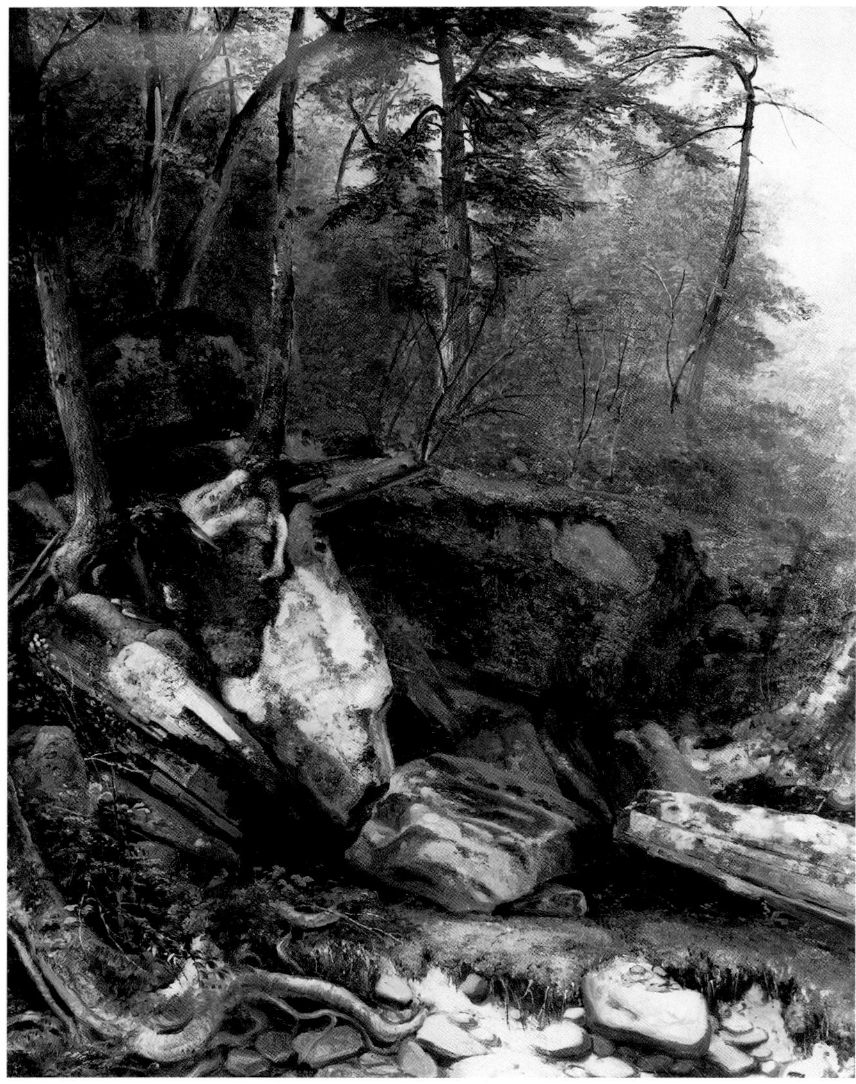

Fig. 30. Asher Durand, *Rocks and Trees in the Catskills*, c. 1850s. Oil on canvas, 21 ½ x 17 in. (54.6 x 43.2 cm). The New-York Historical Society, New York

mation of rocks into soil, and the power of seemingly fragile plants to alter and even destroy the hardest and most durable of materials.

Other studies seem to address death both more directly and more metaphorically. In *Study from Nature: Rocks and Trees* (c. 1856, fig. 31) and *Rocky Cliff* (c. 1860, fig. 32), for example, the rocks are strikingly tomblike. Their forms recall the crumbling, vine-covered sarcophagi of Piranesi's prints (fig. 33), or, more close to home, the classical-revival tombs then being placed in the new rural cemeteries of this country, including Greenwood Cemetery in Brooklyn and Mount Auburn in Cambridge, Massachusetts (figs. 34–35). They recall, too, the lines from "Thanatopsis" in which Bryant makes an explicit equation between the rocks of the earth and human tombs. He refers to the earth as "one mighty sepulchre," while the woods, meadows and brooks, "are but the solemn decorations all / Of the great tomb of man." Perhaps coincidentally, it is about this time, in the middle years of the nineteenth century, that simple, natural, uncarved stones like those in Durand's studies, began to be used as grave markers. In Mount Auburn such stones mark the graves of the sculptor Horatio Greenough and the geologist Louis Agassiz (fig. 36).

Durand's Christian view of death sometimes seems to have colored his rock studies as it did *Thanatopsis.* In *Rocky Cliff,* for example, images of death and decay are paired with images of life and growth. Here the great tomb-shaped mass of cross-bedded sandstone has faulted and slumped, crumbling into ruin before us. Black moss drapes its sides like Victorian funeral crepe, while on the slope just behind it, naked, skeletal limbs of dying trees stand out against the gray sky. Yet in the midst

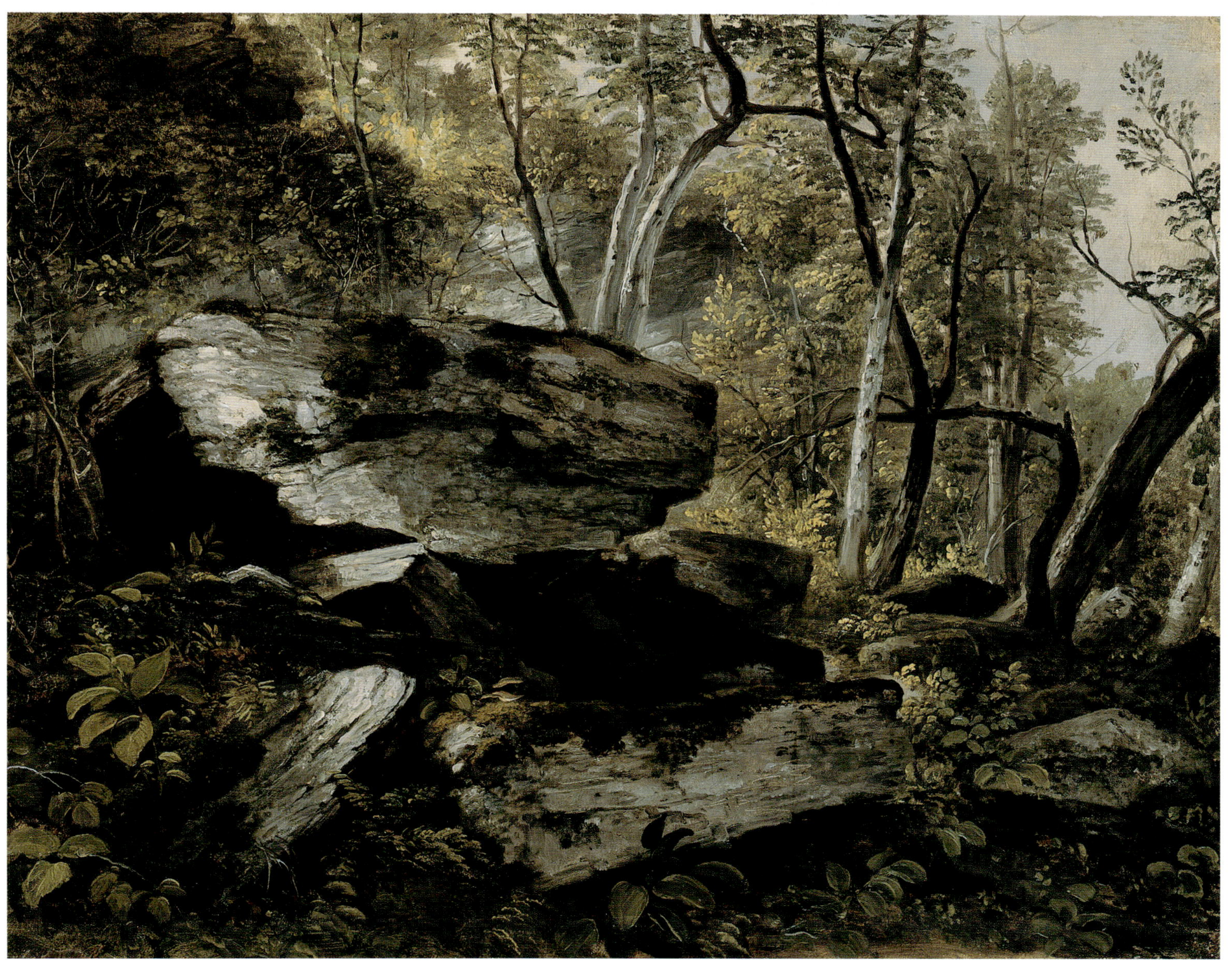

Fig. 31. Asher Durand, *Study from Nature: Rocks and Trees*, c. 1856.
Oil on canvas, 17 x 21 1/2 in. (43.2 x 54.6 cm).
The New-York Historical Society, New York. Gift of Mrs. Lucy Maria Durand Woodman

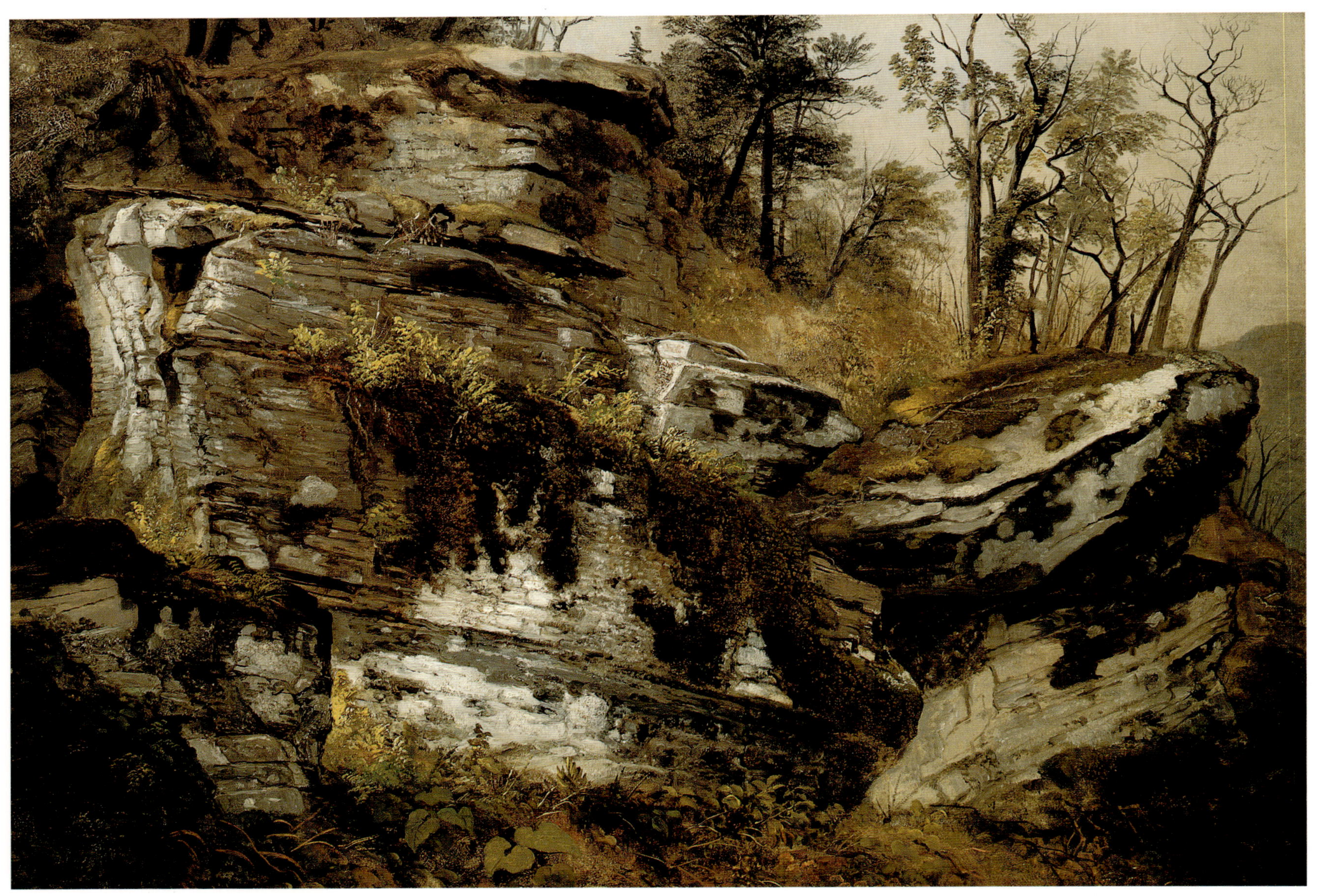

Fig. 32. Asher Durand, *Rocky Cliff*, c. 1860.
Oil on canvas, 16 ½ x 24 in. (41.9 x 61 cm).
Reynolda House, Museum of American Art, Winston-Salem, North Carolina

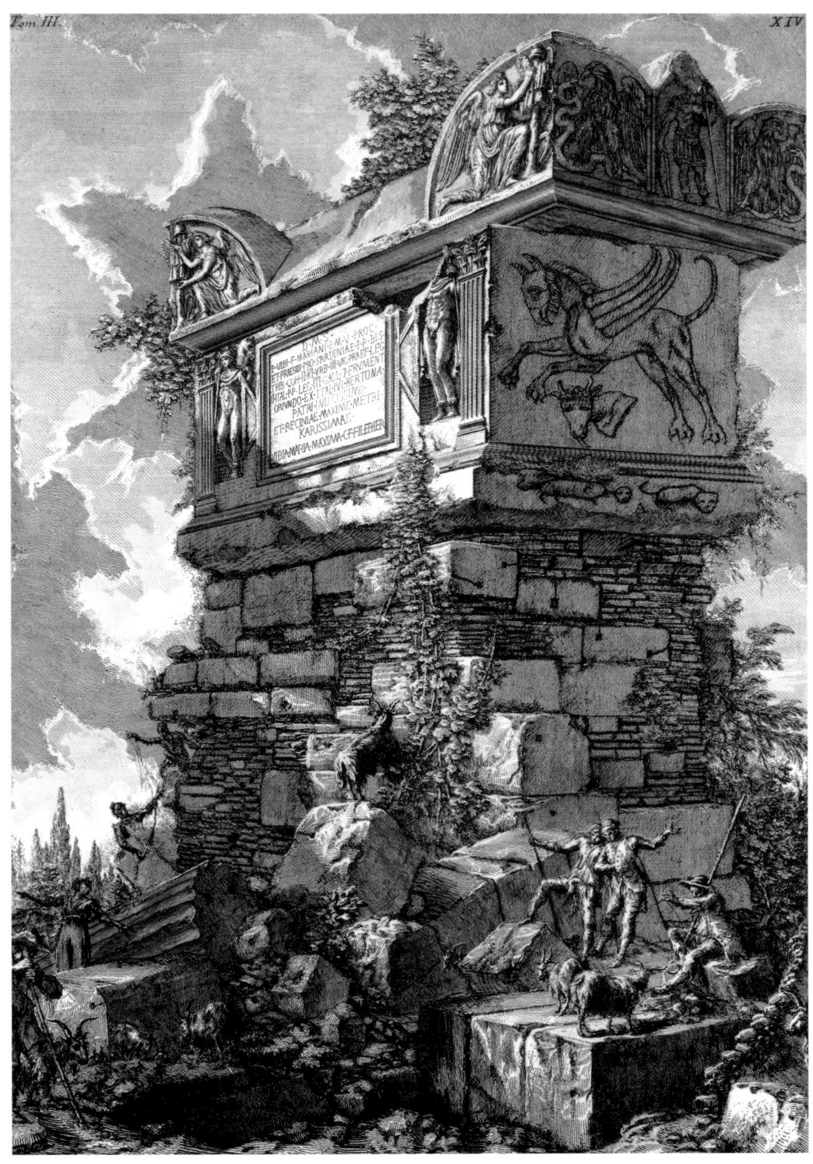

Fig. 33. Giovanni Battista Piranesi (Italian, 1720–1778), *Roman Tomb.* Etching from *Antichità romane* (Rome, 1756), vol. 3, plate 14. National Gallery of Art, Washington, D.C. Rosenwald Collection

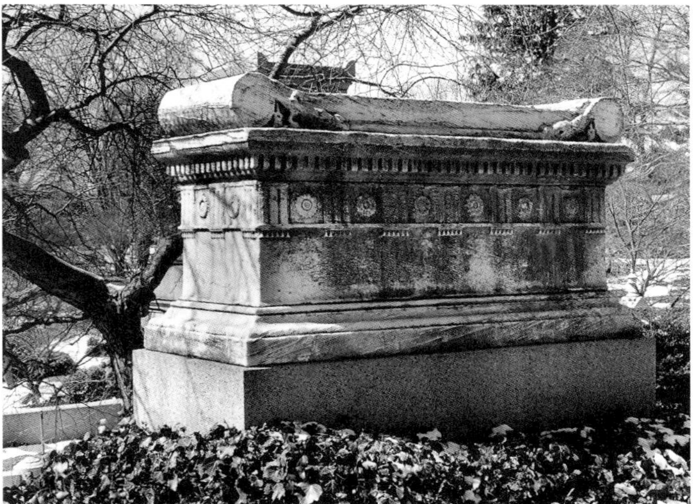

Fig. 34. Tombstone, c. 1836. Mount Auburn Cemetery, Cambridge, Massachusetts

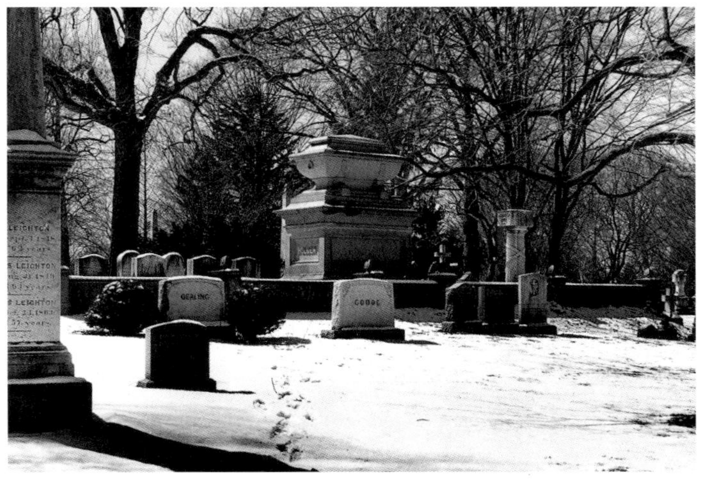

Fig. 35. Tombstones at Mount Auburn Cemetery, Cambridge, Massachusetts

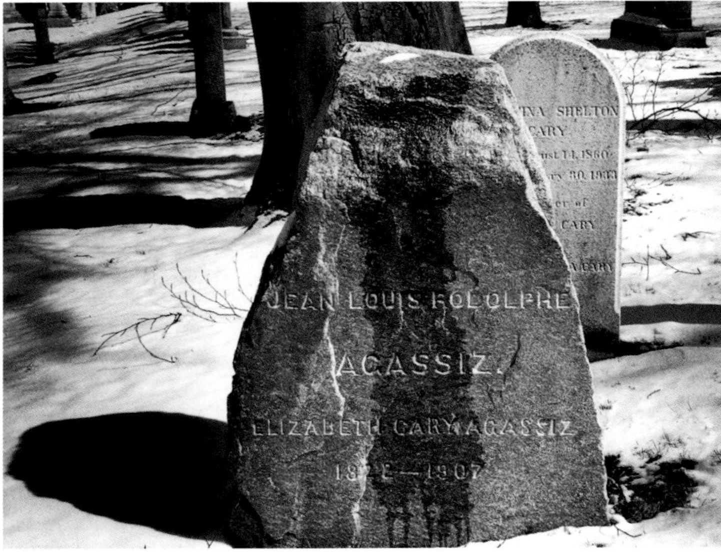

Fig. 36. Stone marking the grave of Louis Agassiz and his wife, Elizabeth Cary Agassiz, Mount Auburn Cemetery, Cambridge, Massachusetts. The stone is an erratic from the Aar Glacier in Switzerland

of this somber scene, new life is taking root. Tender green shoots are sprouting from the dark crevices of the eroding rock, and in the middle of the stand of dying trees a silver-barked birch is raising its leafy branches toward the sky.

The natural cycle of death and rebirth depicted here echoes both the theme and the imagery of Bryant's "The Forest Hymn" (1825), a poem often quoted by Durand. In it, Bryant (who shared Durand's interest in geology) marvels at God's "creation, finished, yet renewed forever."[55] He notes how "Life . . . seats himself upon the tyrant's throne — the sepulchre, / And of the triumphs of his ghastly foe [Death] makes his own nourishment." Durand's image of delicate plants drawing their sustenance from the eroding rock sepulchre seems perfectly matched to Bryant's words.

Drawing on passages from "A Forest Hymn," Durand, in his "Letters," explains how a simple landscape view (like *Rocky Cliff*) can be imbued with moral and spiritual meaning. "[A]mongst the primitive wilds of Nature," he wrote, one comes face to face with evidence of God's continual renewal of His creation. One confronts "'the freshness of the far-beginning' of things which connects us with the past and symbolizes our immortality."[56] Durand's use of the word "symbolizes" implies that for him immortality meant not the purely natural phenomena of new life springing from the moldering corpse, but a more specifically Christian notion of the death of the body and the resurrection of the soul.

If one accepts the interpretation of Durand's paintings offered here, one can see him as participating in a major shift in American attitudes toward death.[57] Beginning in the late eighteenth century and gaining momentum in the early nineteenth century, the intellectual elite in both Europe and the United States cultivated a new, more benign, more optimistic view of death. While earlier generations had fixated on the grotesqueries of the decaying body and the fearful prospect of divine judgement, the new view emphasized the naturalness of death and the release it promised from the cares of earthly existence. Death was "eternal sleep" or a "reunion with loved ones in heaven." One should accept it with quiet resignation or even embrace it with joy.

The rehabilitation of death's image was manifested in multiple ways. "Graveyards" became "cemeteries" (sleeping places); "coffins" gave way to "caskets" (holders of precious things).

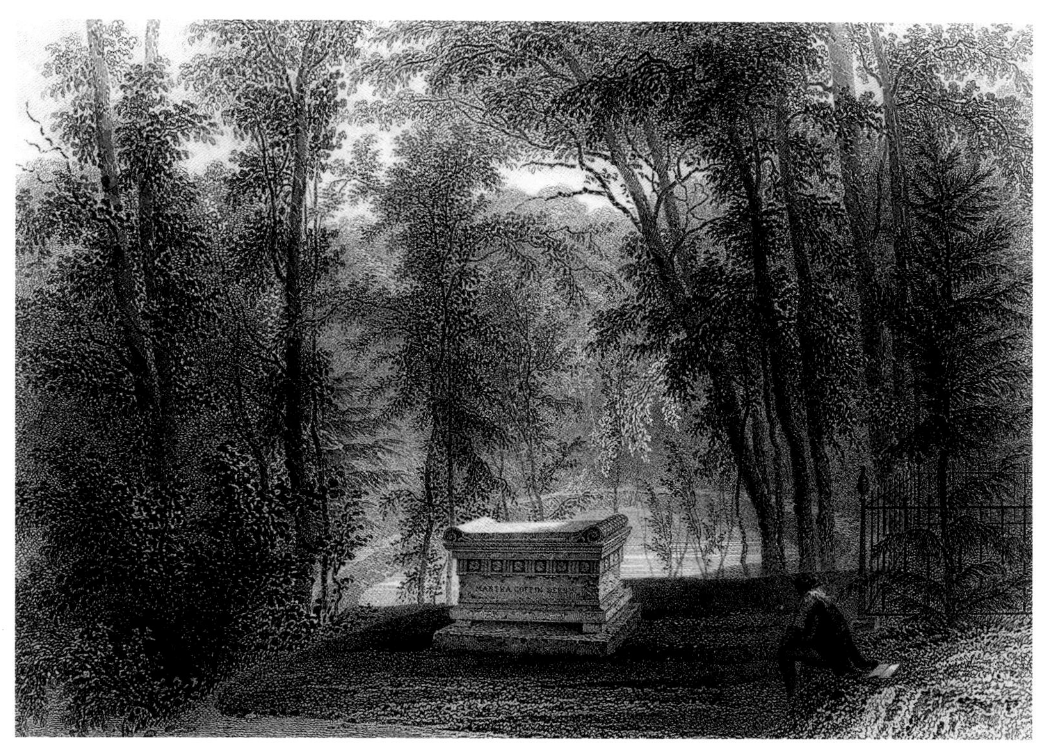

Fig. 37. *Consecration Dell, Mount Auburn Cemetery.* Engraving by James Smillie, from Cornelia W. Walter, *Mount Auburn Illustrated* (New York, 1847)

Grim slate tombstones carved with hollow-eyed skulls were replaced with soft white marble markers decorated with floral swags and sleeping cherubs. Also, beginning in the 1830s, rural cemeteries like Mount Auburn came into vogue. In such places, tasteful classicizing tombs were placed along lushly landscaped paths. Amid wooded dells and quiet reflecting pools, the dead could sleep in peace, while mourners could be soothed and revived by nature's healing influences. Other visitors, drawn by the beauty of the spot and its melancholy associations, would find their ambitions chastened and their emotions "purified and exalted" through meditation on their mortality (fig. 37).[58]

Cornelia Walter, author of *Mount Auburn Illustrated*, wrote in 1847, "The holiness of nature is ever a lofty contemplation; and it is well amidst the quiet wildwood and beneath the forest-shades to be reminded sometimes of death."[59] These words would make a fine epigram for Durand's rock studies. The lessons and pleasures the paintings offer are in many ways similar to those of the rural cemeteries. They remind viewers of the grand cycles of existence and of the transience of earthly things, while consoling mournful thoughts with evidence of the beauty and goodness of God's creation and its intimations of eternal life.

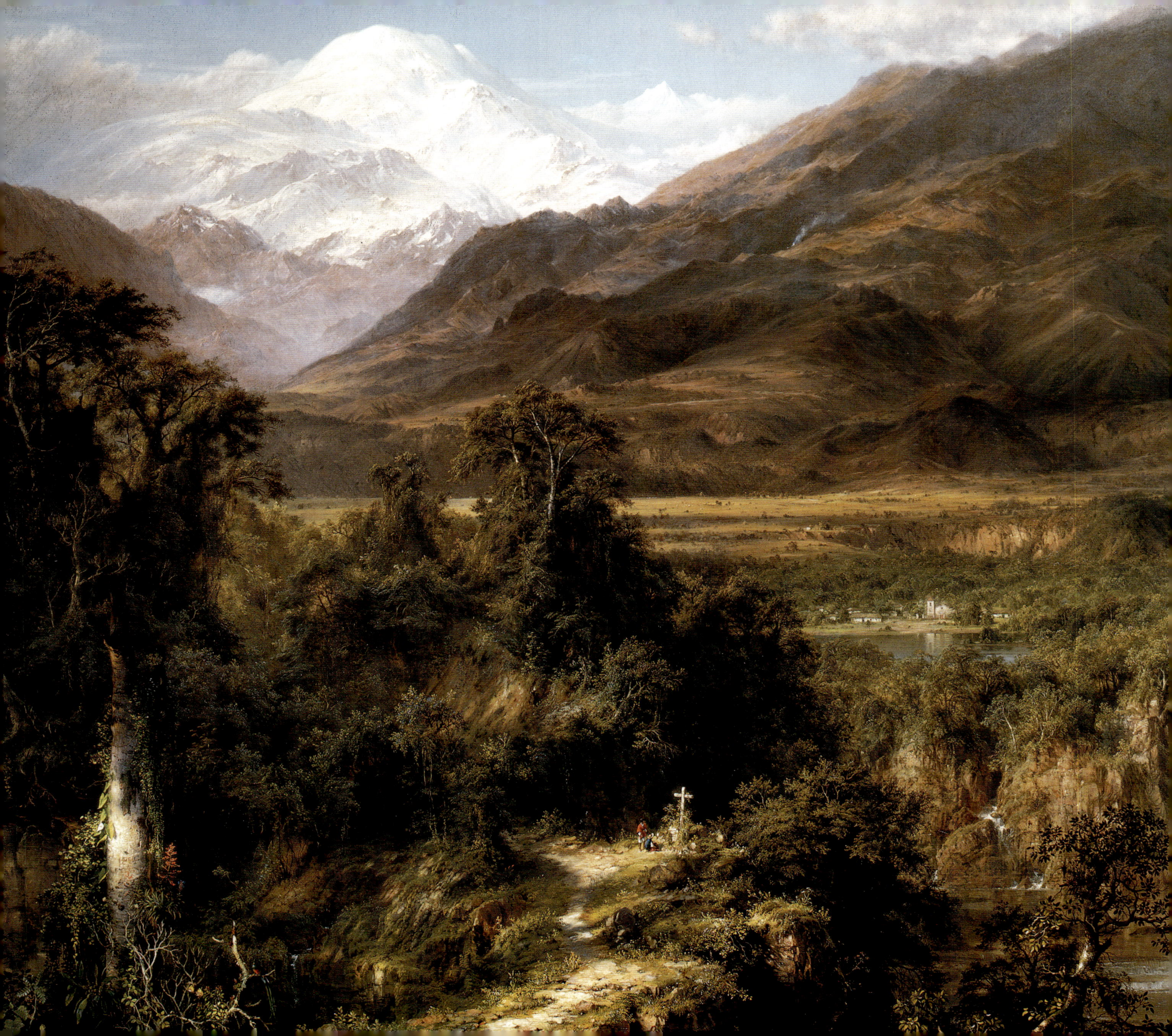

Chapter Three

Frederic Church and the Educational Enterprise

Frederic Church (1826–1900) was born into a society that valued education. In the northern part of the United States, particularly in New England, the surging democratic tide of the second quarter of the nineteenth century brought with it an urgent emphasis on education.[1] Education, it was argued, would prepare the newly enfranchised to assume their responsibilities as citizens; it would also elevate the morals and the intellect of the entire community and prepare Americans to take advantage of the nation's bounties. Those on the upper rungs of the social and economic ladder believed that education would foster social stability; those below saw it as an avenue to social mobility.

With this broad-based support, hundreds of state-supported common schools sprang up across the country (especially in the Northeast and West) in the antebellum era. Public libraries began to open, and numerous lyceums flourished, sponsoring well-attended public lectures by some of the most prominent thinkers of the day, including Ralph Waldo Emerson, Oliver Wendell Holmes, and geologists Louis Agassiz and Charles Lyell. As the nature of these events and institutions suggests, the educational emphasis in this period was not just on schooling children in the rudiments of reading and writing, but on lifelong learning for a wide spectrum of the American populace. Ideally, in keeping with high-minded Victorian civic values, this education was to be morally uplifting and patriotically inspiring as well as intellectually invigorating.

Frederic Church was swept up, both personally and professionally, in this educational enterprise.[2] Personally, he committed himself early on to a life of learning. He taught himself Spanish in his thirties, and all his life read voraciously, amassing a large, impressive library still virtually intact at his home, Olana, near Hudson, New York. Professionally, like many of his contemporaries, he found that the burgeoning demand for educational opportunities offered a chance to both fulfill his civic obligations and turn a profit. He painted a number of mammoth landscape paintings — dense with moral, spiritual, patriotic, historical, and scientific lessons — which he displayed to the public. For about twenty-five cents a head, viewers, sometimes with the aid of printed programs, could be instructed, improved, uplifted, and entertained.

Opposite: Detail of Fig. 40

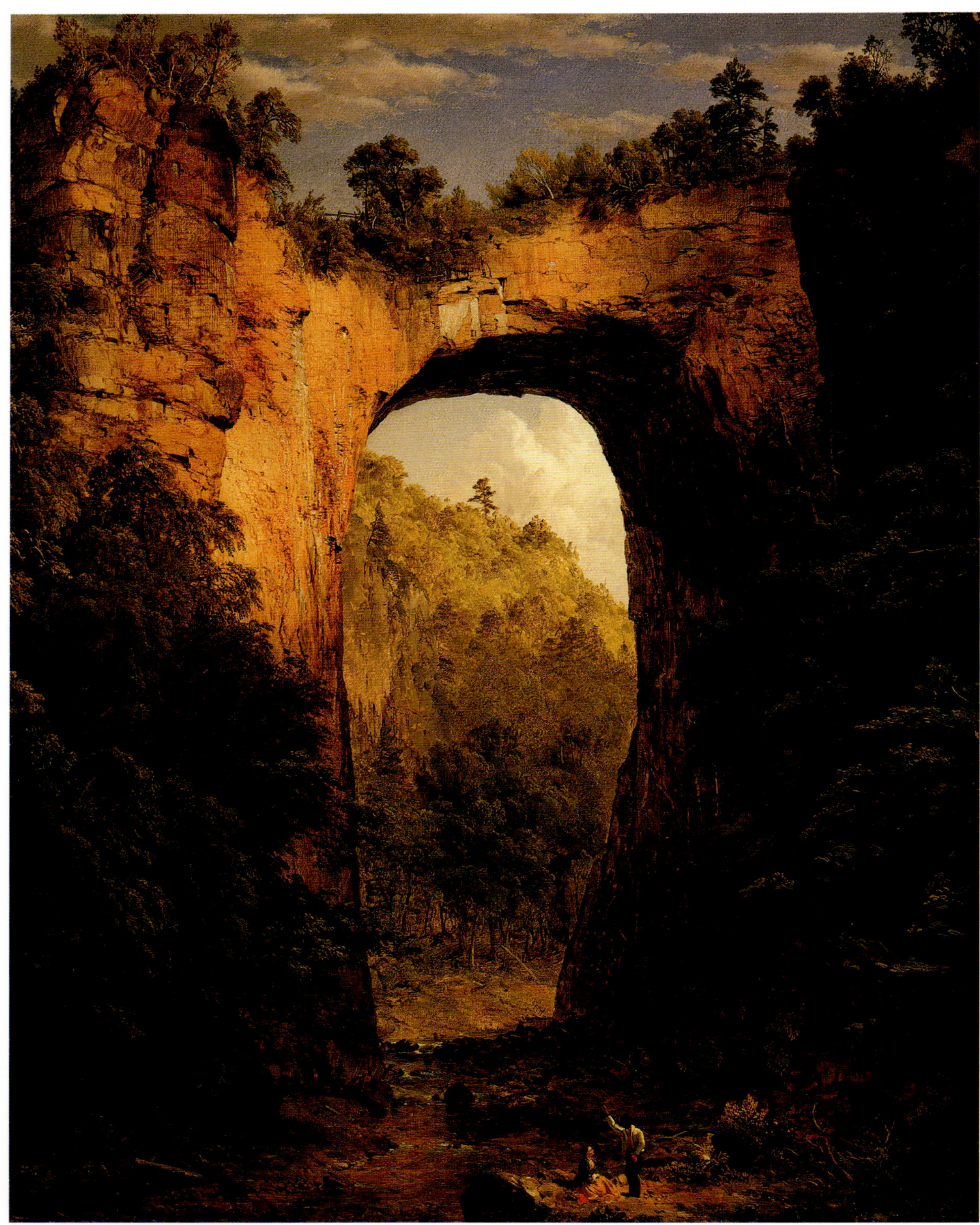

Fig. 38. Frederic Church, *The Natural Bridge, Virginia*, 1852. Oil on canvas, 28 x 23 in. (71.1 x 58.4 cm). Bayly Art Museum, University of Virginia, Charlottesville

Science played a significant part in Church's educational scheme. His own autodidactic enterprise placed considerable emphasis on it. "His taste in reading," the critic Henry Tuckerman noted in 1867, "suggests a scientific bias,"[3] — an observation supported by the contents of Church's library. It includes more than a hundred volumes on scientific subjects, with over twenty on geology, among them William Mather's *Geology of New York* (1843) and Louis Figuier's *The World Before the Deluge* (1865). As the title of Figuier's book suggests, Church (like Cole and Durand) slanted his reading toward those authors who sought to reconcile science and religion.[4] By his own account, Church tried valiantly to keep up with developments in the natural sciences, though in 1883 he threw up his hands in frustration, remarking, "I wish science would take a holiday for ten years so I could catch up."[5]

As Church well knew, he shared his enthusiasm for science with a wide swath of the American public. The brisk sales of popular scientific books, the throngs that crowded the lecture halls to hear talks by Lyell and Agassiz, and the countless herbaria and mineral cabinets that adorned American parlors, offered ample testimony to the public fascination with scientific subjects. In 1851 the conservative New York journal the *Albion* reported, "Science . . . is taking its important place in the scheme of general education; and all the appliances of popular institutions are brought to bear in diffusing a knowledge of these phenomena."[6]

As Church also knew, landscape painting was among the "appliances of popular institutions" that were being enlisted to stimulate and satisfy Americans' desire for scientific knowledge. In the early 1840s, the New York artist Russell Smith was providing Charles Lyell with paintings of American scenery to illustrate his popular geological lectures.[7] Moving panoramas of the Mississippi, Mammoth Cave, and a "Whaling Voyage Round the World" were traveling from city to city in the decades before the Civil War, introducing the American public to the topography of distant places.[8] Church was following in the footsteps of these panoramacists, when he began in the 1850s to send his large canvases of the tropics, and later the Arctic and the Holy Land, on tour to major cities.[9] These canvases were often hailed by the artists' contemporaries for the "lessons" they offered in history, geography, and the natural sciences. The critic Henry Tuckerman, writing in 1864, described Church's pictures as "accessory to and illustrative of natural science."[10]

As Tuckerman's comments suggest, many of Church's canvases were conceived, exhibited, and consumed within the context of popular scientific education. Education was at the heart of Church's work — education of the self and education of others. In preparing himself to create his canvases he assumed the role of student; in presenting them to the public he took on the mantle of teacher.

Of course, to conceive of paintings in a didactic mode was hardly new with Frederic Church. A basic tenet of neoclassical art theory was that paintings should offer the viewer morally and spiritually uplifting lessons — a conception of art's social role that guided the career of Church's own teacher, Thomas Cole. In 1844, the year that Cole undertook Church's tutelage, the elder artist expressed his opinion that landscape should "impress a Sentiment or enforce a moral or religious truth."[11] Church, in his letter of application to Cole, had already stated his commitment to making landscape "rise above the merely descriptive,"[12] and his two years with Cole only deepened his dedication to art's instructive role.

Yet Church also conceived of his educational mission more broadly than Cole had. Cole addressed his canvases to the human conscience; they are the pictorial equivalents of sermons. Church's canvases found their literary analogues in the travelogues and popular scientific texts that lined his library shelves. While suffusing his landscapes with moral, spiritual, and patriotic themes, he at the same time employed them to purvey scientific knowledge. They are full of information about tropical vegetation, Syrian geology, and the electromagnetic phenomena at the earth's poles.

CHURCH, COLE, AND THE LESSONS OF "THE NATURAL BRIDGE"

A comparison of Church's *The Natural Bridge, Virginia* of 1852 (fig. 38) with Cole's *Expulsion from the Garden of Eden* (1828; fig. 11) encapsulates the differences in the art of the two men.[13] Both paintings feature natural bridges and both seek to instruct the viewer, but beyond that they differ markedly. Cole's *Expulsion* presents a biblical scene. In composing the picture, he drew upon the well-established pictorial conventions of the sublime and the beautiful.[14] For Eden, he employed the soft forms, curving lines, and glowing light of the beautiful; for the world beyond Eden's boundaries, he used the sublime's rough textures, jagged forms, and sharp contrasts of light and dark. Narratively joining these two parts of the picture, the tiny figures of Adam and Eve stumble out of Eden into the shadowed, threatening, death-filled world outside the garden.

The most prominent form in the picture — a commanding rock archway — straddles the threshold of paradise. Great beams of light shoot through it, thrusting out toward Adam and Eve as if to hasten their departure. The tiny couple has been expelled through the arch and across another natural bridge that spans the deep chasm between Eden and the hellish, death-filled world beyond. This second bridge is about to collapse, excluding Adam and Eve (and perhaps us, too) from paradise. In this despairing vision of the human condition, Cole underscores the terrible consequences of disobedience to the divine will and the bleakness of the human lot.

In constructing this scene, Cole gave little thought to natural science.[15] The individual plants and rocks and their arrangement on the canvas owe little if anything to the spirit of scientific inquiry. They are unidentifiable in type; the trees are attenuated to a height beyond credence, and the laws of rock formation are blithely ignored in the odd right-angle juncture of the two natural bridges. In shaping these forms Cole sought not to enlighten us about botany and geology, but to choose forms and colors in keeping with the vocabularies of the sublime and the beautiful — the juxtaposition of these two pictorial modes heightening our perception of our enormous loss.

Church's early works often approach the style and spirit of Cole's *Expulsion*, but by 1852, the year he painted *The Natural Bridge*, his art had developed in a different direction.[16] Relinquishing the florid vocabulary of the romantic sublime, Church, in his mature style, moved closer to the limpid language of scientific illustration. Like the illustrators of eighteenth-century scientific travel accounts described by Barbara Stafford, Church seems to have striven for "a plain, rhetorically unornamented, seemingly artless style," which would "forcibly direct the observer's attention away from himself to the individualistics of a dynamic world."[17] In works like *The Natural Bridge*, he intentionally suppressed evidence of his personal interpretation of the subject, avoiding visible brushwork, conventional academic composition, and exaggerated or unnatural forms and colors. If Cole seems to have approached nature with an overflowing heart and a troubled soul, Church's style gives the impression that he apprehended his subject with a cool, clear, rational mind.

Viewing *The Natural Bridge*, we are made to feel, as Church's contemporaries often noted of his work, that we are standing not in front of a picture but before the scene itself. This sensation is enhanced by the artist's choice of subject — a real, localizable, and visitable subject — the Natural Bridge in Rockbridge County, Virginia, over 215 feet tall, once owned by Thomas Jefferson and made famous by him in his *Notes on the State of Virginia*. It is a natural formation carved from the local limestone over thousands of years by Cedar Creek.

Church's clear, direct representation of the site, echoing the style of contemporary scientific drawings, must have enhanced nineteenth-century viewers' trust in the accuracy of the presentation. As in so many scientific illustrations of the era, the subject, in this case the rocky arch of the Natural Bridge, is placed squarely in the center of the canvas. A pellucid light illuminates its exterior, highlighting the rock's unstratified mass (typical of limestone) and drawing attention to its buff-colored surface stained by streaks of white and red, the result of minerals leaching from the stone. A raking light shines on the arch's interior, allowing us to see its uneven, pitted, flaking surface, and reminding us of the arch's slow erosion over time, a perception underscored by the pile of talus at its base. All here is legible and measurable. The details are realized with extraordinary clarity, and small human figures in the foreground allow us to gauge the height of the arch (another device common in scientific illustration).[18]

Looking at this picture, we believe that Church has been on the site, that he has examined it carefully, and that he has faithfully reported his observations to us. He has delivered the facts about the bridge. He has informed us. But is that all he has done? Is there no more to the picture than that — a graphic report on the appearance, formation and composition of the bridge?

The first hint that Church was Cole's attentive pupil (however much he departed from his teacher's style) is the two figures in the foreground. Almost every eighteenth- and nineteenth-century representation of Virginia's Natural Bridge contains human figures: an Indian or two, an astonished white man, or perhaps a fashionably dressed couple.[19] But Church's particular choice of figures seems odd, even incendiary, for his time.

In the center foreground, on the rocky banks of Cedar Creek, a white woman is comfortably seated, her red skirt splayed over the rocks, her head tilted up toward the face of what appears to be a black man standing before her. He, in an easy contrapposto pose reminiscent of famous classical sculptures like the Prima Porta Augustus, gestures toward the natural bridge or perhaps toward the land visible through its arch.

What are we to make of this vignette? — of this white woman seemingly alone in the wilderness with a black man? — of his posture of authority and command, as though imparting information to his attentive companion? Are we to accept this as something seen and recorded on the spot as we do the topographical and geological forms? Is this man simply a guide working for the bridge's owner, informing a visitor about the site? Or might we read this image of seeming racial harmony as an imaginatively conceived detail hinting at another layer of meaning in the work?

To do the latter involves seeing the connection between this work and Cole's *Expulsion*. In Cole's painting the natural bridge forms the gateway to paradise. In Church's picture, it seems to assume the same role. In *The Natural Bridge*, Church has placed the viewer on the eastern side of the arch, looking through its shadowed interior toward a literally glowing vision of the verdant western lands beyond. Just past the arch's shadowed walls is the promised land, the American Eden.[20] Cole, the alienated transplanted Englishman and conscience-stricken Protestant, believed that humans were consigned to death and despair, cut off from paradise. Church, far more optimistic and nationalistic, saw paradise — at least a potential one — spread before him in the wilderness lands of the United States.

In works perhaps known to Church, Edward Hicks deployed an image of the Natural Bridge in a very similar way in a half dozen of his *Peaceable Kingdom* paintings dating from the 1820s through the 1840s (fig. 39).[21] These paintings are rooted in a biblical passage (Isaiah 11:1–16), which prophesies God's establishment of a peaceable kingdom on earth. In that blessed realm He will collect the remnants of His people from Elam, Ethiopia, and other distant lands. There the young of the cow and the bear will lie down together, and all creatures will be led in peace by a little child. Hicks's interpretations of this promised land almost invariably show an open-faced child standing amidst a group of animals: lions, leopards, cows, goats, and lambs, all lounging peacefully in a wood-fringed clearing. In some versions, such as those at Amherst College and Reynolda House, an image of Virginia's Natural Bridge fills the left background, establishing the American location of this promised land. Perhaps the two figures in Church's *The Natural Bridge*, like Hicks's amiable animals, evoke this land where all the races of man and beast will live in harmonious accord. Certainly *The Natural Bridge* offers an optimistic commentary on the future of American civilization.

This sort of nationalistic theme runs through much of Church's work, but it was not one that the artist's contemporaries voiced in their (limited) discussions of *The Natural Bridge*.[22] Then as now, whenever the picture has been discussed at any length it has been to recount the story of Church's 1851 visit to the site with his friend and patron, the avid amateur naturalist Cyrus Field.[23] Field, who eventually purchased the picture, supposedly urged Church to take back samples of the local limestone for reference as he painted; Church insisted that this was unnecessary. Unable to persuade his friend, Field quietly pocketed some samples, and when he compared them with the finished picture, he was astonished at the accuracy with which Church had replicated their appearance.[24]

This often-repeated story serves several purposes. First, it assures us that the painting is rooted in firsthand observation.

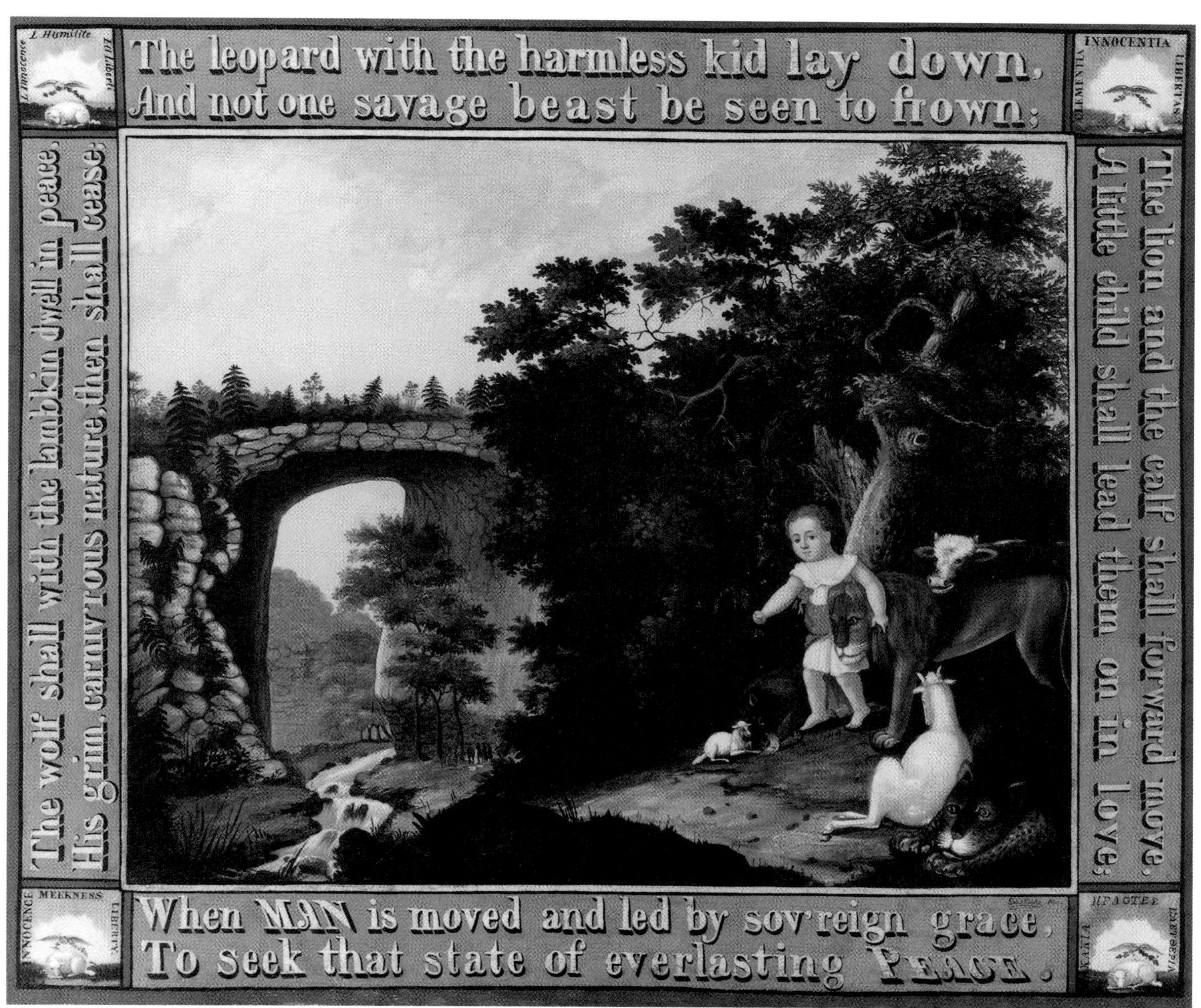

Fig. 39. Edward Hicks, *Peaceable Kingdom*, c. 1825.
Oil on canvas, 30 1/4 x 36 in. (76.8 x 91.4 cm).
Mead Art Museum, Amherst College, Amherst, Massachusetts. Gift of Stephen C. Clark

Second, it impresses on us the power of Church's amazingly retentive memory. (Church's pupil William James Stillman once observed that "his vision and retention of even the most transitory facts of nature passing before him must have been at the max of which the human mind is capable.")[25] Third, it reinforces our sense of the picture's factuality.

CHURCH AS SCIENTIFIC EDUCATOR

Factuality, accuracy, and literalness are words that appear often in nineteenth-century reviews of Church's work. So well known was he for the naturalistic fidelity of his pictorial details that the *Albion*'s art critic, reviewing his *Coast Scene, Mount Desert* in 1863, noted, "It is scarcely praise for Mr. Church to say that the bit of rock in the immediate foreground is a transcript from Nature."[26] Most of the artist's contemporaries (in the pre–Civil War period anyway) greatly appreciated this aspect of his art, praising and valuing his paintings for the "knowledge" they offered—the multitude of facts they conveyed. Many looked to his pictures for information and believed what they found there. In 1859 the artist's friend Theodore Winthrop wrote of Americans' indebtedness to Church for "helping us to a complete knowledge of the exciting and yet indolent beauty of the tropics," while John F. Weir, writing in 1873, found in Church's work "a pictorial manifestation of the scientific facts of nature that is unequalled."[27]

Church took very seriously this informative, educational aspect of his art. Rarely were the exhibitions of his major paintings unaccompanied by some testimony to the reliability of his representations, and his so-called "Great Pictures" such as *The Heart of the Andes* and *The Icebergs* came equipped with descriptive pamphlets meant to heighten the viewer's understanding and appreciation of their factual and thematic content.

In conceptualizing his art's educational mission, Church was encouraged and stimulated by a number of writers, most prominently the great German naturalist Alexander von Humboldt (1769–1859). Many of Church's contemporaries and virtually every scholar since that time have recognized his debt to the naturalist. As many have pointed out, in the second volume of Humboldt's *Cosmos*, one of the most popular scientific books of the nineteenth century (owned by Church in an English translation) appears a section on landscape painting. In this section the author urges artists to join with scientists in the exploration of distant lands—especially tropical South America where Humboldt had adventured from 1799 to 1804. He calls on artists to travel the world, using their paintbrushes to gather data about topography, geology, flora, and fauna. The paintings resulting from these on-the-spot studies could, Humboldt argues, contribute "considerably towards a knowledge of the physiognomy of distant regions, to the taste for voyages in the tropical zones, and to a more active study of nature."[28] Church, Tuckerman observed, entered "with ardor and intelligence" into Humboldt's views.[29]

Other influential writers of the day echoed Humboldt's faith in the instructive potential of landscape painting. John Ruskin, viewing some of Thomas Moran's watercolors and drawings of the American West, remarked that "scenes majestic as these, portrayed with mere and pure fidelity by such scientific means as I have referred to, would form a code of geographic instruction beyond all the former grasp of young people."[30]

In 1864 the American critic James Jackson Jarves observed that if artists would "exhibit a scientific correctness in every particular" of their work then it would be "valuable as an elementary teacher by reason of its alliance with science."[31]

SCIENTIFIC AND SPIRITUAL LESSONS IN "THE HEART OF THE ANDES"

Church's paintings sometimes fulfilled just the functions outlined by Humboldt, Ruskin, and Jarves. When his immensely popular painting *The Heart of the Andes* (1859, fig. 40) was exhibited at the Boston Athenaeum in 1860, the artist's agents, according to the *Boston Transcript*, "very considerately invited the advanced pupils of our Common Schools to view it at a very nominal charge."[32]

Those who visited the painting at the Boston Athenaeum (or at its other public showings in New York, London, Philadelphia, Baltimore, Cincinnati, Chicago, St. Louis, and Brooklyn) encountered a painting full of lessons. These lessons were articulated for visitors in two descriptive booklets available at the door — one by Theodore Winthrop, the other by Cole's biographer, the Rev. Louis L. Noble. Winthrop's 43-page effusively poetic pamphlet makes clear that the lessons offered by the painting are both scientific and spiritual.[33]

The Heart of the Andes is full of information about the natural history of tropical South America. It gives pictorial expression to many of the ideas and observations Church had encountered in Humboldt's writings (and witnessed himself in following Humboldt's path across Colombia and Ecuador in 1853 and 1857). The critic George Sheldon remarked in 1879 that *The Heart of the Andes* and Church's other South American scenes "would make capital illustrations for Humboldt's 'Cosmos,' or any similar text-book of natural science — for Agassiz's works on Brazil, for instance."[34]

Humboldt's sprawling five-volume *Cosmos* has as its immodest aim "a physical description of the universe, embracing all created things in the regions of space and in the earth."[35] Consciously choosing an accessible, animated prose style, Humboldt hoped to make this immense knowledge "the common property of all classes of society."[36] Part travelogue, part scientific text, part social commentary, part personal musing on the harmonious arrangement of the cosmos, the book bulges with facts. It contains tables of barometrical readings, lists of mountains arranged by height, and detailed descriptions of tropical flora, as well as captivating accounts of hibernating boa constrictors bursting through the ground at the beginning of the rainy season. But Humboldt's goal was not to present undigested (if engaging) facts; rather he sought to show the patterns that emerged from all this detail. His aim, he wrote, was "to recognise unity in the vast diversity of phenomena, and by the exercise of thought and the combination of observations, to discern the constancy of phenomena in the midst of apparent changes."[37]

This aim was perhaps best realized in his "geography of plants" — a theory that he articulates in *Cosmos* as well as in his other books about his travels in South America, *Aspects of Nature* and *Personal Narrative of Travels in the Equinoctal Regions* (both of which Church owned and read). In these various books Humboldt argues that plants are not randomly distributed over the earth's crust. Instead they are organized in clear, predictable patterns, with particular types of plants associated with particular soil and climatic conditions. Nowhere, he writes, is this more clearly visible than in the Andes where "different climates are arranged one above the other, stage by stage."[38] Ascending from the lowland jungles to the upland plains to the snowcapped Andean peaks, one passes through a number of what we now call ecological zones, each characterized by different climatic conditions, different geology, and different collections of plants. "Each group of plants," Humboldt writes, "is placed at the height which nature has assigned to it, and we may follow the prodigious variety of forms from the region of palms and arborescent ferns to those of . . . the lichens. These regions form the natural divisions of the vegetable empire."[39] Characteristically for Humboldt, his concern here is not with botany alone, but with the way it intersects with geology, climatology, and other sciences.

Church, as Kevin Avery has noted, gave visual form to this geography of plants in *The Heart of the Andes.*[40] Nineteenth-century viewers would have known this from reading the exhibition pamphlets. The painting shows, Winthrop explains in his booklet, how the Andes "carry on their shoulders the forests and gardens of all climes."[41] "Here," he continues, "narrow upright belts of climate are substituted for the breadths of zone after zone from torrid to frozen regions. All the garden wealth of the tropics, all the domestic charm of the northern plain and field and grove . . . are here combined and grouped at the base and along the flanks of bulky ranges topped with snow and fire."[42]

So closely bound is Church's painting to Humboldt's description of the tropics that not only the overall composition but almost every pictorial detail has its counterpart in Humboldt's words. Like *Cosmos*, this expansive landscape is a synthetic work, a summation and distillation of all that Church had read and observed of the Andean region. And in correspondence with Humboldt's geography of plants, the painting is composed of layered bands, stacked (more or less) one above another, the layers distinguished by light and shadow, as well as by different geological and botanical forms.

The shadowed foreground of this enormous (8′ x 10′) picture depicts an alpine valley, one of those, to use Humboldt's words, "humid and shaded clefts on the slopes of the Cordilleras," home to "the tree-ferns, whose thick cylindrical trunks and delicate leaves stand out in bold relief against the azure sky."[43] In Church's painting the arching fronds of a tree fern, along with a blue-flowered shrub, a large-leaved anthurium and a climbing vine of red passion flowers, frame the lower right corner.

Above this green humid zone (though pictorially still framed by the towering valley trees), lies a narrow, sunlit band of yellow ground. This represents, to use Humboldt's words again, the "cold regions of the Paramos . . . the zone of grasses."[44] From this golden savannah rise the shadowed, grayish purple mass of the Cordillerean slopes. In this gray region, according to Humboldt, "the naked trachyte rock pierces the grassy turf." From here "succeeds the region of perpetual snow," shown by Church in the upper left corner of the picture, where the gray slopes part to reveal a breathtaking vision of the snowy dome of Chimborazo, one of the mightiest of the Andean volcanoes.[45]

Step by ascending step Church has laid out for his viewers

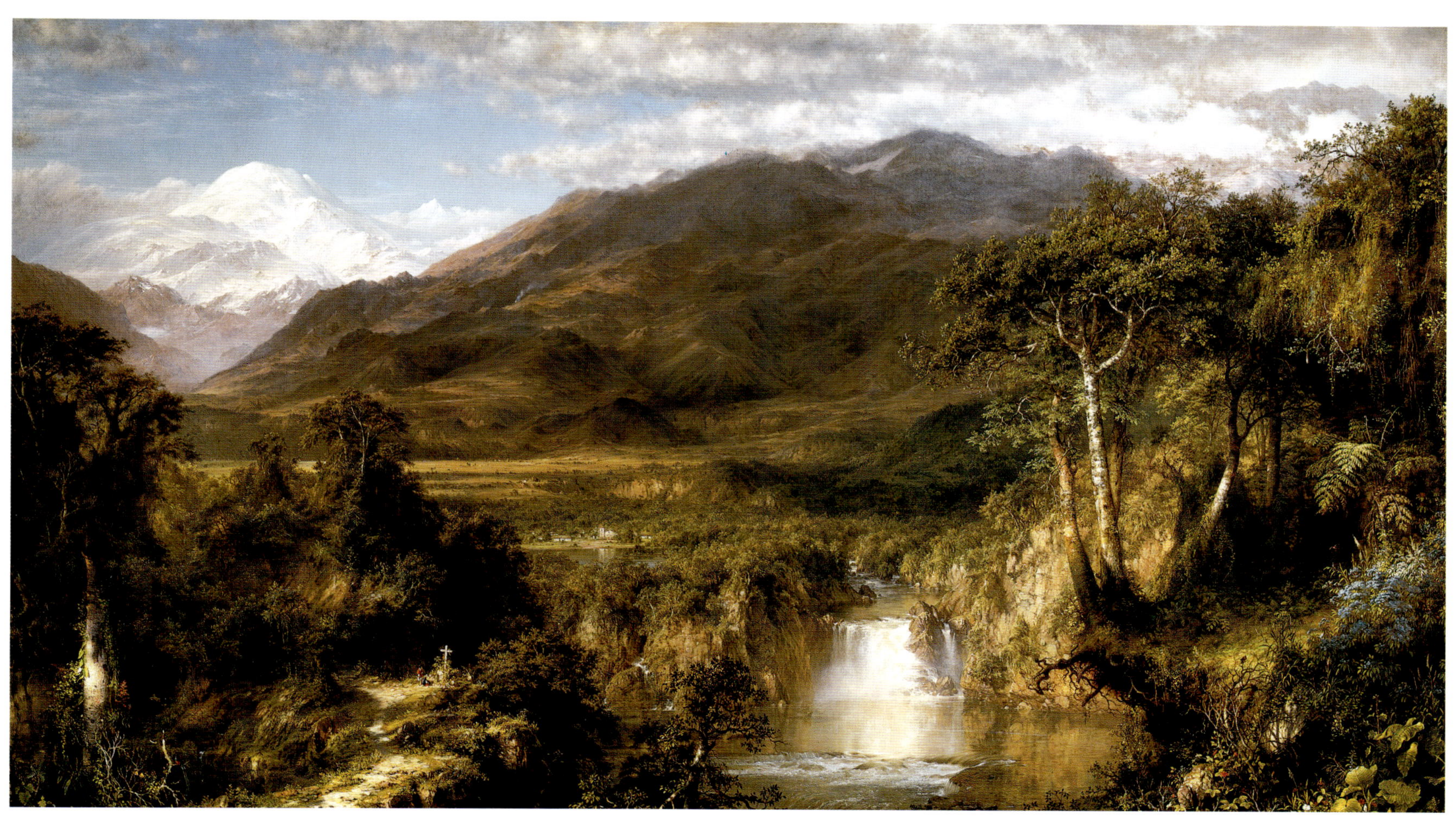

Fig. 40. Frederic Church, *The Heart of the Andes*, 1859.
Oil on canvas, 66 1/8 x 119 1/4 in. (168 x 302.9 cm).
The Metropolitan Museum of Art, New York. Bequest of Mrs. Margaret E. Dows, 1909. (09.95)

Humboldt's geography of plants. He also intended the painting, as Katherine Manthorne has discussed, to evoke the geological dynamics underlying all this varied and luxuriant organic growth.[46] In *Cosmos*, Humboldt emphasized again and again the instability of the earth's crust. It "undergoes," he writes, "great changes in the course of centuries. . . . large plains are . . . raised and sunk. . . . The boundaries of sea and land, of fluids and solids are . . . variously and frequently changed."[47] In *The Heart of the Andes*, the quickly shifting patterns of light and shadow on the rock formations, the jagged, undulating lines of the Cordilleran slopes, and the soft, crumbly texture of the middle ground cliffs, suggest this geological instability.

In his guide to the picture, Winthrop (whom Manthorne notes studied geology at Yale) draws this geological lesson to the viewer's attention. "Here," he writes, pointing to the purple slopes, "are mountain upon mountain; crag climbing on the shoulders of crag; . . . myriad tokens of primeval convulsions; proofs everywhere of change, building, razing, upheaval, sinking, and deliberate crumbling away, and how new ruin restores the strong lines that old ruin weakened."[48]

The processes of geological change are made manifest throughout the picture. Beginning at the top of the canvas, one encounters the snowy mountain, "the type," Winthrop writes, "of the great trachytic domes of the Andes."[49] This volcanic peak suggests the powerful igneous forces that, both Humboldt and Winthrop explain, are responsible for forming new rocks and elevating great segments of the earth's crust. The forces of erosion are emphasized in the lower part of the canvas, especially in one telling detail—the eroded riverbank in the right foreground. There the river has eaten away the soil and rock from under three trees, leaving their water-seeking roots stretching futilely into the air. "Thus," writes Louis Noble in his guide to the painting, "the elements and forces of the earth are forever busy in the apparently infinite task of reducing to a level the primeval erections of violence."[50]

The contemplation of all of these natural forms and forces would, Humboldt argued, carry us "beyond the mysterious boundary which connects the metaphysical with the physical, and lead us into another and higher sphere of ideas."[51] Church seems to have hoped that his painting would likewise uplift the viewer—though he seems to have been animated by a more specifically Christian vision of "uplift" than Humboldt ever embraced.

According to Winthrop and Noble (and Kevin Avery, too), *The Heart of the Andes* embodies a tropical version of *Pilgrim's Progress*, John Bunyan's allegory of a Christian life so popular in nineteenth-century America that Louisa May Alcott, in *Little Women*, had Marmee tuck copies of it under the pillows of her little girls. To journey through the landscape of *The Heart of the Andes*, along the route described by Winthrop, is to imaginatively enact the passage of a Christian through the trials of earthly life toward the spiritual rewards of the next. This allegorical journey begins in the right foreground where a fern-edged path, in Winthrop's words, "conducts us inward to a region as doubtful and dim as the height of the Cordillera above." This route "contrasts with the open road on the left," which leads us past the prominent white cross with its "sweet symbolical meaning" toward the Dome above—the final object of our quest. Before reaching the snowy peak we must ascend

Opposite: Detail of Fig. 40

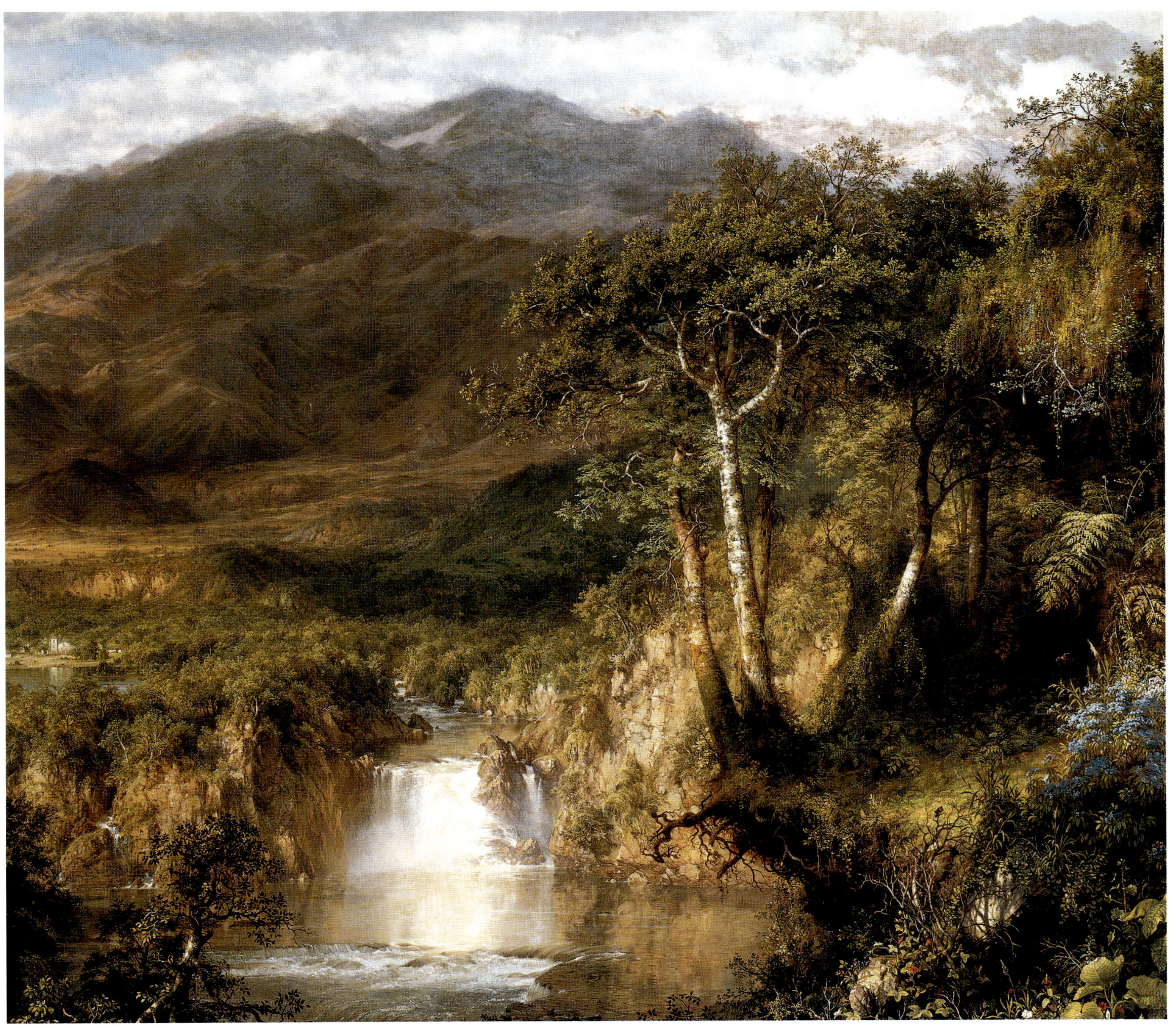

the "central mass of struggling mountain, with a war of light and shade over its tumultuous surface," representing "vigor and toil and perplexity."[52] Passing through this realm, we climb with "one steady movement upward," mounting "nearer and nearer the region of final mysterious battle in clouds and darkness, on the verge of final triumph beyond the veil." Each episode of the picture, writes Winthrop, "guides the mind on to the triumphal crowning spectacle . . . the Dome of snow . . . [the] emblem of permanent and infinite peace."[53]

It is no wonder that Mark Twain, who saw *The Heart of the Andes* in St. Louis, believed that one had to visit it several times to take in all its complexities. "When you first see the tame, ordinary picture," he wrote his brother, "your first impulse is to turn your back upon it, and say 'Humbug'—but your third visit will find your brain *gasping* and straining with futile efforts to take all the wonder in."[54] Tens of thousands of Twain's contemporaries seem to have shared his enthusiasm for the painting. In Boston alone, according to the local papers, more than thirty thousand people stopped by to see it.[55] In some venues people stood in line for hours, waiting to pay their quarters for the privilege of viewing the picture in its massive walnut frame. This frame, designed to resemble the window of an elegant hacienda, draperies pulled back to either side, was meant to place the viewer in a privileged position, inside an Ecuadoran mansion gazing out on a magnificent panoramic view.[56] The *Albion*'s stodgy art critic found this mode of presenting the picture "Barnumesque and altogether objectionable."[57] Objectionable or not, "Barnumesque" was close to the mark.

Though his name is now associated primarily with the Barnum & Bailey Circus, in 1859 Phineas T. Barnum was best known for his immensely popular American Museum, located only a short walk from Church's 10th Street studio. This five-story museum at the corner of Broadway and Ann was much more than a repository of carnivalesque freak shows. It also housed some of the finest "geological, conchological, and ornithological collections . . . in the country," cases of butterflies, two live whales from Labrador, Revolutionary War mementos, along with an entire floor devoted to panoramas, dioramas, and other "large paintings."[58] Its astounding mélange of artistic, historical, and scientific specimens promised the visitor "hours and hours of entertainment, instruction, and moral uplift."[59] Church would certainly have been proud to make the same claim for *The Heart of the Andes*, though perhaps he would have featured the word "entertainment" less prominently. Even so, he understood that entertainment was part of the package he was offering the public.

Church and his agents knew that to make money from the exhibition of single pictures, they would have to draw in a broad spectrum of the public. Promotion and publicity, they understood, would be keys to financial success, and the methods they employed differed little from those used by Barnum and his agents. Both sold informative pamphlets at the door. Both invited socially prominent visitors to their exhibition openings. Both made extensive use of newspaper advertisements and understood the value of reviews—even providing the copy themselves if necessary. The subjects (or in Barnum's case objects) of their exhibitions also have something in common. Church, in choosing subjects for his large exhibition paintings, tended toward those that were both topical and exotic—like tropical South America. Indeed, Winthrop's description of *The Heart of the Andes* sounds like a line from a Barnum publicity leaflet: "The subject is new, the scenes are strange, the facts are amazing."[60]

Barnum encouraged his visitors to bring a certain amount of skepticism to their evaluation of his exhibits. Faced with the strange and unfamiliar, they were prompted to judge what they saw, as Neil Harris has observed, along limited lines: "Is it true or false?" "Is it genuine or contrived?"[61] Perhaps conditioned by men like Barnum, Church's contemporaries often judged his paintings (and those by many other artists of the day) by this same standard. The major difference was that while many left Barnum's exhibits certain that they had been hoaxed or "humbugged" (and delighting in their ability to have discerned the scam), most seem to have left Church's exhibitions satisfied that they had been truthfully informed—and perhaps morally uplifted as well.[62]

THE PATRIOTIC LESSONS OF "COTOPAXI"

With the coming of the Civil War, Church (like Barnum) turned his talents to work that would help promote the Union cause. In *The Natural Bridge* and *The Heart of the Andes* Church had employed his keen observational skills and his knowledge of natural history to uplift his viewers with thoughts of the nation's glorious future and the promise of heavenly reward. In *Cotopaxi* (fig. 41) he drew upon his knowledge of geological forms and geological theory to convey a message of urgent concern to his countrymen.

The picture was begun in 1862 and exhibited to the New York public in March 1863, a time that was for ardent Unionists like Church one of the darkest, most despairing moments in the long, bloody war. The North had suffered defeat after defeat at Shiloh, Bull Run, and Fredericksburg, and the decisive Gettysburg victory was still several months away. *Cotopaxi*, a product of this bleak period, is a large, dramatic painting full of "resounding explosions and . . . torrents of sulphuretted smoke,"[63] as one of Church's contemporaries wrote. It represents an Ecuadorian volcano that Church had visited on his South American treks. Against a pearly morning sky, the perfect cone of Cotopaxi bursts into violent eruption. Thick black smoke roils southward from its summit, almost blotting out the yellow sun, reminding the *Albion*'s critic of "the war-clouds rolling dun."[64] A lurid light stains the level lava plain in front of the volcano and turns the middle-ground lake a bloody red. A waterfall, fed by the lake's waters, tumbles into the great chasm that splits the foreground.

A number of scholars, led by David Huntington, have recognized the connection between this painting and the Civil War.[65] The splitting, shattering, and dissolution of the land in the picture evokes the situation of the nation, while the volcanic imagery echoes the trembling fears of the country's inhabitants. Yet at the same time that the painting evokes the fears and anxieties of the moment, it also, Huntington argues, holds out the promise of Union victory. The picture, he says, is a "geological parable" that prophesies the outcome of the conflict. He argues that the luminous light of the "newly risen sun" burning through the darkness and the calm sky beyond the black plumes promise the ultimate redemption of the nation.[66]

While agreeing with Huntington's interpretation of the

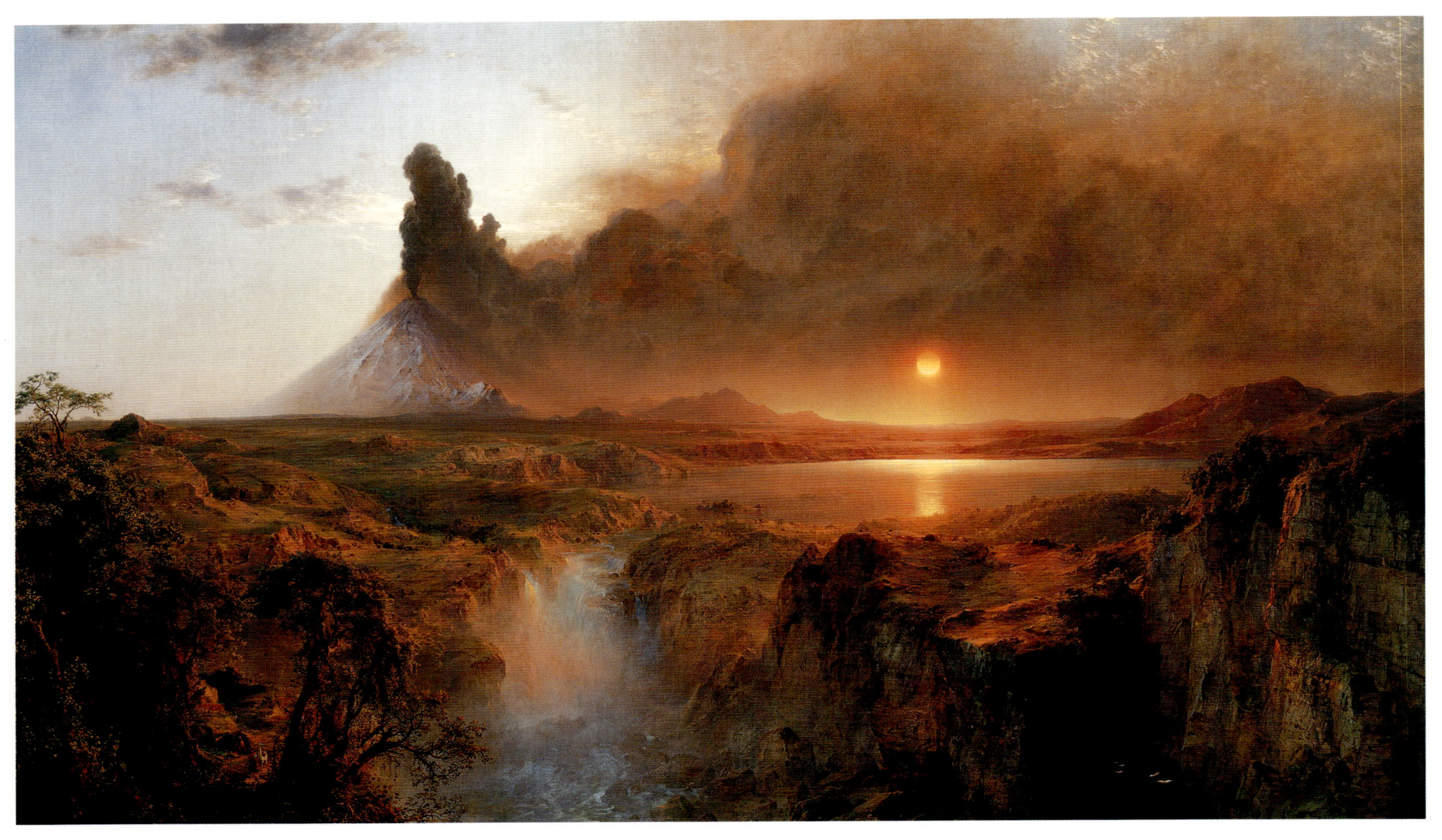

Fig. 41. Frederic Church, *Cotopaxi*, 1862.
Oil on canvas, 48 x 85 in. (121.9 x 215.9 cm).
The Detroit Institute of Arts. Founders Society Purchase, Robert H. Tannahill Foundation Fund, Gibbs-William Fund, Dexter M. Ferry Jr. Fund, Merrill Fund, Beatrice W. Rogers Fund, and Richard A. Manoogian Fund

painting, I want to elaborate on the part of his argument that he left undeveloped, the way in which this is a "geological parable," or the way in which Church drew on geological ideas to convey his themes.

The painting is a revelation of the geological agencies that have shaped the earth.[67] It describes the harmonious workings of the great rock cycle—the phases of erosion, deposition, and volcanic upheaval that have shaped the surface of the planet. Volcanic forces are, obviously, represented by Cotopaxi itself (a fiery furnace in which new rocks are forged). The forces of erosion are represented by the numerous streams that cut across the level lava plain, culminating in the great mist-shrouded waterfall. The falls (a perfect symbol for the forces of erosion) are dissolving hard rock into the fertile soil that supports the tangle of greenery in the left foreground. The third component of the rock cycle — deposition (the piling up of sediments) — is displayed in the layered structure of the foreground cliffs. Thus we see spread out before us the evidence of God's wise plan for the continual rejuvenation of our planet.

But what does this have to do with the Civil War? In this great rock cycle, so wisely devised by the Creator, violence plays an important role. It is part of the process of creation; it is necessary for the continuation of life. By analogy, the violence of the Civil War can be seen as part of God's plan, as something necessary for the rejuvenation of the nation. Just as God sent the Flood to chastise and renew humankind, so He visited the Civil War on Americans to cleanse them of their sins and prepare them for a new birth, for a renewal of the nation. The painting, as Huntington said, offers viewers "nature's type for the regeneration of America."[68] In 1863 it called on Americans to accept as God-given the great sacrifices that were being demanded of them, and it held out a promise of ultimate reward.

To many nineteenth-century educators, Church included, education meant not simply the acquisition of skills and the mastery of facts, but also the elevation of morals, the inculcation of patriotic pride and the understanding of one's civic responsibility. In paintings such as *Cotopaxi*, *The Heart of the Andes*, and *The Natural Bridge*, Church was able to convey scientific facts and theories while simultaneously using them to achieve these higher ends. In putting his great scientific knowledge to this use, he remained to the end the pupil of Thomas Cole.

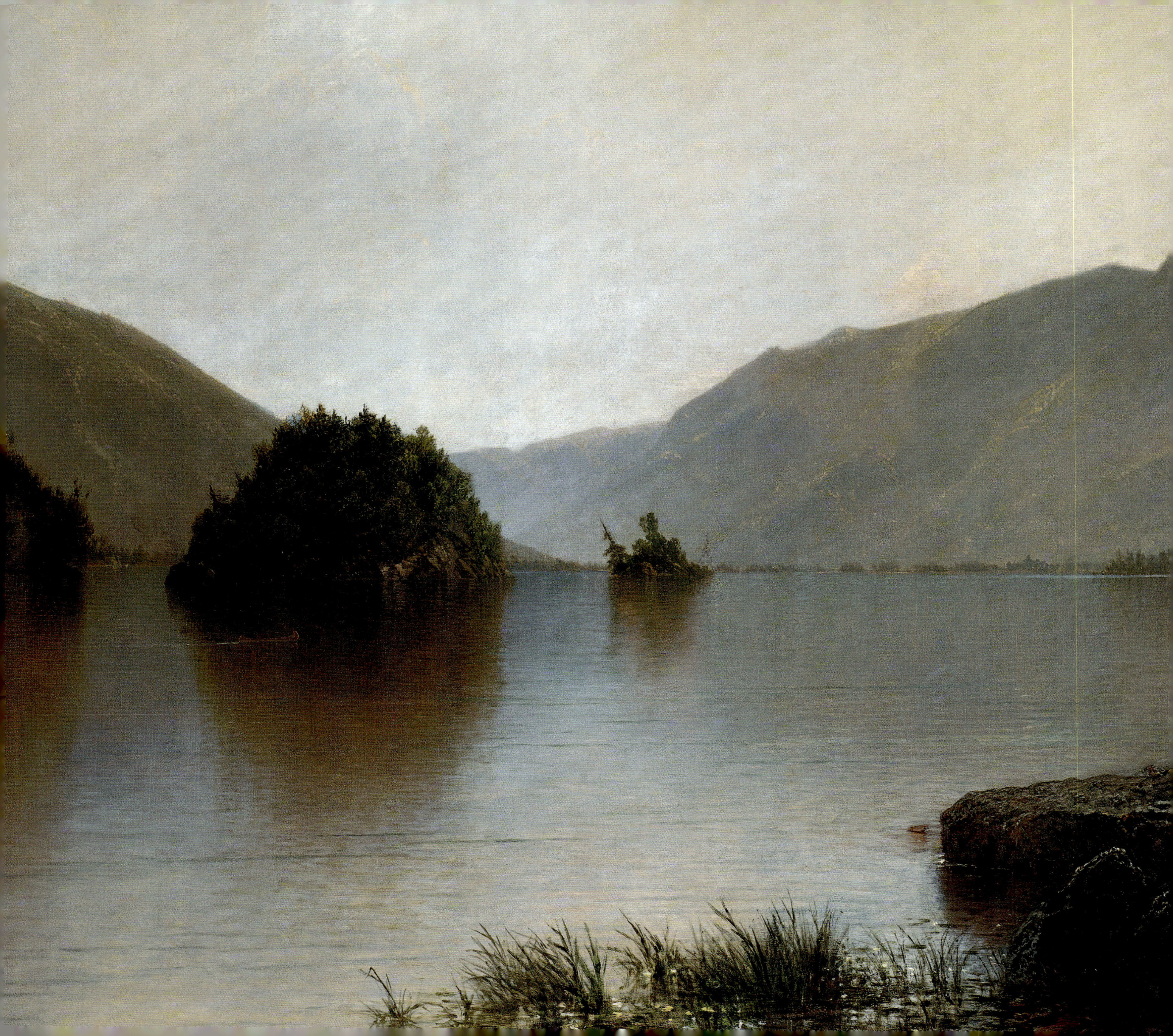

Chapter Four

John Kensett, Geology, and Landscape Tourism

John F. Kensett (1816–1872), affable and urbane, fond of good company, soft beds, and fine cigars, was well suited to be a painter of the touristic landscape.[1] He trained his pencil on Niagara Falls, Mount Washington, the Hudson Highlands, and Lake George, all sites on the standard tourist routes at mid-century, and all within an easy distance of railroad stations, steamboat landings, and comfortable hotels. While Frederic Church was swatting flesh-eating insects in the Andean jungles, Kensett was enjoying the evening breezes on the veranda of one of the era's great white hotels, relaxing after a day of sketching in the nearby countryside.

If Church's paintings find their literary correlatives in Humboldt's *Cosmos*, Kensett's find theirs in the period's guidebooks. As one of his contemporaries said, he offered "the public their favorite Murray's guide-book topography."[2] Such guidebooks, which were pouring off the presses in the mid-nineteenth century in response to the burgeoning tourist trade, promoted three major ways of appreciating America's natural scenery: aesthetically, as pictures; historically, for its associations; and scientifically (especially geologically) for the lessons it offered about the structure of nature and the operation of its laws. Kensett crafted his paintings to both allude to and accommodate these varied experiential modes.

Commercial tourism had just begun to develop in the United States in the 1820s.[3] During that same decade, a native school of landscape painters was forming, and geology was emerging as a fashionable pastime. Almost from the start, these three ventures became intimately intertwined, each influencing, impacting, and responding to the others. Geologists and the popular geological enthusiasms of the period came to play a significant part in shaping the tourist's itinerary and experiences, and, beyond that, the subject matter and even compositional modes of artists like Kensett who oriented their work toward the tourist scene. Kensett's career exemplifies the alliance between landscape painting, geology, and scenic tourism that was so critical to the financial viability of many mid-century artists.[4]

Opposite: Detail of Fig. 48

KENSETT AND THE TOURIST MARKET

From the very beginning of his career Kensett recognized the value of landscapes in the tourist market. In the 1840s when he was living in Europe, honing his skills as a landscape painter, he kept his pockets filled — or at least tried to keep them filled — by selling images to travelers on the Grand Tour. He wrote at the time of his ambition to choose and paint scenes "for exhibition at home, or for such travelers as may be disposed to purchase on the spot."[5] After his return to the United States in 1847, he continued to be involved with the tourist trade. In 1852 he produced dozens of landscape vignettes to illustrate *Lotus Eating*, a travel book about the major tourist sites of the northeastern United States, authored by his friend George William Curtis. These tiny wood engravings, interspersed through the text, describe touristic amenities such as the teahouse on one of the islands in the midst of Lake George, the piazza of the luxurious "United States" hotel in Saratoga, and the boardwalk that extended out over the rapids to the rim of Niagara Falls (fig. 42).

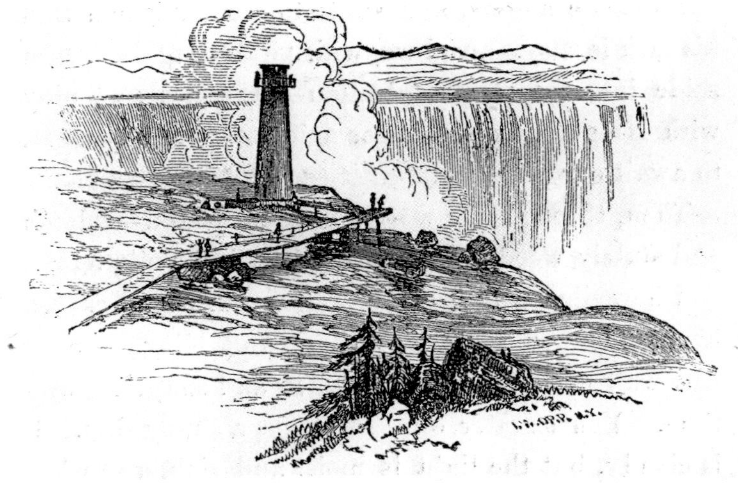

Fig. 42. Landscape vignette of Niagara Falls. Wood engraving after John Kensett, from George William Curtis, *Lotus-Eating: A Summer Book* (New York: Harper and Brothers, 1852)

All through his career, Kensett's works were bound to the traveling and vacationing habits of his well-to-do contemporaries. His landscapes often served them as touristic mementos and souvenirs of summer vacations. These are not mammoth exhibition pictures like Church's *Heart of the Andes*; they are, for the most part, parlor-sized paintings, meant to be hung over mantelpieces and side tables and intended for intimate viewing with family and friends. While Church was offering his viewers the drama of exploration and discovery, Kensett was providing the pleasures of recollection and reminiscence. When the art critic Henry Tuckerman visited Kensett's studio in the mid-1860s, he referred to the artist's paintings of the Rhode Island coast as "charming memorials of a favorite summer haunt," adding "we retrace at our ease our summer wanderings in his studio."[6] In 1855 a reviewer for *Putnam's Magazine*, commenting on one of Kensett's images of White Mountain scenery, remarked: "Of all our readers, to whom the mountains of New Hampshire have this summer been an enchanted region, we hope there is not one who, in looking upon such a picture, would not feel that it made his memories more beautiful."[7] In 1860 Kensett's patron, the Boston lawyer Charles Loring, wrote to thank the artist for sending the pictures of the scenery near his summer home in Beverly, Massachusetts:

> I had them immediately suspended in my sitting room, and it happened that the Academy of Arts and Sciences held a social meeting at my house that evening, giving a fine opportunity to display them. I need not tell you that they were very much admired and especially by those familiar with the inspirations of the Beverly Shore. . . . it will really be an addition to the charms of my home and the pleasures of my life to have these charming illustrations of scenes so dear to me, so constantly before my eyes, when removed from them in winter.[8]

THE TRAVEL INDUSTRY'S EXPLOITATION OF ART

While Kensett's bank account benefited considerably from his engagement with the touristic enterprise, the travel industry sought to benefit from its engagement with him. Almost from the inception of America's scenic tourism industry in the 1820s its members recognized the positive impact artists could have on their business. As landscape painters tromped through the American wilderness in search of new subjects for their pencils and brushes, they discovered beauty spots and tamed them through the use of aesthetic conventions into scenes that could be transferred to canvas, engaging in a process that Alan Wallach has called "aesthetic pioneering."[9] They took raw nature and transformed it into "scenery"; they took a nature new to art and shaped it into a cultural artifact that could be visually consumed by an educated public.[10] The compelling images of America's natural landscape that resulted from this process created in viewers a desire to see the "originals" for themselves.

Seeking to capitalize on this process, hoteliers and railroad company executives hired artists to paint the scenery around their hotels and along their tracks (and sometimes to offer art lessons to their guests), while guidebook authors commissioned views to illustrate their texts. The California landscape painter William Keith produced advertising images for the Northern Pacific Railroad;[11] Thomas Moran's paintings of the Grand Canyon were used to promote business on the Sante Fe Railroad;[12] Aaron Draper Shattuck worked with and for the proprietors of the Walcott House in North Conway, New Hampshire;[13] T. Addison Richards wrote and illustrated numerous guidebooks, and the list could go on and on. A nineteenth-century innkeeper in New Hampshire's White Mountains, Samuel W. Thompson, testified to the artist's role in boosting tourism: "Yes, to the landscape artist more than to any other one is due the present prosperity of North Conway. This one man [an unnamed painter] was enthusiastic, others saw his pictures or heard of them and came to this wonderfully beautiful place."[14]

The physical labor that the artists expended in blazing trails to scenic sites likewise benefited tourists and tourism. As one nineteenth-century journalist pointed out, "The summer of 1849 was spent by Messrs. Casilear and Kensett at Haines Falls and Kaaterskill Clove [in the Catskill Mountains] and their ladders and paths were the first by which that portentous gorge was rendered easy of access."[15]

By the mid-nineteenth century, guidebooks were even promoting the artists themselves as tourist attractions. In

"A Sabbath on the Catskills," an article anthologized in several nineteenth-century guidebooks to the Catskill region, the Reverend Theodore L. Cuyler directed his readers to the spot where Frederic Church was building his new home (the mansion we now know as "Olana"). He also pointed out that "haunt of genius," "the studio of Cole [in the village of Catskill], from which came forth the immortal 'Voyage of Life,' and in which still remain the unfinished 'Cross and the World.'"[16] Sighting live artists under their white umbrellas sketching in the countryside became an image to be collected on one's vacation, like spotting a moose or a rare fern. Though sometimes the artists were not hard to sight at all; Kensett described trying to paint at Niagara Falls with fifty tourists peering over his shoulders.[17]

GEOLOGISTS AND THE TOURIST INDUSTRY

Although geologists themselves never became scenic attractions as the artists did, the tourist industry nonetheless took an eager interest in their work. Those geologists involved in the many state and national geological surveys of the mid-nineteenth century recognized the potential economic value of scenic beauty, and prospected for fine views as well as mineral deposits as they pushed their way through the nation's wilderness. Edward Hitchcock, for example, head of the Massachusetts Geological Survey, devoted a whole section of his final report to the state's "Scenographical Geology," which an enterprising publisher quickly turned into a guidebook to the state's natural wonders. As the publisher explained in his preface to the volume, for those "in our cities and towns, who are in the habit of making excursions into the country during the summer, this sketch may serve as a convenient guide."[18]

Geologists were also valuable to the tourist industry in other ways. The survey leaders were generally anxious to generate popular enthusiasm for their publicly sponsored work. To that end, they published highly readable accounts of their adventures and discoveries. Ferdinand Hayden, for example, leader of the Geological and Geographical Survey of the Territories, recounted his travels in the Yellowstone region in a series of articles for *Scribner's Monthly* in the early 1870s. Clarence King, a member of the California Geological Survey and later head of the Fortieth Parallel Survey, authored the lively and widely read *Mountaineering in the Sierra Nevadas* (1872), describing his exploits with the survey among the snow-capped western peaks. Such publications were of great value to the tourist industry since, like landscape paintings, they had the potential to charge readers' imaginations, creating a desire to visit the described locales. The topographical information in the surveys' official reports was also extremely valuable to entrepreneurs of the tourist industry as they plotted their railroad lines and sited their hotels. Indeed, the surveys' work was so valuable to railroad companies in particular that their executives vigorously lobbied the United States Congress and state legislatures to continually renew the surveys' appropriations.

KENSETT'S PATRONS AND THE TOURIST INDUSTRY

While supporting geological fieldwork, the travel industry also solicited the attention of artists, sometimes going to

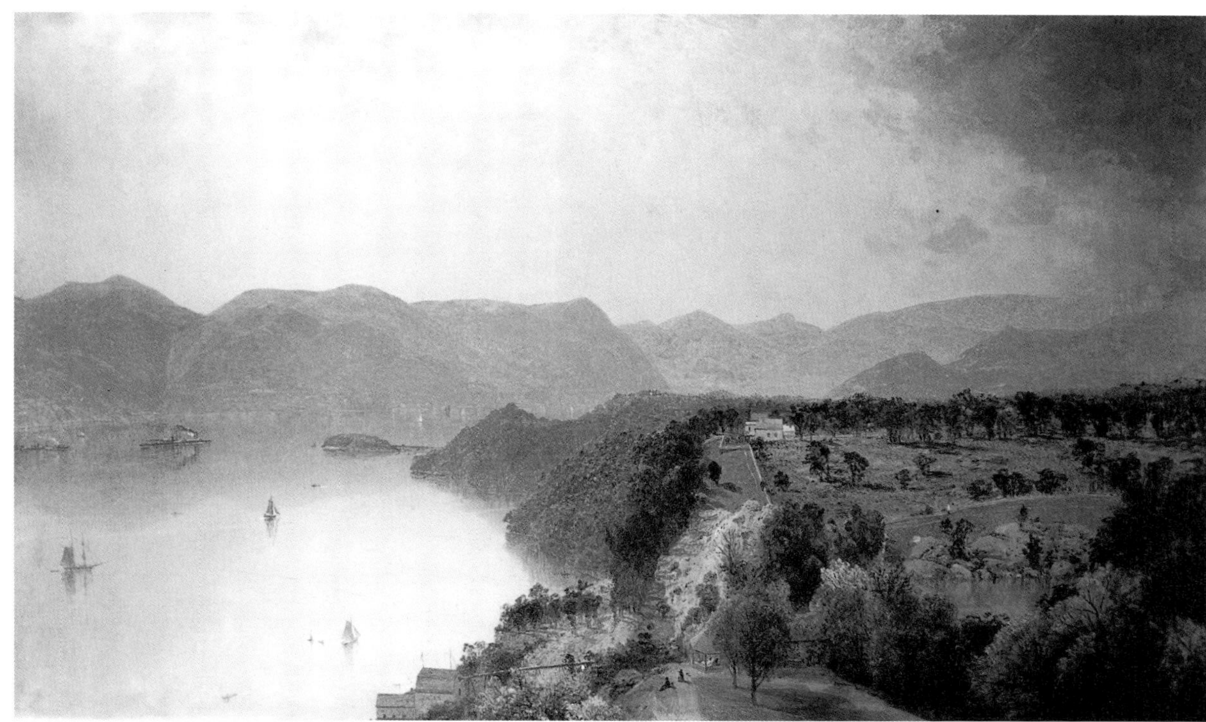

Fig. 43. John Kensett, *View from Cozzens Hotel near West Point*, 1863. Oil on canvas, 20 x 34 in. (50.8 x 86.4 cm). The New-York Historical Society, New York

great lengths and expending considerable sums of money to do so. In 1858 Kensett, along with about two dozen other artists and photographers, was invited by the Baltimore and Ohio Railroad for an all-expenses-paid tour of the scenery along the company's tracks from Baltimore to Wheeling, West Virginia.[19] Six luxuriously appointed cars with staterooms, writing tables, and a continually replenished buffet table, were placed at their disposal, all in the hope that the artists would be moved to memorialize the views from the train's windows and around its station stops. The B&O's largesse was ill-spent on Kensett, who seems never to have painted a scene inspired by that trip. But other of his patrons were more fortunate.

Among the successful acquisitors of his works were many who were deeply involved in the tourist trade.[20] Robert M. Olyphant, Kensett's good friend and most loyal patron, headed the Delaware and Hudson Railroad Company, the New York and Canada Railroad Company, and the Lake George Steamboat Company, all of which catered to tourists.[21] Another patron, Abraham M. Cozzens, made his fortune in the New York hotel trade. Purchaser of at least eleven paintings by Kensett, he was an ardent supporter of American landscape painters, believing that their works had the potential, among other things, to invigorate the tourist trade by advertising the attractions of American scenery.[22]

In the 1850s Cozzens constructed a large, luxurious hotel on the bluffs of the Hudson near West Point. At Cozzens's invitation, Kensett visited the hotel at least twice, once in the 1850s and again in 1863. The second visit seems to have been made

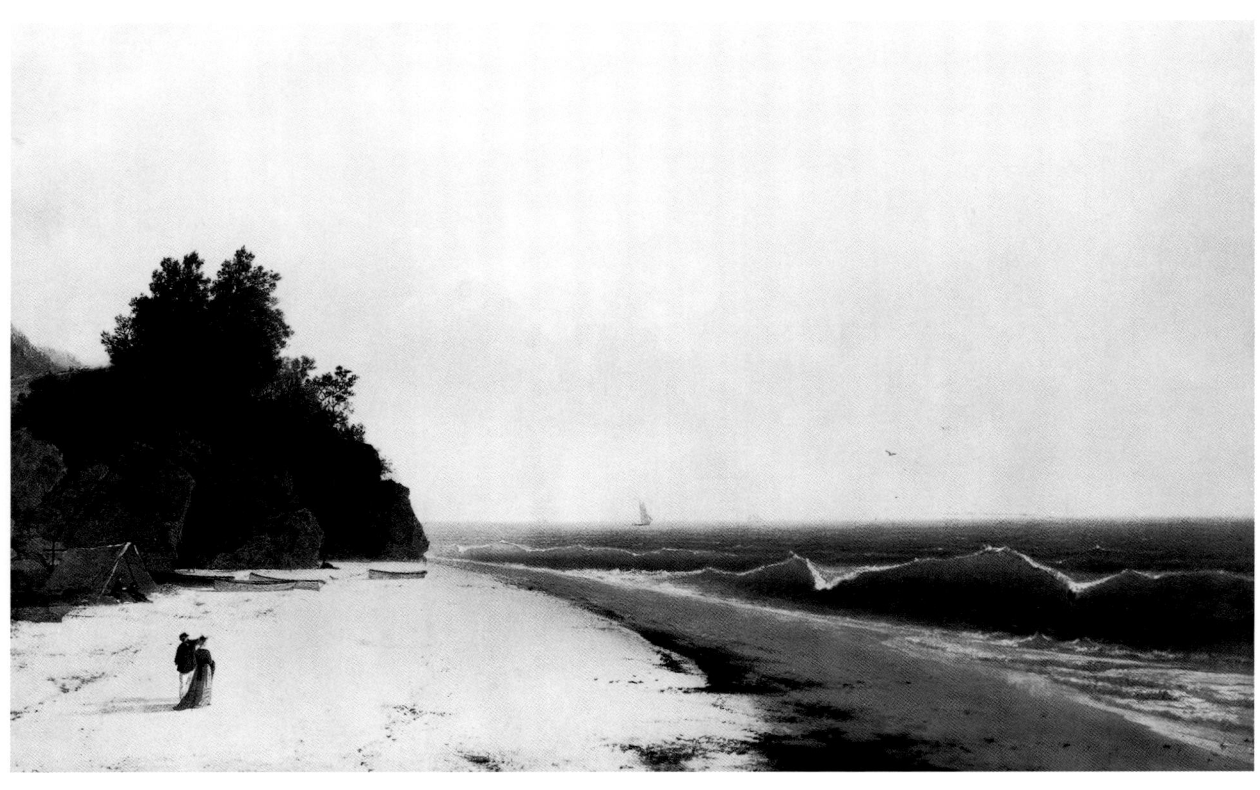

Fig. 44. John Kensett, *Coast Scene with Figures (Beverly Shore)*, 1869. Oil on canvas, 36 1/4 x 60 1/4 in. (92 x 153 cm). Wadsworth Atheneum, Hartford, Connecticut. The Ella Gallup Sumner and Mary Catlin Sumner Collection Fund

to take sketches for his painting *View from Cozzens Hotel near West Point* (1863, fig. 43).[23] The picture describes a hazy afternoon in late summer or early autumn as the trees are just beginning to shade from green to pale yellow and red. From an elevated vantage point, presumably at or near Cozzens Hotel, we gaze out over a panoramic vista. To the right we see the rocky, wooded top of the bluff, its surface punctuated by substantial dwellings, an inviting lake, and a small gazebo from which ladies look out, as we do, over the Hudson toward the "rude cliffs" on the opposite side where one can find one of the area's most famous geological sights, a "remarkable range of precipices of trap rock."[24] The placid gray surface of the river is dotted with sailboats, rafts, and steamships. These small details evoke the leisurely pleasures of a late summer sojourn at Cozzens Hotel.

The hotel itself is not shown. Kensett usually excluded from his landscape paintings the most obvious signs of tourism: the summer homes, the railroad stations, the teahouses, the boardwalks, and the carriage stops that were becoming such conspicuous features along the tourist routes. These omissions were almost certainly calculated to enhance that sense of intimate engagement with nature so prized at the time. However, despite these omissions Kensett consistently incorporated signals that his are landscapes of leisure. One of the most important of these signals is the choice of figures. Like the vacation resorts themselves, Kensett's paintings tend to be populated by fashionably dressed women. Often accompanied by elegant gentlemen, they stroll along the shores and rest in the shade of spreading oaks (fig. 44). Kensett also tended to work with an artistic vocabulary of horizontal forms, soft light, and subdued colors that led his contemporaries to describe his paintings as "gentle," "lyrical," "delicate," "sweet," "soft," "smooth," and "calm," words which in the nineteenth century had distinctively feminine connotations.[25] Their "feminine" characteristics mark them as civilized landscapes, as tamed and domesticated spots where one could laze away a sultry afternoon.

KENSETT AND THE TOURISTIC GAZE

The efficacy of Kensett's paintings as touristic mementos and as stimulants to the tourist industry can be attributed, at least in part, to the close correspondence between the ways he presented American nature and the ways his fashionable traveling patrons consumed it. To understand how these well-to-do tourists approached natural scenery we cannot do better than look at the era's guidebooks, many of them written by and for members of this set. Such texts, as Kenneth Myers has pointed out, "provided vocabularies and interpretive frameworks that largely defined the content of individual tourists 'personal' responses to the sites."[26] Authors of this literature took seriously their role in mediating the public's experiences. Thomas Starr King, author of one of the most famous guidebooks to the White Mountains, explained that his aim was to help his readers "appreciate landscape more adequately."[27]

The Aesthetic Experience of the Touristic Landscape

Mid-century authors of tourist guides, as was noted earlier, promoted three major ways of experiencing places: aesthetic, associationist, and scientific. The aesthetic mode of viewing nature had its roots in the eighteenth-century English concept of the picturesque. As originally conceived, the picturesque involved appreciating natural scenery by mentally composing it into pictures resembling well-known works by such artists as Claude Lorrain. These "living landscape paintings" were evaluated by their creators according to criteria established for the judgment of art: was the image well framed? was the composition balanced? were the colors harmonious? When Jane Austen's fashion-conscious characters in *Northanger Abbey* admired the countryside around Bath, speaking approvingly of its "foregrounds, distances, and second distances; side-screens and perspectives; lights and shades," they were participating in the picturesque vogue.

Guidebook authors helped their readers appreciate American nature in picturesque terms. In *The White Hills* (1859), Starr King describes New Hampshire's White Mountains as a natural art gallery through which his readers can wander at leisure. His object, he explains, is to direct them to the places "where the best pictures are to be seen."[28] The selection of choice vantage points was considered a crucial first step in the aesthetic objectification of the land. As William Cullen Bryant notes in his preface to the first volume of *Picturesque America* (1872), "People in search of the picturesque should under-

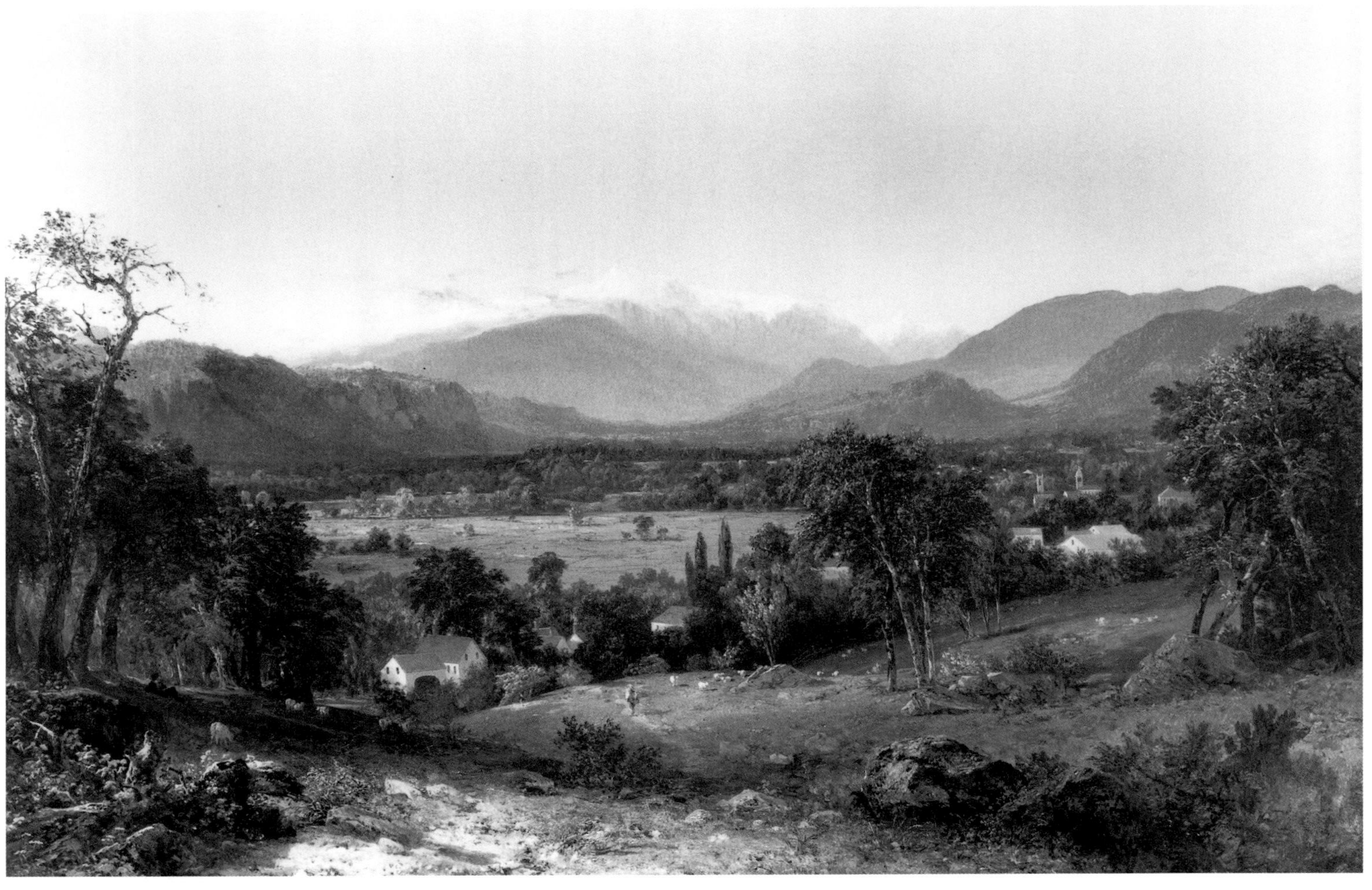

stand the importance of selecting suitable points of view."[29] Starr King added to this the importance of viewing the scene at the right time of day and under appropriate weather conditions. He often advised his readers on such matters, recommending viewing a spot at sunset, or mid-afternoon, or just after a shower, when the colors, the patterns of light and dark, and the softness or clarity of forms would most nearly resemble a painted image.

The painted images he had in mind were preeminently those by American landscape painters like Kensett. Indeed a number of guidebook authors, including Starr King, assumed that Kensett's paintings were well-enough known that their readers could use them as models in composing their mental landscapes. Authors even steered their readers to places where they could see "a Kensett." Starr King pauses beside the "Artist's Brook" in his tour of the Saco Valley, to point out "an over-

Opposite: Fig. 45. John Kensett, *The White Mountains from the Valley of Conway,* 1851. Oil on canvas, 41 x 63 3/8 in. (104.1 x 159.9 cm). Davis Museum and Cultural Center, Wellesley College, Wellesley, Massachusetts. Gift of Mr. and Mrs. James B. Munn (Ruth C. Hanford, '09) in the name of the class of 1909

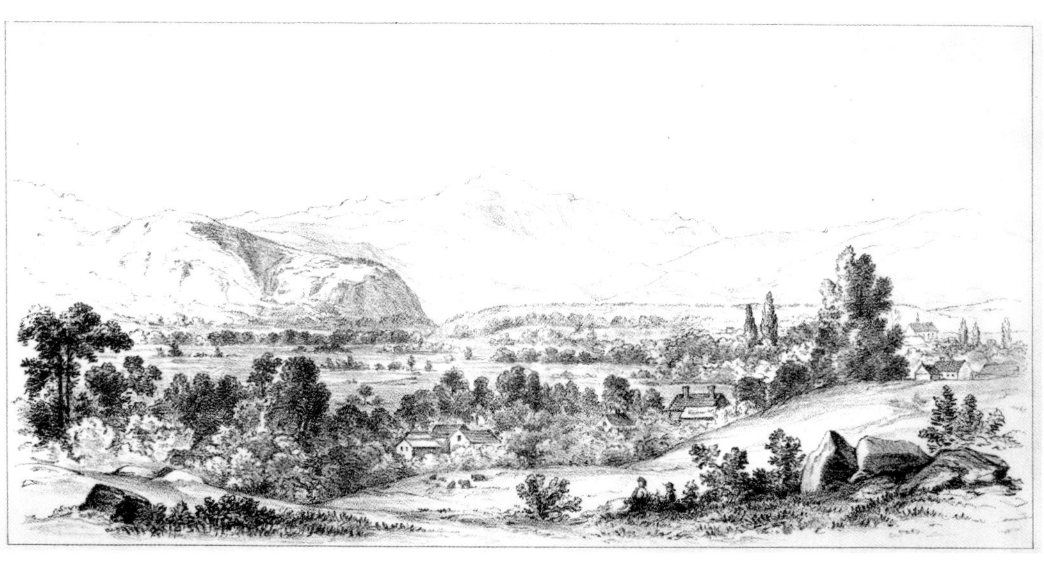

Fig. 46. "The White Mountains from North Conway." Frontispiece to Benjamin Willey, *Incidents in White Mountain History* (Boston: Nathaniel Noyes, 1856)

hanging beech with marbled stem, such as Kensett loves to paint."[30] In *Lotus Eating* Curtis describes one of his traveling companions hiking near Catskill Falls where he "glanced among the trees, and from time to time, announced 'a Kensett,' as a broad bit of mossed rock, or a shapely stretch of trees with the mountain outline beyond, recalled the poetic accuracy and characteristic subjects of that artist."[31] Still another author, Charles Rockwell, in *The Catskill Mountains and the Region Around* (1867), describes a hike to Haines Falls, noting: "Descending the brook, you pass over ledges and boulders of gray lichened stone, such as Kensett loves and paints better than any man in America."[32]

These passages suggest that Kensett's paintings helped to shape the way his viewers responded to the natural world—inciting them to mentally frame and compose bits of the countryside to recall the sort of images they had found in his works. He provided models for looking at the countryside in pictorial terms. One could easily argue that virtually all landscape images have this effect, but Kensett's works seem to have played a particularly prominent role in this process. This is in part because some of the places he depicted, such as the White Mountains, were just becoming popular with tourists, thus allowing his paintings to participate in the initial cultural appropriation of the sites, conditioning the way later visitors approached them. His *White Mountains from the Valley of Conway* (1851, fig. 45), for example, an engraving of which was distributed by the American Art Union in 1851, established the view across the valley of Conway toward Mount Washington as one of the must-see sights on a White Mountain itinerary. From the 1850s onward, variations on Kensett's composition illustrated many guidebooks to the area, including Benjamin Willey's *Incidents in White Mountain History* (1856, fig. 46).

Furthermore, the topographical, geological, and botanical specificity of Kensett's works encouraged observers to make direct connections between the painted images and actual places. He almost always gave his paintings site-specific titles *(Bash Bish Falls, Mount Chocorua, Newport Coast)*, and his faithful rendition of mountain profiles as well as his care in replicating trees and rocks allowed his viewers to easily match painting and place. The Reverend William Furness, writing for the *Home Journal* in 1851, explained why well-rendered topographical views like Kensett's could be so much more satisfying than more fanciful "compositions": "We gaze upon a picture portraying some country spot—we detect some resemblance to places we have visited and immediately we are lost in a revery of pleasant recollections in which the spirit bathes as in a stream and is refreshed." But, he laments, in "our visits to [young artists'] studios, we too often find them engaged on 'composition'—the infallible signs of which are gigantic blue and purple mountains, violently opposed by tall and massive trees. Of course such artistic productions remind us of nowhere, and hence enjoy the unenviable felicity of remaining on the hands of their projectors."[33]

The Associationist Experience of Landscape

The second mode of appreciating natural scenery, the historic or associationist mode, was, like the picturesque, rooted in eighteenth-century British aesthetic theory. In his 1790 essay *On the Nature and Principles of Taste*, the Scottish philosopher Archibald Alison argued that the pleasure we derive from looking at nature and art arises not from something inherent in the objects viewed but rather from the associations, the trains of ideas and emotions, that they generate. The more numerous and profound the associations, Alison argues, the greater will be the pleasure of the viewer.[34]

The problem this posed for Americans was that, according to numerous eighteenth- and nineteenth-century pundits, the American land had no associations. John Ruskin, for instance, attributed the United States' "deficiency in landscape" to the country's "want of historical associations."[35] Thomas Cole in his 1836 "Essay on American Scenery" refers to "what has been considered a grand defect of American scenery—the want of associations such as arise amidst the scenes of the old world."[36]

American guidebook authors were eager to dispel this notion of national inadequacy, inundating their readers with lengthy accounts of the historic events, the legends, the literature, and the art associated with particular American spots. In his essay "Highlands and Palisades of the Hudson," written for Bryant's *Picturesque America*, E. L. Burlingame insists that he must "say something of the associations which, besides its beauty, make [the region] a place full of interest to every traveler through the Hudson's scenery." He then regales his readers with detailed accounts of the Revolutionary War struggles acted out along its shores. Next he moves to literary associations, informing his readers that they are "in the very land of [Washington] Irving now, the whole region is peopled with the creations of his fancy."[37]

Few were the guidebook authors who did not include such literary and historical references. Guides to the Catskills almost invariably included excerpts from the writings of Washington Irving, James Fenimore Cooper, and William Cullen Bryant, while travel literature about the White Mountains inevitably recounted the story of the tragic demise of the Willey family, the Indian legend of "The Curse of Chocorua," and tales of early exploration and settlement, with occasional allusions to the short stories of Nathaniel Hawthorne.

Landscape painters could accommodate this associationist mode of landscape appreciation in a number of ways. They could choose to people their landscapes with figures enacting the stories and events associated with the place depicted. Thomas Cole sometimes chose this tack, as he did in his print of the Legend of Chocorua (fig. 47) or in his painting of Crawford Notch with its allusions to the Willey Disaster (fig. 25). This approach had the virtue of creating associations for those viewers who lacked them and gave those who knew the stories the pleasure of seeing them acted out on the canvas. But it also tended to limit the ways that the viewer could experience the image, fixing the associations on a particular event. It did not easily allow for the layering and multiplication of associations that Alison argued so greatly increases the viewer's pleasure.

Topographic landscapes devoid of figures also accommodated associationism by allowing viewers to call to mind any associations they might have with the depicted spot (indeed associationist theory was rooted in this mnemonic response to place). Like a stage devoid of actors, such images opened up possibilities by allowing the viewer to write the script and people the scene with the varied creations of his or her own fancy.

Unlike Cole, Kensett seems never to have illustrated particular legends, stories, or historic events in his landscape paintings. Yet he sometimes included small details presumably intended to spark the viewer's imagination, eliciting a train of associations. This is perhaps best exemplified in *Lake George* (1869, fig. 48), one of the largest and most stunning of his works.

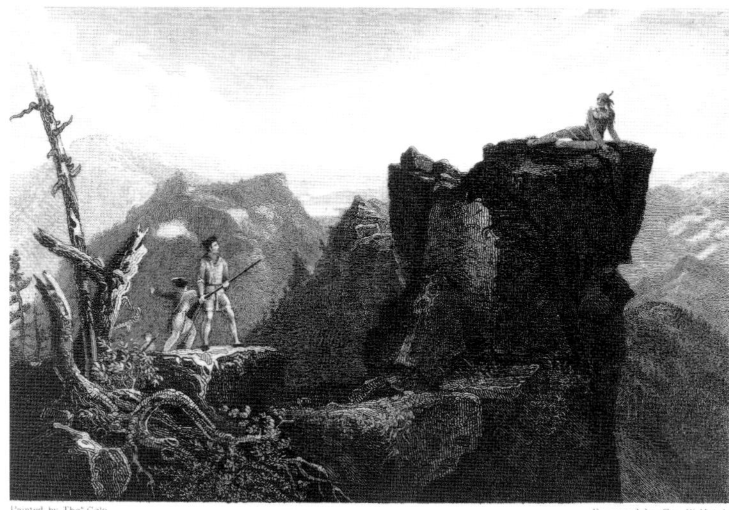

Fig. 47. George W. Hatch, *Chocorua's Curse.* Engraving after Thomas Cole, *Corway Peak, New Hampshire,* 1829. From S. G. Goodrich, *The Token, A Christmas and New Year's Present* (Boston: Carter and Hendee, 1830). The Huntington Library, San Marino, California

Painted in muted hues of gray and green, it depicts a soft, still, misty scene in New York's Adirondack Mountains. The calm surface of Lake George, filling the lower third of the canvas, stretches outward from a roughly textured foreground patch of rocks, reeds, and water lilies. Toward the far shore, soft green mounds of wooded islands rise from the water. Beyond them, ringing the lake, are glacier-sculpted hills, their shapes shrouded in the gray clouds of a passing shower. The

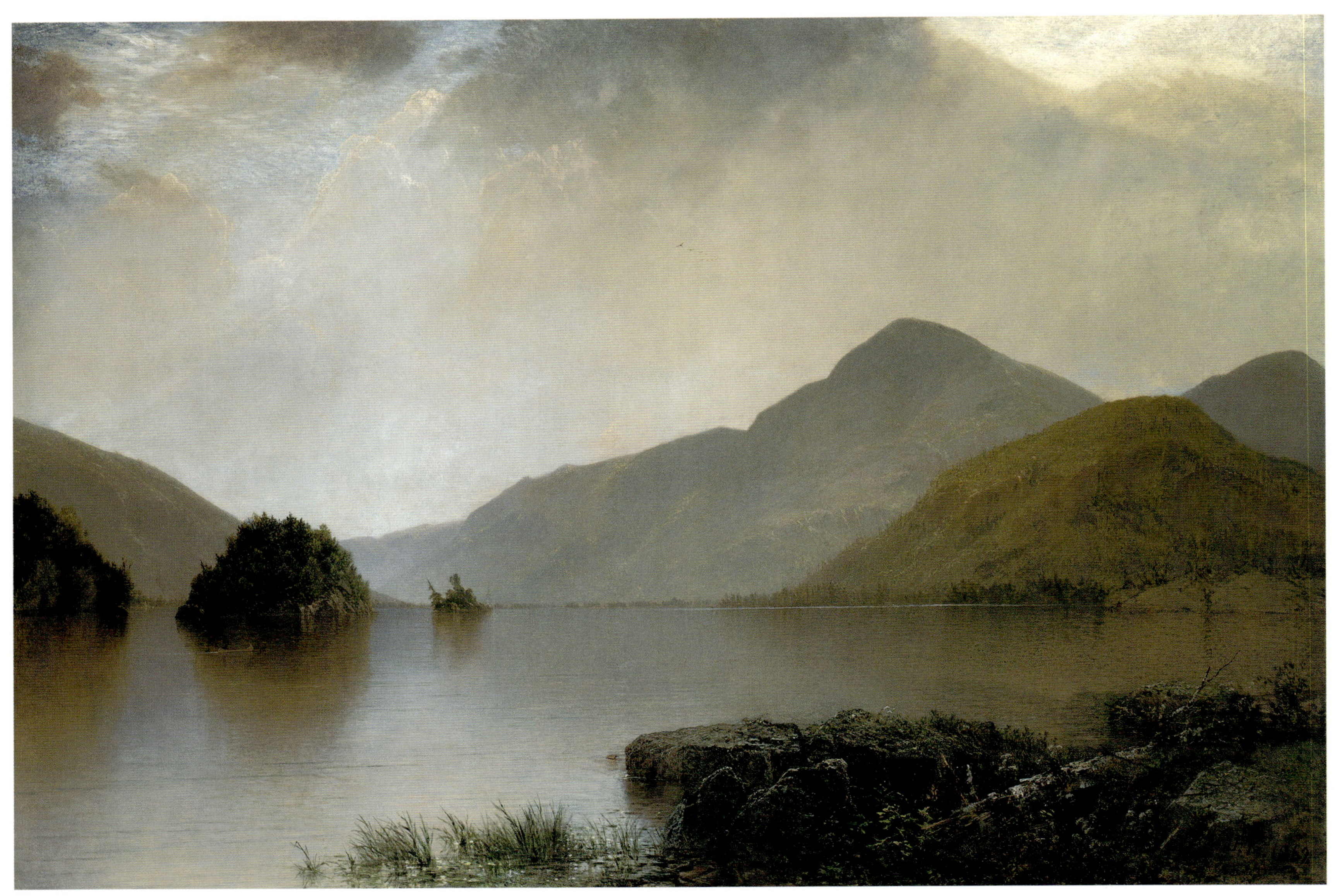

Fig. 48. John Kensett, *Lake George*, 1869.
Oil on canvas, 44 1/8 x 66 3/8 in. (112.1 x 168.6 cm).
The Metropolitan Museum of Art, New York. Bequest of Maria DeWitt Jessup, 1915. (15.30.61)

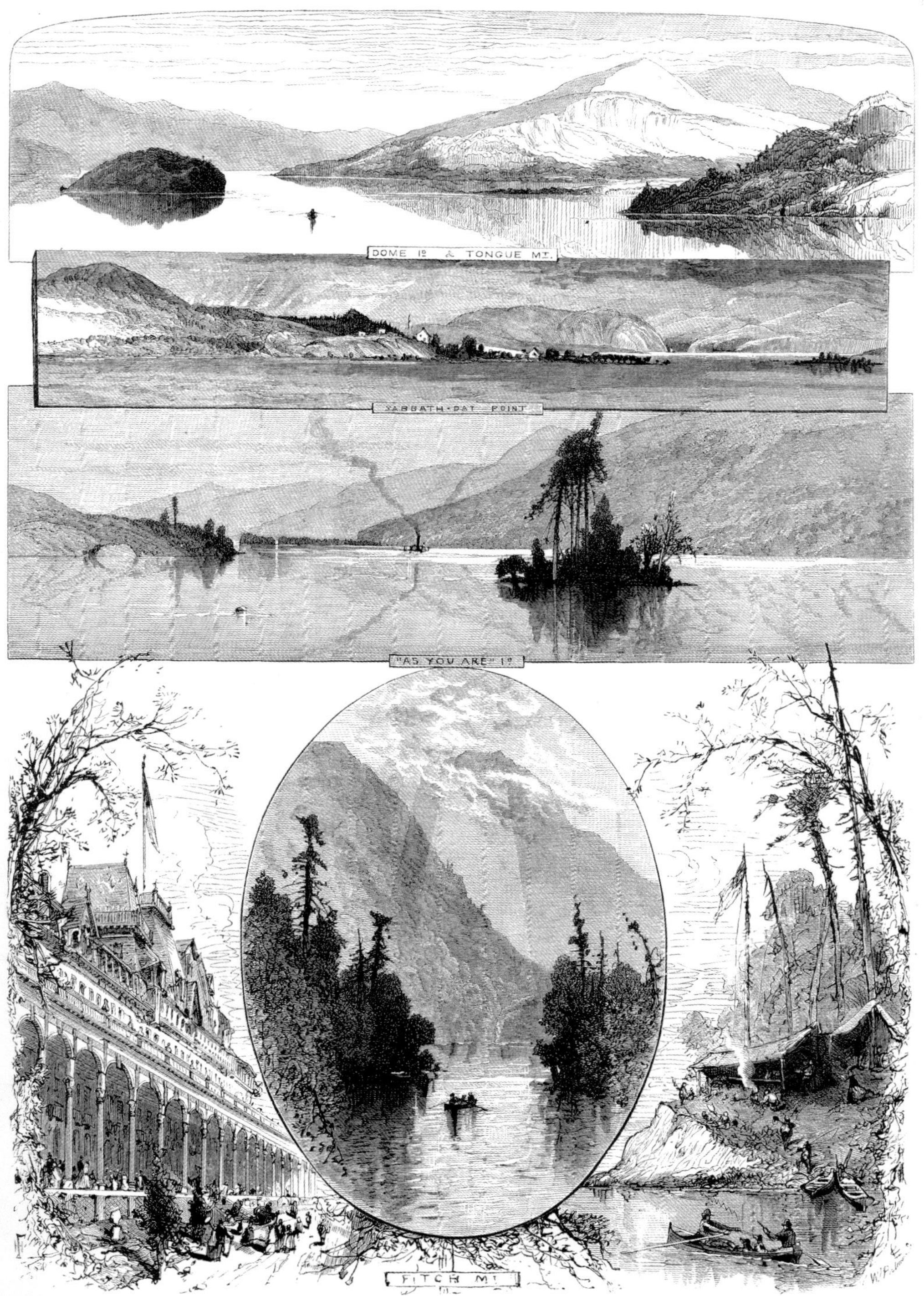

Fig. 49. "Scenes on Lake George." Illustration from William Cullen Bryant, ed., *Picturesque America*, vol. 2 (New York: D. Appleton, 1874)

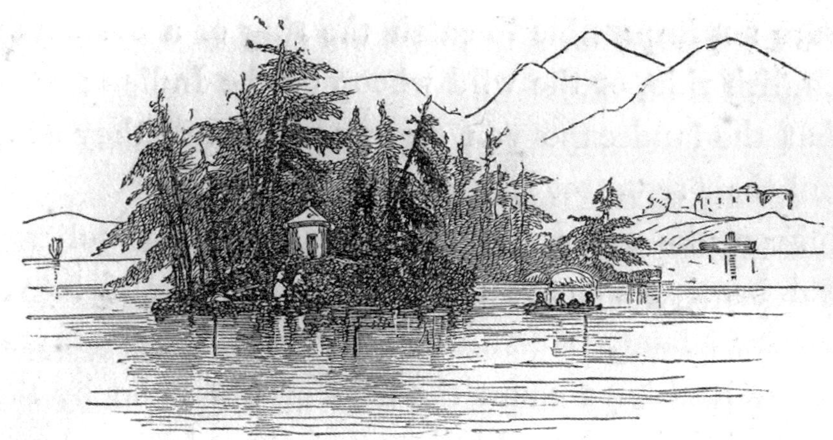

Fig. 50. Landscape vignette of Lake George. Wood engraving after John Kensett, from George William Curtis, *Lotus-Eating: A Summer Book* (New York: Harper and Brothers, 1852)

air seems to be heavy with moisture, and the atmosphere tinged with the anticipation of a change in the weather. In the upper sky, sunlight burns through the precipitation offering glimpses of blue sky and lacy white clouds. The drama of the painting seems to hinge on this atmospheric shift, this change in the weather—until one notices the tiny figure of an Indian guiding his canoe past one of the islands on the far left. This small, unobtrusive detail then evokes a flood of associations—with the early history of the United States, with the military skirmishes of the French and Indian Wars, and with the novels of James Fenimore Cooper—exactly those associations touted by every nineteenth-century guidebook to the area.

In *Lotus-Eating*, Kensett's friend Curtis describes how such associations crowd into the mind of a viewer standing on the shores of Lake George: "You might well fancy the populace of the primeval forest yet holding those retreats. You might still dream on the twilight that it were not impossible to catch the ring of a French or English rifle, or the wild whoop of the Indian; sure that the landscape you see, was 'the same they saw and their remotest ancestors.'"[38]

In his essay on Lake George for *Picturesque America*, O. B. Bunce likewise recalls the lake's colonial history: "It is a stirring picture that comes up before the imagination—this placid sheet, these sylvan shores, all astir with the 'pomp and circumstance of war.'"[39] But for him, the literary associations were equally powerful: "Lake George has many associations as well as charms. Few places in our country are more associated with historical reminiscences, or so identified with legend or story. . . . Cooper has peopled the shores of this lake with the creations of his fancy. Who can wander along its shores without thinking of Cora and Alice, and Hawkeye, and, more than all, of that youthful figure in whose melancholy eyes is foreshadowed the fate of the last of the Mohicans."[40] Through his inclusion of the figure of the Indian, Kensett stirs, in those who know the stories, these same grandiloquent musings.

Kensett further enhanced the associational possibilities of this scene by deliberately excluding the gigantic white hotels, teahouses, and steamships that then dotted the shores and plied the waters of this popular resort (fig. 49). He had made these tourist facilities a central feature in his landscape vignettes for Curtis's *Lotus-Eating* (fig. 50), but their inclusion in *Lake George* would have fixed the viewer's thoughts on the sybaritic delights of a contemporary vacation rather than on the literary and historical associations of the site.

The Scientific Experience of the Touristic Landscape

The third mode of appreciating American nature touted by guidebook authors was the scientific. While the picturesque demanded that the viewer step back from a scene in order to objectify it as a "picture," and associationism vaulted the viewer's mind out of his or her immediate environment into the contemplation of literature and history, the scientific mode almost always began with an intense engagement with the local scene. With a botanical guide in his pocket and a rock hammer in his pack, the scientifically engaged traveler minutely inspected his environment, categorizing its manifold components and picking up specimens to press in his albums or mount in his mineral cabinet.

Guidebook authors tended to enthusiastically promote this scientific engagement with the landscape. This is hardly surprising when one realizes that a sizable number of them were geologists. Benjamin Silliman, Josiah Dwight Whitney, Edward Hitchcock, Clarence King, Ferdinand Hayden, William H. Brewer, and John Muir were among the many nineteenth-century geologists to write popular guidebooks and travelogues.

Silliman's *Remarks Made on a Short Tour Between Hartford and Quebec in the Autumn of 1819* (1820) was one of the first guidebooks to what became known as the "northern tour." Although Silliman originally conceived of the volume as a personal account of his journey rather than a guidebook, by the time of the publication of the second edition in 1824 he had clearly recognized its utility for tourists, noting in the preface that he had inserted many remarks that he hopes will "add to the value of the work as a *pocket companion for travellers.*"[41]

As a geologist, Silliman laced his book with observations about the geological features along his route, and he explains why the traveler ought to take note of these: "The geological features of a country, being permanent—being intimately connected with its scenery, with its leading interests, and even with the very character of its population, have a fair claim to delineation in the observations of a traveller."[42] To further justify his inclusion of scientific information, he remarks that this practice "however unusual to us, is now common in Europe."[43] But though he could claim the stamp of European approval, he still worried that his readers would not find his geological observations compelling, and so assures them that he has set the geological notices off from the main text so that they "may, without inconvenience, be omitted by those to whom they are uninteresting."[44]

While Silliman felt somewhat apologetic and defensive about his inclusion of scientific observations, later authors felt no such qualms, even making these remarks the major interpretive thread of their texts. Such books played a very important role in the travel literature of the mid-nineteenth century, encouraging particular modes of vision—scientific habits of looking and thinking—that shaped the way travelers responded to the world around them.

This became a very popular way of appreciating nature in the mid-nineteenth century, so much so that the enthusiastic amateur naturalist became a stock character in the period's travel literature. In *The White Hills*, Starr King recounts a trip to Tuckerman Ravine with a number of companions, among them a "prominent Boston gentleman [who] graced our company with his enthusiasm for science—one of the modern regiment of Solomons, knowing every shrub and weed, from the cedar to the hyssop."[45]

Even the guidebook authors who were not scientists usually found some way to encourage or at least accommodate this passion for natural history. Starr King included in *The White Hills* a guide to White Mountain flora compiled for him by the botanist Edward Tuckerman. Moses Sweetser, the author of another White Mountain guidebook, enlisted the geologist J. H. Huntington to write a section on the area's geology, including a list of rock types and their locations. For those readers desiring even more geological information, Sweetser helpfully recommended "Hitchcock's noble volumes on the *Geology of New Hampshire,*" which they could purchase "at the office of the town clerk" in North Conway.[46] John Dix in *A Handbook of Newport and Rhode Island* (1852) directed ladies to the places where the "choicest specimens of seaweed may be gathered" and pointed out where to find "the most beautiful of mosses, such as keen admirers of the cryptogamic species would scarcely pass by without specimenizing."[47]

However, as guidebook authors were quick to point out, the scientific mode of appreciating a place need not end with "specimenizing." Geological facts in particular have the potential to act in an associationist way to carry the mind of the viewer beyond the immediate environment, allowing him or her to re-create scenes from the ancient past. The geologist Edward Hitchcock in his *Sketch of the Scenery of Massachusetts* describes the "rich and delightful associations" that the contemplation of geological features could yield to those able to read them. The mind of the geologically informed observer, he writes, is "carried back through immense periods of past time, during which natural causes were operating to produce the scenery before him: and he witnesses in imagination that spot, assuming peculiar and widely diverse aspects; and sees how wisely each change was adapted to bring it to its present state."[48]

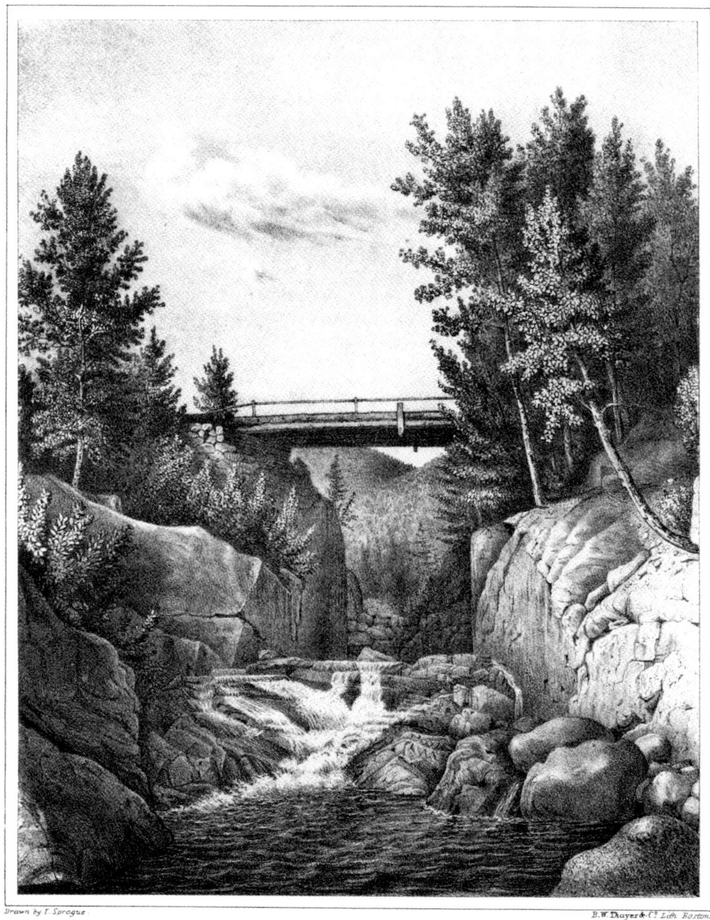

Fig. 51. Isaac Sprague (American, 1811–1895), *Nancy's Bridge, near the White Mountains.* Lithograph. Illustration from William Oakes, *Scenery of the White Mountains* (Boston: Crosby and Nichols, 1848), plate 13

Guidebook authors were ready to assist those tourists who could not decipher a site's geological history on their own. William Oakes, author of the lushly illustrated *Scenery of the White Mountains*, was particularly adept at this. In his short essay accompanying a lithograph of Nancy's Bridge (fig. 51), he recounts, as did virtually every guidebook author who wrote about the site, the tragic story of Nancy, the jilted servant who froze to death near the spot as she was pursuing her departed lover. But to this he added the story of the geological history of the place:

> The plate before us is a most accurate representation of a beautiful specimen of the trap dike of geologists. The granite crust of the earth has been lifted and cracked, and into that fissure thus formed, the hot liquid matter has been injected from below, cooling afterwards into trap rock. In the course of time the trap rock falls to pieces, and is carried way by the force of water, leaving the perpendicular walls of granite on each side standing, with an empty space between. In the present case the trap rock is conspicuous in the bed of the little rapid and broken stream, called Nancy's river, which comes down from its sources two or three miles distant in the opposite mountains.[49]

For those who passed their vacations in passionate contemplation of nature's forms, a painting that replicated to some extent that mode of vision, recalling the plants and rocks they had examined and collected, would have for those viewers increased associative powers. A precise description of a rock or a tree or a bit of representative topography could unleash a flood of memories, carrying the viewer's mind back to a particular spot. When the art critic Henry Tuckerman first encountered Jasper F. Cropsey's *Greenwood Lake, New Jersey* (1845), he said, "I knew it belonged to New Jersey from the character of the rocks, familiar to all who have wandered along the Passaic."[50]

KENSETT AND THE SCIENTIFIC GAZE

The intense particularity of Kensett's paintings with their precise descriptions of topographical forms and their close attention to plant species and geological formations seems to acknowledge and cater to this way of apprehending the world. His friend and fellow artist Daniel Huntington wrote that Kensett "studied the characteristic points in every place he visited. . . . If you are a lover of the sea you will find the rocks and beaches of Nahant, Newport, and Beverly."[51] As Huntington implies, Kensett consistently recorded on his canvases the diversity of nature's forms: the rugged granites of the White Mountains (fig. 52), the tall limestone bluffs of the Mississippi (fig. 53), and the eroded shales and sandstones of the Catskills (fig. 54). Not only was Kensett true to broad topographical features but he was equally attuned to smaller lithologic details. His delight in the specificity of rock types is evident in many of his works, especially in those such as *Niagara Falls* (c. 1851–52, fig. 55) in which he disregards the more conventional panoramic views to zero in on a bit of rock or wood. Here he describes not the sublime vista of the falls from the rim, but the slabs of rock found at their base.

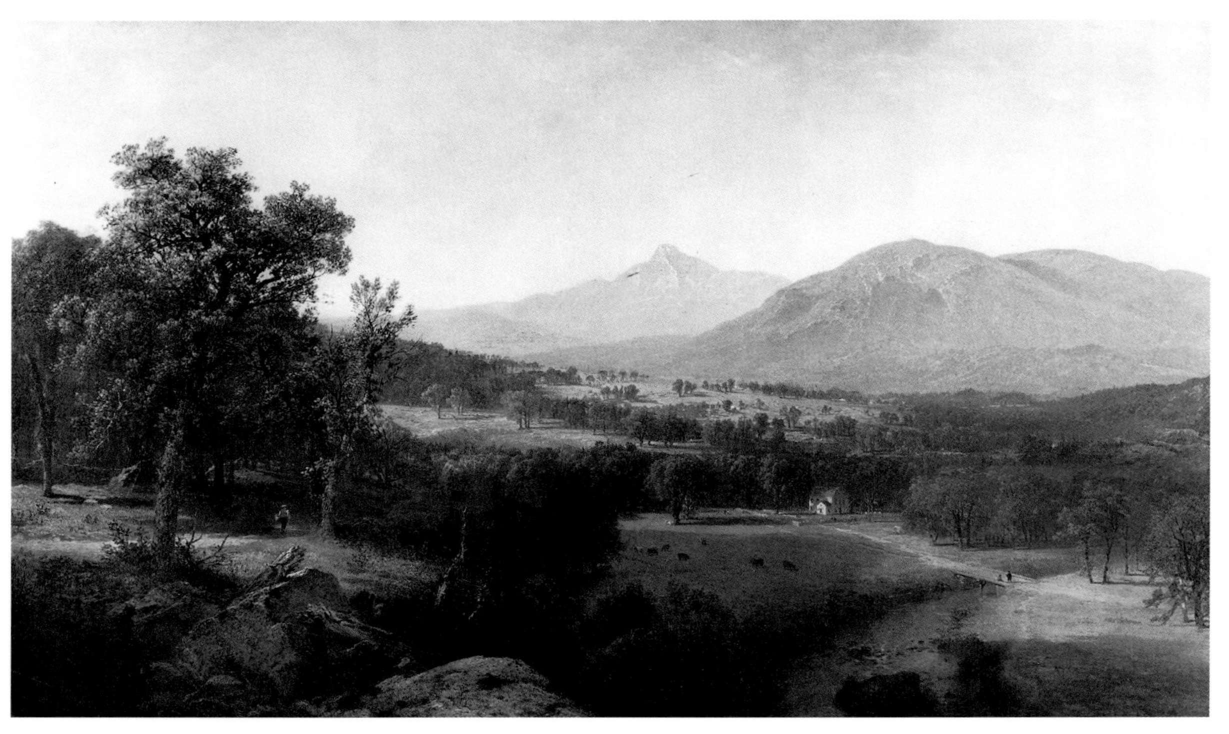

Fig. 52. John Kensett, *Mount Chocorua*, 1864–66. Oil on canvas, 48 x 84 in. (122 x 213.4 cm). The Century Association, New York

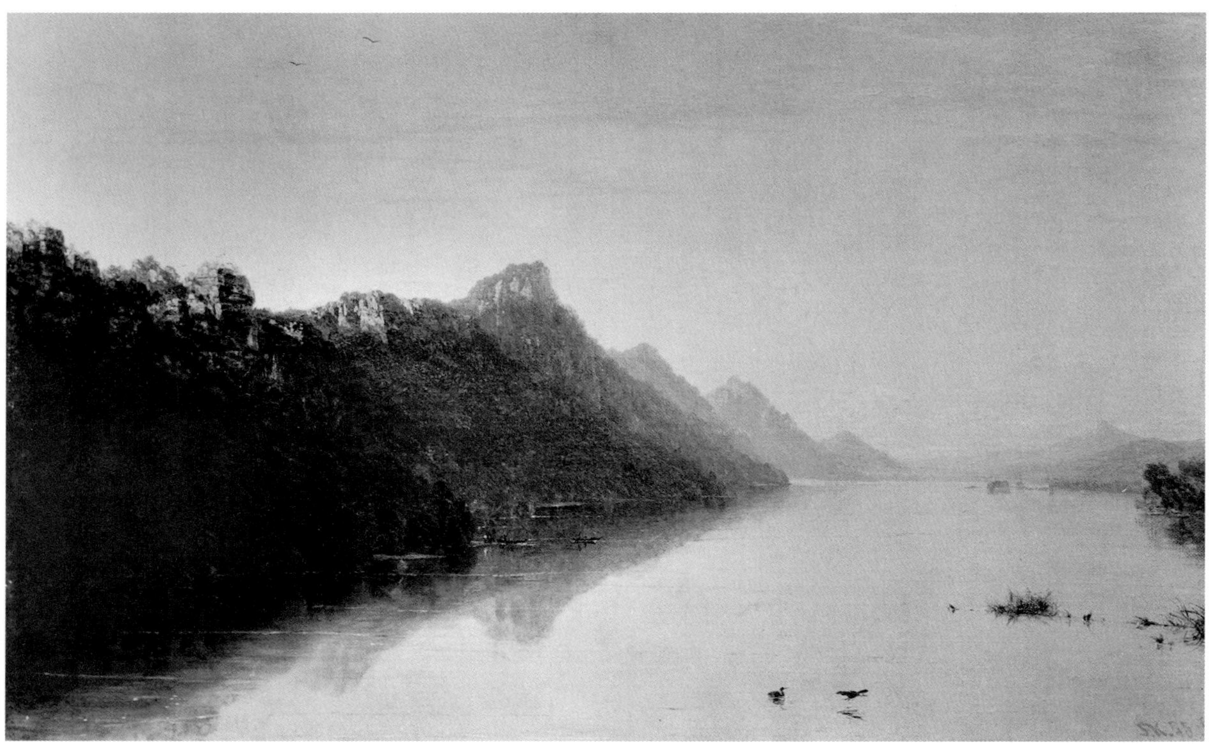

Fig. 53. John Kensett, *Upper Mississippi*, 1855. Oil on canvas, 18 3/8 x 30 1/4 in. (46.7 x 76.9 cm). The Saint Louis Art Museum. Eliza McMillan Fund

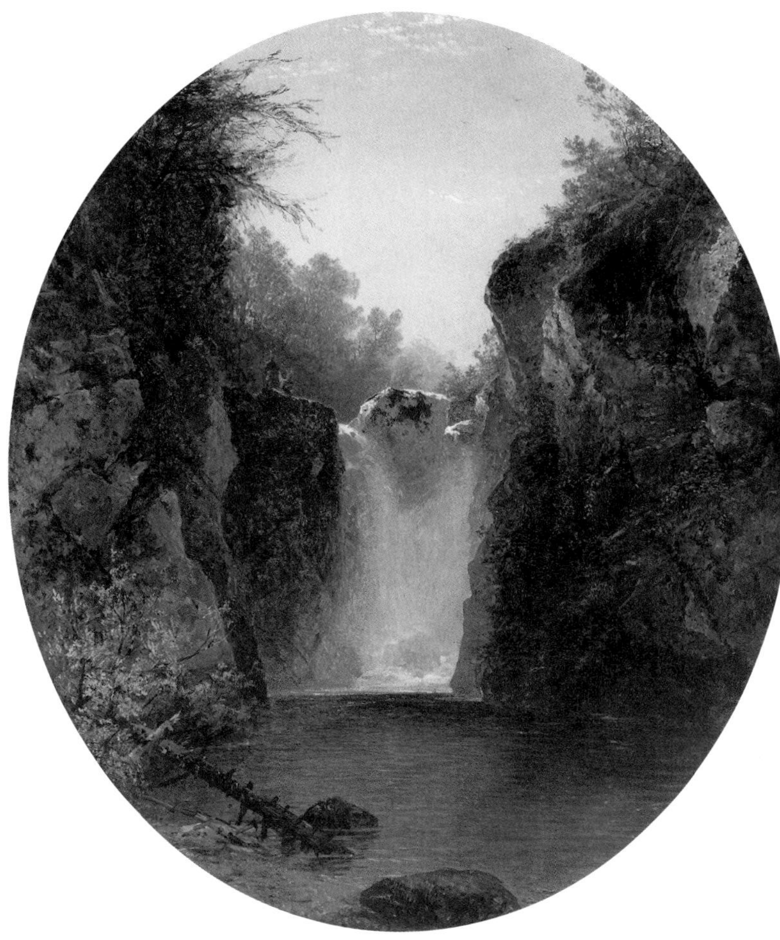

Fig. 54. John Kensett, *The Fawn's Leap*, 1859. Oil on canvas, 30 1/4 x 25 1/4 in. (76.8 x 64.1 cm). Mead Art Museum, Amherst College, Amherst, Massachusetts. Gift of Herbert W. Plimpton: The Hollis W. Plimpton, Class of 1915, Memorial Collection

The particularity of Kensett's view has a parallel in a description from a contemporary travelogue. R. E. Garczynski in his essay "Niagara" for *Picturesque America* carries his readers over the edge of the falls, dragging them down into the whirlpool below where, "we find ourselves . . . among huge masses of fragments, principally of gypsum, of a very hard character. . . . These blocks are of all sizes, from slabs weighing many tons to pieces no larger than one's hand. Mingled with them are granite boulders, whose pink hue makes them conspicuous among the gray gypsum. All of them are partially covered with a thick velvety moss."[52]

Kensett, too, takes us into the ravine to examine these stone slabs, but while Garczynski has focused on granite and gypsum, Kensett describes the sedimentary rocks (limestone, sandstone, and shale in particular—fragments of the local bedrock) that are more commonly found along the river's banks.[53]

The unusual composition of Kensett's *Niagara* painting, with the crisply delineated stone slabs filling the foreground and the hazy view of Niagara in the left background, demands an oddly bifurcated gaze. It is virtually impossible to take in simultaneously both the rocks and the falls; we focus on one or the other. This split vision may perhaps be associated with different modes of appreciating the scenery. The rocks themselves seem to demand scientific scrutiny—a visual analysis of their color, texture, bedding patterns, and fracture planes that allow their identification. In fact, the placement of a sharply focused specimen against a more sketchily defined background that indicates the environmental origins of the specimen was a well-established convention in scientific illustration when Kensett painted this view (fig. 56).

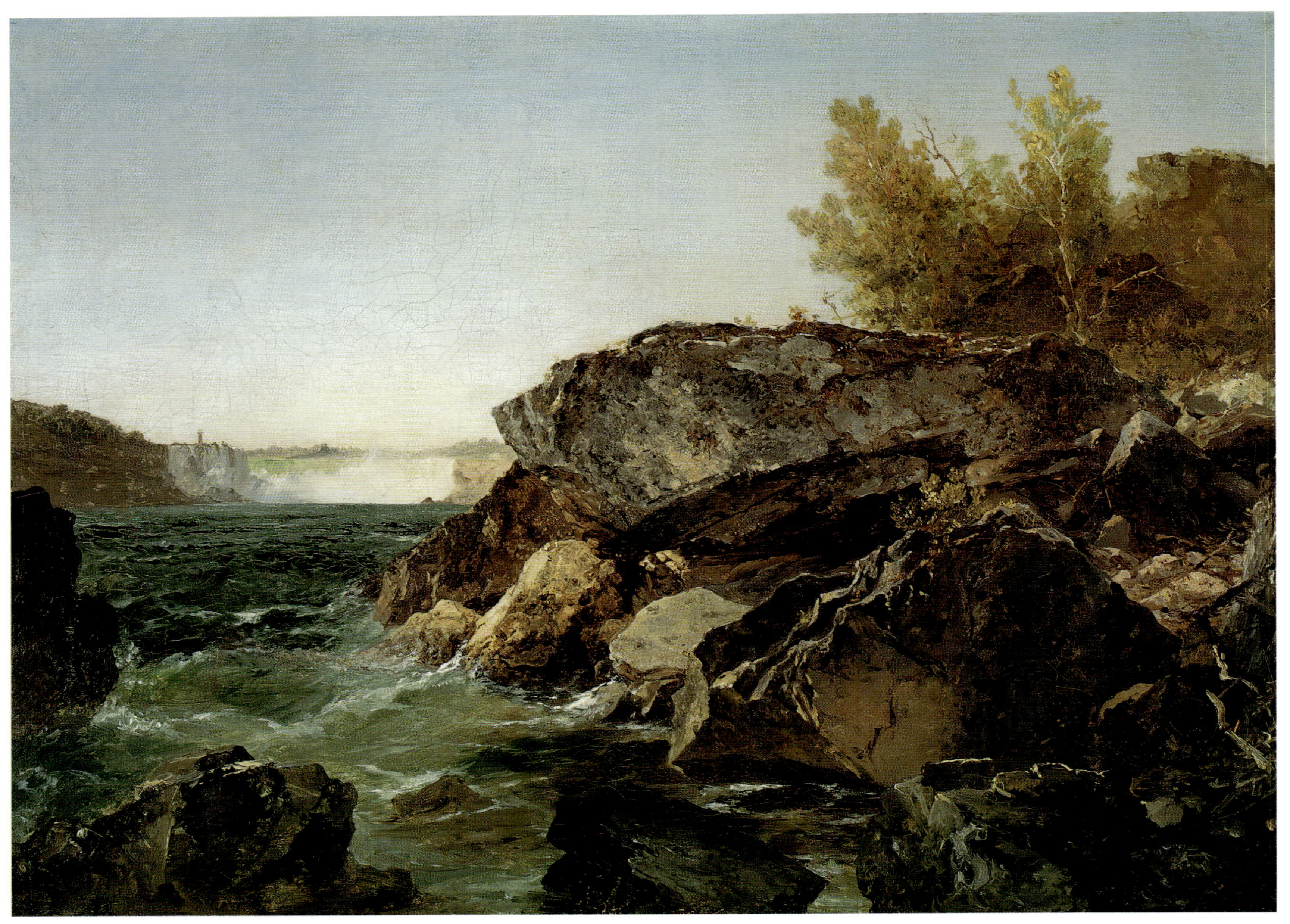

Fig. 55. John Kensett, *Niagara Falls*, c. 1851–52.
Oil on canvas, 17 x 24½ in. (43.1 x 62.2 cm).
Mead Art Museum, Amherst College, Amherst, Massachusetts

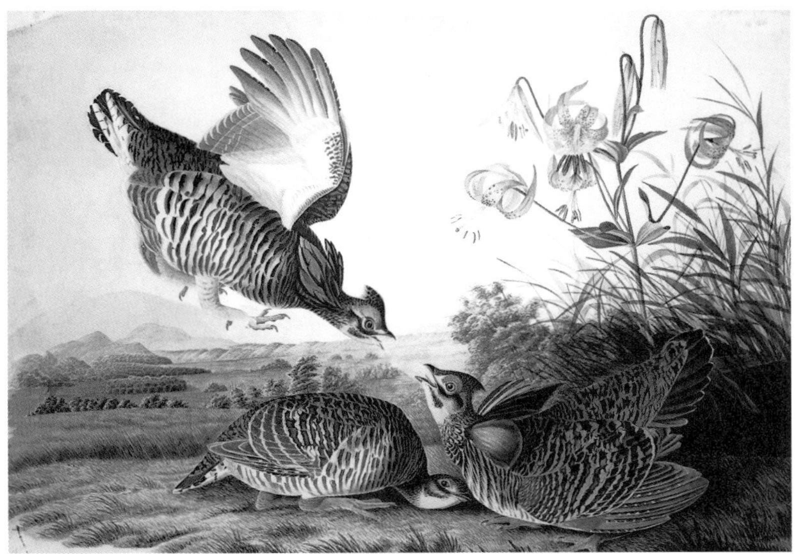

Fig. 56. John James Audubon (American, 1785–1851), *Greater Prairie-Chicken*. Watercolor, 25 x 35 7/8 in. (63.5 x 91 cm). The New-York Historical Society, New York

But as our gaze shifts to the background, the scientific mode of vision gives way to the picturesque. The rocks lose their individual identities to become shadowed frames for the panoramic vista of the falls. Just as tourists in search of the picturesque were encouraged to do when visiting the actual site, we find ourselves creating multiple pictures for ourselves when perusing Kensett's singular canvas.

One might also interpret the distant view of the falls in yet another way — as alluding to the site's geological history. Nineteenth-century tourists traveled to Niagara for an experience of the sublime, for the frisson of fear that comes from confronting something far more powerful than oneself. Part of their perception of Niagara's power lay in their awareness of its extraordinary erosive force. Almost every nineteenth-century guidebook to the site called attention to the way the falls are "eating away, year by year, at the rocky ledge over which the waters hurl their strength."[54] Visitors were sometimes actual witnesses to this process as new bits of the cataract's rim were constantly tumbling into the gorge. One of the most exciting events at Niagara in the nineteenth century was the collapse of the famous Table Rock (long a favorite point from which to view the falls) into the swirling rapids. In Kensett's painting, the tumbled boulders in the foreground are the detritus left by the falls' erosion of its gorge. As we follow the path of the green waters back toward the cascade, we are moving through time, visually reenacting the falls' recession.

Kensett's contemporaries enthusiastically praised his geological renderings. Henry Tuckerman and Clarence Cook, then two of the most prominent American critics, admired his "rock-portraits" and commented on their truthfulness and freedom from conventional handling.[55] The critic for *Literary World* was also a fan: "As a painter of rocks we know of no one superior to Kensett."[56] While applauding Kensett's attention to the specificities of individual rocks, his contemporaries also admired his ability to evoke geological processes and geological history. To Kensett's friend Dr. Osgood, the artist's rocks spoke eloquently of the passage of time and the effects of erosion: "That rock whispers to you the secret of earth, and sea, and sky. Its surface speaks out of the mysterious life of nature which glows in that rich color like blood in the cheek, and those stains, and seams, and moss are the impressions which ages have left upon that stony face under the changes of the air, water, and light."[57]

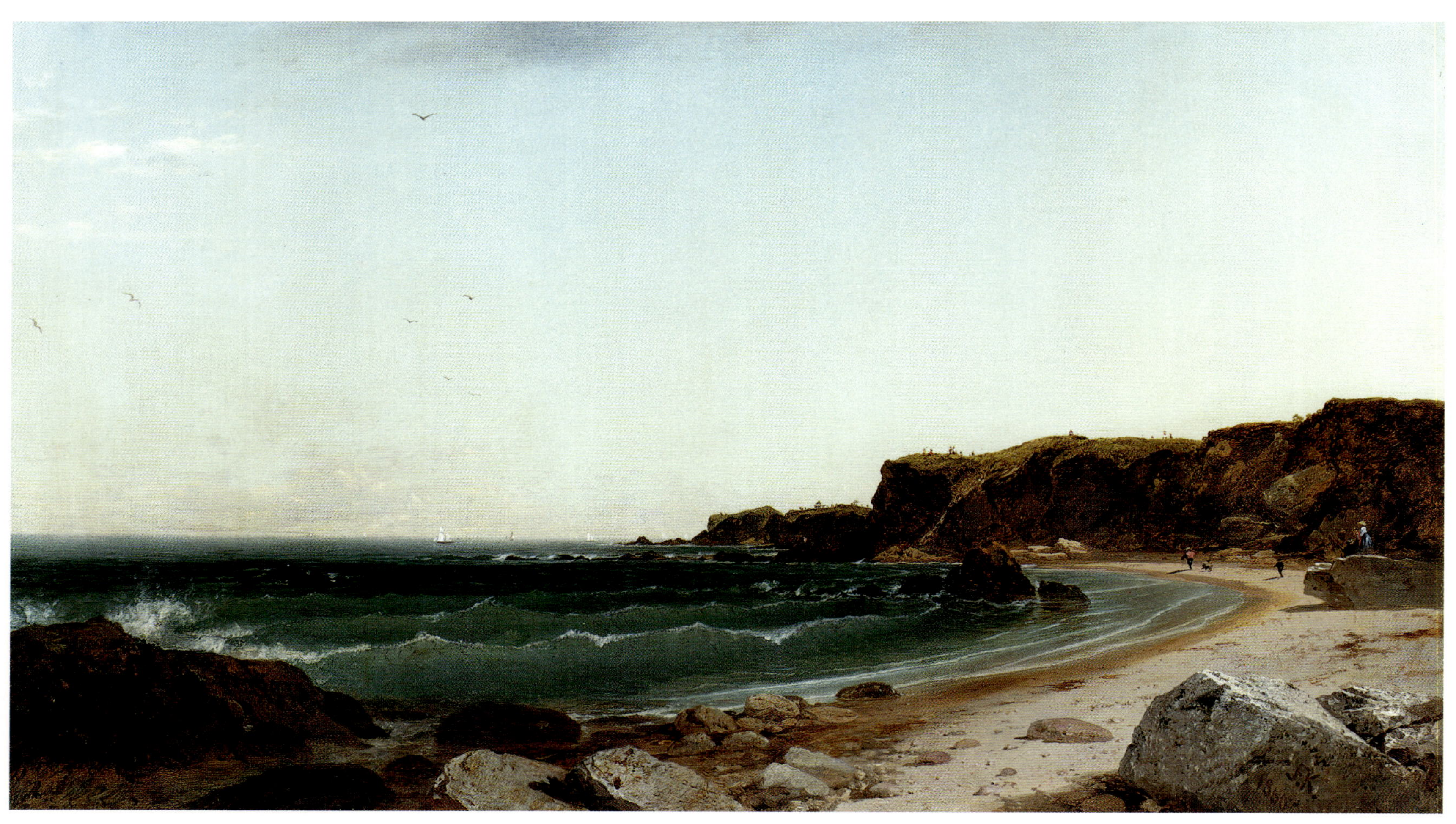

Fig. 57. John Kensett, *Forty Steps, Newport, Rhode Island*, 1860.
Oil on canvas, 20 1/8 x 36 in. (51.1 x 91.4 cm).
Jo Ann and Julian Ganz Jr.

In *Forty Steps, Newport, Rhode Island* (1860, fig. 57), Kensett displays his ability to evoke geological forces at work and to suggest the past and future states of a landscape. The painting describes a crescent-shaped beach bordered by lines of brown bluffs. The waves that roll rhythmically onto the beach are deceptively gentle, for they are slowly devouring the embracing cliffs. The surf has already eaten well into the prominent background bluff, leaving behind a low string of deep brown rocks. Just in front of these lies a second chain of rocks — the remains of another cliff, which is being buffeted into oblivion.

Standing and sitting along the tops of the bluffs and walking along the shore are well-dressed ladies and gentlemen, tiny figures that remind us that Newport was then one of the most fashionable watering holes in the United States. Placing us on the beach with these privileged observers, Kensett directs our attention — as theirs may have been directed — to the geology of the scene.

The piles of rocks strewn across the foreground are precisely described, varying from angular granitic blocks to softly rounded, reddish stones (perhaps sandstone). Their forms are angled into the scene, but they do more than frame the view and direct us into its depths. Because they are so prominently placed, highlighted with flecks of white pigment, and described with such precision, they demand our scrutiny. They invite us to linger over their forms, puzzling out their identities and histories. Their fragmentary nature also turns our thoughts to the destructive powers of nature.

Beyond these stones, the V-shape of the water cuts into the land like the tip of a knife, emphasizing its erosive power. Meanwhile, thin white borders of foaming surf outline the dark lumps of crumbled cliff. Ironically, the foam, which we think of as evanescent, is painted with crisp, sharp lines, while the rocks and bluffs are composed of soft scumbled strokes. This contrast heightens our sense of the rocks' mutability as they are endlessly pummeled by the ocean waves.

Kensett's juxtaposition of these pictorial geological musings with the numerous figures of tourists seems to imply that Newport's visitors could or did look at the scene in this way. Nineteenth-century guidebooks certainly promoted this geological view of Rhode Island's coastal scenery. A number of them echo Kensett's comments on its evanescent nature. John Dix, for instance, in his *A Hand-book of Newport and Rhode Island* (1852) describes the "jagged-edged shores" of Narragansett Bay "which, in the course of centuries, have been worn into high bluffs, rounded ledges, and smooth beaches, by the silent but surely progressive actions of wind and wave."[58] At the same time, though, Dix singles out the site as being "picturesque" — encouraging viewers to read it as a painting. Thus Dix's text, like Kensett's picture, points to that peculiar intersection of art, tourism, and geology that characterized the culture of landscape appreciation in mid-nineteenth-century America.

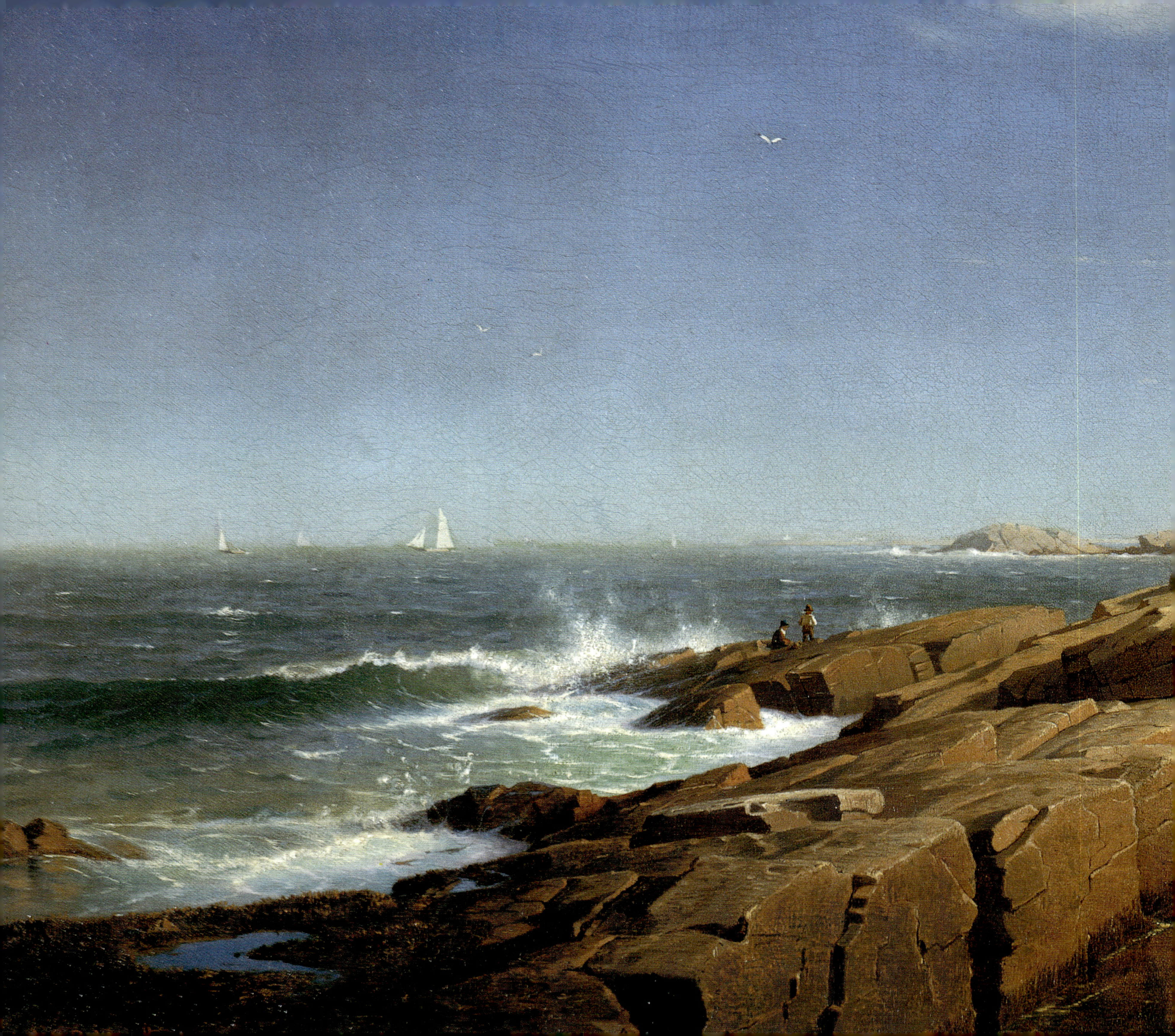

Chapter Five

William Stanley Haseltine and the Rocks at Nahant

In the mid-1860s, William Stanley Haseltine (1835–1900) painted more than sixteen pictures of the coastal rocks in Nahant, Massachusetts.[1] The Brooklyn Museum's *Rocks at Nahant* and the Terra Museum's *Rocks at Nahant*, both dated 1864, are typical of the series (figs. 58–59). Smooth expanses of reddish rock fill the foreground and middle ground of the canvases. The stones are lit by sunny summer skies, their scratched and polished surfaces tilted upward for our contemplation. A long, sloping diagonal separates the rocks from the deep blue ocean whose foaming waves break gently against the coast in the middle distance. A pair of tiny figures fish and converse on the middle-ground rocks, while a boat sails serenely across the long horizon.

These are unusual paintings. Most pictures of coastal scenes focus on pounding surf or on the dramatic light effects of the shore. In Haseltine's canvases, however, the slabs of ruddy rock, much more so than the sea or the sky, command the observer's attention.

These paintings, odd as they are, found ready buyers among the artist's contemporaries. According to Haseltine's daughter, at one point the artist received so many orders for these rocky scenes that "he lacked time to paint anything else."[2] What accounts for the popularity of these pictures? Why did Haseltine focus on Nahant? Why did he lay such stress on the rock formations? To answer these questions we need to look to both social history and the history of science. Geology, particularly the teachings of the great naturalist Louis Agassiz, provides one key to the meaning and the popularity of the images. Fashion, wealth, and social distinction provide another.

The Social Cachet of Nahant

The mid-nineteenth century has been vaunted as the "era of the common man," a time of democratization when social mobility increased and social distinctions blurred. Yet as recent scholarship has repeatedly demonstrated, class lines were at least as clearly drawn in this period as they had been before.[3] In few places was this social stratification more apparent than in the era's summer resorts. Upper-crust vacationers traveled to Saratoga, Newport, and the Berkshires not to broaden their

Opposite: Detail of Fig. 58

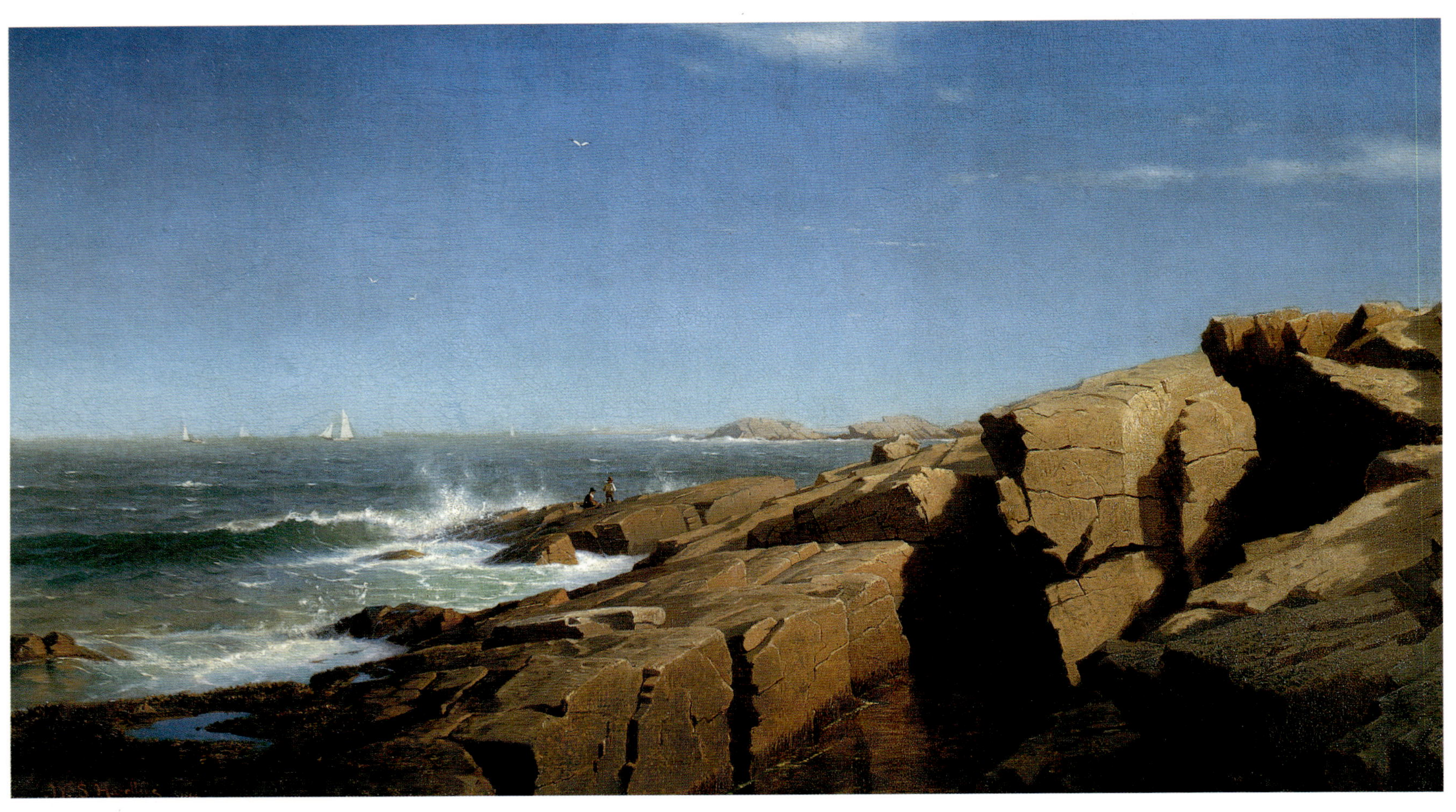

Fig. 58. William Stanley Haseltine, *The Rocks at Nahant*, 1864.
Oil on canvas, 22 1/8 x 40 1/8 in. (56.2 x 101.9 cm).
Brooklyn Museum of Art. Dick S. Ramsay Fund, A. Augustus Healy Fund, and the Healy Purchase Fund B

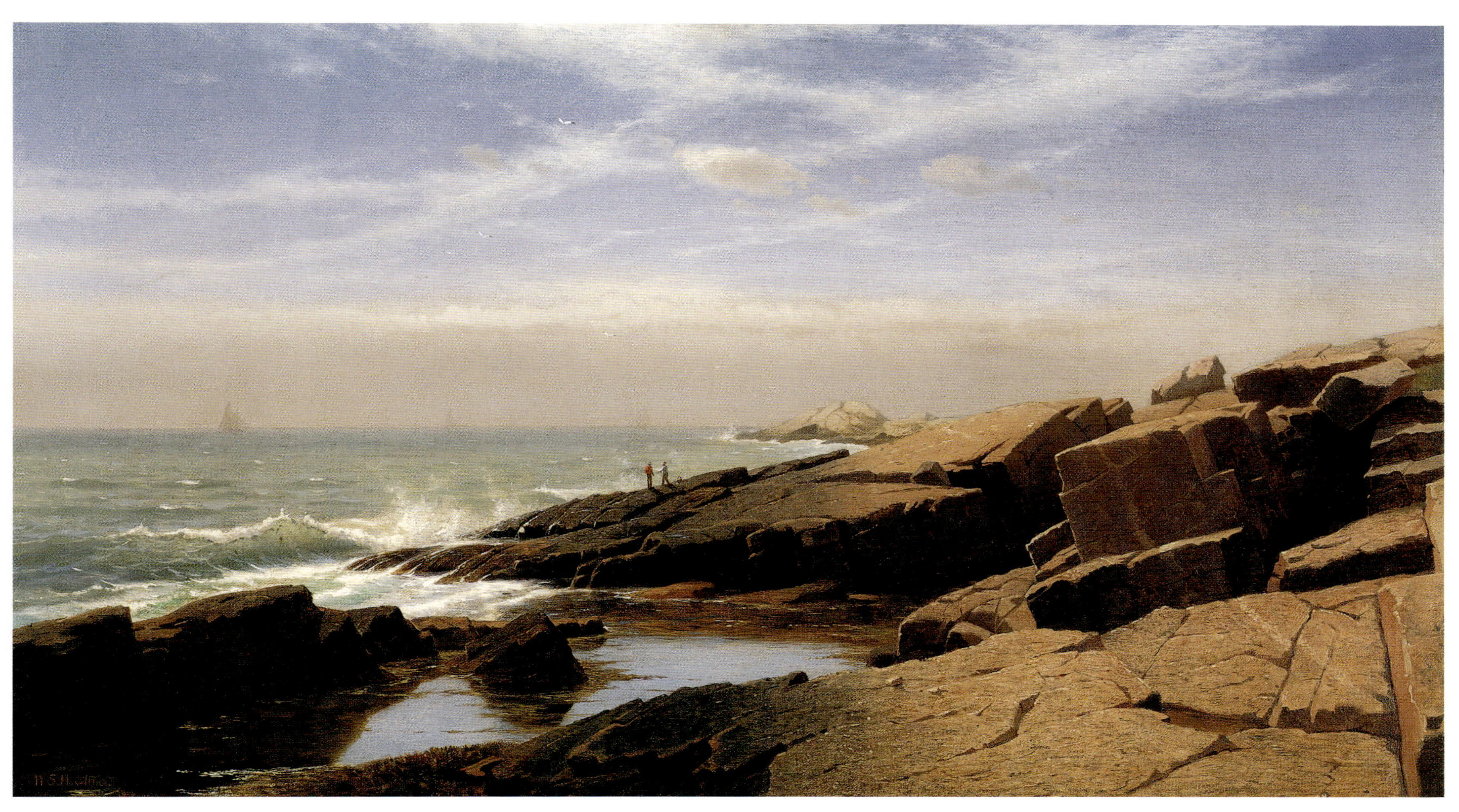

Fig. 59. William Stanley Haseltine, *The Rocks at Nahant*, 1864.
Oil on canvas, 22 3/8 x 40 1/2 in. (56.8 x 102.9 cm).
Terra Museum of American Art, Chicago. Daniel J. Terra Collection, 1999.65

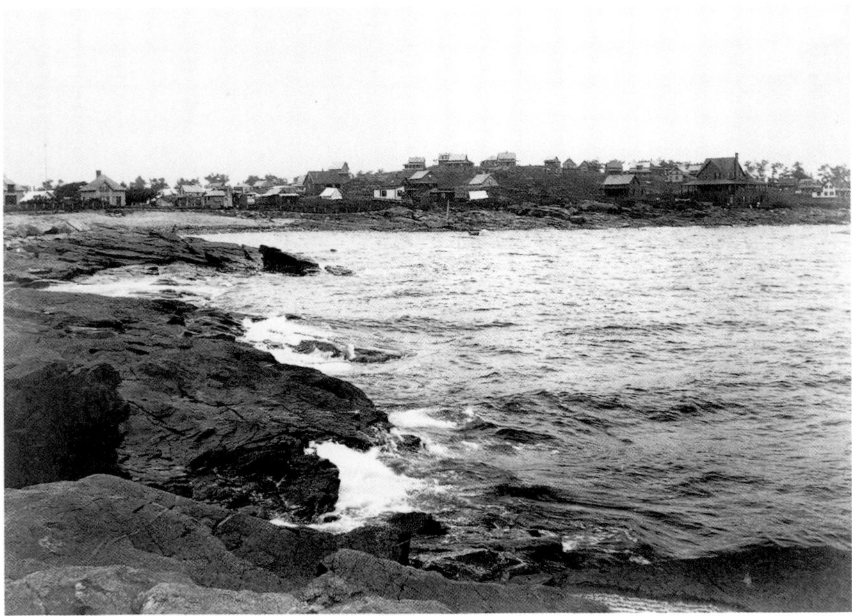

Fig. 60. Cottages at Coral Beach, Nahant, Massachusetts, n.d. Photograph by C. H. Newall. Courtesy of the Society for the Preservation of New England Antiquities, Boston

life experiences nor to meet people of different classes and cultures, but to solidify relationships with members of their own social set. This was certainly the case at Nahant.

Nahant is a narrow peninsula that juts into Massachusetts Bay about fifteen miles north of Boston. In the nineteenth century the cream of New England society (along with sundry New Yorkers and assorted Southerners) summered along its shores.[4] The Perkinses, Cabots, and Eliots began to build "cottages" there in the 1820s (fig. 60). The substantial stone hotel, erected by Thomas Handasyd Perkins in 1821, catered to the likes of Daniel Webster, Charles Sumner, William Appleton, David Sears, George Bancroft, and George Ticknor (fig. 61). This first generation of "Nahanters" was composed primarily of professional men: industrious entrepreneurs and accomplished statesmen.

By mid-century, when Haseltine visited the peninsula, Nahant society was dominated by a new generation—by men of letters, the Brahmin intellectual set. Buoyed by inherited wealth, this next generation based their claims to social distinction not only on money and family lineage but, even more so, on cultural accomplishments.[5] Included in this group were many of those men and women who made Boston at mid-century the intellectual capital of the United States: the writers Henry Wadsworth Longfellow, Oliver Wendell Holmes, George William Curtis, James Russell Lowell and John Greenleaf Whittier, the essayist and renowned wit Thomas Gold Appleton, the historian John Lothrop Motley, the social reformer Julia Ward Howe, and the scientist Louis Agassiz. All sought respite from the summer heat on Nahant's rockbound coast.

Little is known of Haseltine's sojourns on Nahant, yet it seems clear that he cast his lot with this Brahmin set. During the summer of 1864 *Watson's Weekly Art Journal* reported, "Haseltine divides his time between fashion and the sea at Nahant."[6] Although the artist was not a Boston blue blood, he had much to recommend him to this elite crowd: his genealogy, his educational credentials, his artistic accomplishments, and his years in Europe.

Oliver Wendell Holmes once wrote, "other things being equal, in most relations of life I prefer a man of family."[7] Haseltine was such a man. Although he was born and raised in Philadelphia, his father came from old Massachusetts stock. His

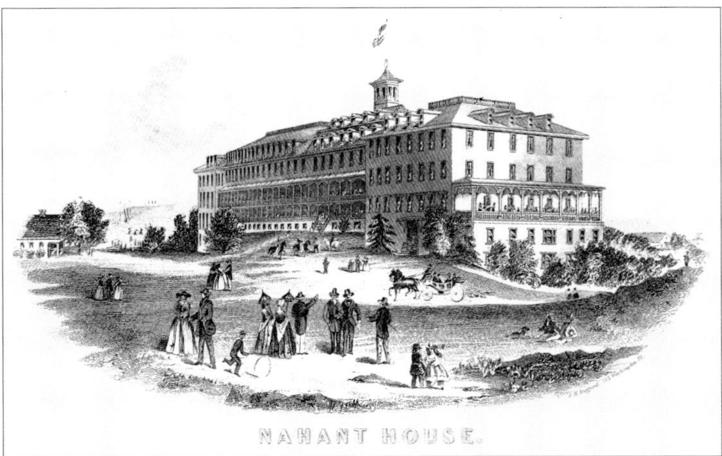

Fig. 61. *Nahant House*, c. 1855. Engraving after a lithograph by John H. Bufford (American, 1835–1871). Courtesy of the Society for the Preservation of New England Antiquities, Boston

ancestors had landed in Boston in 1637 and had founded the towns of Rawley, Bradford, and Haverhill.[8] Not only were the Haseltines well established, they were also well-to-do. In the mid-nineteenth century William's father, John, was one of the wealthiest men in Philadelphia, with assets assessed in 1846 at over $100,000.[9]

In addition to this respectable pedigree, Haseltine also possessed a Harvard degree. Male Nahanters were, by and large, Harvard men. Most studied there; many, including Longfellow, Lowell, Holmes, and Agassiz, taught there. A Harvard diploma, as Frederic Jaher has remarked, "could be a passport for those not entitled by lineage to membership in [Boston's] urban aristocracy."[10] Haseltine earned his passport with his graduation from Harvard in 1854. During his college years he came in contact with many of those who summered in Nahant. He studied modern languages with Longfellow and perhaps natural history with Agassiz; his classmates included Nahanters Charles Francis Adams, Alexander Agassiz (Louis's son), John Chandler Bancroft (George's son), Charles Jackson Paine, and Robert C. Winthrop, as well as various Eliots, Lawrences, Lowells, and Perkinses who may have belonged to those families who summered on Nahant. Any one of these men could have introduced Haseltine to the resort. Adams, Bancroft, and Winthrop are especially likely candidates since, according to Haseltine's daughter, they remained his lifelong friends.[11]

Haseltine's lineage and Harvard degree were not his only social assets. The Brahmin elite worshiped both European culture and artistic accomplishment, and Haseltine could claim marks in both categories. By the early 1860s he was an established artist, exhibiting regularly at such locations as the Pennsylvania Academy of the Fine Arts, the Boston Athenaeum, the National Academy of Design, the Salmagundi Club and the Century Association. In 1859 he had been elected a member of the prestigious Century Association, which Mark Twain called "the most unspeakably respectable club in the United States, perhaps."[12] There he shared membership with a number of Nahanters, including Oliver Wendell Holmes and George Bancroft. He could also boast of a European training, including two years in Dusseldorf and a year in Italy. In the later 1860s he began to spend more and more time abroad, eventually settling in Rome. There he maintained his ties to the Brahmin set, for instance, attending a dinner for Henry Wadsworth Longfellow in 1869.[13]

Haseltine's paintings of Nahant asserted his membership

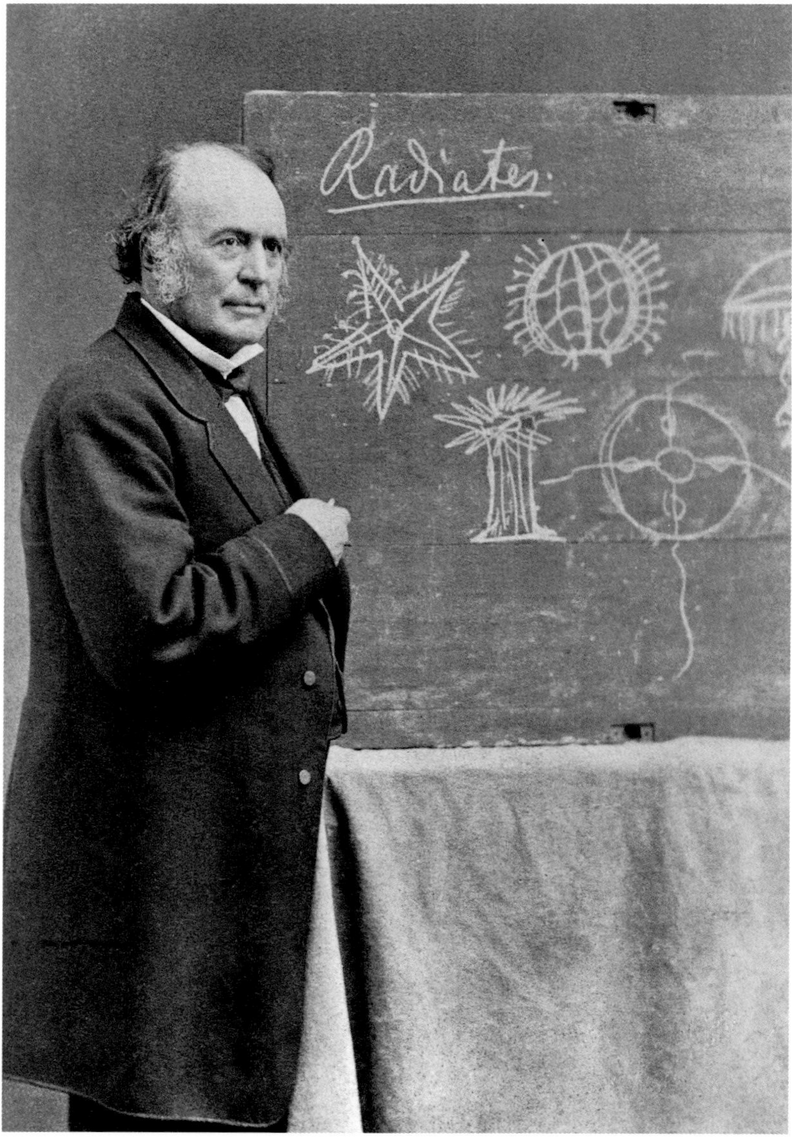

Fig. 62. *Louis Agassiz Lecturing*, c. 1861. Photograph by Carleton Watkins. Museum of Comparative Zoology, Harvard University, Cambridge, Massachusetts

in this elite group and announced his access to one of the most exclusive and prestigious of summer resorts. For those who purchased the works, including, it seems, Nahanter Thomas Gold Appleton, they may have filled a similar function by alluding to the owner's social status.[14] On a more personal level, and probably more important, they could serve, as Kensett's paintings did, as mementos of summer vacations, as reminders of sunny days on the rocks. The paintings, indeed, contain numerous references to summertime pleasures: bright blue skies above surging surf, tiny sailboats, and small figures disporting on the rocks.

AGASSIZ AND THE GEOLOGICAL ATTRACTIONS OF NAHANT

Nahant's status as a fashionable watering place may well account for Haseltine's choice of the peninsula as a subject for his brush. It does not, however, explain his almost obsessive focus on the rock formations. In most of the Nahant paintings, slabs of smooth-topped igneous stone dominate the canvases. Their weathered faces are turned toward us, inviting our scrutiny. To understand Haseltine's interest in and treatment of these stones we need to look to the teachings of one of Nahant's most famous residents: Louis Agassiz.

In the 1850s and 1860s the Swiss-born Agassiz was considered America's outstanding naturalist (fig. 62).[15] He had arrived in this country in 1846 with a grant from the King of Prussia to study the natural history of North America. During his first year in the United States he delivered a series of public lectures in major cities along the eastern seaboard. These met with resounding success. In New York, Horace Greeley of the *Tribune* told his readers, "Never have our citizens enjoyed the opportunity of acquiring so large a measure of knowledge of the laws of nature . . . as these lectures will afford them."[16] In Boston the lectures were so popular that on some evenings as many as five thousand people turned out to hear them, and Agassiz often had to deliver two lectures a night in order to accommodate the crowds.[17] Among the most attentive members of Agassiz's audience was the Boston patriarch John Amory Lowell. He was so impressed by Agassiz that he decided to entice him to remain in America by endowing a special professorship for him at Harvard. In 1848 Agassiz accepted the position and made Boston his home for the rest of his life.

In 1846 Agassiz was thirty-nine years old. Handsome, charming, sophisticated, a master of six languages, and an intimate of some of the greatest scientific men in Europe (including Alexander von Humboldt and Charles Lyell), he was well equipped to win the admiration of Boston society. Indeed, he immediately became a favorite with the Boston-Cambridge intellectual set. The Cabots and Lowells vied to have him as a dinner guest. Longfellow and Emerson were enthralled by his conversation and declared him one of the most brilliant men of their day. Not only did they find his grasp of scientific matters astonishing, but his religious and philosophical beliefs were well attuned to their Unitarian-Transcendentalist creed. Although he attended church infrequently, Agassiz was a deeply religious man who drew much of his spiritual sustenance from nature. To him, science was not a dry accumulation of facts but a means to understanding the thoughts of the Creator. The role of the scientist, he felt, was to decipher nature's innermost workings and uncover proofs of God in nature. Everywhere he looked in the natural world, he saw signs of divine benevolence and indications that "a God infinitely wise [is] regulating Nature according to immutable laws which He has Himself imposed on her."[18] He staunchly maintained these views even after the publication of Darwin's *Origin of the Species* in 1859. In fact he became one of most outspoken anti-Darwinians in the United States. He felt that the geologic record did not support Darwin's theory of evolution. Even more important, he could not accept the chasm which it was creating between religion and science, between God and nature. This stance hurt his reputation in the scientific community, but it seems to have enhanced his popularity with the general public of his day.

In 1850 Agassiz cemented his ties to the Boston Brahmin set by marrying Elizabeth Cary, daughter of blue blood Thomas Graves Cary and granddaughter of the successful merchant and Nahant developer Thomas Handasyd Perkins. It was during a summer sojourn on Nahant that Agassiz first pressed his courtship of Lizzie Cary; after their marriage they usually made the spot their summer home (fig. 63). The peninsula became for Agassiz an outdoor research laboratory. He launched extensive investigations into its geology, fish, and flora. He found the geology particularly enthralling, for here the sculpting hands of fire and ice were visible at every turn. The bedrock was shot through with igneous dikes, evidences of intense volcanic activity in the remote past. The surface topography, on the other hand, revealed everywhere the marks of ancient ice sheets.

These signs of glaciation were of particular interest to

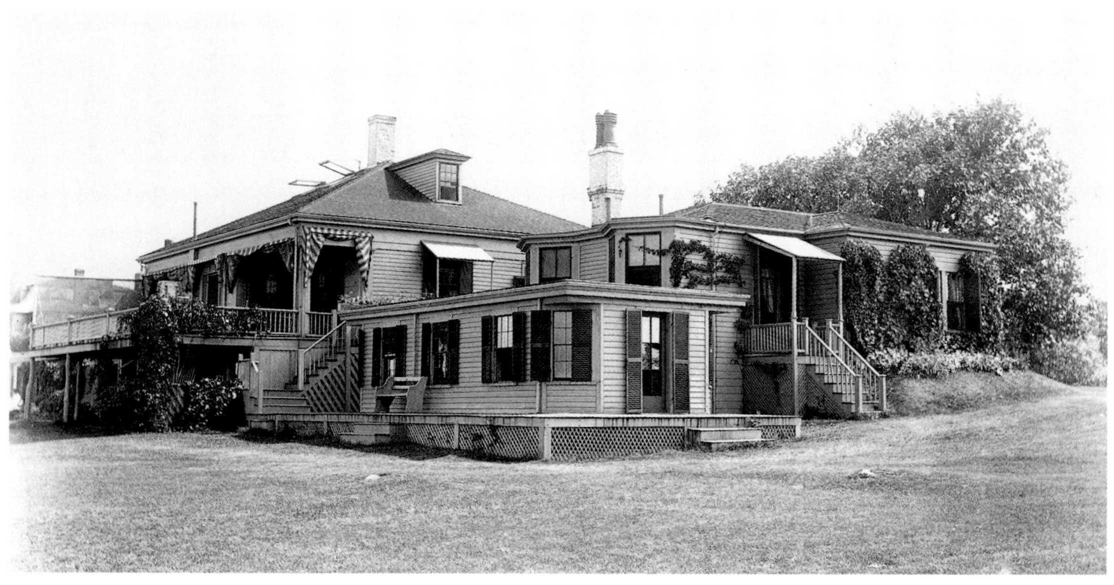

Fig. 63. Agassiz's house at Nahant, 1907. Photograph by Baldwin Coolidge. Courtesy of the Society for the Preservation of New England Antiquities, Boston

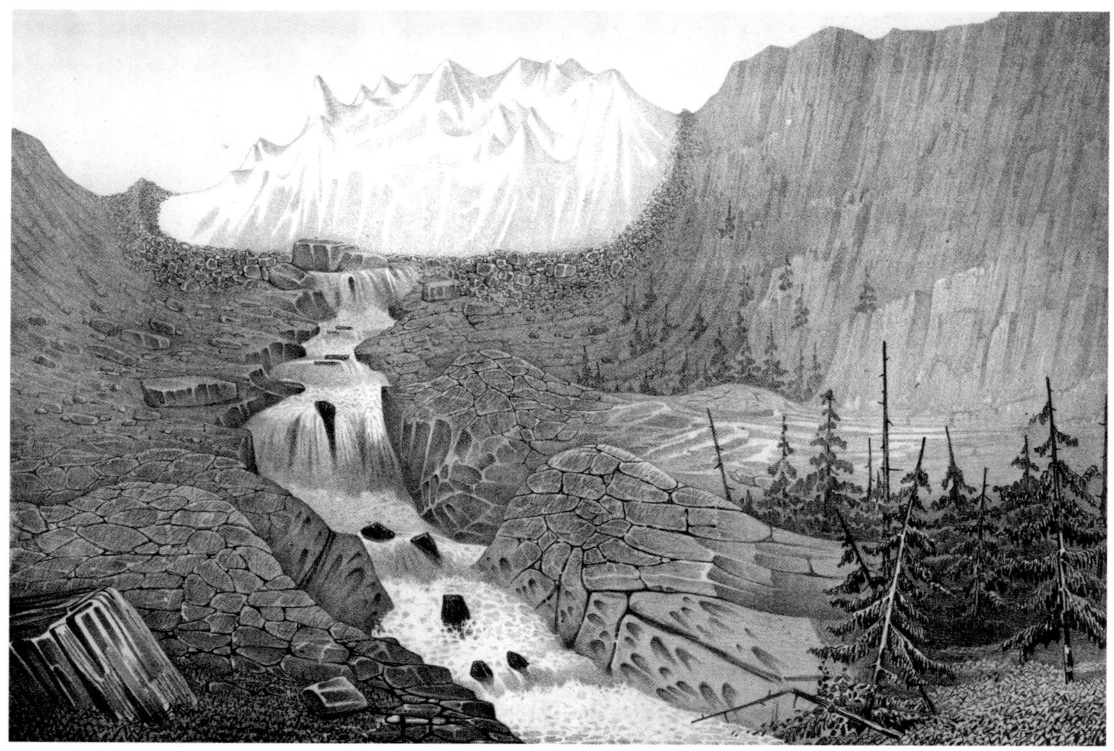

Fig. 64. *Glacier de Viesch.* Plate 9 from Louis Agassiz, *Étude sur les Glaciers* (1840)

Agassiz. In fact he was the first to recognize them as such. Glaciology was one of his central interests and the field in which he made his most lasting contributions to science. He was the first to conceive of an "ice age" and also the first to explain the extremely important role ice played in sculpting the topography of the planet. He first presented his revolutionary ice-age hypothesis in Neuchatel, Switzerland, in 1837. On 24 July of that year he told the assembled members of the Swiss Academy of Natural Sciences that a great geological winter had once fallen over the earth. During this period, he said, an immense ice sheet had extended from the North Pole to the Mediterranean Sea. This great glacier, he claimed, was responsible for creating the erratic boulders, U-shaped valleys, and sheered and polished rocks that had for so long been attributed to another great cataclysm: the Deluge or Noah's Flood.[19]

Agassiz's audience was skeptical. The theory, to them, sounded far-fetched and fantastic. Undeterred by this response, Agassiz continued his researches and in 1840 published his monumental memoir on glaciers, *Étude sur les Glaciers*. This book, with its hefty text and lavish illustrations, did much to win converts to Agassiz's cause. The plates, much admired at the time, offer depictions of Swiss glaciers and the ways they have sculpted the land. Plate 9, for example, a view of the "Glacier de Viesch," shows a glacier that has receded from the foreground of the print to the background (fig. 64). The drawing clearly indicates that as the ice melted it left in its wake smoothed and polished rocks, erratic boulders, a U-shaped valley, and a pronounced terminal moraine (the rocky debris deposited at the forward edge of a glacier).

The prominent Massachusetts geologist Edward Hitchcock acquired this book in 1841. Although he had long been an avid supporter of the Deluge theory, he read Agassiz's book with enthusiasm and later that year described his response to it in an address before the American Geological Society: "While reading this work . . . I seemed to be acquiring a *new geological sense* and I [now] look upon our smoothed and striated rocks, our accumulations of gravel, and the *tout ensemble* of diluvial phenomena with new eyes."[20] In subsequent years many other Americans would have the same response as they, too, learned, through Agassiz's theory, to read their landscape with new eyes.

In North America, Agassiz was delighted to find conclusive proof for his theory of a universal ice age. The same signs of glaciation that he had observed in Switzerland were evident in Nova Scotia, in Michigan, and in Massachusetts. All along the Massachusetts coast he found the tracks of ancient glaciers. These, he felt, were especially evident at Nahant. Erratics (rocks carried some distance from their place of origin and then deposited by the ice as it receded) were visible all over the peninsula, while the flat-topped rocks beside the shore (the same rocks that Haseltine painted) bore unmistakable proofs of the grinding and shearing action of glaciers. To Agassiz, their smooth and polished faces were mirrors of the past.

The always voluble and communicative Agassiz shared his discoveries with friends and public alike. Visitors to his summer home were unlikely to escape without a discourse on the peninsula's natural history. When Ralph Waldo Emerson dropped by for a visit in the late 1860s, he had no sooner walked in the door than Agassiz took him by the arm and escorted him out to the rocks for a lecture on the local geology. Fellow Nahanter Julia Ward Howe recalled of the naturalist: "his continued presence among us gave a new impetus to the study of natural science. In his hands the record of the bones and fossils became a living language, and the common thought was enriched by the revelation of the wonders of the visible universe. Agassiz's was an expansive nature, and his great delight lay in imparting to others the discoveries in which he had found such intense pleasure."[21] Under Agassiz's tutelage, the study of natural history became one of the pleasures of summer on Nahant.

In 1854 Agassiz treated the residents of Nahant's fashionable hotel to a Sunday evening discourse on the peninsula's geology. This was recorded and published by his fellow Harvard professor Cornelius Felton. On that occasion Agassiz commented, "To the student of nature, Nahant is a geological museum in miniature, in which he may examine on a small scale all the great features of the globe."[22] He went on to trace Nahant's geological history from the aquatic origin of the original sedimentary beds, to their alteration by volcanic forces, to the final shaping action of the ice sheets.

Agassiz's observations on Nahant geology reached a wider audience through a series of articles on glaciers and glaciology published in the *Atlantic Monthly* in 1863 and 1864 (at the same time that Haseltine was working on his Nahant series). The July 1864 issue carried his essay about the ice period in America. In this article Agassiz pointed to the Nahant coast as an excellent place to witness the effects of glacial action. "In our granitic regions," he wrote, "as, for instance, at Nahant, the smooth surface of many of the rocks . . . shows that the same inexorable saw [the ice sheet] . . . has passed over them. . . . These marks may be traced everywhere, . . . not only to the water's edge, but beneath it."[23] Haseltine's paintings describe in exquisite detail these same ice-sheared rocks.

Haseltine was well aware of Nahant's geological history. In the latter part of his life, when he was living as an expatriate in Italy, he often told his daughter that he longed to see again "the glacier-lined rocks of the New England coast."[24]

Haseltine's familiarity with Nahant's geology probably began during his student years at Harvard. He attended the college when Agassiz's popularity there was at its height. The scientist's texts were used in the natural history course required of Harvard juniors, and in Haseltine's senior year Agassiz offered a special lecture course for his class on the geology of the ice age. Henry Adams, who sat in on the course, has testified to its appeal. In his autobiography (which is written in the third person), Adams contrasted his general dissatisfaction with Harvard with his great delight in Agassiz's class: "The four years passed at Harvard were, for his purposes, wasted. . . . The only teaching that appealed to his imagination was a course of lectures by Louis Agassiz on the Glacial Period and Paleontology, which had more influence on his curiosity than the rest of the college instruction altogether."[25]

Because there are no attendance records for Harvard lectures during this period, we cannot know for certain if Haseltine took the course. Yet his interest in natural science (evidenced by his membership in the Harvard Natural History Society) together with his friendship with Alexander Agassiz (his classmate and president of the Natural History Club) suggest that he would have been drawn to the lecture hall. If so, this would

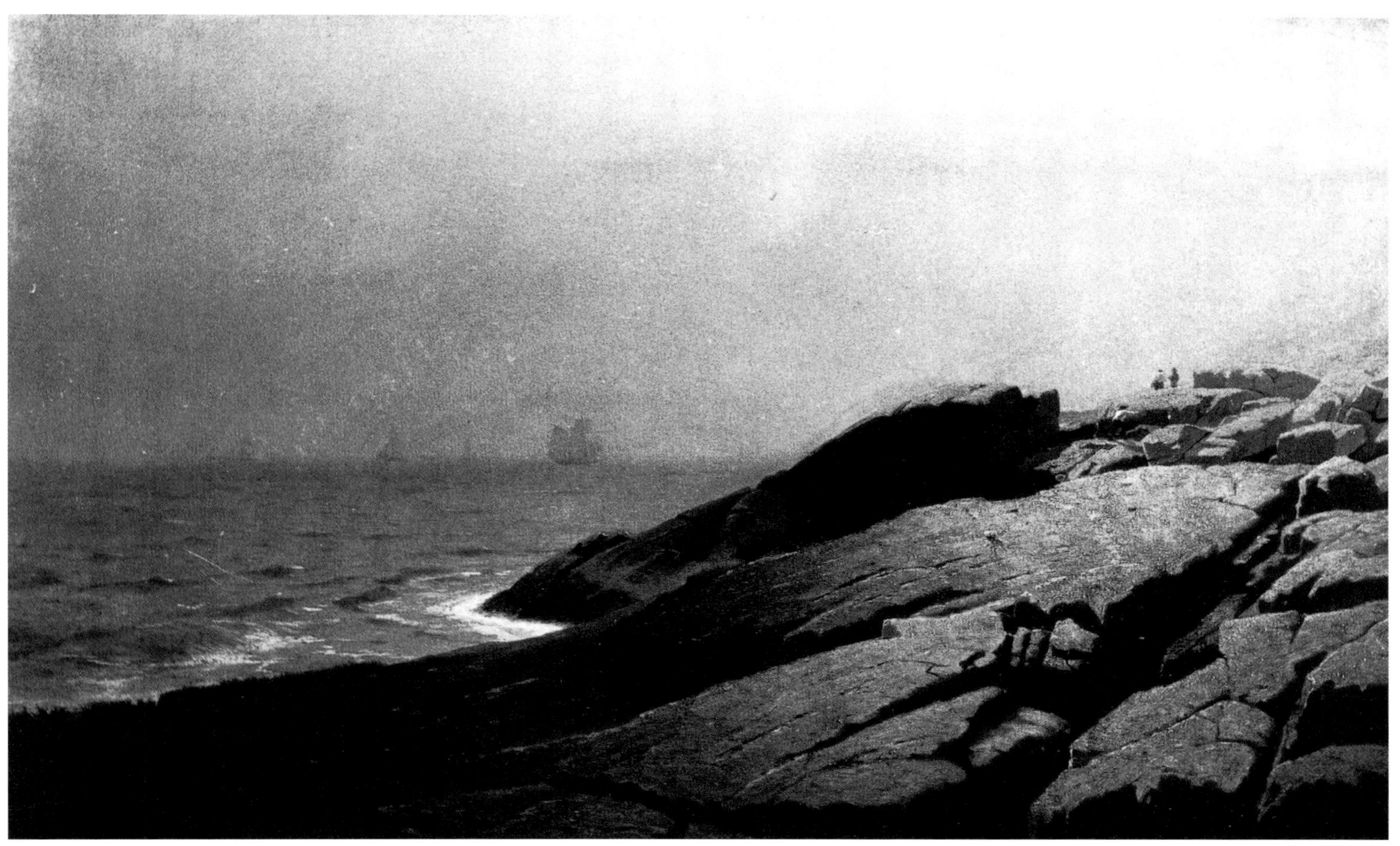

Fig. 65. William Stanley Haseltine, *Nahant Rocks, New England*, 1864. Oil on canvas, 17 x 29 in. (43.2 x 73.7 cm). The Washington County Museum of Fine Arts, Hagerstown, Maryland. Gift of Mrs. Helen Haseltine Plowden, London, England

be particularly significant since Nahant is the place Agassiz took his Harvard classes to show them the effects of glacial action.

In later years Haseltine would recognize a close relationship between art and science. He once said, "Every real artist is also a scientist . . . and an artist [like a scientist], is not satisfied until his work is a true expression of what he feels to be real; detail is of equal importance to the artist as to the scientist; both eschew vagueness and eliminate that which is irrelevant and meretricious."[26]

The desire that Haseltine expresses in this passage to eliminate unnecessary detail in order to concentrate on the essential is evident in the Nahant paintings (figs. 65–66). In almost all of these pictures the artist has stripped away the usual

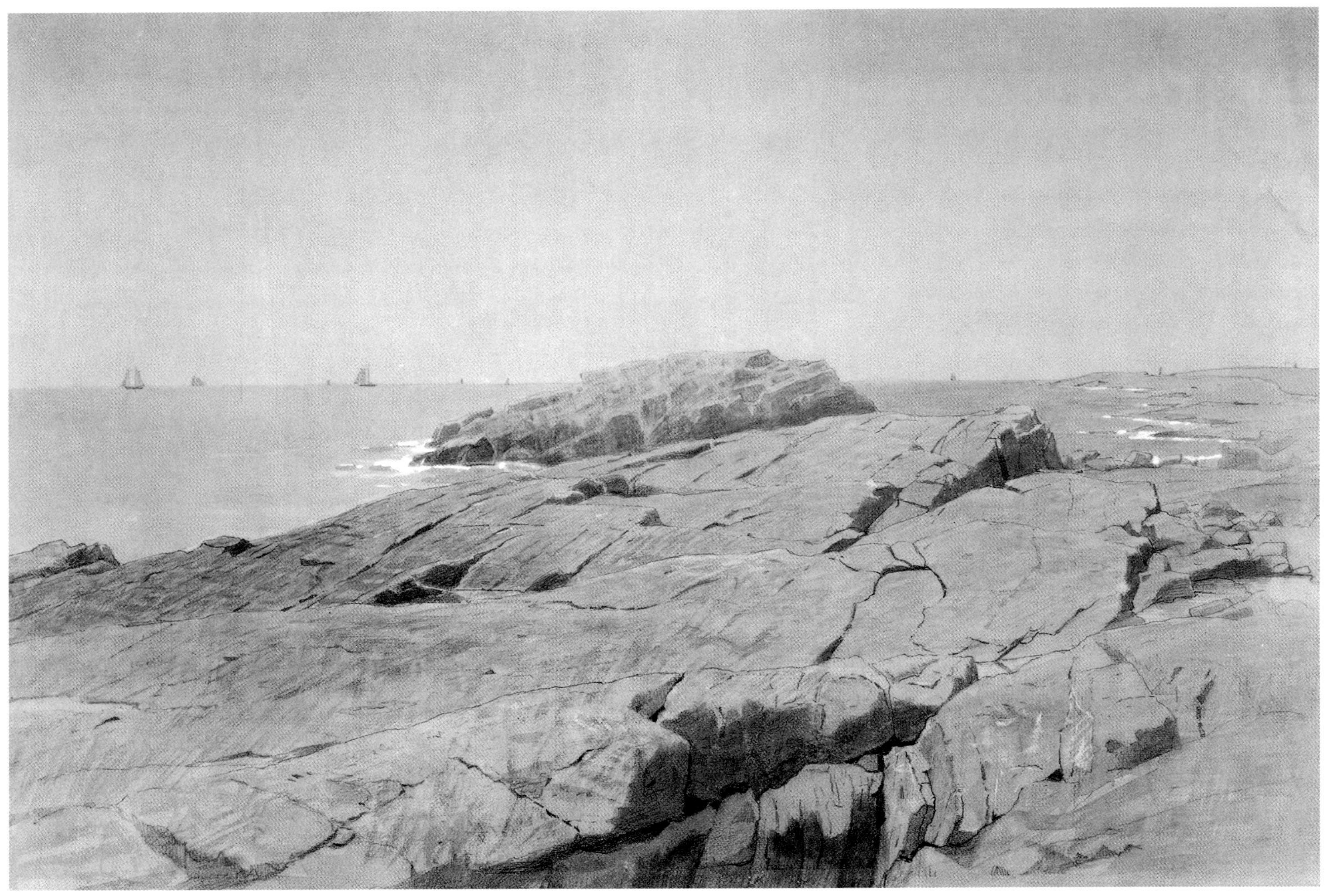

Fig. 66. William Stanley Haseltine, *Rocks at Nahant*, c. 1864. Pencil and watercolor on paper, 14 1/4 x 20 7/8 in. (36.2 x 53 cm). Museum of Fine Arts, Boston. Gift of Maxim Karolik

seashore detritus. The rock formations are presented to us swept clean of extraneous matter; their pristine, polished surfaces are like the pages of a geological text open for our perusal.

"Everything in nature," Haseltine once remarked, "is worth painting, provided one has discovered the meaning of it. The picture will then tell its own story."[27] In the case of the Nahant paintings, the story which they seem to be trying to tell is the story of the rocks, their fiery birth and icy middle age. By presenting these rocks so prominently in his canvases, Haseltine invites us to reenact in our minds the story of their formation.

Haseltine probably intended his Nahant canvases not only

to evoke the peninsula's geological history, but also to call to mind Agassiz and his teachings at and about Nahant. It was, after all, the naturalist who had first shown both the artist and his other adopted countrymen how their land had been shaped by the advancing glaciers of the great ice age, and his name was intimately associated with both the ice-age concept and Nahant. In the 1860s, when Haseltine was producing this series, Agassiz's name was known to virtually every educated American. His strong and vocal support of the Union during the Civil War, together with his deep religiosity, ardent love of American nature, and staunch opposition to Darwinian evolution, had made him a cultural hero of great magnitude.[28] At that time, a painting of a glaciated landscape (and of Nahant in particular) would have called to mind his name and his virtues almost as surely as a view of Mount Vernon invoked images of George Washington. This would certainly have been true of the circles in which Haseltine moved.

In commenting on the Nahant paintings, Haseltine's contemporaries often remarked on both their geological content and their relation to Agassiz. In 1864 a critic for *Watson's Weekly Art Journal* commented, "Agassiz pronounces the rocks of Nahant to be the oldest on the globe, and that they are of volcanic origin. Mr. Haseltine fully conveys their character in his pictures, and no one who has wandered over those huge masses of rough red rock, and watched the waves breaking against them, could fail to locate, from his studies, the very spot he has delineated."[29] Henry Tuckerman praised Haseltine's "rock portraits," writing: "Few of our artists have been more conscientious in the delineation of rocks; their form, superficial traits and precise tones have been given with remarkable accuracy. . . . There is a history to the imagination in every brown, angle-projecting slab."[30]

According to Haseltine's daughter, the artist "became known as a painter who possessed an uncanny knowledge of sea-coloring and rock formations, and was often asked if he had studied geology."[31] In 1893 the president of the Fine Arts Committee of the Columbian Exposition wrote an article about Haseltine in which he discussed both the great demand for the images and their geological content: "The lovers of art in America, and especially in Eastern Massachusetts, will remember with pleasure the paintings of the rocks at Nahant, made by William Stanley Haseltine during his sojourn there, twenty years ago. These paintings were so much in demand, that the artist was unable to produce them in sufficient numbers; they were executed in a manner which revealed a comprehensive knowledge of rock formation."[32]

These forces of rock formation—volcanic heavings and glacial action—that Haseltine's contemporaries apprehended in his pictures lend a sublime edge to the taut canvases. The juxtaposition of tiny figures against the massive rocks heightens the effect, introducing a poignant note into what might otherwise be drily scientific compositions. At the same time, these figures call our thoughts from the remote geological past into the human present, reminding us of the pleasures of a summer sojourn on the rocks at Nahant—pleasures that include these geological musings.

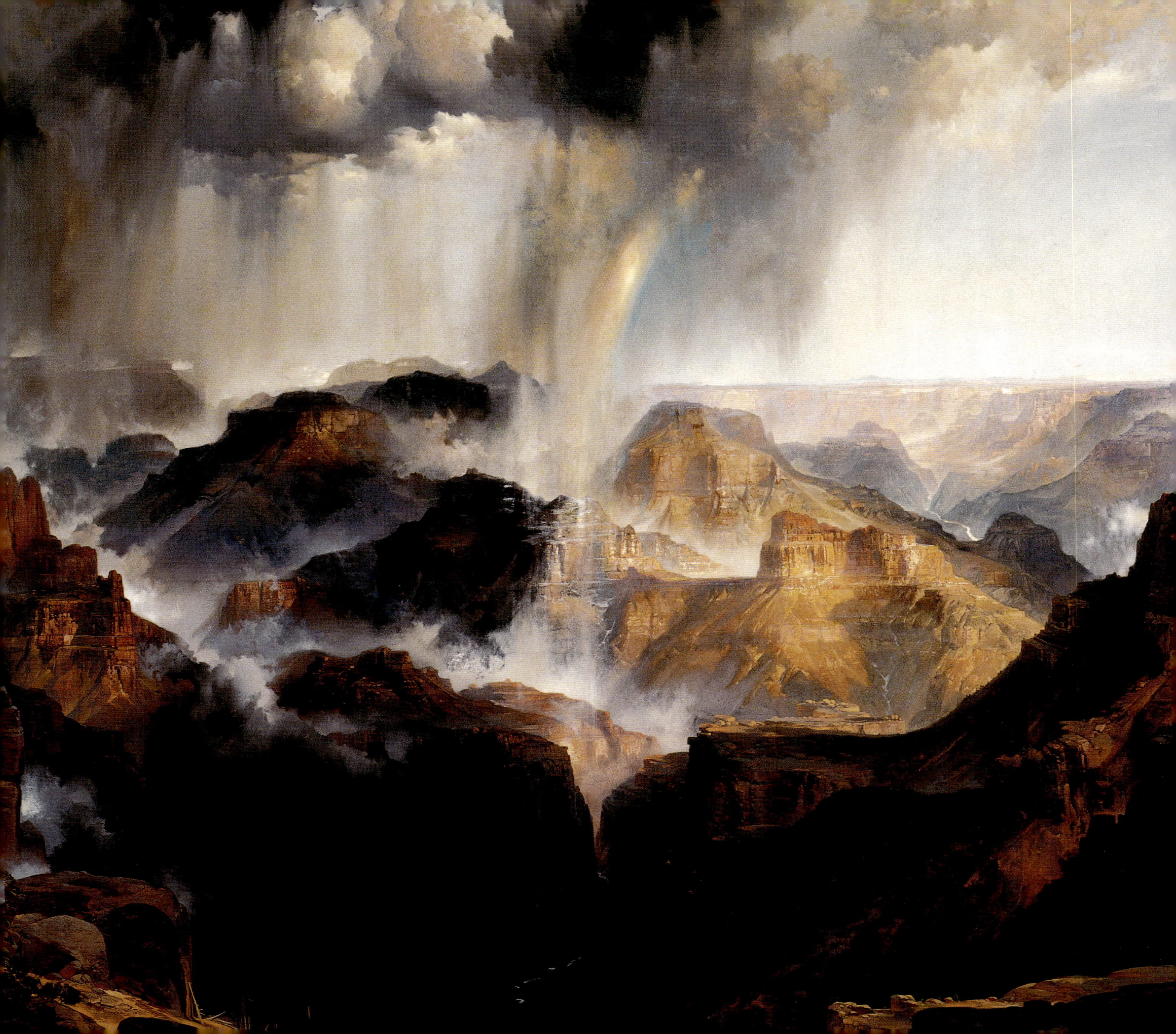

Chapter Six

THOMAS MORAN AND THE WESTERN SURVEYS

IN EARLY JULY 1871 Thomas Moran (1837–1926), a slight, wiry thirty-four year old, alighted from a stagecoach in Virginia City, Montana Territory.[1] He immediately set off in search of the nearby encampment of Ferdinand Hayden's Geological and Geographical Survey of the Territories, whose members were then marshalling their forces for a reconnaissance of the Yellowstone region (fig. 67).

When Moran walked into their camp, he joined not only that particular survey party but also the sizable coterie of landscape painters who found berths on the geological surveys of the nineteenth century. Their ranks numbered in the dozens. Some of these men, such as John Henry Hill (1839–1922), a staff artist on Clarence King's Fortieth Parallel Survey, were paid employees; others, like Moran, were guests, who hooked up with surveys for a variety of reasons, probably chief among them the relative safety and convenience of the surveys as a way to penetrate the unpainted, unphotographed landscape of the backcountry.[2]

On these surveys, artists and scientists were brought into intimate contact for weeks, sometimes months, at a time. They

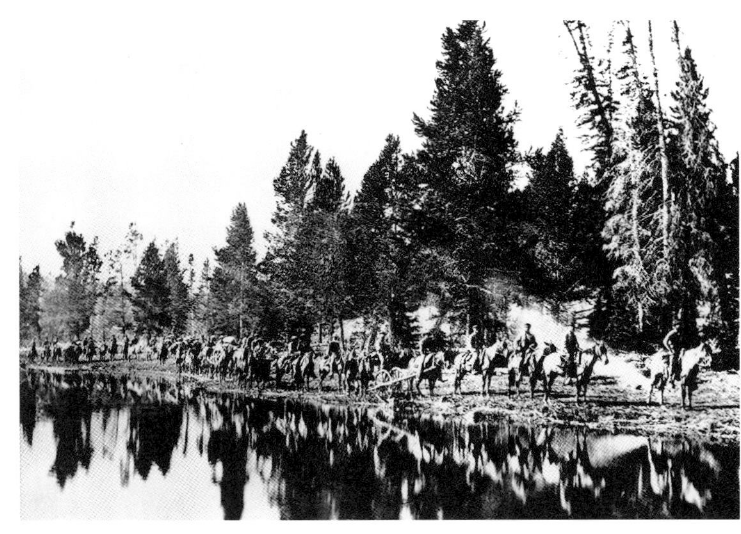

Fig. 67. *Pack Train of the U.S. Geological Survey*, 1871. Photograph by William Henry Jackson. National Park Service, Yellowstone National Park

shared the same bread-and-bacon meals and faced the same hardships and dangers. Together they coped with hailstorms, baking heat, foul water, tarantulas, rattlesnakes, and hostile Indians. As they rode along the trails, dried their socks beside

Opposite: Detail of Fig. 72

the fire, and labored over their reports, they also shared their insights into the lands through which they traveled. They had much to learn from each other since their work was directed toward the same ambitious ends: the observation, collection, and analysis of information that would elucidate the American land, chart its ancient history and topography, map its natural resources, detail its scenic attractions, in short, make it known.

The survey artists' work should not be seen as playing an ancillary role in this endeavor, serving only to "illustrate" others' discoveries. It was, rather, one of many avenues to knowledge engaged by the surveys' members. Photographing, sketching, and painting were alternate modes of collecting samples, taking notes, performing analyses, and making reports. As all the survey leaders recognized, some types of information are more easily collected and conveyed by visual means. The particular shape of a mountain peak, the configuration of a fossil tooth, or the precise relationship of one stratigraphic unit to another are just a few examples of the sort of information that is more readily comprehended through a sketch or a photograph than through words.

The artists' work was also deployed for other ends beyond the scientific aims of the survey. The survey leaders often used it to publicize and promote their achievements, while many businesses found other ways to exploit the images. Publishers of popular journals sought to boost their circulations by including survey-derived images of recently explored lands. Railroad company executives, western land agents, and a host of other commercial venturers also used the artists' images to help them sell their products and services. In multiple ways the artists helped to make the western lands available for consumption. As Peter Hales has pointed out, "the activity of looking became both precedent and substitute for other forms of acquisition."[3] Joni Kinsey, in her exemplary *Thomas Moran and the Surveying of the American West*, explains very well how Moran's work was exploited for commercial ends. This chapter, though much indebted to Kinsey's work, focuses more on the scientific context in which Moran's great paintings of the West were conceived, executed, and understood.

THE GEOLOGICAL SURVEYS

Between 1867 and 1879, four major government-sponsored geological and geographical surveys were active in the western United States: Hayden's Survey of the Territories (under the aegis of the Interior Department), King's Fortieth Parallel Survey (under the Army), Lieutenant George Wheeler's Geographical Surveys of the Territories West of the 100th Meridian (also under the Army), and John Wesley Powell's Geographical and Topographical Survey of the Colorado River of the West (under the Smithsonian and then the Interior Department). These four expeditionary forces are now known collectively as the Great Surveys.[4]

With much the same mission and occasionally covering much the same ground, these surveys competed fiercely for public attention and federal funds. The work of the survey artists played a part in this competition, being used, among other things, to garner public and legislative support. Its efficacy is implied by the survey leaders' eager efforts to sign on the most talented of these men. This meant that sometimes the artists themselves became objects of inter-survey competition. Moran, for example, found himself awkwardly situated in 1872 and 1873 when both Hayden and Powell sought to secure his services for their expeditions. And the competition for artists was just one area in which the survey leaders sought to outmaneuver their fellows. Finally, in 1879, after reports of such incidents as two rival survey parties jostling each other as they tried to set up their surveying equipment on the same mountain peak, the government put a stop to the squabbling and duplicated efforts by consolidating the four groups into the United States Geological Survey, under the direction of Clarence King.

But before this consolidation, Thomas Moran three times went West under the auspices of the Great Surveys. Two times he traveled with Hayden (1871, 1874), once with Powell (1873). Accompanying these men, Moran had rare opportunities to see the land through their eyes and under their guidance. They encouraged him to perceive it geologically, to comprehend the processes at work in shaping the land before him, and to envision the past scope and present action of those forces. In the paintings resulting from those trips, Moran revealed the impact their scientific vision had on him. He described landscapes in the process of creation, living landscapes with pasts, presents, and futures. The three most famous paintings that emerged from those trips: *The Grand Canyon of the Yellowstone* (1872, fig. 71), *The Chasm of the Colorado* (1873–74, fig. 72), and *The Mountain of the Holy Cross* (1875, fig. 73) dramatize the geological forces that have shaped and are shaping the land: the generative work of fire, the erosive force of water, and the sculpting power of ice.

In drawing attention to the evolutionary character of the land and to the forces involved in its transformation, Moran's paintings aligned themselves with the uniformitarian geological theories embraced by both Hayden and Powell. These scientists ascribed to the by then widely (though by no means universally) accepted theories of the English geologist Charles Lyell. In his most famous book, *Principles of Geology* (1830–33), Lyell (as was noted in chapter 2) argued that the earth's surface is not inert but is constantly evolving, passing through continuous cycles of erosion, deposition, and uplift. In contrast to the rival catastrophist theory which held that geologic change occurs by a series of sudden cataclysmic events (the biblical Flood for example), Lyell's uniformitarian theory held that this change occurs slowly over great periods of time, and that the processes that have shaped the earth in the past are essentially the same that we see operating in the present. The present, in Lyell's theoretical system, is the key to the past. The earth is dynamic, continually transforming itself. Through an understanding of the processes that are now shaping the crust, we can both decipher the earth's past and predict its future. This, in the briefest and broadest terms, is the geological theory that seems to underlie Moran's western landscapes.

RUSKIN AND TURNER

Moran was primed to see the landscape in these dynamic, evolutionary terms years before he met Hayden and Powell. As a teenager he had encountered the works of the British artist J.M.W. Turner, and, more important, had encountered

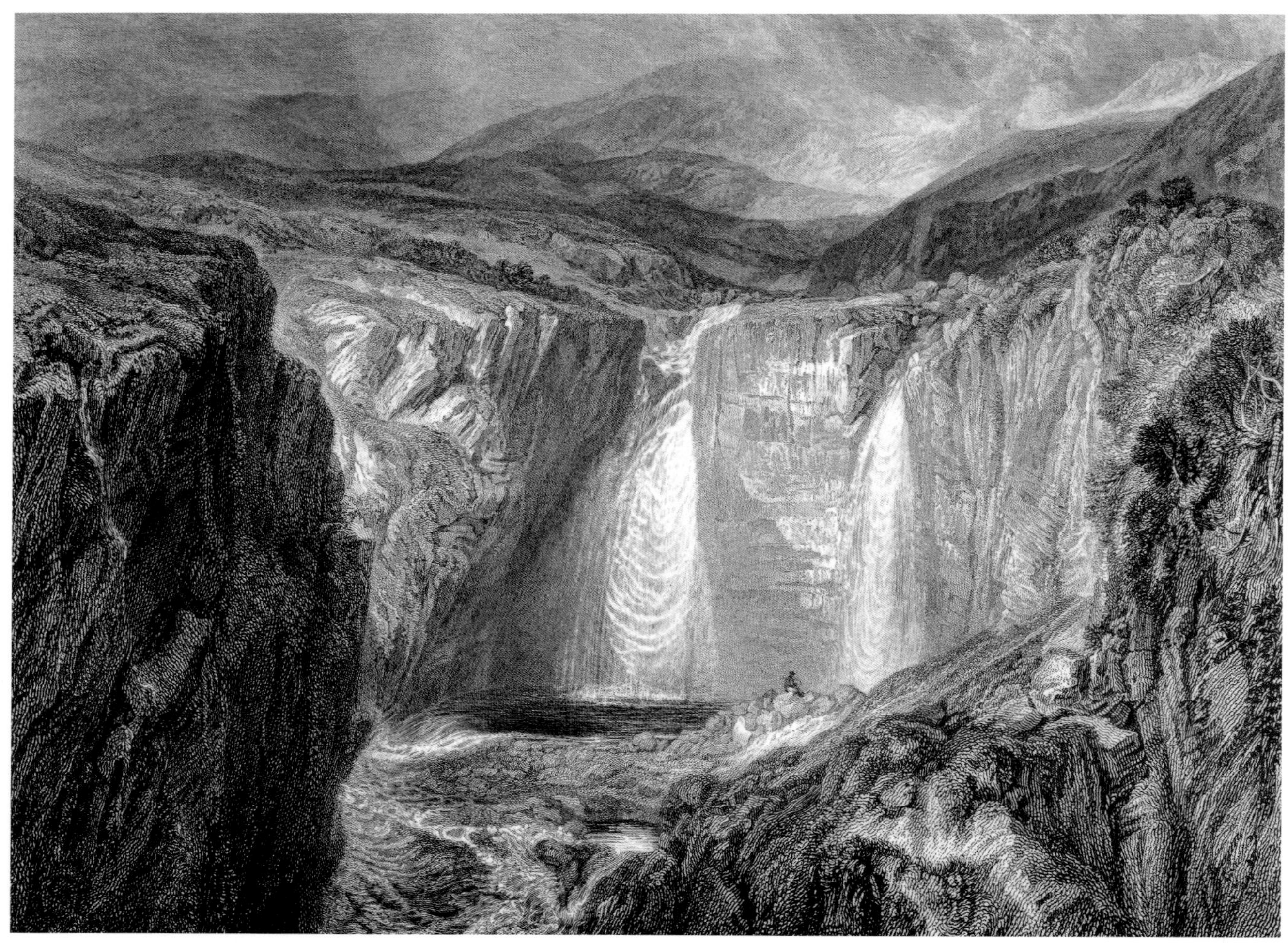

Fig. 68. J.M.W. Turner, *The Upper Falls of the Tees, Yorkshire.* Engraving by Edward Goodall for *Picturesque Views in England and Wales* (London, 1827). Fogg Art Museum, Harvard University Art Museums, Cambridge, Massachusetts. Gray Collection of Engravings Fund

them with John Ruskin as his guide. Turner and Ruskin (who was familiar with Lyell's work) were to shape Moran's perceptions of nature and art, his theoretical vision, and his technical means.[5]

Moran seems to have been introduced to Turner through Ruskin's *Modern Painters* (1843–1860). Like so many American artists of his time, Moran was very familiar with this work, though he focused on somewhat different aspects of Ruskin's advice than other painters, such as Durand, had done. In these volumes, Ruskin argues for Turner's supremacy as a landscape artist and presents his works as models for younger artists to follow. Ruskin bases his case for Turner's greatness on the artist's unsurpassed fidelity to nature. Turner, he avows, "paints more of nature than any man who ever lived."[6]

Through the several thousand pages of *Modern Painters*, Ruskin marshals evidence to support this assertion, pointing out Turner's perception of the minutest facts of nature, such as the way limbs branch from the trunks of trees and the way rivers cut their banks. He urges young artists to follow Turner's example in keenly attending to nature's forms. "Every class of rock, every kind of earth, every form of cloud," he admonishes, "must be studied with equal industry, and rendered with equal precision."[7]

Yet to Ruskin, this perfect fidelity was not the end and aim of landscape art. "[B]ecause such accurate knowledge is necessary," he writes, "it does not follow that . . . it is valuable in itself, and without reference to high ends."[8] True greatness lies in moving beyond fidelity to detail, or rather using this faithfully perceived detail to convey the artist's impressions, his interpretations of his subject, the high and holy lessons embedded in the natural world. "It is not," writes Ruskin, "detail sought for its own sake . . . but it is detail referred to a great end, sought for the sake of the inestimable beauty which exists in the slightest and least of God's works, and treated in a manly, broad and impressive manner."[9] In truly great art "minutiae of detail" is reconciled with "grandeur of impression."[10] In Turner's works, according to Ruskin, one finds the fullest expression of this reconciliation.

Again and again Ruskin directs the reader to Turner's prints and paintings for examples of the highest achievements in landscape art. Through these examples he explains the various components of Turner's greatness. Of particular relevance to Moran's works and his developing interest in geology is a point Ruskin makes in the first volume of *Modern Painters*: "the great quality of Turner's drawings which more especially proves their transcendent truth, is the capability they afford us of reasoning on past and future phenomena."[11] To exemplify this point, he turns our attention to Turner's engraving of *The Upper Falls of the Tees, Yorkshire* (fig. 68):

> With this drawing before him the geologist could give a lecture upon the whole system of aqueous erosion, and speculate as safely upon the past and future states of this very spot, as if he were standing and getting wet with the spray. He would tell you at once, that the waterfall is in a state of rapid recession; that it once formed a wide cataract just at the spot where the figure is sitting on the heap of débris; and that when it was there, part of it came down by the channel on the left, its bed still marked by the delicately chiselled lines of fissure.[12]

Ruskin tells us elsewhere that Turner conveys the historical and living character of the landscape by seizing "the governing and leading lines" that "rule the swell, and fall and change of the mass." These lines, he writes, "show us in a mountain, first how it was built or heaped up; secondly how it is now being worn away, and from what corner the wildest storms strike it. . . . This," he concludes, "is vital truth."[13] When he refers to the "historical character" of the landscape, he does not allude, as earlier theorists such as Sir Joshua Reynolds would have been alluding, to the acts of human history that had been played out in the scene, but to the past life of the earth itself.

According to Ruskin, Turner's works reveal to us the "operation of the great laws of change, which are the conditions of all material existence, however apparently enduring." Through Turner's works, Ruskin tells us, we come to see that even the "hills, which as compared with living beings seem 'everlasting' are in truth as perishing as they."[14] Turner's landscapes convey the eternal changefulness of nature and its perpetual transience, and through this heighten our perception of the tentative, tangential place that humans occupy in this world.

With Ruskin's guidance, Moran fully grasped this aspect of Turner's work and went on to convey similar ideas in his own art (though for the most part avoiding Turner's more despairing themes). Like Turner (at least Turner as understood by way of Ruskin), Moran sought to depict the specificities of rocks, trees and clouds, while also evoking the processes of land formation and the changefulness of the earth's crust. He conveyed these ideas and perceptions in a style so deeply rooted in a faithful study and conscientious copying of Turner's paintings and prints (as recommended by Ruskin) that his works have occasionally been mistaken for those of the English master.[15] From Turner's prints came Moran's energized, quavering, flexible line. From Turner's watercolors and oils came his radiant light effects, his thin translucent veils of pure color, and his hazy indistinctness of forms (though he never carried this quite as far as Turner). With these devices, Moran suggested nature's flux, the sinking, splitting, and heaving of the earth's crust, the sense of a world half-formed.

Ruskin's definition of artistic greatness stayed with Moran throughout his life. Until his death, Moran continued to believe that great landscape art is and ought to be rooted in a thorough knowledge of the natural world. In an article written for *Brush and Pencil* in 1903, Moran presented his Ruskinian theory of art. In what is now the best-known passage from the article, he writes:

> Knowledge in art is the power behind the hand-work. Eyesight is nothing unless backed by brains.
>
> In condensed form, this is my theory of art. In painting the Grand Canyon of the Colorado and its wonderful color scheme . . . I have to be full of my subject. I have to have knowledge. I must know the geology. I must know the rocks and the trees and the atmosphere and the mountain torrents and the birds that fly in the blue ether above me.[16]

Moran's lifelong commitment to a Ruskinian geological truth is also suggested in an incident recalled by one of the painter's contemporaries, a younger artist named Gustave Buek. In an article written for the *Mentor* in 1924, Buek recounted that he once took a friend to visit Moran's New York studio. The friend was captivated by an unfinished painting of a western scene on Moran's easel. This painting, according to Buek, "had been boldly laid in in broad masses and looked quite different from one of his finished paintings." The friend sought to purchase it in its unfinished state, but Moran adamantly refused "saying that the painting, as it was, was not correct as to geological facts and consequently could not leave his studio in that state."[17]

All this is to say that when Moran hooked up with Hayden's survey that summer in 1871, he arrived well equipped to both perceive and depict all the natural forms and forces that he might encounter in the course of the survey's work. He was alert to the living character of the landscape and sensitive to the specificities of geological formations (Ruskin, after all, had informed him that generalizing granite and slate is just as absurd as generalizing a man and a cow.)[18]

THE HAYDEN SURVEY (1871)

With five-hundred-dollar advances from both Richard Watson Gilder, editor of *Scribner's*, and Jay Cook, president of the Northern Pacific Railroad (both of whom hoped to take full advantage of the images resulting from the trip), Moran was able to apply for a berth on Hayden's 1871 Yellowstone expedition with the assurance that he could pay his own way. Hayden, an ambitious and politically astute man, promptly and graciously acceded to Moran's request and later made ample use of the artist's works. Indeed, as Joni Kinsey has persuasively demonstrated, all the parties involved were to benefit considerably from Moran's participation.

Although Moran had to keep the agendas of all his benefactors in mind as he created his Yellowstone images, this chapter concentrates on his interactions with Hayden and the other survey scientists, and the ways these interactions shaped Moran's works and their public reception.

Hayden's impact seems to have been extensive. He set the itinerary for the survey's work, controlling the terrain to which Moran was exposed and thus the broad range of subjects from which he would select his images. Hayden also sometimes guided Moran to particular sites that he hoped would spark the artist's imagination, and he shared with Moran his perception of those places. Moreover, his involvement with the artist did not end when Moran left the survey's field camp. Once Moran was back in his studio, Hayden continued to correspond with him, to visit him, and to comment on the works in progress. Once the images were completed, he appeared at the official openings, sometimes giving talks about the works to those assembled. He also seems to have participated in the creation of broadsides describing the paintings that were distributed at the exhibitions. In addition, he wrote texts that accompanied many of Moran's mass-produced images — not only the official survey reports, but also an article for *Scribner's*, and the letterpress text for a set of chromolithographs after Moran's Yellowstone paintings published by Louis Prang. Thus, through lectures and texts and conversations, Hayden played a major role in shaping the discursive framework within which Moran's works were understood in their time.

MORAN ON THE SURVEY

Aside from his drawings and paintings, Moran left scanty records of his first summer in the Yellowstone region. His diary of the month-long expedition is only three pages long. Yet these sources — when pieced together with the records left by other expedition members — allow us to gain a general sense of Moran's experiences that summer and the extent of his engagement with the expedition's scientific mission.

Most of Moran's days on the survey were spent working side by side with the expedition's photographer, William Henry Jackson. Then in his second year with the survey, Jackson was

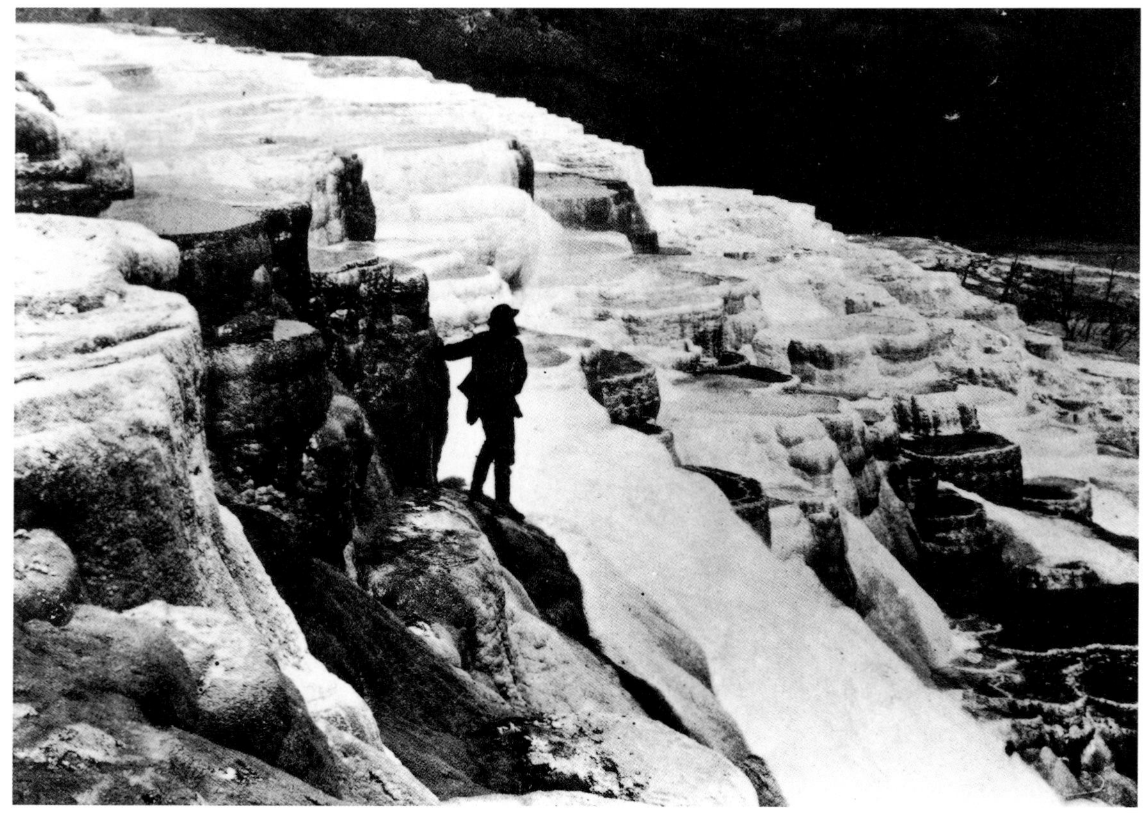

Fig. 69. *Thomas Moran at the Geyser Basin*, 1871. Photograph by William Henry Jackson. National Park Service, Yellowstone National Park

Opposite: Fig. 70. Thomas Moran, *Extinct Craters, Gardiner's River*, 1871. Pencil, watercolor, and opaque color on paper, 5 x 9 1/2 in. (12.7 x 24.1 cm). National Park Service, Yellowstone National Park. Gift of George D. Pratt, Mrs. Henry Strong, Mr. John D. Rockefeller Jr., Col. Herbert J. Slocum

to become Moran's lifelong friend and a companion on many future journeys. On this trip Moran must have learned much from Jackson about balancing the demands of science and art. In Jackson's contract, he agreed to "cooperate with . . . F. V. Hayden in every way possible for the advancement of Geological and Geographical Science."[19] In taking his photos, he sought out views "of distinctive interest, from a scenic as well as a geological standpoint."[20] Although Hayden allowed Jackson considerable freedom, he would sometimes request specific subjects. As Jackson noted in his diary of his 1870 expedition with Hayden, "I unpacked my outfit several times to photograph the rock formations the Doctor [Hayden] indicated."[21]

Moran and Jackson sometimes left the main party, striking out on their own in search of views. At other times they worked side by side with the scientists, as they did at the Great Geyser Basin (fig. 69). A passage in Jackson's diary of the 1870 survey, on which the painter Sanford Gifford was a guest, gives some indication of the way the geologists' revelations could shape the artists' perception of the landscape. Of a day in the Badlands in southwest Wyoming, he wrote: "While Gifford

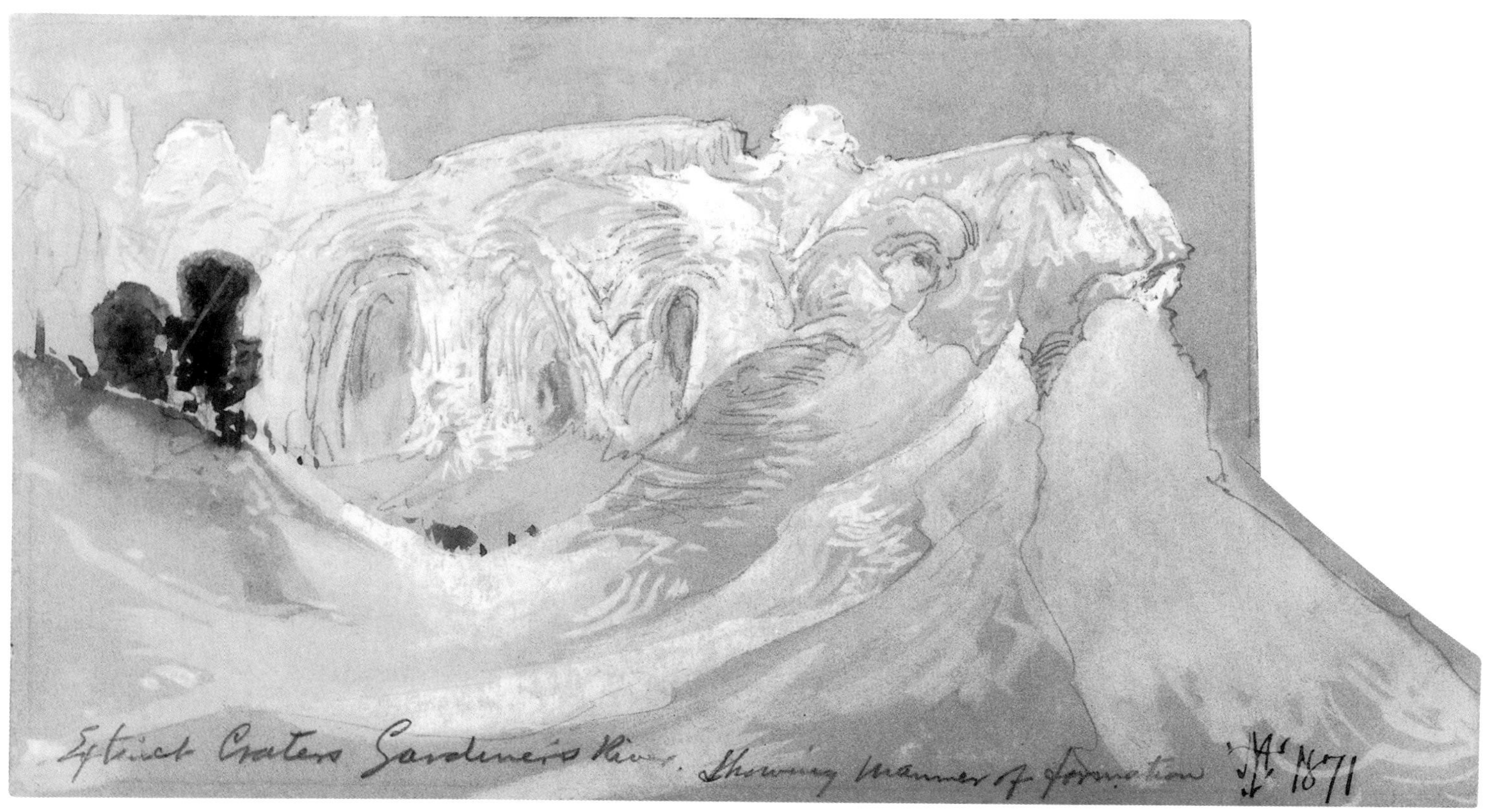

and I were making pictures of the interesting scenes, the geologists under Hayden were digging for fossils. They collected a wagon load of ancient turtles, shellfish, and other creatures that lived in the great inland sea that once covered this section of this country."[22]

While on the survey, Jackson quickly became comfortable with scientific terminology, filling his diaries with remarks about the geological character of the country through which they were traveling. Moran was soon doing the same. The sketches he made on that 1871 trip are annotated with phrases such as "shaly rock" and "Basaltic Hill."[23] Even after he left the survey, Moran continued to describe the places he visited in geological terms. On a trip to the Tetons with his brother Peter in 1879, he recorded in his journal observations such as, "The opposite mountain rises 5000 feet above the river with a granite base surmounted by sandstone & capped with tremendous precipices of limestone."[24]

Beyond this attention to lithology, Moran's sketches and writings from the 1871 trip also reveal a sensitivity to the historical, evolutionary character of the landscape. On his drawing

Extinct Craters, Gardiner's River (1871, fig. 70), he wrote, "Showing manner of formation." And indeed, the nested arcs of white wash suggest the slow buildup of calcareous deposits over time. Even Moran's choice of medium — a watercolor wash, in which the large grains of pigment settle out of the water to adhere to the dark paper — evokes the process by which the craters were formed. One of Moran's contemporaries, gazing over his watercolors of Yellowstone's geysers and hot springs, also found himself thinking about the manner of their formation and, like Moran, saw them in uniformitarian terms. He muses in his review on "the singularly shaped beds of mineral matter deposited by the springs, and the lovely lofty terraces built by the slow and silent action of the waters." [25]

"THE GRAND CANYON OF THE YELLOWSTONE"

At Yellowstone, Moran saw, as one can see at few places on earth, a landscape in the throes of creation. In the geyser fields, he stepped gingerly over a thin crust of newly hardened rock, fearful that at any moment it would split beneath his feet. He walked beside bubbling mud pots and gazed on spouting geysers, rapidly eroding gorges, and tumbling avalanches of loose mud and rocks. Some years after that trip, he wrote, "The impression then made upon me by the stupendous & remarkable manifestations of nature's forces will remain with me as long as memory lasts." [26]

The paintings that resulted from that expedition emphasize the metamorphic character of the extraordinary region. They are pictures about change, about the dynamic, evolutionary character of the earth, and about the transformatory powers of nature and art. The largest and most famous of these paintings is *The Grand Canyon of the Yellowstone* (1872, fig. 71). This huge (7′ x 12′) canvas depicts what Hayden called, with qualification, "the greatest wonder of all." [27] Its subject is the Lower Falls of the Yellowstone River and the deep gorge that the plunging river has carved through the area's brilliantly colored volcanic rocks.

In traditional picturesque fashion, Moran framed his panoramic view of the falls and canyon with shadowed wings of earth. To the right rises a tall, vertical mass of dark volcanic rock, to the left a broad flat plateau which supports a forest of towering evergreens. Between these wings opens a view of the V-shaped walls of the canyon, their slopes punctuated by shining white pinnacles of rock and small stands of skeletal firs. At the base of the canyon flows a turquoise river. Following it backwards, one arrives at the falls, their height magnified by an ascending spume of spray that reaches to the top of the canvas. This spume cuts in two the long horizontal line of the plateau that forms the painting's high horizon. On this plateau, toward the left, tiny columns of jetting water mark the presence of the geyser fields.

Moran marshaled every aspect of this picture — the subject, the forms, the technique — to convey the transforming powers of time and the forces of nature. His concern with the geological history of the site is evident, for example, in his chosen style, which evokes the processes of creation as much as their products. The wavering, trembling, crackling lines and the liquid brushstrokes, even the continually gradated shifts from light to dark, announce the unstable, transitory nature of the scene and the changefulness of matter.

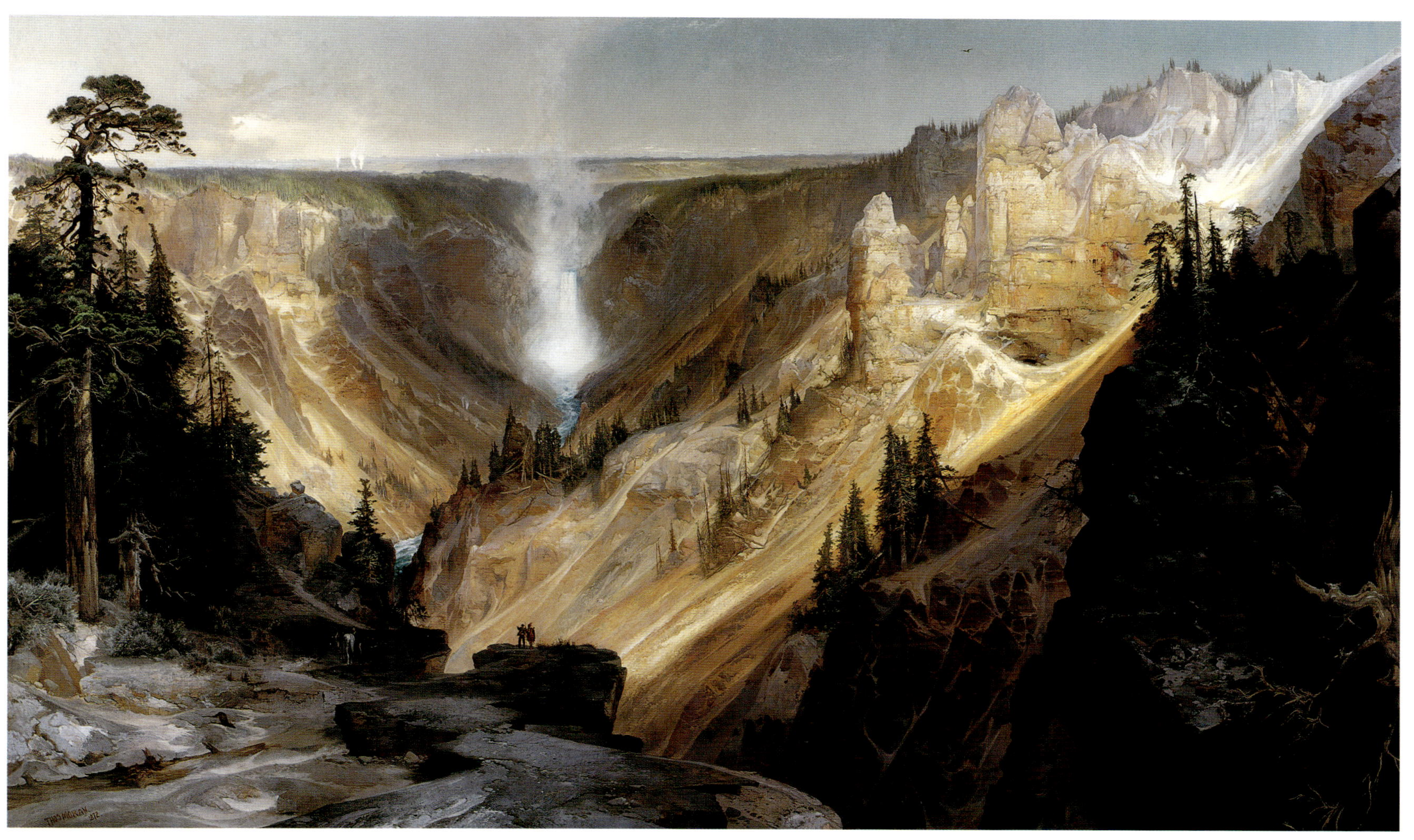

Fig. 71. Thomas Moran, *The Grand Canyon of the Yellowstone*, 1872.
Oil on canvas, 84 x 144 in. (213.4 x 365.8 cm). Smithsonian American Art Museum, Washington, D.C. Lent by the Department of the Interior Museum, Washington, D.C.

Moran's concern with the metamorphic character of the land is especially evident in the details of the painting. In the left foreground, tiny figures stand on the lip of an ancient lava flow. This dark layer of stone winds out toward the canyon's rim. Its undulating shape makes it seem to flow like the lava from which it was formed, reminding us of the once viscous state of the rock. Beside it churns the water of a stream so gray and silt-laden that it seems to be made of liquid earth, again evoking thoughts of the metamorphosis of matter. In this section of the canvas it is very difficult to tell where the water ends and the rock begins. They seem to merge into each other. Placed side by side, the stream and the ledge of igneous rock evoke the eternal conflict between the forces that raise the land and those that wear it away.

Even Moran's paint handling evokes geological processes. In creating the left foreground ledge, he applied his paint in layers, some rough, some smooth, some brown, some gray, with the lower layers showing through the ones above, replicating the process by which the ledge itself was formed. The layering of pigment here reminds us of the slow accumulation of strata over time. But creation in Moran's work is continually paired with images of destruction. On the right side of the canvas the softness of many of the forms, and the jagged, tremulous lines that crackle across the surface of many of the formations suggest the crumbling of rock and its breakdown into dirt and debris.

Other aspects of the picture remind us of the rock-creating work of igneous forces. Besides the winding band of solidified lava in the foreground, the picture's hot colors — the incandescent white and sulphurous yellow of the canyon's walls and the bright blue of the river — together recall the colors of flames and remind us of the fiery temperatures of volcanic forces. Meanwhile, on the cliffs, long strokes of oily pigment — streams of molten gold — run down toward the water. These strokes describe the avalanches of soft, crumbling volcanic rock that tumble down the canyon walls, but at the same time they suggest the lava that once spilled over the land. Moran's contemporaries noted these allusions to volcanic action. A writer for the Washington *Republican*, reviewing *The Grand Canyon of the Yellowstone* in 1872, interpreted the long yellow brushmarks as "boiling fountains of sulphur and iron . . . [which] pour down their wealth of magic coloring in lava-like streams of soft drift."[28] Here intimations of creation and destruction are unified in a single image.

All of these details allude to changes and transformations taking place in the fullness of geological time, but Moran also alludes in this painting to changes taking place in the much shorter time frame of human existence. On the foreground ledge, for example, stand two figures: an Indian and a white man. They face in different directions. The white man stands with his back toward us, gesturing toward the light-filled canyon, toward the future. The Indian faces us, with his hands at his sides, looking into the shadowed foreground, or into the past. To Moran and other Euro-Americans of his generation, this detail must have suggested a major historical shift, the end of the "savage state" and the arrival of "civilization." Other details suggest changes of other sorts. The framing of the canvas with a dead, denuded tree on the right and a tall, vigorous evergreen on the left, and the pairing of a dead deer by the foreground stream with a live bear in the woods just beyond it suggest changes in the states of matter not only from liquid to solid, and hard to soft, but from life to death.

Looking closely at the canvas, we also become aware of another sort of transformation: the artist's extraordinary ability to create rocky ledges and turbid streams from bits of ground-up minerals and oil. Richard Watson Gilder, the editor of *Scribner's* who helped to finance Moran's trip to the Yellowstone, was particularly struck by this magical mutation. He visited Moran's studio as the canvas was taking shape, and marveled at the transformation of pigment into earth, air, and water, and the analogies between this and the creation of the earth.[29] He wrote: "Watching the picture grow was like keeping one's eye open during the successive ages of world creation —from darkness to the word Good. The outline was thrown upon the bare canvas in a single day. Afterward great streaks of, to me, meaningless color flashed hither and thither. I saw only hopeless chaos. Then blue sky appeared; by and by, delicate indications of cloud, mist, mountains, rock and tree crept down the canvas."[30] Creation, transformation, metamorphosis, change — these are the central themes of the painting, whether manifested in the artist's talents in creating such paintings or in nature's powers to shape such scenes.

The Public Reception of the Painting

In creating *The Grand Canyon of the Yellowstone*, Moran was deeply concerned with the accuracy of the geological facts he was presenting. In March 1872, as the painting was taking shape in his studio, he wrote to Hayden requesting the geologist's judgement on the picture's scientific content:

> I cannot feel confident about it [the painting] until *you* have seen it. In fact I cannot finish it until you have seen it, as your knowledge of nature and her workings would make your judgment on the truths of the picture of far greater value to me than that of any other man in the country. Your knowledge of cause and effect in nature, would point out to me many facts connected with the place that I may have overlooked, and if your duties or time allow you to come and see the picture you would add another to the many great obligations I am under to you.[31]

The next month Moran again asked for Hayden's help.[32] Whether the geologist rendered this service or not (and he presumably did) the completed painting was a scientific as well as an aesthetic success. Clarence Cook, writing for the *New York Tribune*, declared, "it does not need the testimony of learned geologists . . . to convince us of the truthfulness of the [picture]."[33] Perhaps, as Cook argues, this testimony was unnecessary, but Moran and his supporters made sure that it was provided. At the public unveiling of the picture in New York on 2 May 1872, Hayden was in attendance, offering "an impromptu description of the picture . . . [showing] point by point, the artist's devoted adherence to facts."[34]

Few were the reviews of the painting (and there were many) that did not mention Hayden's assertion of the artist's truthfulness. And few were the reviews that did not devote considerable space to the picture's geological content. To Russell Sturgis of the *Nation*, it was "a picture that explains the marvels of geological formation and natural chemistry, it is a chart of physical geography."[35] To Clarence Cook, "if the picture had no other merit it had this, that a mine of scientific illustration is to be found in it."[36]

Most reviews began with a lengthy description of the picture's geological and topographical subject. One critic wrote:

> On these tremendous walls we read — and he who knows most geology reads most clearly — the whole history of their building. For, though it is, in fact, destruction that has made them, as it has made all rocky river banks; yet, as they stand, they convey rather the idea of battlements piled up with Titan art than awful trophies of the power of moving water. It is hard to believe that the slender stream, whose blue makes so delightful a key-note to the color of the picture, and which seems to be there only for its beauty . . . should be, in fact, the physical cause of all this stupendous transformation. But so it is. The river has eaten its way down to the present level. It once flowed along yonder plain, out of which the geysers are spouting their foam-fountain; and the cataract shows us the work still going on. The canyon will be lengthened in that direction — the fall receding — until there comes a rib of rock too hard to be so easily worn away.[37]

While this particular article focused the viewer's attention on the work of erosion, other authors emphasized the volcanic character of the depicted country. One mentions that the area Moran has painted "was the center of volcanic action in ages past, and its shores are still fringed with systems of geysers and boiling springs of a very active character." On the extreme right of the painting, this author continues, "a section of the basaltic formation is fully exposed."[38] In another review entitled "On the Easel: Art Among the Volcanic Wonders of the West," a reporter for the *New York Evening Mail* informs his readers that they "will be best prepared to understand and appreciate this painting" if they "read the remarkable series of papers descriptive of the 'Wonders of the Yellowstone,' published in *Scribner's Monthly* last year and . . . in the February number of this year."[39] Both are articles that detail the geological, especially the volcanic origins of the spot.

The articles in *Scribner's*, the detailed reviews, and the "testimony of learned geologists" must have, for many viewers, shaped their perception of the picture, directing their attention toward its geological content, the testimony it offers to the mutability and ultimate evanescence of all matter, as well as to the continually evolving character of the earth's surface.

"THE CHASM OF THE COLORADO"

The Grand Canyon of the Yellowstone was purchased by the Federal Government for $10,000 in 1872 and hung prominently in the U.S. Capitol building. Two years later the government acquired (again for $10,000) a pendant to the Yellowstone painting: Moran's *Chasm of the Colorado* (1873–74, fig. 72). Sharing the gigantic size of the Yellowstone picture (7′ x 12′), it also, like the earlier painting, testifies to Moran's fascination with earth-shaping processes, though the emphasis this time is on water rather than fire. Also in keeping with the Yellowstone painting, *The Chasm of the Colorado* grew out

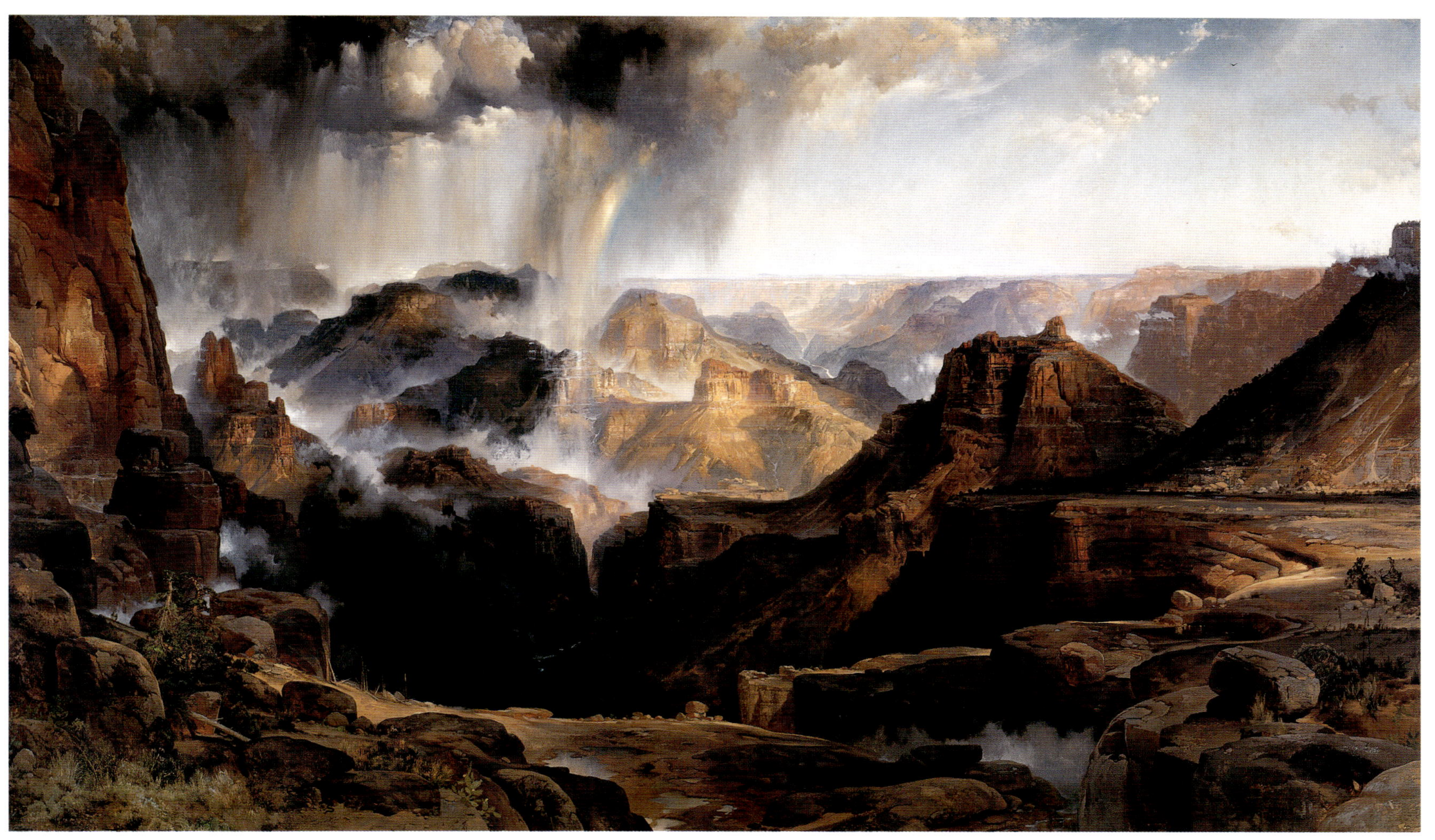

Fig. 72. Thomas Moran, *The Chasm of the Colorado*, 1873–74.
Oil on canvas, 84 x 144 in. (213.4 x 365.8 cm).
Department of the Interior Museum, Washington, D.C.

of Moran's experience on one of the western surveys, in this case Powell's Geographical and Topographical Survey of the Colorado River of the West.

Major Powell led his survey party into the canyon country of Utah and Arizona in the summer of 1873. Moran and the journalist J. E. Colburn spent over a month with them, exploring the arid regions around the Grand Canyon and what is now Zion National Park. During that time, under the guidance of Powell and the other survey scientists, Moran continued his geological education. The letters he wrote from the field as well as the paintings that resulted from the trip offer evidence of his adeptness as a pupil.

In his letters to his wife, Mary, he detailed a few of the rigors of the trip, including tarantulas creeping over his saddlepack and rattlesnakes gliding between the legs of survey members, things, he reported with some restraint, that "made us a little uncomfortable at night." He also described to Mary the geology of the countryside. Writing from Kanab on 13 August, he told her of passing through "a volcanic country full of old craters & lava."[40] A few days later he had arrived at the Grand Canyon itself: "The whole gorge for miles lay beneath us and it was by far the most awfully grand and impressive scene I have ever yet seen. . . . The color of the Grand Cañon itself is red, a light Indian Red, and the material sandstone and red marble and is in terraces all the way down. All above the cañon is variously colored sandstone mainly a light flesh or cream color and worn into very fine forms."[41]

Not only did Moran quickly and accurately perceive the rock types that formed the canyon, he also learned much about the geological processes that had created it. Some years later he explained the canyon's formation: "A feature of the Colorado worthy of note is that it is about the same level as it always was, the country gradually rising and the river cutting down with a pace equal to the uprising of the land."[42] This was exactly how Powell had explained the canyon's formation in his official survey report. In that report he argued that contrary to what one might expect, the canyon was not formed by the river burrowing ever deeper into the stratified rock, but by the river remaining at the same level while the land rose up around it (or, as Elizabeth Childs has explained even more clearly, the river acted like a whirling stationary saw, against which the earth gradually pushed up).[43] Powell added that while the main canyon was created by this interaction of river and rising earth, many of the other geological features: the buttes, the pinnacles of rock, the side canyons (all so prominent in Moran's picture), were formed primarily by the action of raindrops. "[N]o human hand," he wrote, "has placed a block in all those wonderful structures. The rain drops of unreckoned ages have cut them all from solid rock."[44] As both Joni Kinsey and Elizabeth Childs have made clear, it is exactly this theory of the land's formation that Moran gave form to in *The Chasm of the Colorado.* In the picture, he concentrates his efforts on describing the sculpting action of rushing, running, falling, dripping water. Everywhere the work of aqueous erosion is evident.

From a vantage point high on the north rim of the Kaibab Plateau, the viewer looks out over miles and miles of arid canyonland. A broad sandstone ledge, more than 5,000 feet above the rushing Colorado River, forms the foreground of the painting. On the left, a reddish wall of rock rises from behind a pile of boulders. A rattlesnake winds its way between the loose stones, and a few prickly pear cacti and stunted firs have taken tenuous root in their crevices. On the edge of the rim, rounded sandstone boulders balance precariously, reminders, as Kinsey has noted, of "transition and change."[45] The ledge ends abruptly, plunging into a black chasm — not the Grand Canyon itself, but, according to a contemporary broadside, "a lateral chasm communicating with the Grand Canyon, but unprovided with water, except from the chance effect of storms."[46] The Colorado River, a thin white ribbon, appears and disappears between the serrated plateaus in the center of the picture.

Heightening the tension, a violent thunderstorm sweeps across the bleak scene. Alternating bands of brilliant sunshine and deep shadow mark its progress over the landscape. It has recently passed over the foreground ledge, leaving puddles in the sandstone depressions, their surfaces smooth enough to reflect the gray sky above. To the left, over the gloomy mouth of the canyon, water cascades from black-bottomed clouds like a celestial waterfall. The descending torrents beat against the naked brown rocks, continuing the work of erosion that has been progressing for millions of years. To the right of the thunderclouds the sky has cleared, and sunlight sparkles across the distant plateau country. In the very center of the picture a partial rainbow fringes the storm clouds, a sign, Kinsey argues, of hope and redemption in this barren desolate land described by one critic as an "appalling chaos of cliffs and chasms."[47]

The fast-moving storm clouds, the shifting patterns of light and dark, the tentatively balanced boulders, and the dying firs on the plateau rim all underscore the transitory appearance of the scene, reminding us of the changes continually wrought by natural processes. Numerous details allude in particular to the work of water in crafting and recrafting the scene. In the foreground, the gray-white pools of water catch the viewer's eye, their rounded contours echoing the water-smoothed shapes of the dark rocks beside them. Prominent, too, are the low-lying clouds — some so heavy with moisture that they have sunk into the canyons, their presence recalling the water that has cut the chasms from the solid rock. Most obviously, the violent thunderstorm dramatizes the work of aqueous erosion. The sheets of water descending from the storm clouds are forming instant waterfalls on the middle-ground peaks. These gleaming silver streams are cascading into the chasm, carving the rock as they descend. This detail, as Childs has pointed out, echoes a passage in Powell's official report: "A little shower falls, and the water gathers rapidly into streams, and plunges headlong down the steep slopes, bearing with it loads of sand."[48]

The close connection between Powell's words and Moran's images was hardly coincidental. Moran consulted with Powell as he worked on the canvas, much as he had with Hayden on the Yellowstone picture, and Powell later expressed great satisfaction with the results. "[I]t not only [missing word] the truth," Powell wrote, "but it displays the beauty of the truth." He was especially struck by "the curve of the amphitheater on the right. . . . While it is an effective feature in the picture, it is also a geological section; the great columns in the further angle; the well-defined bedding; the beveling down of the edges of the beds in the middle of the curve; the water stains — all of the details have been carefully studied."[49]

In his lengthy remarks about the painting, Powell underscores the tentative nature of each element of the scene: the vegetation, the water pockets, and the land itself. Of the dying evergreens in the lower left corner of the canvas, which Powell calls "very effective," he writes, "The home of the fir is on the plateau above, where they abound and grow to giant form, but occasionally they find their way down to a lower level, tempted by some local gathering of moisture; but in the progress of the erosion of these chasms by storm, places favorable to their growth are soon drained, when they wither and their dead trunks remain to attest to the ever-changing conditions under which such vegetation must flourish."[50]

The water pockets left by the passing shower, gleaming in the center foreground, Powell notes, will "soon evaporate under the power of the southern sun." Of the topography, he says that Moran chose a "place where the side of the plateau had been deeply eroded by a cataract stream." Together these details describe a place that has changed in the past, is changing in the present, and will continue to change in the future.

Powell's words were repeated in numerous reviews of the painting, encouraging the public to read it in these same geological terms. They certainly affected one visitor to a private exhibition of the painting, who remarked: "This strange and wild scene, it should be bourne in mind, is not the work of volcanic action or upheaval force, but simply the quiet and progressive work of erosion by water — thousands and thousands of years have witnessed the progress of the work."[51]

"THE MOUNTAIN OF THE HOLY CROSS"

In August 1874, a year after he returned from the Grand Canyon, Moran headed west again, this time with the Hayden survey. His ambition that summer was to reach the fabled Mountain of the Holy Cross and record its image on yet another of his enormous canvases. This peak, on the western slopes of the Rocky Mountains about 100 miles from Denver, has emblazoned on its eastern flank a white cross formed by two intersecting snow-filled crevasses. Moran's friend William Henry Jackson had photographed the peak in 1873 on assignment with the Hayden survey. When Moran saw Jackson's images he resolved, according to Thurman Wilkins, to paint a picture of it, which would "rival, if not excel, his panoramas of Yellowstone and the Colorado chasm."[52] He found this snowy mountain cross an irresistible subject. At a time when religious skepticism was on the rise and Darwinian science was dealing daily blows to the unity of God and nature, the pure white cross, hidden amid the undefiled peaks of the West, seemed to offer compelling testimony to the sanctity of nature and the immanence of the divine.

The major painting that resulted from Moran's 1874 journey was *The Mountain of the Holy Cross* (1875, fig. 73). The artist was pleased enough with the painting that he planned to exhibit it together with the Yellowstone and Colorado pictures at the Philadelphia Centennial in 1876.[53] These three pictures share not only their large scale and topographically striking subjects, but also their scientific content. With *The Mountain of the Holy Cross,* Moran again was concerned with geological processes, but instead of fire and water, this canvas evokes the work of snow and ice. As the broadside published to coincide with the picture's exhibition in New York explained, the picture is full of evidences of "glacial action of a former period."[54]

The glacial geology of the Holy Cross valley was described

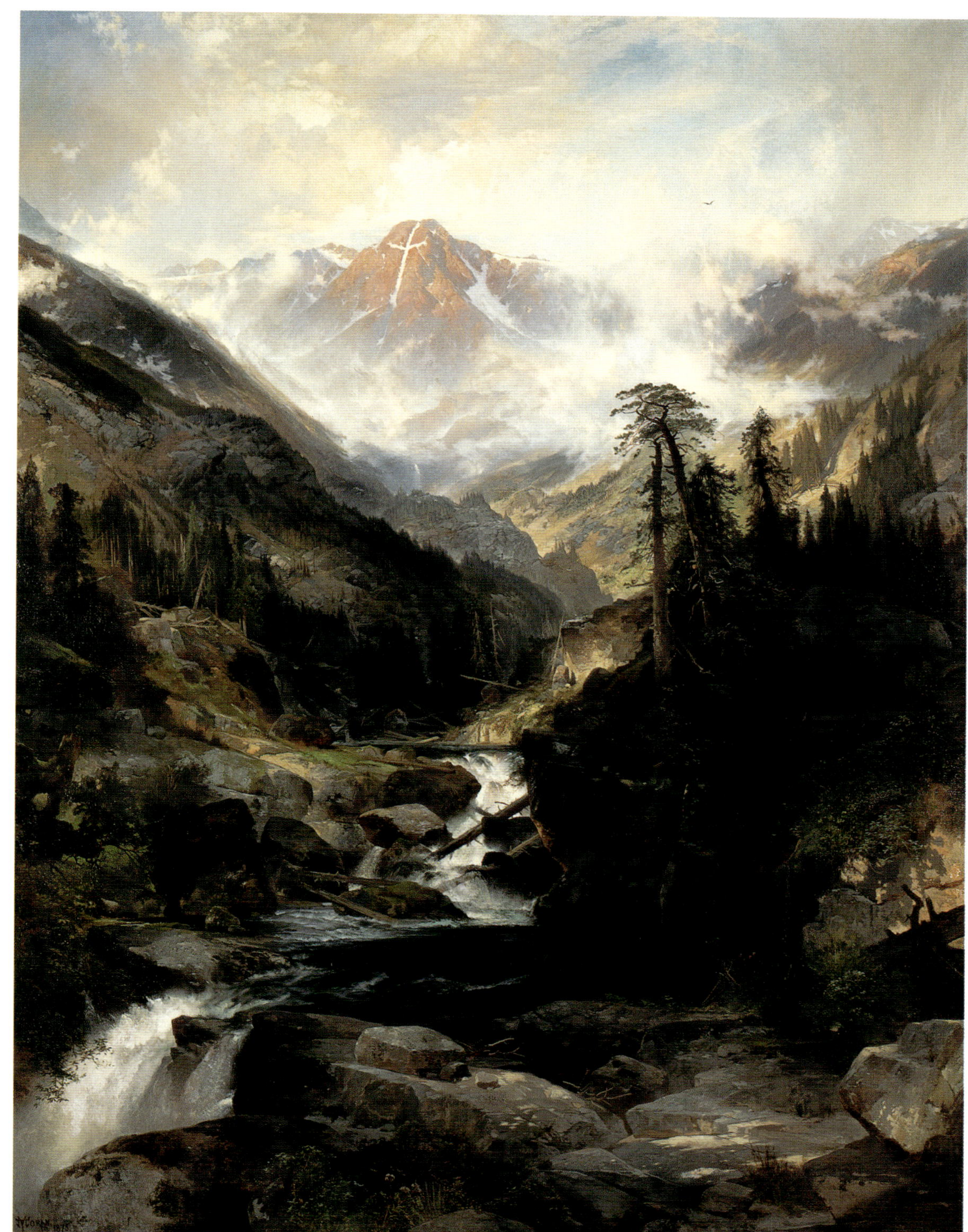

Fig. 73. Thomas Moran, *The Mountain of the Holy Cross*, 1875. Oil on canvas, 82 1/8 x 64 1/4 in. (208.6 x 163.2 cm). Autry Museum of Western Heritage, Los Angeles

by Hayden in one of his popular publications: *The Yellowstone National Park, and the Mountain Regions of Portions of Idaho, Nevada, Colorado, and Utah* (1876). The book was illustrated with chromolithographs of Moran's paintings, including *The Mountain of the Holy Cross*. Of the scene described by Moran, Hayden wrote: "This valley, which now forms the rocky bed of the torrent, was once the bed of an ancient glacier, and its bottom and sides, for a distance of 2000 feet or more, are rounded and scarred by the action of ice." Most striking of the valley's glacial features, he noted, are the ice-sculpted "roches moutonnées."

> Looking down the valley from the summit of the mountain, the eye rests upon one of the most remarkable illustrations of what are called in Switzerland "Roches Moutonnées," or "sheep-backed rocks," so called because they look at a distance like a flock of enormous recumbent sheep. These rocks which are scattered irregularly over the valley, vary in height from ten to fifty feet, and the interstices between them are covered with fallen pines, sometimes forming a network several feet high.[55]

Most contemporary reviews of Moran's *The Mountain of the Holy Cross* mention the icy history of the spot and direct the viewers' attention to particular evidences in the painting of the work of glaciers past. One reviewer pointed out that around the summit of the mountain "lie irregular snow-fields, with at least one century-old glacier, showing at the picture left of the peak."[56]

The artist himself in his letters from the site revealed his knowledge of the area's geology: "The descent into the valley was even steeper than the ascent had been but was freer from fallen timber. We got down all right and without accident, but Horror!! the way up the valley was infinitely worse than anything we had yet encountered. A swamp, covered with the worst of fallen logs & projecting through which were the *Roche Moutonnée* or Sheep Rocks, rounded & smooth & slippery, varying from 10 to 40 feet high."[57]

The roches moutonnées figure prominently in the completed canvas, and Moran took pride in their delineation. These granite outcroppings with their smoothed and furrowed surfaces "are realized," he once said, "to the farthest point I could carry them . . . I elaborated them out of pure love of rocks. I have studied rocks carefully and like to represent them."[58]

At least three different narratives are embedded in *The Mountain of the Holy Cross* and these "rounded & smooth & slippery" rocks are central to all of them. The first is a personal narrative of the artist's (and the survey's) physically grueling yet ultimately triumphant conquest of the site—the story Moran told with such enthusiasm in the passage from his letters just quoted; the second a scientific narrative of the site's geological past; the third a Christian narrative of spiritual triumph over adversity. In the first narrative, the rocks testify to the difficulties the explorers faced and the obstacles they overcame; in the second, they evoke the grinding polishing action of ancient glaciers, which, like the explorers, inched their way over the landscape, carving out paths through the wilderness; in the third, they emblematize the trials encountered on the journey through life.

Opposite: Detail of Fig. 73

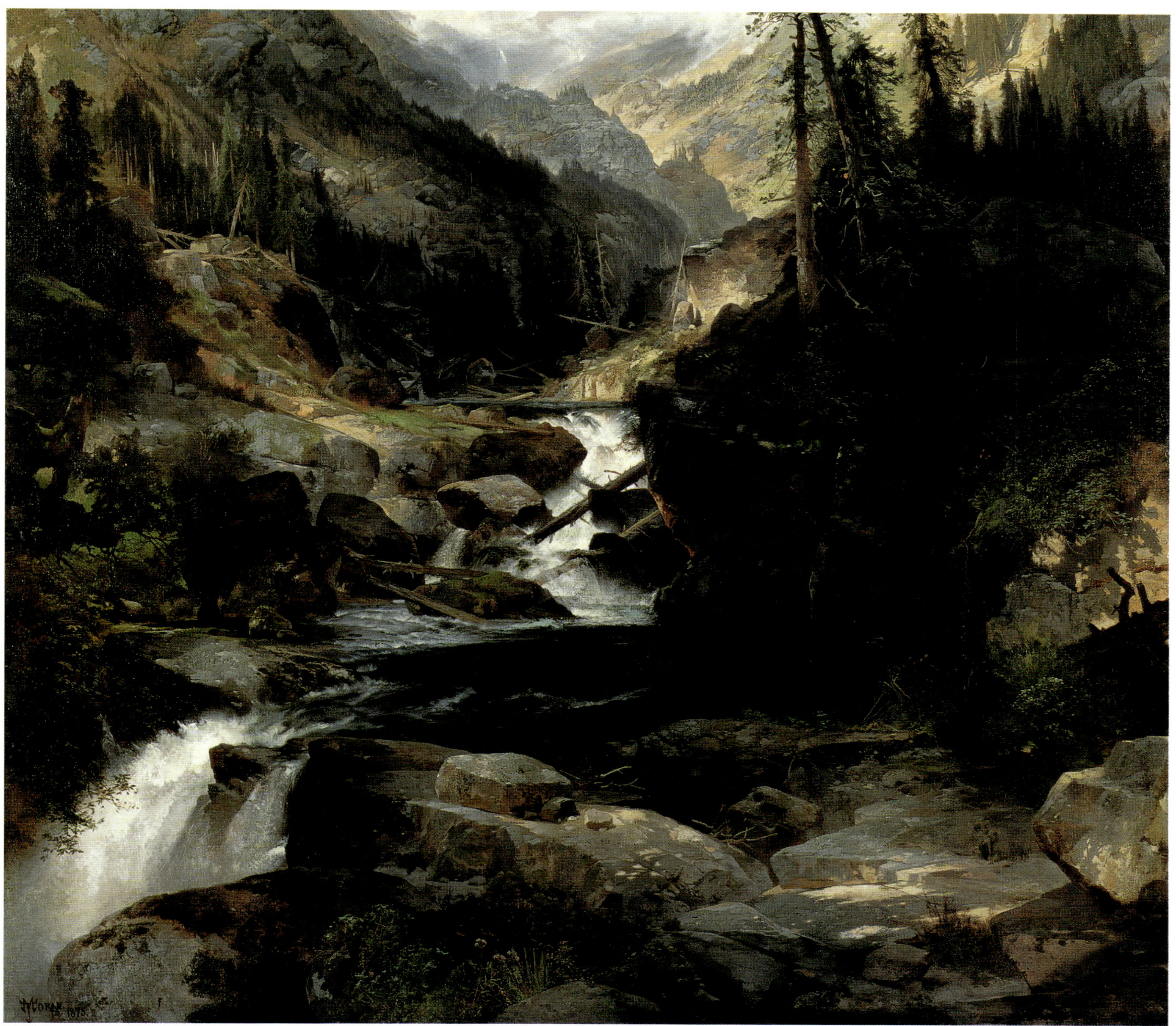

Even more important to these narratives than the roches moutonnées is the shining white path, the principal organizing motif of the picture, which winds its way up (and down) the surface of this large vertical canvas (7 feet tall). Formed, in the lower part of the composition, by the foaming waters of Holy Cross Creek, this path is framed on either side by dark masses of ice-sheared rock and evergreen forest. Its course is often broken by fallen timber and slick moss-covered boulders, and sometimes it becomes lost behind bends in the rugged landscape. From the lower left corner, it climbs up a series of cascades until it reaches a waterfall in the distance. There the path merges with a wreath of white mist, which simultaneously rings the cross and masks and mystifies the approach to it. The white form of the cross is tilted backwards slightly, pointing up into the heavens. The journey up the canvas is clearly, as Joni Kinsey has discussed, a sort of "pilgrim's progress," a natural allegory for the struggles of a Christian on the path to redemption, the same trope that animated Church's *Heart of the Andes* (as discussed in chapter 3).[59]

At the same time, the white path suggests the glacial history of the spot. If one follows it down rather than up, it recalls the white glaciers that once flowed down from the mountain summits to carve the landscape below. This geological story was noticed and commented on in many contemporary reviews of the painting; indeed it was noted far more often than the picture's more obvious Christian symbolism — though not always in terms of approbation.

This painting, so full of spiritual and geological lessons, enjoyed considerable popularity in its day and was reproduced often in many different forms and formats. Yet despite this positive popular reception, by the time of its public unveiling in 1875 authoritative critical opinion was turning decidedly against such "sensation pictures," as they were called at the time. Such pictures, many critics were arguing, were too much about science and exploration and too little about art. They were imbued with too many facts and too few sentiments.

An 1875 review of *The Mountain of the Holy Cross* in the *Boston Daily Advertiser*, while lengthy, offers an excellent summary of the emerging critical consensus on such paintings. The writer seems to be reacting against the publicity surrounding the painting's public exhibition in Boston that fall. The audience, he felt, was being told all too much about the artist's hardships in reaching the site and of the extent to which the image is true to the topography and geology of the region. The painting, he writes,

> professedly calls for public approbation, more particularly for its merits as a portrait of the scene it represents than from its attributes as a work of art. We learn that the Mountain of the Holy Cross is in the heart of the Rocky Mountains of Colorado, and in an almost impenetrable wilderness. . . .
>
> All this is very interesting to know; it adds weight to the testimony that the picture is an authentic portrait. But . . . it does not yet drop one grain into the scale of its worth as an artistic production. As a geological chart, showing mountain formation and traces of glacial action, it will have its attractions; as a photographic likeness of a remote corner of the Rocky Mountains, interesting from its curious peak of rock archi-

> tecture . . . it will also count numbers of admirers. And with all this it may be far from being a great picture, in the best sense of the word. It is unfortunate, both for the author of the picture and the public, that they should be introduced to each other in such a way. That the artist should bring a certificate of his physical energy and courage, of his admiration for curious natural formations, and, above all, of his willingness to foster the spirit which prompts so many of us to cry continually of anything American — "the best in the world, the largest in the world," — that he should present this certificate rather than the recommendation that he is a man of refined taste and strong sentiment, is, it is plain, unfortunate for all parties concerned.[60]

Such reviews stung Moran, who felt himself unjustly accused of literalism and lack of sentiment. He saw himself as an interpreter of nature, not an imitator. Literal fidelity, he continually asserted, was not his aim. "Art is not Nature," he told a reporter in 1879; "an aggregation of ten thousand facts may add nothing to a picture, but be rather the destruction of it. The literal truth counts for nothing; . . . The mere restatement of an external scene is never a work of art, is never a picture."[61] He did not set out to transcribe particular views, but to convey to the observer through his complex, carefully crafted studio compositions "the impression produced by nature on himself."[62] Yet the abundant quantities of sharply focused detail in his paintings, their convincing plunges into space, and their compelling atmospheric perspective — all contributing to the verisimilitude that seemed to efface the artist's presence — combined with his enlistment of the "testimonies of learned geologists" to their "truth," suggested to many late-nineteenth-century critics that Moran had lost sight of art in his dedication to science.

Sentiments like those expressed by the Boston critic were both cause and effect of the unraveling ties between art and science, most particularly between geology and landscape painting, in the last decades of the nineteenth century. Increasingly artists were expected to emphasize formal features above subject matter, and sentiment above fact. And by sentiment, these critics did not mean the awe-inspiring sublime (an emotion that shaped all of Moran's canvases and that had become entwined with American nationalism and manifest destiny). Instead they sought a quieter, more personal sentiment, expressed in a more individual and preferably more modern style. Moran's paintings, as full of revelations as they are — revelations about topography, and geology, and the mutability of matter, about the creative work of water, fire, and ice — no longer suited the informed taste of the time.

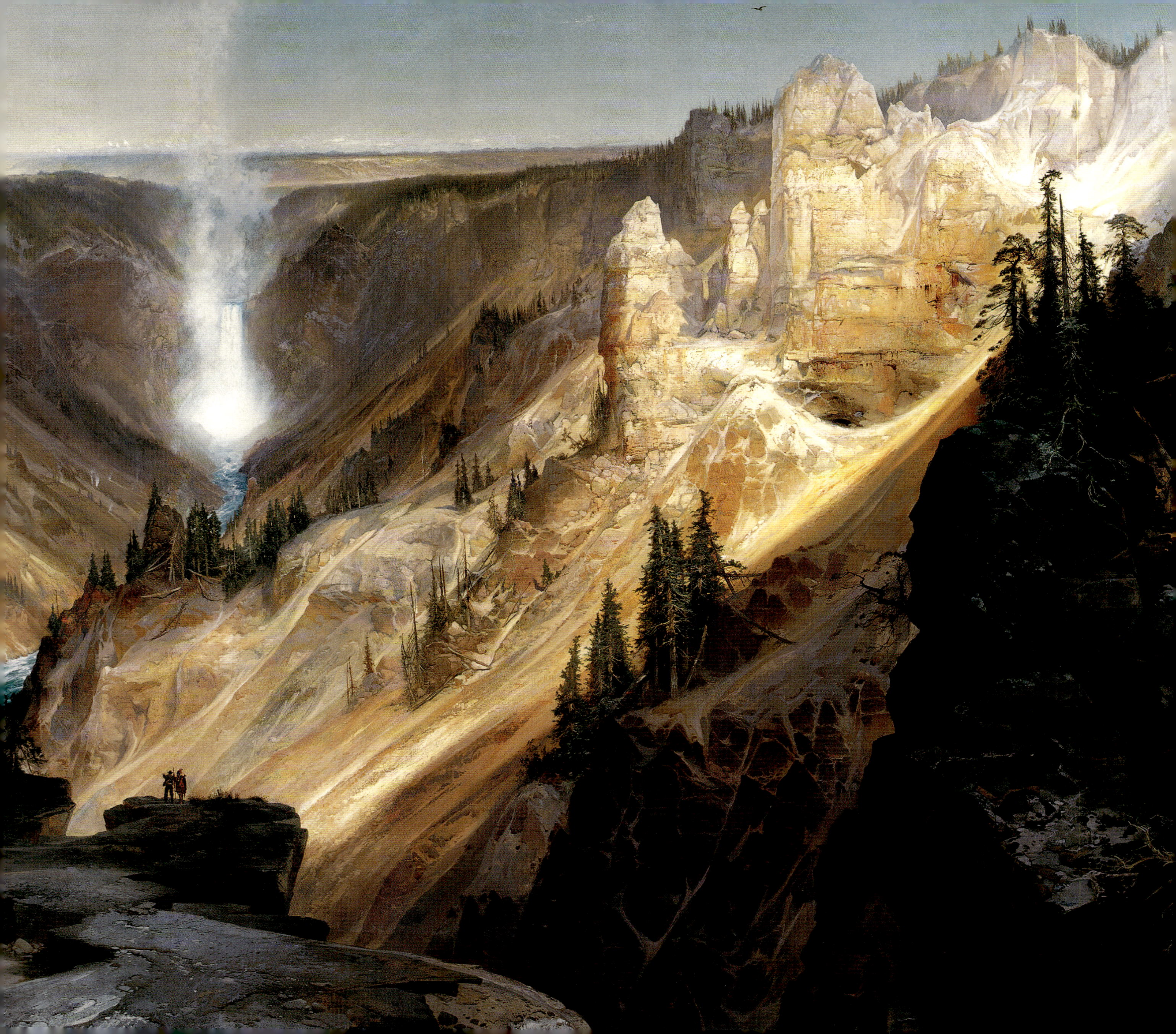

Conclusion

NO MESSY PUBLIC DIVORCE marked the demise of the marriage of geology and landscape painting in nineteenth-century America. Instead, by the 1870s they had begun to drift slowly and quietly apart. Aging artists and critics, including many discussed in this book, carried their geologically informed methods of imaging and critiquing landscapes into the early decades of the twentieth century. Thomas Moran, for example, until his death in 1926, continued to paint landscapes exploring the dynamic characteristics of the earth's crust. His brushwork softened, and his later canvases often seem suffused with longing for the vanishing West of his younger days, yet they continue to be informed by his knowledge of geology. Indeed, in 1924 the geologist Edward Orton Jr. was thrilled to acquire Moran's *Petrified Forest* (1904), which he intended for the walls of The Edward Orton Memorial Library of Geology in Columbus, Ohio. The painting, he wrote the dealer, exactly suited his needs since it "illustrates rather strikingly the well known geological process by which fossils are preserved."[1]

But despite Orton's enthusiasm, by the turn of the century Moran was generally considered a conservative artist, clinging to the ideas of a past era. Those landscape painters who came of age in the decades after the Civil War, many working in the imported Barbizon and Impressionist modes, had little interest in geology or indeed in any of the natural sciences.

This declining interest can be attributed to many causes: shifts in public taste, the rise of new artistic imperatives, and changes in geology itself. Since to treat this topic thoroughly would require another book, this short conclusion will attempt only to sketch in some of the factors that opened and widened the gulf between landscape painting and geology in the closing decades of the nineteenth century.

Geology was a very different science in 1900 than it was in 1825.[2] In the early nineteenth century, geology was a young and exciting science bound in many ways to revealed religion. Its practitioners' revelations—including the expansion of the age of the earth, the re-creation of vanished species, and the reconstruction of ancient ice ages—captured the public's imagination. Amateurs crowded the field certain that they could make meaningful contributions to its advancement.

Opposite: Detail of Fig. 71

Fashionable gentlemen kept mineral cabinets, collected fossils, and read the latest geological literature. Many of the period's most prominent geologists, including Benjamin Silliman, Charles Lyell, Louis Agassiz, and Ferdinand Hayden, actively encouraged this public involvement. They wrote books and articles intended for public consumption and traveled the lecture circuits with popular accounts of their latest discoveries.

By the end of the nineteenth century, geology had lost some of its popular appeal and almost all of its aristocratic cachet. It was becoming simultaneously too familiar and too arcane. Geology texts aimed at general readers continued to appear, and the Chautauqua Movement carried on the work of the earlier lyceums by sponsoring occasional lectures by geologists. But the novelty of the science's earlier discoveries had worn off (indeed, they were being incorporated into standard school curricula), and the new questions geologists were investigating, such as orogeny (how mountains are formed) and microscopical petrography, though interesting, did not have the same potential to shake people's perceptions of their place on the planet.

Geology was also becoming more professionalized, the domain of credentialed experts rather than inquisitive amateurs. This was tied to the growing rigor of geological training, with the serious pursuit of the science often requiring the use of specialized equipment and a knowledge of upper-level mathematics and chemistry. As university departments of geology began to flourish and as professional societies and professional journals developed, geologists began more and more to speak *to* each other and write *for* each other rather than for the public. The literature grew more complex and technical, the vocabulary more abstruse, making it difficult for the average reader to decipher. Rising standards for entrance to national and international geological societies also worked to exclude many laymen. Their enthusiasm dampened by these developments, many members of the public (at least the scientifically inclined, along with the popular journals that catered to them) began to turn their attention to some of the newer, human-centered sciences, including psychology and optics.

For artists, it was the elite's loss of interest in geology that had the greatest impact. When Thomas Cole launched his career in the 1820s, geology was the province of the wealthy, educated, exhibition-going, art-buying segment of the American populace; it thus behooved him to know something about it. By the late nineteenth century, with geology being taught in the public schools, knowledge of it no longer identified one as a member of the upper class. Wealthy Americans had by then turned to other ways of distinguishing themselves from the masses, conspicuous consumption (so distasteful to Cole's patrons) chief among them. Many of these fashionable men and women, instead of passing their vacations hiking the Catskills or the White Mountains picking up specimens for their mineral cabinets, traveled to Europe, buying Old Master paintings and Louis XV chairs to fill their palatial mansions. Landscape painters seeking to appeal to this class had to reorient themselves, turning from realistic representations of the American wilderness toward European subjects and European styles. John Durand, son of Asher Durand, explained the declining fortunes of his father and the other members of what he called "The American School" of landscape painting:

> Through the profits of mines, railway enterprises, and cattle-raising, it [a wave of wealth] ran mountain high. A new generation of energetic men indifferent to Eastern ideals spring up, and craving new outlets for the expenditure of their fortunes as well as new criterions of social distinction, find these in the adoption of a taste for art. Western millionaires begin to buy French pictures right and left. . . . Native students, finding foreign art in the ascendent, abandon original perceptions and imitate the methods and aims of a foreign school.[3]

When their upper-crust patrons abandoned geology, artists lost one of their major motivations for studying it.

Other changes in geology were also rendering it less useful and less accessible to artists. In the early part of the nineteenth century, geology was still closely tied to natural history, its methodology revolving around observation, collection, and classification. Its findings, rooted in visual description, could be readily expressed through the pictorial language of drawing and painting. As geology became more a science of analysis and experimentation, concerned with the chemical components of matter and with calculations as much as observations, its insights were no longer so easily expressed through art.

The disentanglement of geology from religion also dampened its usefulness for artists. In the transcendentalist view of nature, so pervasive in the United States in the mid-nineteenth century, each natural form was invested with spiritual meaning. It was a work of God, a physical manifestation of the Creator's thought. The contemplation of nature was an avenue to divinity, a way of apprehending God. Geology could thus be seen as a pious pursuit, leading to a deeper understanding of the laws of creation and of God's will.

Ironically, geology and the other natural sciences helped undermine this spiritual view of the world. In 1851 Ruskin wailed, "If only the geologists would let me alone, I could do very well, but those dreadful Hammers! I hear their clink at the end of every cadence of Bible verses."[4] A few years later, Darwin's theories, too, were leveling blows at the union of religion and science. In evolutionary theory, individual trees and animals were presented not as careful creations of God but as the result of random combinations of the gene pool. Looking at nature through Darwinian eyes, it no longer seemed an expression of God's beneficent spirit, but a raw, violent, aggressive realm governed by impersonal laws. Because of these developments, Carol Christ argues, "Victorians gradually came to perceive nature as a collection of disparate forms with nothing to offer but the experience of their own sensations."[5] As natural forms were divested of their spiritual meanings, they lost some of their resonance as pictorial elements. No longer could they be counted on — as Cole, Durand, and Church had counted on them — to evoke moral and spiritual ideas.

Artists' loss of faith in science as a conduit to the Creator was paralleled by scientists' loss of faith in the ability of artistic representations to capture the truths of nature. This was tied to shifting attitudes toward the role of human subjectivity in the perception and representation of natural phenomena.[6] In the romantic era, artists and scientists alike recognized and even celebrated the subjective nature of human vision. Both believed that they brought to their observations of the natural world a shaping intelligence, a transforming passion, that allowed them to see beyond and beneath the surface of things. It allowed them to apprehend the larger patterns operating in nature, to sort out the telling facts from the others, and to discover the larger moral and spiritual lessons embedded in the natural world. Scientists, accepting and valuing the transformatory powers of the observer's gaze, were happy to embrace artistic interpretations of nature, making use of them in their own work to illustrate reports and so forth.

But in the late nineteenth century, scientists became extraordinarily wary of the role of human subjectivity in the scientific enterprise, so wary that they sought to suppress it as far as possible. Fearful that the interposition of the observer's subjectivity could dangerously distort the object or phenomena perceived, they sought ways to "let nature speak for itself."[7] Objectivity of the sort that Lorraine Daston and Peter Galison have labeled "noninterventionist" or "mechanical" objectivity (an objectivity that "attempts to eliminate the mediating presence of the observer") came to assume the status of a moral imperative in scientific circles. Seeking images that could be "certified free of human interference, [scientists] turned to mechanically produced images to eliminate suspect mediation."[8] They embraced images produced by spectroscopes, X-ray machines, and cameras, believing that these mechanical devices could screen out the contaminating subjectivities of their operators. For many scientists of this era (though certainly not all) the photograph with its potential for sharply focused, almost infinite detail became "a primary metaphor for objective truth."[9]

While scientists were calling for images that could be produced without the distorting interference of human intelligence and sentiments, artists were moving in the opposite direction, embracing their subjective responses to the natural world. Even before the Civil War, some American artists had begun to chafe at the strictures they felt were imposed on them by the prevailing realist aesthetic. They felt that critical demands for strict adherence to physical facts suppressed their creativity, stifled their imaginations, and transformed them into slaves of nature. Literal fidelity, they argued, was often achieved at the expense of higher qualities such as composition, organization, and coloring. The language of art was sacrificed to the language of nature. The English Pre-Raphaelite Edward Burne-Jones, in describing his views on direct transcripts from nature, expressed the thoughts of many American artists: "I suppose by the time the 'photographic artist' can give us all the colours as correctly as the shapes, people will begin to find out that the realism they talk about isn't art at all but science; interesting, no doubt, as a scientific achievement but nothing more. Someone will have succeeded in making reflections in a looking glass permanent under certain conditions. What has that to do with art?"[10]

To invest their representations of nature with human meaning, landscape painters in the later nineteenth century shifted their emphasis from natural facts to their subjective apprehension, from the forms themselves to the feelings and sensations they aroused. Instead of mirroring nature, the canvas would mirror the state of the artist's mind. Universals came to be sought "not in the objects of perception but in the categories of perception, in imaginative activity."[11] Émile Zola's definition of Impressionism: "Nature seen through a temperament" succinctly expresses this new approach to painting the natural world—this new valuation and valorization of the artist's individual subjectivity in confrontation with nature.

While Church and Durand had sought to efface their artistic presence and give beholders the impression that they were standing before nature rather than a picture, in the late nineteenth century artists deliberately asserted their roles as mediators of their scenes, calling attention to themselves through visible brushstrokes, exaggerated colors, and other pictorial devices. Style, and the individuality and originality of that style, came to be seen as more important than subject matter in evaluating the meaning and content and quality of a painting; the things represented mattered less than how they were represented. Instead of a communal attempt to create didactic works that would educate and elevate the public and fan the formation of a coherent national identity, landscape painting came to be regarded more as an avenue for personal expression, and the stronger the artistic personality and the greater the originality of the work, the higher its perceived "quality."

James McNeill Whistler, a leader of the Art for Art's Sake movement that promoted the artist's liberation from subject matter, argued that a painting is first and foremost an arrangement of lines and shapes and colors; there is no need for it to teach a lesson or tell a story; it is enough for it to offer a pleasing, harmonious composition of forms. A knowledge of geology was of little service to artists creating works within this new value system. As abstraction swept the American art world in the opening decades of the twentieth century, geology faded from the picture.

Notes

ABBREVIATIONS

AAA	Archives of American Art, Smithsonian Institution, Washington, D.C.
DIA	Detroit Institute of Arts, Detroit, Michigan
NYSL	New York State Library, Albany

INTRODUCTION

1. Review of Parker Cleaveland's *An Elementary Treatise on Mineralogy and Geology*, *North American Review* 5 (September 1817): 409–10.

2. Samuel L. Metcalf, "The Interest and Importance of Scientific Geology as a Subject for Study," *Knickerbocker* 3 (April 1834): 227.

3. *New England Magazine* (April 1835) quoted in Dennis R. Dean, "The Influence of Geology on American Thought and Literature," in *Two Hundred Years of Geology in America: Proceedings of the New Hampshire Bicentennial Conference on the History of Geology*, ed. Cecil J. Schneer (Hanover, N.H.: University Press of New England, 1979), 293; *American Journal of Science* 41 (October 1841): 271.

4. On the popularity of geology in Great Britain see Lynn Barber, *The Heyday of Natural History, 1820–1870* (London: Jonathan Cape, 1980); Charles Coulton Gillispie, *Genesis and Geology* (Cambridge, Mass.: Harvard University Press, 1951). On European artists' fascination with geology see Timothy F. Mitchell, *Art and Science in German Landscape Painting, 1770–1840* (New York: Oxford University Press, 1993); Charlotte Klonk, *Science and the Perception of Nature* (New Haven, Conn., and London: Yale University Press, 1996); Barbara Maria Stafford, *Voyage into Substance: Art, Science, Nature and the Illustrated Travel Account, 1760–1840* (Cambridge, Mass.: MIT Press, 1984).

5. On the status of the natural sciences in nineteenth-century America see George H. Daniels, *American Science in the Age of Jackson* (New York: Columbia University Press, 1968); Nathan Reingold, *Science in American Society: A Documentary History* (New York: Hill and Wang, 1964); Elizabeth B. Keeney, *The Botanizers: Amateur Scientists in Nineteenth-Century America* (Chapel Hill: University of North Carolina Press, 1992); Sally Gregory Kohlstedt, "Parlors, Primers, and Public Schooling: Education for Science in Nineteenth-Century America," *Isis* 81 (1990): 425–45; and Kohlstedt's "Curiosities and Cabinets: Natural History Museums and Education on the Antebellum Campus," *Isis* 79 (1988): 405–26.

6. Gillispie, *Genesis and Geology*, 39–40.

7. Louis Agassiz, *Principles of Zoology* (Boston: Gould, Kendall, and Lincoln, 1848), 206.

8. *North American Review* 42 (April 1836): 425.

9. A great deal has been written about the complex relationship between geology and religion in the nineteenth century. See, for example, Gillispie, *Genesis and Geology*; John Hedley Brooke, "The Natural Theology of the Geologists: Some Theological Strata," in *Images of the Earth*,

ed. L. J. Jordanova and Roy S. Porter, *Boston Society for the History of Science Monographs*, vol. 1 (1979), 39–64; Herbert Hovenkamp, *Science and Religion in America, 1800–1860* (Philadelphia: University of Pennsylvania Press, 1978); *Science and Religious Belief: A Selection of Recent Historical Studies*, ed. C. A. Russell (London: University of London Press, 1973).

10. See Barbara M. Cross, *Horace Bushnell: Minister to a Changing America* (Chicago: University of Chicago Press, 1958), especially 120–21.

11. Charles Lyell, *Principles of Geology*. 3 vols. (New York: D. Appleton, 1859), 1:60–61 (first published in London, 1830–33).

12. "Professor Hitchcock's Report on the Geology, etc. of Massachusetts," *North American Review* 42 (April 1836): 425.

13. Henry Adams, *The Education of Henry Adams: An Autobiography* (1906; Boston: Houghton Mifflin, 1918), 225.

14. "Geological," *Knickerbocker* 60 (August 1862): 140.

15. Richard Shafer Trump, "Life and Works of Albert Bierstadt" (Ph.D. diss., Ohio State University, 1963), 109.

16. Fitz Hugh Ludlow, *The Heart of the Continent* (Cambridge, Mass., 1870), 288, quoted in Trump, "Life and Works," 109.

17. "The Yellowstone National Park," *Scribner's Monthly* 4 (May 1872): 120–21.

18. Louis Agassiz, *Geological Sketches* (Boston: Fields, Osgood, and Co., 1866), 1.

19. Charles Lyell, *Travels in North America in the Years 1841–2* (New York: Wiley and Putnam, 1845), 1:15.

20. Metcalf, "Interest and Importance," 226.

21. Ibid.

22. Review of William Swainson's *Study of Natural History*, *North American Review* 41 (October 1835): 409.

23. Jules Marcou, *Life, Letters, and Works of Louis Agassiz* (New York: MacMillan and Co., 1896), 281.

24. G. W. Featherstonhaugh, *Geological Report of an Examination of the Elevated Country between the Missouri and Red Rivers* (Washington, D.C.: Gales and Seaton, 1835), 11.

25. Lyell, *Travels in North America*, 1:13–14.

26. Benjamin Silliman, "Address Before the American Association of Geologists and Naturalists," *American Journal of Science* 43 (October 1842): 236.

27. Quoted in Franklin W. Kelly, "Myth, Allegory, and Science: Thomas Cole's Paintings of Mount Etna," *Arts in Virginia* 23 (1983): 13.

28. Louis Agassiz, *Contributions to the Natural History of the United States* (Boston: Little, Brown and Co., 1857–62), 1:x.

29. S. S. Schweber, "Scientists as Intellectuals: The Early Victorians," in *Victorian Science and Victorian Values: Literary Perspectives*, ed. James Paradis and Thomas Postlewait (New Brunswick, N.J.: Rutgers University Press, 1985), 1.

30. The artists, writers, critics, and geologists discussed in this book are all men, and men definitely dominated these fields in the mid-nineteenth century. There were, however, at least a few women who can be located at the intersection of art and geology. Cecilia Beaux (1855–1926), for example, began her career creating lithographs of fossils to illustrate the geological reports of the distinguished paleontologist Edward Cope. See Cecilia Beaux, *Background with Figures* (Boston: Houghton Mifflin, 1930), 75–83.

31. Century Association members in the second half of the nineteenth century included the geologists Clarence King, S. F. Emmons, James D. Hague, and O. C. Marsh and the artists Asher B. Durand, John F. Kensett, Frederic Edwin Church, Albert Bierstadt, and Sanford Gifford. Century Association membership information was provided by Rodger Friedman, Librarian of the Century Association, in correspondence of June 1987. The Saturday Club, which included Louis Agassiz, Ralph Waldo Emerson, and Henry David Thoreau, did not have any artists on its membership roster, but several painters, including Kensett and William James Stillman, attended dinners and other functions with the club members.

32. William H. Truettner, "The Genesis of Frederic Edwin Church's *Aurora Borealis*," *Art Quarterly* 31 (Autumn 1968): 272.

33. For an excellent discussion of Peale's museum and his scientific activities, see David R. Brigham, *Public Culture in the Early Repub-*

lic: Peale's Museum and Its Audience (Washington, D.C.: Smithsonian Institution Press, 1995), and Charles Coleman Sellers, *Mr. Peale's Museum* (New York: W. W. Norton, 1980).

34. Diary of Manasseh Cutler, 13 July 1787, quoted in Charles Coleman Sellers, *Charles Willson Peale: The Early Life (1741–1790)* (Philadelphia: The American Philosophical Society, 1947), 1:261. David Brigham informed me that Peale later replaced this diorama with scientifically ordered display cases.

35. Quoted in Sellers, *Mr. Peale's Museum*, 62.

36. Brigham, *Public Culture*, 108–9.

37. I am grateful to David Brigham for this information.

38. Peale's excavation of the mastodon and the painting that resulted from it are discussed in Sellers, *Mr. Peale's Museum*, chapter 5; Lillian B. Miller, "Charles Willson Peale as History Painter: *The Exhumation of the Mastodon*," *American Art Journal* 13 (Winter 1981): 47–68; John H. Ostrom, "Mr. Peale's Missing Mastodon," *Discovery* 17 (1983–84): 3–9.

39. Ostrom, "Peale's Mastodon," 3, 6.

40. These ideas are discussed by Miller, "Peale as History Painter," 50–52.

41. The idea of extinction had not yet been generally accepted, and many Americans, including Thomas Jefferson, believed that mastodons would be found roaming America's western frontier. On Jefferson's interest in paleontology and in mastodons in particular see Dumas Malone, *Jefferson and the Ordeal of Liberty* (Boston: Little, Brown, 1962), chapter 22, and, also by Malone, *Jefferson the President: Second Term 1805–1809* (Boston: Little, Brown, 1974), 172–73.

42. Miller, "Peale as History Painter," 62–3.

43. For an excellent discussion of this painting, see Roger B. Stein, "Charles Willson Peale's Expressive Design: *The Artist in His Museum*," in *New Perspectives on Charles Willson Peale*, ed. Lillian B. Miller and David C. Ward (Pittsburgh: University of Pittsburgh Press for the Smithsonian Institution, 1991), 167–218.

44. Carleton Mabee, *The American Leonardo: A Life of Samuel F. B. Morse* (New York: Alfred A. Knopf, 1943), 83; Edward Lind Morse, *Samuel F. B. Morse: His Letters and Journals* (Boston: Houghton Mifflin, 1914), 1:239, 270.

45. Michael Quick, *American Portraiture in the Grand Manner: 1720–1920*, exh. cat. (Los Angeles County Museum of Art, 1981), 140.

46. Ibid.

47. Morse, *Samuel F. B. Morse*, 2:437. The lectures were published and Morse's directions for the establishment of the series are printed in the prefaces to these volumes. See, for example, Henry Calderwood, *The Relations of Science and Religion: The Morse Lecture, 1880* (New York: Robert Carter, 1881), v–vi.

48. Barbara Novak in *Nature and Culture: American Landscape and Painting, 1825–1875* (New York: Oxford University Press, 1980; rev. ed. 1996) called attention to nineteenth-century American artists' interest in geology. Her chapter "The Geological Time-Table: Rocks" was one of the starting points for this book. Other scholars, including William H. Truettner, Ellwood C. Parry III, Franklin Kelly, Katherine Manthorne, Joni Kinsey, Elizabeth Childs, and Virginia Wagner, whose specific publications are cited in other notes, have also contributed greatly to our knowledge of the interrelationship of geology and American landscape painting.

49. Quoted in Paul Staiti, "Accounting for Copley," in *John Singleton Copley in America*, exh. cat. (New York: Metropolitan Museum of Art, 1996), 35.

50. On science as "an essential mental discipline" in the mid-nineteenth century, see Kohlstedt, "Parlors, Primers, and Public Schooling."

CHAPTER ONE

This chapter is an expanded and revised version of an essay that first appeared in Amy R. W. Meyers, ed., *Art and Science in America: Issues of Representation* (San Marino, Calif.: Huntington Library, 1998).

1. Cole's fossil hunting with his friend William A. Adams is mentioned in a letter from Cole to Adams of May 1838. Thomas Cole Papers,

New York State Library, Albany (hereafter NYSL), box 1, folder 3; on microfilm at the Archives of American Art (hereafter AAA), roll ALC1.

2. "Professor Emmons' survey" is cited twice in Cole's papers, once in his 1837 "Catskill, New York" Sketchbook, Detroit Institute of Arts (hereafter DIA) (AAA, roll D39, frame 844), and again in a notebook entry for 8 July [1837 or 1838], NYSL, box 6, folder 2 (AAA, roll ALC3). "Comstock's Geology" is on a list of books in Cole's possession, DIA (AAA, roll D6, frame 265). This book is probably J. L. Comstock's *Outlines of Geology* (Hartford, Conn.: D. F. Robinson and Co., 1834). Ellwood C. Parry III and Frank Kelly have also argued that Cole was acquainted with Charles Lyell's famous book *Principles of Geology* (1830–33), and Barbara Novak has pointed out that Cole could hardly have missed the many articles on geology in the periodical literature of the day. See Parry's "Acts of God, Acts of Man: Geological Ideas and the Imaginary Landscapes of Thomas Cole," in Cecil J. Schneer, ed., *Two Hundred Years of Geology in America: Proceedings of the New Hampshire Conference on the History of Geology* (Hanover, N.H.: University Press of New England, 1979), 60–61; Kelly's "Myth, Allegory, and Science: Thomas Cole's Paintings of Mount Etna," *Arts in Virginia* 23 (1983): 12–13; Novak's *Nature and Culture: American Landscape and Painting, 1825–1875* (New York: Oxford University Press, 1980; rev. ed. 1996), 57.

3. On Cole's relationship with Silliman, see Ellwood C. Parry III, "Thomas Cole's Ideas for Mr. Reed's Doors," *American Art Journal* 12 (Summer 1980): 37–38.

4. *American Journal of Science and Arts* 18 (July 1830): 210–11, quoted in Ellwood C. Parry III, "Recent Discoveries in the Art of Thomas Cole," *Antiques* 120 (November 1981): 1164.

5. Cole's description of Niagara Falls can be found in his 1828 New York Sketchbook, DIA (AAA, roll D39, frames 193–94). The description of Kaaterskill Falls is quoted in Louis Legrand Noble, *The Life and Works of Thomas Cole* (1853; reprint, Cambridge, Mass.: Harvard University Press, 1964), 258. On volcanic formations, see "Visit to Volterra," journal entry for 31 August 1831 (NYSL, box 4, folder 3; AAA, roll ALC2).

6. Entry for 7 October 1835 from the journal "Thoughts and Occurrences," reproduced in Marshall Tymn, ed., *Thomas Cole: The Collected Essays and Prose Sketches* (St. Paul, Minn.: John Colet Press, 1980), 136–37.

7. Joshua Reynolds, quoted in *Discourses on Art*, ed. Robert R. Wark (New Haven, Conn., and London: Yale University Press, 1975), 41–42.

8. Quoted in Matthew Baigell, *Thomas Cole* (New York: Watson Guptill, 1981), 13.

9. From the sketchbook "Thoughts and Occurrences," NYSL, box 6, folder 2 (AAA, roll ALC3).

10. *Diary of Philip Hone, 1826–1851*, ed. Allan Nevins (New York: Dodd, Mead and Co., 1936), 445.

11. Dixon Ryan Fox, *The Decline of the Aristocracy in the Politics of New York* (New York: Columbia University, 1919); Alan Wallach, "Thomas Cole and the Aristocracy," *Arts Magazine* 56 (November 1981): 94–106.

12. Samuel L. Metcalf, "The Interest and Importance of Scientific Geology as a Subject for Study," *Knickerbocker* 3 (April 1834): 227.

13. On the history of this group, see Fox, *Decline of the Aristocracy*, and Frederick Cople Jaher, *The Urban Establishment: Upper Strata in Boston, New York, Charleston, Chicago, and Los Angeles* (Urbana: University of Illinois Press, 1982).

14. Quoted in Jaher, *Urban Establishment*, 35.

15. Wadsworth's geological interests are discussed in Parry, "Recent Discoveries," 1162.

16. On Cole's relationship to Wadsworth, see *The Correspondence of Thomas Cole and Daniel Wadsworth*, ed. J. Bard McNulty (Hartford: Connecticut Historical Society, 1983).

17. On Featherstonhaugh's contributions to American geology, see George P. Merrill, *The First One Hundred Years of American Geology* (New Haven, Conn., and London: Yale University Press, 1924), 136–39.

18. Information on Cole's relationship with Featherstonhaugh is drawn largely from Ellwood C. Parry III, *The Art of Thomas Cole: Ambition and Imagination* (Newark: University of Delaware Press, 1988), 28–30.

19. Amos Eaton to Benjamin Silliman, 18 May 1829, quoted in Ethel M. McAllister, *Amos Eaton: Scientist and Educator* (Philadelphia: University of Pennsylvania Press, 1941), 294; Simon Baatz, "'Squint-

ing at Silliman': Scientific Periodicals in the Early American Republic, 1810–1833," *Isis* 82 (June 1991): 223–44, offers further details of Featherstonhaugh's unsavory character.

20. The officers of the American Geological Society are listed in *American Journal of Science and Arts* 2 (1820): 141. See also Chandos Michael Brown, *Benjamin Silliman: A Life in the Young Republic* (Princeton, N.J.: Princeton University Press, 1989), 310. I am indebted to Alan Wallach for calling my attention to the connections between Gilmor, Silliman, and the American Geological Society.

21. "Catalogue of the Library of the Late Robert Gilmor" (Baltimore: Joseph Robinson, 1849). Copy in the library of the Peabody Institute, Baltimore. Janet Headley kindly brought this catalogue to my attention.

22. Parry, *Art of Thomas Cole*, 62.

23. Quoted in Ibid., 64.

24. Ella M. Foshay, "Luman Reed, A New York Patron of American Art," *The Magazine Antiques* 138 (November 1990): 1074–85.

25. Mrs. Jonathan Sturges, *Reminiscences of a Long Life* (New York, 1894), 158–60, quoted in Parry, *Art of Thomas Cole*, 178; Ella M. Foshay, *Mr. Luman Reed's Picture Gallery* (New York: Harry N. Abrams, 1990), 39.

26. McAllister, *Amos Eaton*, 276.

27. Alan Wallach, "Thomas Cole and the Aristocracy," *Arts Magazine* 56 (November 1981): 94–106. My account of Cole's childhood and of the formation of his class consciousness is based on this article.

28. Quoted in Wallach, "Thomas Cole and the Aristocracy," 95.

29. Ibid., 95.

30. See, for example, the listing of genres by rank in "The Exhibition of the National Academy of Design, 1827," *The United States Review and Literary Gazette* 2 (July 1827): 244, quoted in Parry, *Art of Thomas Cole*, 52–53.

31. C. R. Leslie to Cole, 11 May 1835, NYSL, box 2, folder 4 (AAA, roll ALC1).

32. On the changing course of geology in the nineteenth century, see Mott T. Greene, *Geology in the Nineteenth Century* (Ithaca, N.Y.: Cornell University Press, 1982); Rachel Laudan, *From Mineralogy to Geology: The Foundations of a Science, 1650–1830* (Chicago: University of Chicago Press, 1987); and Charles Coulton Gillispie, *Genesis and Geology* (Cambridge, Mass.: Harvard University Press, 1951). On Featherstonhaugh's views, see his *Geological Report of an Examination of the Elevated Country between the Missouri and Red Rivers* (Washington, D.C.: Gales and Seaton, 1835).

33. On Silliman, see Brown, *Silliman*.

34. *Diary of Philip Hone*, 209.

35. Ibid., 504.

36. See NYSL, box 1, folder 4: Letters from Thomas Cole to William A. Adams dated March, October, and December 1839 requesting fossil specimens for Silliman; and box 3, folder 1: Letter from A. N. Skinner to Cole dated September 1839 mentioning a visit by Cole to Silliman.

37. Quoted in John C. Greene, "Protestantism, Science, and American Enterprise: Benjamin Silliman's Moral Universe," in *Benjamin Silliman and His Circle*, ed. Leonard G. Wilson (New York: Science History Publications, 1979), 17–18.

38. Ibid.

39. Benjamin Silliman, *Outline of the Course of Geological Lectures Given in Yale College* (New Haven, Conn., 1820).

40. Parry, in "Acts of God," points out Cole's inclusion of erratic boulders in *The Last of the Mohicans* paintings and *The Course of Empire* series, though without drawing a connection between these stones and the Deluge theory. Parry's article was one of the starting points for this chapter.

41. Parry, *Art of Thomas Cole*, 64.

42. Comstock, *Outlines of Geology*, 80.

43. NYSL, box 5, folder 2 (AAA, roll ALC3).

44. Sketchbook inscribed "New York 1827," NYSL, box 6, folder 3 (AAA, roll ALC4). Although the sketchbook is dated 1827, it covers several subsequent years.

45. Hosack owned one of the earliest mineral collections in the United States, and he also collected fossils, which he forwarded to the Royal Academy of Science in London. See Stephen Dow Beckham,

"Colonel George Gibbs," in Wilson, ed., *Benjamin Silliman and His Circle*, 31; and "Letters of Mr. Brongniart with Remarks," *American Journal of Science* 3 (1821): 225. In the late eighteenth and early nineteenth centuries, fossils were believed by many to be remains of the Flood; see Gillispie, *Genesis and Geology*.

46. Much has been written about *The Course of Empire* series. See Angela Miller, "Thomas Cole and Jacksonian America: *The Course of Empire* as Political Allegory," *Prospects* 14 (1989): 65–92; Alan Wallach, "Thomas Cole: Landscape and the Course of American Empire," in William H. Truettner and Alan Wallach, *Thomas Cole: Landscape into History* (New Haven, Conn., and London: Yale University Press and National Museum of American Art, Smithsonian Institution, Washington, D.C.), 23–112; Alan Wallach, "Cole, Byron, and the Course of Empire," *Art Bulletin* 50 (December 1968): 376; Parry, *Art of Thomas Cole*, 137–87.

47. Cole to Luman Reed, 18 September 1833. Quoted in Wallach, "Cole, Byron," 376.

48. See A. Hallam, *Great Geological Controversies* (New York: Oxford University Press, 1983), especially chapter 2, "Catastrophists and Uniformitarians."

49. Miller, "Thomas Cole and Jacksonian America." This subject is also addressed by Alan Wallach in his essay "Thomas Cole: Landscape and the Course of American Empire," in Truettner and Wallach, *Thomas Cole: Landscape into History*, 23–112.

50. These fears were pervasive among the educated elite in the decades before the Civil War. George M. Frederickson, *The Inner Civil War* (New York: Harper and Row, 1965), and Lawrence Kohl, *The Politics of Individualism* (New York: Oxford University Press, 1989), offer many examples.

51. B [probably George Barker], untitled reminiscence of Luman Reed, Luman Reed Papers, New-York Historical Society, 50. Quoted in Truettner and Wallach, *Thomas Cole: Landscape into History*, 38.

52. David Lawall, *Asher Brown Durand: His Art and Art Theory in Relation to his Times* (New York: Garland Publishing, 1977), 198.

53. Charles Grier Sellers, *The Market Revolution: Jacksonian America, 1815–1846* (New York: Oxford University Press, 1991), 5.

54. I am grateful to Alan Wallach for the Clotho reference.

55. Quoted in Truettner and Wallach, *Thomas Cole: Landscape into History*, 90.

56. Ibid., 92.

57. Quoted in Wallach, "Cole, Byron," 378.

58. My information about Crawford Notch and the Willey Disaster is based largely on John Sears, *Sacred Places: American Tourist Attractions in the Nineteenth Century* (New York: Oxford University Press, 1989), chapter 4. Sears reproduces Cole's painting of Crawford Notch in this chapter but does not discuss it. For a fuller account of the Willey Disaster, see Eric Purchase, *Out of Nowhere: Disaster and Tourism in the White Mountains* (Baltimore: Johns Hopkins University Press, 1999).

59. John Carver, *Sketches of New England* (New York: E. French, 1842), 90–91. "We reached the Notch just after noon. The entrance of the chasm is formed by two rocks standing perpendicularly at the distance of twenty-two feet from each other . . . This opens you into a narrow defile, extending two miles in length, between two huge cliffs, apparently rent asunder by some great convulsion of nature. This convulsion, Dr. Dwight thinks, was that of the deluge, since there are no proofs of volcanic action anywhere in this region."

60. Cole, journal entry for autumn 1828, quoted in Franklin Kelly, *American Paintings of the Nineteenth Century, Part I*, The Collection of the National Gallery of Art Systematic Catalogue Series (New York: Oxford University Press, 1996), 94.

61. Quoted in Sears, *Sacred Places*, 80.

62. Though it is not certain that Cole read Hawthorne's story, he was always interested in the literary and historical associations of the places he painted and intentionally hunted down references to them. *Twice-Told Tales* was Hawthorne's first successful volume and was published at least partially through the efforts of Cole's Boston patron Samuel Griswold Goodrich, who liked to think of Hawthorne as his protégée. (In fact, in the late 1820s and early 1830s, Goodrich drew on the tal-

ents of both Cole and Hawthorne to fill his publications, including *The Token* and *New England Magazine.*) On Cole's relationship with Goodrich, see Parry, *Art of Thomas Cole*, 37, 54, 85–86.

Franklin Kelly in his entry on this painting in *American Paintings of the Nineteenth Century*, 87–95, also suggests that it may allude to Hawthorne's short story. In his eloquent essay, Kelly adds another layer of meaning to the painting by explaining its origins as a companion piece to *Landscape Composition, Italian Scenery*.

63. Noble, *Life and Works*, 301–2. See also Kenneth James LaBudde, "The Mind of Thomas Cole" (Ph.D. diss., University of Minnesota, 1954), 192–93.

64. Matthew Baigell, in his brief discussion of this painting in *Thomas Cole* (New York: Watson-Guptill, 1981), 60, mentions the stumps and describes them as showing "the violence man has done to nature." For a more general discussion of the meaning of the stump in nineteenth-century American landscape painting, see Nicolai Cikovsky Jr., "'The Ravages of the Axe': The Meaning of the Tree Stump in Nineteenth-Century American Art," *Art Bulletin* 61 (December 1979): 611–26; and Novak, *Nature and Culture*, chapter 8.

65. Novak, *Nature and Culture*, 157.

CHAPTER TWO

1. Anyone who works on Durand owes a debt to David Lawall's magisterial thesis, *Asher Brown Durand: His Art and Art Theory in Relation to His Times* (New York: Garland Publishing, 1977) and to his *Asher B. Durand: A Documentary Catalogue of the Narrative and Landscape Paintings* (New York: Garland Publishing, 1978).

2. Letter from Caroline Durand to her brother John. Asher Durand Papers, New York Public Library, Manuscript Division (AAA, roll N20, frames 1018–21).

3. Eleanor Jones Harvey, *The Painted Sketch: American Impressions from Nature, 1830–1880*, exh. cat. (Dallas: Dallas Museum of Art in assoc. with Harry N. Abrams, 1998), 18. Harvey offers an excellent account of the ascendancy of sketches and studies from preparatory works to independent works of art, with particular attention to Durand's critical role in this development.

4. *Literary World* 3 (13 May 1848): 287, quoted in Lawall, *Durand: A Documentary Catalogue*, 69–70.

5. Clarence Cook, *Art and Artists of Our Time* (New York: Selmar Hess, 1888), 3:295.

6. John Ruskin, *Modern Painters*, 5 vols., vols. 3–7 in *The Works of John Ruskin*, ed. E. T. Cook and Alexander Wedderburn (London: G. Allen, 1903–12), 3:39.

7. Letter 3, *The Crayon* 1 (31 January 1855): 66.

8. There may also be a piece of green phyllite in the center of the stream. The rocks in Durand's paintings were identified for me by E-an Zen, Nicholas Ratcliffe, and their colleagues at the U.S. Geological Survey, Reston, Virginia, and by Ellis Yochelson and Anita Harris of the Museum of Natural History, Smithsonian Institution. I am very grateful to them for their help.

Carol T. Christ, *The Finer Optic: The Aesthetic of Particularity in Victorian Poetry* (New Haven, Conn., and London: Yale University Press, 1975) offers an excellent discussion of the aesthetic and philosophical dimensions of this shift toward particularity, which is evident in literature as well as in art.

9. On Ruskin's influence in the United States, see Roger B. Stein, *John Ruskin and Aesthetic Thought in America, 1840–1900* (Cambridge, Mass.: Harvard University Press, 1967); Linda S. Ferber and William H. Gerdts, *The New Path: Ruskin and the American Pre-Raphaelites*, exh. cat. (Brooklyn Museum, 1985); Virginia Wagner, "John Ruskin and Artistical Geology in America," *Winterthur Portfolio* 23 (Summer/Autumn 1988): 151–67; David Howard Dickason, *The Daring Young Men: The Story of the American Pre-Raphaelites* (Bloomington: Indiana University Press, 1953).

10. Durand acquired the first volume of *Modern Painters* within months of its publication, sharing it with his fellow artists John Casilear and Francis Edmonds. He later owned a complete set. See John Durand

to Asher Durand, 22 August 1844, Durand Papers, New York Public Library (AAA, roll N20, frame 201).

11. Ruskin, *Modern Painters*, 3:34–55.

12. William Blake, "Auguries of Innocence," (c. 1803), *Blake: The Complete Poems*, 2nd ed., ed. W. H. Stevenson (London and New York: Longman, 1989), 589.

13. Ruskin, *Modern Painters*, 1:624.

14. Ruskin, *Modern Painters*, 3:38.

15. Ibid., 3:35. Although Ruskin's works are full of passages encouraging a close, scientific examination of nature, from the 1850s onward his feelings about the sciences become increasingly ambivalent as he began to fear that they could have "a tendency to chill and subdue feelings, and to resolve all things into atoms and numbers." (*Modern Painters* 5:386–87). On Ruskin's attitude toward the sciences, see Frederick Kirchhoff, "A Science against Sciences," in *Nature and the Victorian Imagination*, ed. U. C. Knoepflmacher and G. B. Tennyson (Berkeley and Los Angeles: University of California Press, 1977).

16. On Ruskin's interest in geology see his *Deucalion and Other Stories in Rocks and Stones*, vol. 26, *Works of John Ruskin*, ed. Cook and Wedderburn (1906), especially the introduction; also Anthony Lacy Gully, "Sermons in Stone: Ruskin and Geology," in Susan P. Casteras et al., *John Ruskin and the Victorian Eye* (New York: Harry N. Abrams, 1993).

17. Ruskin, *Modern Painters*, 1:425.

18. Ibid., 1:333.

19. Letter 9, *The Crayon* 2 (11 July 1855): 16.

20. Letter 2, *The Crayon* 1 (17 January 1855): 34.

21. Letter 9, *The Crayon* 2 (11 July 1855): 16.

22. On Hugh Miller, see Charles Coulton Gillispie, *Genesis and Geology* (Cambridge, Mass.: Harvard University Press, 1951); Lynn Barber, *The Heyday of Natural History, 1820–1870* (London: Jonathan Cape, 1980).

23. Hugh Miller, *The Old Red Sandstone* (Boston: Gould and Lincoln, 1858), 1. First published in London, 1841.

24. Ibid., 7–8.

25. Ibid., 10.

26. Barber, *Natural History*, 231.

27. Miller, *Sandstone*, 267–69, quoted in Barber, *Natural History*, 232.

28. On geological debates over the age of the earth, see A. Hallam, *Great Geological Controversies* (New York: Oxford University Press, 1983); Stephen J. Gould, *Time's Arrow, Time's Cycle: Myth and Metaphor in the Discovery of Geological Time* (Cambridge, Mass.: Harvard University Press, 1987); Stephen Toulmin and June Goodfield, *The Discovery of Time* (Chicago: University of Chicago Press, 1965).

29. Quoted in Gillispie, *Genesis and Geology*, 46.

30. Miller, *Sandstone*, 68–69, quoted in Gillispie, *Genesis and Geology*, 175.

31. Miller, *Sandstone*, 172.

32. Baden Powell, *Christianity without Judaism* (London, 1857), 257–58, discussed and quoted in Gillispie, *Genesis and Geology*, 181.

33. Letter 2, *The Crayon* 1 (17 January 1855): 34.

34. Letter 9, *The Crayon* 2 (11 July 1855): 17.

35. On Lewes, see Bruce Haley, *The Healthy Body and Victorian Culture* (Cambridge, Mass.: Harvard University Press, 1978); on Channing, see Lawall, *Durand: His Art and Art Theory*, 527.

36. Quoted in Paul F. Boller, *American Transcendentalism, 1830–1860: An Intellectual Inquiry* (New York: G. P. Putnam's, 1974), 72.

37. Letter 2, *The Crayon* 1 (17 January 1855): 34.

38. Ibid.

39. John Durand, *The Life and Times of A. B. Durand* (1894; reprint, New York: Da Capo Press, 1970), 179.

40. Letter 4, *The Crayon* 1 (14 February 1855): 98.

41. *New Mirror* 2 (2 March 1844): 350–51, quoted in Lawall, *Durand: A Documentary Catalogue*, 41.

42. Letter 3, *The Crayon* 1 (31 January 1855): 66.

43. Letter 7, *The Crayon* 1 (2 May 1855): 274.

44. Ibid.

45. Letter 9, *The Crayon* 2 (11 July 1855): 17.

46. *Biographical Sketches of the Leading Men of Chicago* (1868), 597–604. I am grateful to Wendy Greenhouse for this information.

47. Mark Skinner to Durand, 1 November 1854, quoted in Lawall,

Durand: A Documentary Catalogue, 104.

48. Andrew Jackson Downing, *Rural Essays* (New York: R. Worthington, 1881), 111.

49. Andrew Jackson Downing, *A Treatise on the Theory and Practice of Landscape Gardening* (New York: Putnam, 1849), 410.

50. Andrew Jackson Downing, *The Cultivator* 8 (September 1841): 145, quoted in Kenneth Blair Hawkins, "The Therapeutic Landscape: Nature, Architecture, and Mind in Nineteenth-Century America" (Ph.D. diss., University of Rochester, 1991), 26.

51. Quoted in David Schuyler, *Apostle of Taste: Andrew Jackson Downing, 1815–1852* (Baltimore: Johns Hopkins University Press, 1996): 78–79. Schuyler discusses Downing's work for the New York and New Jersey state lunatic asylums.

52. John Durand, *A. B. Durand*, 179.

53. Ibid., 177.

54. Lawall, *Durand: His Art and Art Theory*, 537.

55. On Bryant's interest in geology, see Donald A. Ringe, "William Cullen Bryant and the Science of Geology," *American Literature* 26 (January 1955): 507–14.

56. Letter 9, *The Crayon* 2 (11 July 1855): 17.

57. On antebellum views of death and on the rural cemetery movement, see Blanche Linden-Ward, *Silent City on a Hill: Landscapes of Memory and Boston's Mount Auburn Cemetery* (Columbus: Ohio State University Press, 1989); David Stannard, ed., *Death in America* (Philadelphia: University of Pennsylvania Press, 1975); Thomas Bender, "The Rural Cemetery Movement: Urban Travail and the Appeal of Nature," *New England Quarterly* 47 (June 1974): 196–211.

58. Zebedee Cook Jr., *An Address Pronounced Before the Massachusetts Horticultural Society* (1830), quoted in Linden-Ward, *Silent City*, 182.

59. Quoted in Linden-Ward, *Silent City*, 167.

CHAPTER THREE

1. On the history of American education in the nineteenth century, see Carl Bode, *The American Lyceum: Town Meeting of the Mind* (New York: Oxford University Press, 1956); Sally Gregory Kohlstedt, "Parlors, Primers, and Public Schooling: Education for Science in Nineteenth-Century America," *Isis* 81 (1990): 425–45; Lawrence A. Cremin, *American Education: The National Experience, 1783–1876* (New York: Harper and Row, 1980); Frederick J. Antczak, *Thought and Character: The Rhetoric of Democratic Education* (Ames: Iowa State University Press, 1985); B. Edward McClellan and William J. Reese, eds., *The Social History of Education* (Chicago: University of Illinois Press, 1988); Rush Welter, *American Writings on Popular Education: The Nineteenth Century* (New York: Bobbs-Merrill, 1971).

2. The literature on Frederic Church is rich and extensive. Particularly important for this chapter have been David Carew Huntington, "Frederic Edwin Church, 1826–1900: Painter of the Adamic New World Myth" (Ph.D. diss., Yale University, 1960); Huntington's *The Landscapes of Frederic Edwin Church* (New York: G. Braziller, 1966); and his "Church and Luminism: Light for America's Elect," in *American Light*, ed. John Wilmerding, exh. cat. (Washington, D.C.: National Gallery of Art, 1980); Franklin Kelly, et al., *Frederic Edwin Church*, exh. cat. (Washington, D.C.: National Gallery of Art, 1989); Franklin W. Kelly and Gerald L. Carr, *The Early Landscapes of Frederic Edwin Church, 1845–1854* (Fort Worth, Tex.: Amon Carter Museum, 1987); Franklin W. Kelly, *Frederic Church and the National Landscape* (Washington, D.C.: Smithsonian Institution Press, 1988); Katherine Manthorne, *Creation and Renewal: Views of Cotopaxi*, exh. cat. (Washington, D.C.: National Museum of American Art, 1985); Kevin Avery, *Church's Great Picture: The Heart of the Andes* (New York: Metropolitan Museum of Art, 1993); Angela Miller, *The Empire of the Eye: Landscape Representation and American Cultural Politics, 1825–1875* (Ithaca, N.Y.: Cornell University Press, 1993); Gerald L. Carr, *Frederic Edwin Church: The Icebergs*, exh. cat. (Dallas Museum of Fine Arts, 1980).

3. Henry T. Tuckerman, *Book of the Artists: American Artist Life* (New York: G. P. Putnam, 1867), 371.

4. Stephen J. Gould, "Church, Humboldt, and Darwin," in Franklin Kelly, et al., *Frederic Edwin Church*, 106, points out Church's general

bias against materialist science, especially evident in his exclusion of Darwin's *Origin of Species* from his library shelves.

5. Quoted in Carr, *Church: The Icebergs*, 13.

6. *The Albion* 10 (12 April 1851): 177.

7. "Russell Smith Memoirs," Smith Family Papers (AAA).

8. On the panorama vogue, see Kevin J. Avery, "Whaling Voyage Round the World: Russell and Purrington's Moving Panorama and Herman Melville's 'Mighty Book,'" *American Art Journal* 22 (1990): 50–78; Angela Miller, "Spaces as Destiny: the Panorama Vogue in Mid-Nineteenth-Century America," in *World Art: Themes of Unity in Diversity*, ed. Irving Lavin. 3 vols. (University Park, Penn.: University of Pittsburgh Press, 1989), 3:739–44; Lee Parry, "Landscape Theater in America," *American Art Journal* 59 (1971): 52–61.

9. Church's relationship to the panoramacists is discussed in Kevin J. Avery, "*The Heart of the Andes* Exhibited: Frederic E. Church's Window on the Equatorial World," *American Art Journal* 18 (1986): 52–72.

10. Tuckerman, *Book of the Artists*, 370.

11. Quoted in Kelly and Carr, *The Early Landscapes*, 32.

12. Ibid.

13. For a thorough analysis of Cole's *Expulsion* and its companion piece, *The Garden of Eden*, see Franklin Kelly, *Thomas Cole's Paintings of Eden* (Fort Worth, Texas: Amon Carter Museum, 1994).

14. On Cole's familiarity with these conventions, see Earl A. Powell III, "Thomas Cole and the American Landscape Tradition: The Naturalist Controversy," *Arts Magazine* 52 (February 1978): 114–23; Kelly, *Thomas Cole's Paintings of Eden*.

15. His inclusion of the natural bridges (as well as the erupting volcano beyond them) may have been informed by his knowledge of catastrophist geology, which held that geological change occurs through sudden cataclysmic events. (Catastrophist geology still held sway in American scientific circles in the 1820s.) Natural bridges, for example, were generally ascribed in this theory to an abrupt splitting of bedrock by an earthquake or even lightning strike. The violence and danger associated with their formation thus fit well the stormy mood of Cole's scene. Later in Cole's career, however, as Franklin Kelly and Ellwood C. Parry III have argued, Cole may well have been swayed by Lyell's uniformitarian theories; see chapter 1, note 2.

16. For an excellent discussion of Church's artistic relationship to Cole see Kelly, *Frederic Church and the National Landscape*, esp. chapter 1.

17. Barbara Maria Stafford, *Voyage into Substance: Art, Science, Nature, and the Illustrated Travel Account, 1760–1840* (Cambridge, Mass.: MIT Press, 1984), 28–29.

18. Church's presentation of the natural bridge with its emphasis on the eroding walls inside the arch and the piles of talus at its base, suggests his allegiance to the geological theory of uniformitarianism, rather than the catastrophism Cole had embraced in the early part of his career (when he painted *Expulsion*). Unlike catastrophists who believed that geological change occurred through sudden cataclysmic events, uniformitarians, with Charles Lyell foremost among them, argued that these changes occurred slowly over great periods of time, and the processes that shaped the earth in the geologic past are essentially the same as those operating today.

19. See the illustrations in Pamela H. Simpson, *So Beautiful an Arch: Images of the Natural Bridge, 1787–1890*, exh. cat. (Lexington, Va.: Washington and Lee University, 1982).

20. Much has been written about Church and others' perception of America as the new Eden. See, for example, Huntington, *The Landscapes of Frederic Edwin Church*; R.W.B. Lewis, *The American Adam: Innocence, Tragedy, and Tradition in the Nineteenth Century* (Chicago: University of Chicago Press, 1955).

21. For a recent study of Hicks's *Peaceable Kingdom* paintings, see Carolyn Weekley, *The Kingdoms of Edward Hicks* (Williamsburg, Va.: Colonial Williamsburg Foundation, 1999).

22. Many authors have discussed the nationalistic themes in Church's art. See especially Huntington, *Landscapes of Frederic Edwin Church*, and Kelly, *Frederic Church and the National Landscape*.

23. Field owned a natural history cabinet that included 1,500 speci-

mens of rocks and minerals. See Virginia Wagner, "The Idea of Geology in American Landscape Painting, 1825–1875" (Ph.D. diss., University of Delaware, 1987), 151.

24. Kelly, et al., *Frederic Edwin Church*, 46; Simpson, *So Beautiful an Arch*, 27; Linda S. Ferber and William H. Gerdts, *The New Path: Ruskin and the American Pre-Raphaelites*, exh. cat. (Brooklyn Museum, 1985), 246; Isabella Field Judson, *Cyrus W. Field: His Life and Work* (New York: Harper & Bros., 1896), 39.

25. William James Stillman, *The Autobiography of a Journalist*, 2 vols. (Boston: Houghton, Mifflin, 1901), 1:114.

26. "Fine Arts. National Academy of Design. Second Notice," *The Albion* 41 (2 May 1863): 213.

27. Quoted in Ila Weiss, *Poetic Landscape: The Art and Experience of Sanford Gifford* (Newark: University of Delaware Press, 1987), 136. Like many post–Civil War critics, Weir, besides noting the extraordinary factual content of Church's art, also lamented its paucity of poetic and emotional effects.

28. Alexander von Humboldt, *Cosmos: A Sketch of a Physical Description of the Universe*, 5 vols., trans. E. C. Otté (London: Henry G. Bohn, 1849–52), 2:456. This is the edition owned by Church.

29. Tuckerman, *Book of the Artists*, 370.

30. *The Letters of John Ruskin, 1827–1869*, in *The Works of John Ruskin*, ed. E. T. Cook and Alexander Wedderburn (London: G. Allen, 1903–12), 36:329.

31. James Jackson Jarves, *The Art Idea* (1864; reprint, ed. Benjamin Rowland Jr., Cambridge, Mass.: Harvard University Press, 1960), 86.

32. Huntington, "Frederic Edwin Church," 10.

33. That Church should combine scientific and religious teachings in his work was completely in keeping with the educational trends of his time. As Cremin explains in *American Education: The National Experience, 1783–1876*, by the 1840s and 1850s a generalized Protestant piety had become an integral part of the American vernacular, and the responsibility for teaching that piety to all Americans became the central task of a newly constructed configuration of educational institutions.

34. George W. Sheldon, *American Painters* (New York: D. Appleton, 1879), 13.

35. Humboldt, *Cosmos*, 1:x.

36. Ibid., 1:32.

37. Ibid., 1:43.

38. Ibid., 1:12.

39. Alexander von Humboldt, *Personal Narrative of Travels to the Equinoctal Regions of America during the Years 1799–1804*, trans. Thomasina Ross (London: Henry G. Bohn, 1852), 1:xvi.

40. Avery, *Church's Great Picture*.

41. Theodore Winthorp, *A Companion to The Heart of the Andes* (New York: D. Appleton, 1859), 4.

42. Ibid., 12.

43. Humboldt, *Cosmos*, 1:13.

44. Ibid., 1:14.

45. Ibid.

46. Manthorne, *Creation and Renewal*, 31–51.

47. Humboldt, *Cosmos*, 1:153.

48. Winthrop, *Companion*, 23.

49. Ibid., 17.

50. Quoted in Manthorne, *Creation and Renewal*, 42.

51. Humboldt, *Cosmos*, 5:3.

52. Winthrop, *Companion*, 38, 22.

53. Ibid., 43, 22.

54. Twain to Orion Clemens, 18 March 1861, in *Mark Twain's Letters*, ed. Edgar Marquess Branch et al. (Berkeley and Los Angeles: University of California Press, 1988), 1:116–17.

55. Avery, *Church's Great Picture*, 41.

56. The frame and other aspects of the painting's exhibition are discussed by Avery, "*The Heart of the Andes* Exhibited"; and Kelly et al., *Frederic Edwin Church*, 57–58.

57. Quoted in Avery, *Church's Great Picture*, 38.

58. Neil Harris, *Humbug: The Art of P. T. Barnum* (Boston: Little Brown, 1973; reprint, Chicago: University of Chicago Press, 1981),

esp. 165.

59. Ibid., 55.

60. Winthrop, *Companion*, 6.

61. Harris, *Humbug*, 78.

62. In contrast to Church, Bierstadt often found himself attacked for offering landscape subjects that were false or contrived. In May 1865 *The New Path* castigated the artist for his *Mount Hope*: "Unfortunately for Mr. Bierstadt, and all other painters who endeavor to substitute their own ideas for nature's perfection of color and form, the Rocky Mountains have been photographed, and geologists have been there too, on government surveys; . . . and we have the authority of these same geologists, when we say that this picture is a caricature, and not a true portraiture of the country" (2:75).

63. "Fine Arts: Art in America," *The Albion* 41 (19 September 1863): 453.

64. "Fine Arts: Mr. Church's Cotopaxi," *The Albion* 41 (21 March 1863): 141.

65. See, for example, Huntington, "Church and Luminism," 179–81; Manthorne, *Creation and Renewal*, 48–51; Angela Miller, *Empire of the Eye*, 132–35.

66. Huntington, "Church and Luminism," 179–81.

67. Manthorne, *Creation and Renewal*, offers an excellent discussion of the way volcanoes were perceived as forces of both destruction and creation.

68. Huntington, "Church and Luminism," 180.

CHAPTER FOUR

1. The scholarly literature on Kensett is surprisingly scant. Among the important publications are John Paul Driscoll and John K. Howat, *John Frederick Kensett: An American Master*, exh. cat. (Worcester, Mass.: Worcester Art Museum, 1985); Kathleen Motes Bennewitz, "John F. Kensett at Beverly, Massachusetts," *American Art Journal* 21, no. 4 (1989): 46–65; Mark White Sullivan, "John F. Kensett, American Landscape Painter" (Ph.D. diss., Bryn Mawr College, 1981); John K. Howat, *John Frederick Kensett, 1816–1872*, exh. cat. (New York: Metropolitan Museum of Art, 1968).

2. [Russell Sturgis?], "Fine Arts: The Kensett Relics," *The Nation* 16 (20 March 1873): 204.

3. On the history of nineteenth-century American tourism see Dona Brown, *Inventing New England: Regional Tourism in the Nineteenth Century* (Washington, D.C.: Smithsonian Institution Press, 1995); John Sears, *Sacred Places: American Tourist Attractions in the Nineteenth Century* (New York: Oxford University Press, 1989).

4. The intersection of tourism and landscape painting has been eloquently discussed by Kenneth Myers, *The Catskills: Painters, Writers, and Tourists in the Mountains, 1820–1895* (Yonkers, N.Y.: Hudson River Museum of Westchester, 1987), as well as by other scholars including Joni Kinsey, *Thomas Moran and the Surveying of the American West* (Washington, D.C.: Smithsonian Institution Press, 1992); Donald D. Keyes, *The White Mountains: Place and Perception*, exh. cat. (Durham: University Art Galleries, University of New Hampshire, 1980); Pamela J. Belanger, *Inventing Acadia: Artists and Tourists at Mount Desert*, exh. cat. (Rockland, Maine: Farnsworth Art Museum, 1999).

5. Kensett to Elizabeth Kensett, 3 January 1844, quoted in Driscoll and Howat, *John Frederick Kensett*, 57.

6. Henry T. Tuckerman, *Book of the Artists: American Artist Life* (New York: G. P. Putnam, 1867), 512–13.

7. *Putnam's Magazine* (1855): 332, quoted in Sullivan, "John F. Kensett," 89.

8. Charles Loring to Kensett, 1860, John F. Kensett Papers (AAA, roll N68-84, frame 22).

9. William H. Truettner and Alan Wallach, *Thomas Cole: Landscape into History* (New Haven, Conn., and London: Yale University Press and National Museum of American Art, Smithsonian Institution, Washington, D.C., 1994), 51.

10. On this process see Myers, *The Catskills*, esp. 19.

11. "William Keith, Thomas Hill, Albert Bierstadt," from "Cali-

fornia Art Research," vol. 2, first series, from WPA Project 2874 OP 65-3-3632, San Francisco, 1937 (AAA, roll NDA Cal I, no frame numbers).

12. Kinsey, *Thomas Moran and the Surveying of the American West*; Sandra D'Emilio and Suzan Campbell, *Visions and Visionaries: The Art and Artists of the Sante Fe Railway* (Salt Lake City: Gibbs Smith, 1991).

13. Keyes, *The White Mountains*, 54.

14. Quoted in Ibid., 44.

15. "John W. Casilear," unidentified newspaper clipping, c. 1858 (AAA, roll NY59-29, frame 364).

16. Rev. Theodore L. Cuyler, "A Sabbath on the Catskills," in *The Scenery of the Catskill Mountains* (New York: D. Fanshaw, 1864), 48. This essay also appears in Rev. Charles Rockwell's *The Catskill Mountains and the Region Around* (New York: Taintor Bros., 1867).

17. Jeremy Elwell Adamson, *Niagara: Two Centuries of Changing Attitudes, 1697–1901*, exh. cat. (Washington, D.C.: Corcoran Gallery of Art, 1985), 51.

18. Edward Hitchcock, *Sketch of the Scenery of Massachusetts with Plates from the Geological Report of Professor Hitchcock* (Northampton, Mass.: J. H. Butler, 1842).

19. "An Excursion on the Baltimore and Ohio Railroad," *The Crayon* 5 (July 1858): 208–10.

20. This is noted by Mark Sullivan, "John F. Kensett, American Landscape Painter" (Ph.D. diss., Bryn Mawr College, 1981). This thesis offers much evidence of Kensett's involvement with tourism and was one of the catalysts for this chapter.

21. Sullivan, "John F. Kensett," 50.

22. Ibid., 52.

23. Ibid., 92.

24. Theodore Dwight, *The Northern Traveller and Northern Tour*, 5th ed. (New York: Goodrich and Wiley, 1834), 17.

25. In using these words to describe Kensett's paintings, and in continually insisting that the pictures were embodiments of Kensett's own "sweet" and "gentle" personality, his contemporaries were perhaps alluding in a coded way to his homosexuality. Certainly neither the artist nor any of his acquaintances ever made any definitive statement about his sexual orientation, but many pointed out that he never married and lived for most of his adult life with a male friend, Louis Lang.

26. Myers, *The Catskills*, 36.

27. Thomas Starr King, *The White Hills: Their Legends, Landscape, and Poetry* (Boston: Crosby & Nichols, 1862), vii. First published 1859.

28. Starr King, *The White Hills*, 8.

29. William Cullen Bryant, ed., *Picturesque America*, vol. 1 (New York: D. Appleton, 1872), 8.

30. Starr King, *The White Hills*, 169.

31. George William Curtis, *Lotus-Eating: A Summer Book* (New York: Harper and Brothers, 1874), 55. First published 1852.

32. Rockwell, *The Catskill Mountains*, 345.

33. Rev. William Furness's address to the Philadelphia Art Union, quoted in "Art and Artists," *Home Journal* (9 August 1851): 3.

34. Archibald Alison, *Essays on the Nature and Principles of Taste*, 3rd. ed. (London: Longman, 1812). On American artists' interest in associationism, see Earl A. Powell III, "Thomas Cole and the American Landscape Tradition: Associationism," *Arts Magazine* 52 (April 1978): 113–17.

35. Ruskin to William James Stillman, c. 1851. *The Letters of John Ruskin, 1827–1869*, vol. 36, *The Works of John Ruskin*, ed. E. T. Cook and Alexander Wedderburn (London: G. Allen, 1912), 125.

36. Thomas Cole, "Essay on American Scenery" (1836), in John W. McCoubrey, *American Art 1700–1960: Sources and Documents* (Englewood Cliffs, N.J.: Prentice-Hall, 1965), 108.

37. Bryant, *Picturesque America*, 2:17–18.

38. Curtis, *Lotus-Eating*, 130–31.

39. O. B. Bunce, "Lake George and Lake Champlain," in Bryant, *Picturesque America*, 2:267.

40. Ibid., 264.

41. "Preface to the Second Edition" of Benjamin Silliman's *Remarks Made on a Short Tour between Hartford and Quebec in the Autumn of 1819* (New Haven, Conn.: S. Converse, 1824), n.p.

42. Silliman, *Remarks*, 1.

43. Ibid.

44. Ibid.

45. Starr King, *The White Hills*, 345.

46. Moses Foster Sweetser, ed., *The White Mountains: A Handbook for Travellers*, 9th ed. (Boston: Ticknor & Co., 1888), 20.

47. John Dix, *A Hand-book of Newport and Rhode Island* (Newport: C. E. Hammett, Jr., 1852), 44.

48. Hitchcock, *Sketch of the Scenery*, 5.

49. William Oakes, *Scenery of the White Mountains* (Boston: Crosby and Nichols, 1848), n.p.

50. Tuckerman, *Book of the Artists*, 539.

51. Quoted in Bennewitz, "John F. Kensett," 61.

52. R. E. Garczynski, "Niagara," in *Picturesque America*, ed. William Cullen Bryant (New York: D. Appleton, 1872), 1:444.

53. This was pointed out to me by Maria Nadakavukaren Waller, Geology Department, Wellesley College.

54. Garczynski, "Niagara," 435.

55. Tuckerman, *Book of the Artists*, 374; Clarence Cook, *Art and Artists of Our Time*, 3 vols. (New York: Selmar Hess, 1888), 3:294.

56. "The National Academy," *Literary World* 6 (27 April 1850): 423.

57. *Proceedings at a Meeting of the Century Association Held in Memory of John F. Kensett, December, 1872*, 20.

58. Dix, *Hand-book*, 38.

CHAPTER FIVE

This chapter is a revised and expanded version of an essay that first appeared in *Nineteenth Century* 14, no. 1 (1994): 3–9.

1. Both the dating and the identification of the Nahant paintings are problematic. The similarity of Haseltine's views of the Massachusetts and Rhode Island coasts often makes it difficult to precisely determine the site depicted. Yet it is certain that Haseltine painted more than sixteen views of Nahant. In April 1866 Haseltine offered for auction sixteen paintings of Nahant at the "American Artist's Sale" at Miner & Sullivan's Gallery [Marc Simpson et al., *Expressions of Place: The Art of William Stanley Haseltine*, exh. cat. (The Fine Arts Museums of San Francisco, 1992), 177]. Since Haseltine had sold Nahant paintings before this date (including three paintings that he borrowed from collectors for the 1865 exhibition at the National Academy of Design), he must have executed more than sixteen.

As to the dating of the pictures, there are securely dated Nahant paintings from 1864 and 1865. Helen Haseltine Plowden in *William Stanley Haseltine: Sea and Landscape Painter* (London: Frederick Muller, 1947) reproduces an oil sketch of Nahant that she dates to 1862. Another painting depicting either Nahant or Narragansett, Rhode Island, is dated 1863 (Henry Fuller Collection). Marc Simpson, in assembling a chronology of Haseltine's life, was able to document only one Nahant trip by Haseltine, in the summer of 1864. However, in July of 1862 and 1863 Haseltine was in Cambridge, Massachusetts, for his Harvard class reunions and could well have visited Nahant at those times. [Harvard Class Reports, Class of 1854. Harvard University Archives.] If he did not, the 1862 and 1863 paintings must be either misdated or mistitled.

2. Plowden, *William Stanley Haseltine*, 29–30.

3. Douglas T. Miller, *Jacksonian Aristocracy* (New York: Oxford University Press, 1967); Edward Pessen, *Riches, Class, and Power Before the Civil War* (Lexington, Mass.: D. C. Heath, 1973); Ronald Story, *The Forging of an Aristocracy: Harvard and the Boston Upper Class, 1800–1870* (Middletown, Conn.: Wesleyan University Press, 1980).

4. Information on Nahant is drawn from several sources: Stanley C. Paterson and Carl G. Seaburg, *Nahant on the Rocks* (Nahant, Mass.: Nahant Historical Society, 1991); Alonzo Lewis, *Picture of Nahant* (Lynn, Mass.: J. B. Tolman, 1845); *Nahant: A Collection from Sundry Sources of Some Noteworthy Descriptions of the Town* (Lynn, Mass.: John MacFarlane, 1899); Henry Cabot Lodge, *An Historical Address* (Nahant, Mass.: Town of Nahant, 1904).

5. See Frederick Cople Jaher, *The Urban Establishment: Upper Strata in Boston, New York, Charleston, Chicago, and Los Angeles* (Urbana: Uni-

versity of Illinois Press, 1982), chapter 2.

6. "Movements of Artists," *Watson's Weekly Art Journal* 1, no. 14 (30 July 1864): 213, quoted in Marc Simpson et al., 171.

7. Oliver Wendell Holmes, *The Autocrat at the Breakfast Table* (Boston: Houghton Mifflin, 1858), 20.

8. Plowden, *William Stanley Haseltine*, 23–24.

9. Pessen, *Riches*, 329.

10. Jaher, *Urban Establishment*, 17.

11. Plowden, *William Stanley Haseltine*, 28.

12. Quoted in Angela Miller, *The Empire of the Eye: Landscape Representation and American Cultural Politics, 1825–1875* (Ithaca, N.Y.: Cornell University Press, 1993), 75.

13. *Daily Evening Transcript* (Boston, 27 February 1869): 2:1. Merl M. Moore kindly brought this article to my attention.

14. A painting by Haseltine titled "The Shore" and listed as belonging to "T. Appleton" was exhibited at the Boston Athenaeum in 1863.

15. Information on Agassiz, unless otherwise noted, is drawn from Edward Lurie's excellent biography *Louis Agassiz: A Life in Science* (Chicago: University of Chicago Press, 1960).

16. *New York Daily Tribune* (3 October 1847), quoted in Ibid., 142.

17. Lurie, *Louis Agassiz*, 126.

18. Louis Agassiz, *Comparative Physiology* (1861), quoted in Gerald Carr, *Frederic Edwin Church: The Icebergs* (Dallas Museum of Fine Arts, 1980), 12.

19. Although Agassiz's theory is still accepted, it has been considerably modified. For instance, Agassiz envisioned only a single ice age while today geologists believe that the earth has endured many glacial periods. Agassiz also exaggerated the geographical extent of the ancient ice sheets and was mistaken about the mechanics of glacial movement. For further information on this subject, see Albert V. Carrozi's introduction to his English translation of Agassiz's *Etudes sur les Glaciers*. (*Studies on Glaciers* [New York: Hafner Publishing, 1967].)

20. *The American Journal of Science* 41 (October 1841): 232.

21. Julia Ward Howe, *Reminiscences, 1819–1899* (Boston: Houghton Mifflin, 1899), 182–83.

22. *Nahant: A Collection of Sundry Sources*, 43, quoted in Marc Simpson et al., 23.

23. Louis Agassiz, "The Ice Period in America," *Atlantic Monthly* 14 (July 1864), 89.

24. Plowden, *William Stanley Haseltine*, 173.

25. *The Education of Henry Adams: An Autobiography* (1906; Boston: Houghton Mifflin, 1918), 14.

26. Plowden, *William Stanley Haseltine*, 168.

27. Ibid., 169.

28. It is profoundly ironic that such a devout man did so much to sever the connections between science and religion; that was certainly not his intention. In propounding the ice-age theory he did not mean to deny the historical validity of the Flood. His point was that the geologic features then pointed to as proofs of its occurrence were in fact remnants of glaciers. He did not argue that there had been no Flood, only that there was as yet no geological evidence of it. Despite his good intentions, his ice-age theory was one of the many blows that science dealt religion in the nineteenth century. It was one of the theories that tended to undermine a literal reading of the Bible and discredit it as an accurate account of the earth's history.

29. "Among the Studios," *Watson's Weekly Art Journal* 1, no. 24 (8 October 1864): 372, quoted in Marc Simpson et al., 17.

30. Henry Tuckerman, *Book of the Artists: American Artist Life* (New York: G. P. Putnam, 1867), 556–57.

31. Plowden, *William Stanley Haseltine*, 83.

32. Quoted in Ibid., 174.

CHAPTER SIX

1. Important critical writings on Moran include Nancy K. Anderson et al., *Thomas Moran*, exh. cat. (Washington, D.C.: National Gallery of Art, 1997); Joni Kinsey, *Thomas Moran and the Surveying of the American West* (Washington, D.C.: Smithsonian Institution Press, 1992); Anne

R. Morand, Joni Kinsey, and Mary Panzer, *Splendors of the American West: Thomas Moran's Art of the Grand Canyon of the Yellowstone* (Birmingham, Ala.: Birmingham Museum of Art, 1990); Carol Clark, *Thomas Moran: Watercolors of the American West* (Austin: University of Texas Press for the Amon Carter Museum of Western Art, 1980).

2. Many American artists served on or traveled with the surveys. Their ranks included the American Pre-Raphaelite painter John William Hill (1812–1879), a topographical artist for the New York State Geological Survey from 1836–41, and his son John Henry Hill with King's survey; Russell Smith who worked for both the Pennsylvania and Virginia Geological Surveys in the 1840s; Sanford Gifford who had accompanied Hayden's survey west in 1870; and Gilbert Munger who traversed the Sierras and Great Basin with King in about 1869–70. On the Hills, see Linda S. Ferber and William H. Gerdts, *The New Path: Ruskin and the American Pre-Raphaelites*, exh. cat. (Brooklyn: Brooklyn Museum, 1985), 166, 180; on Russell Smith, see "Russell Smith Memoirs," Smith Family Papers, AAA, roll 2038; on Sanford Gifford, see Ila Weiss, *Poetic Landscape: The Art and Experience of Sanford R. Gifford* (Newark: University of Delaware Press, 1987); on Gilbert Munger, see Patricia Trenton and Peter Hassrick, *The Rocky Mountains* (Norman: University of Oklahoma Press, 1983), 157, 159, 369, and J. Gray Sweeney, *American Painting at the Tweed Museum of Art and Glensheen* (Duluth: University of Minnesota, 1982), 50–52.

3. Peter B. Hales, *William Henry Jackson and the Transformation of the American Landscape* (Philadelphia: Temple University Press, 1988), 69.

4. For an excellent discussion of the surveys, see William H. Goetzmann, *Exploration and Empire* (New York: W. W. Norton, 1966); also Richard A. Bartlett, *Great Surveys of the American West* (Norman: University of Oklahoma Press, 1962).

5. The connections between Moran, Ruskin, and Turner have been discussed by many scholars. William H. Truettner, "'Scenes of Majesty and Enduring Interest': Thomas Moran Goes West," *Art Bulletin* 58 (1976): 241–59, offers the most eloquent discussion of the subject. See also Thurman Wilkins, *Thomas Moran: Artist of the Mountains* (Norman: University of Oklahoma Press, 1966); Kinsey, *Thomas Moran and the Surveying of the American West*, ch. 1; Clark, *Thomas Moran*; Richard Ladgast, "Thomas Moran, NA," *Truth* 19 (September 1900): 212 (AAA, NTM-1, frame 349).

6. John Ruskin, *Modern Painters*, in *The Works of John Ruskin*, ed. E. T. Cook and Alexander Wedderburn (London: G. Allen, 1903–12), 1:48.

7. Ibid., 1:34.

8. Ibid., 1:37.

9. Ibid., 1:32.

10. Ibid., 1:32–33.

11. Ibid., 1:487.

12. Ibid., 1:488.

13. Ibid., 4:238; John Ruskin, *Elements of Drawing*, in *The Works of John Ruskin*, ed. Cook and Wedderburn, 91.

14. Ruskin, *Modern Painters*, 4:176.

15. Moran's allegiance to Turner has been amply documented elsewhere. As a young man, Moran acquired Turner's *Liber Studiorum* and *The Rivers of France*, as well as other books with plates by the artist, and diligently copied them. In 1861 he went to England with the primary objective of studying Turner's works, which he continued to do throughout his career. See Clark, *Thomas Moran*, 8–9; Morand et al., *Splendors*, 11, 46; Wilkins, *Thomas Moran*, 21–22, 37–38; Sheldon, *American Painters*, 123; Thomas Moran Papers, East Hampton Free Library, East Hampton, N.Y. (AAA, roll N-TM1, frames 90, 94).

16. Thomas Moran, "Knowledge a Prime Requisite in Art," *Brush and Pencil* 12, no. 1 (April 1903): 14–16.

17. Gustave Buek, "Thomas Moran, N. A., The Grand Old Man of American Art," *The Mentor* (August 1924), quoted in Fritiof Fryxell, ed., *Thomas Moran: Explorer in Search of Beauty* (East Hampton, N.Y.: East Hampton Free Library, 1958), 67–68.

18. Ruskin, *Modern Painters*, 1:34.

19. Quoted in Hales, *William Henry Jackson*, 72.

20. William Henry Jackson in collaboration with Howard R. Driggs,

The Pioneer Photographer: Rocky Mountain Adventures with a Camera (Yonkers-on-Hudson, N.Y.: World Book Co., 1929), 83.

21. Ibid., 80.

22. Ibid., 89.

23. These notations are included on a sketch of the Yellowstone region from 1871 in the collection of the Cooper-Hewitt National Design Museum, New York, accession number 1917.17.11.

24. Quoted in Fritiof Fryxell, "Thomas Moran's Journey to the Tetons in 1879," *Augustana Historical Society Publications* 2 (1932): 37–46, in Thomas Moran Papers, East Hampton Free Library (AAA, N-TM3).

25. "Mr T. Moran's Sketches." Unidentified clipping from a scrapbook, Thomas Moran Papers, East Hampton Free Library (AAA, roll N-TM4, frame 600).

26. Quoted in Wilkins, *Thomas Moran*, 65.

27. Ferdinand V. Hayden, "The Wonders of the West — II: More about the Yellowstone," *Scribner's Monthly* 3, no. 4 (February 1872): 392.

28. "Moran's Yellowstone Canyon," *Republican* [Washington, D.C.], May 1872, clipping in the Moran Papers, East Hampton Free Library (AAA, roll N-TM1, frame 163).

29. This is discussed in Truettner, "Scenes of Majesty," 244.

30. R. W. Gilder, *Scribner's Monthly* (June 1872), quoted in Truettner, "Scenes of Majesty," 244.

31. Moran to Hayden, 11 March 1872 (National Archives, RG 57, mfm 623, roll 2, frames 468–70), quoted in Kinsey, *Thomas Moran*, 64.

32. Kinsey, *Thomas Moran*, 64.

33. "Fine Arts," *New York Tribune* (3 May 1872), clipping in the "Thomas Moran Scrapbook," Milch Gallery Papers (AAA, roll N/730, frame 62).

34. Ibid.

35. [Russell Sturgis?], "The Yellowstone Picture," *The Nation* 15 (5 September 1872): 157.

36. "Fine Arts," *New York Tribune* (3 May 1872).

37. Unidentified clipping, Moran Papers, East Hampton Free Library (AAA, roll N-TM4, frame 602).

38. "Moran's Picture: The Canon of the Yellowstone," unidentified clipping, Moran Papers, East Hampton Free Library (AAA, roll N-TM4, frame 600).

39. Clipping dated 25 March 1872, "Thomas Moran Scrapbook," Milch Gallery Papers (AAA, roll N/730, frame 30).

40. Moran to Mary Nimmo Moran, 13 August 1873, in *Home Thoughts from Afar: The Letters of Thomas Moran to Mary Nimmo Moran*, ed. Amy O. Bassford (East Hampton, N.Y.: East Hampton Free Library, 1967), 37.

41. Ibid., 39–40.

42. Unidentified clipping from Utah newspaper, 9 June 1900, in Moran Papers, East Hampton Free Library (AAA, roll N-TM4, frame 603).

43. Elizabeth C. Childs, "Time's Profile: John Wesley Powell, Art, and Geology at the Grand Canyon," *American Art* 10 (Spring 1996): 7–33.

44. John Wesley Powell, *Exploration of the Colorado River of the West* (1875), 174, quoted in Goetzmann, *Exploration and Empire*, 565–66.

45. Kinsey, *Thomas Moran*, 98.

46. "Chasm of the Colorado, by Thomas Moran," broadside published in conjunction with the painting's exhibition at M. Knoedler & Co., New York, Moran Papers, East Hampton Free Library (AAA, roll N-TM4, frame 604).

47. "Art," *Appleton's Journal* 11 (30 May 1874): 700.

48. Childs, "Time's Profile," 25.

49. Unidentified newspaper clipping signed "J. W. Powell," Thomas Moran Scrapbook, Milch Gallery Papers (AAA, roll N/730, frame 70).

50. Ibid.

51. "The Chasm of the Colorado," unidentified newspaper clipping, Moran Papers, East Hampton Free Library (AAA, roll N-TM4, frame 605).

52. Wilkins, *Thomas Moran*, 96.

53. Kinsey, *Thomas Moran*, 141.

54. Milch Gallery Papers (AAA, roll N/730, frame 68).

55. F. V. Hayden, *The Yellowstone National Park, and the Mountain*

Regions of Portions of Idaho, Nevada, Colorado and Utah (Boston: L. Prang, 1876), 37.

56. "The Mountain of the Holy Cross," Thomas Moran Scrapbook, Milch Gallery papers (AAA, roll N730, frame 37).

57. *Home Thoughts*, ed. Bassford, 51.

58. Sheldon, *American Painters*, 125.

59. Kinsey, *Thomas Moran*, chapter 8.

60. "The Fine Arts," *Boston Daily Advertiser*, 11 November 1875, clipping in the Thomas Moran Scrapbook, Milch Gallery Papers (AAA, roll N730, frame 44).

61. "American Painters," *The Art Journal* n.s. 5, no. 50 (February 1879): 43.

62. Moran, quoted in Fryxell, *Thomas Moran*, 64.

CONCLUSION

1. Edward Orton Jr. to C. H. Meinhard, Howard Young Galleries, New York, 29 December 1924 (AAA).

2. On geology's place in late nineteenth-century American culture, see Mott T. Greene, *Geology in the Nineteenth Century: Changing Views of a Changing World* (Ithaca, N.Y.: Cornell University Press, 1982); Richard Paul Boekenkamp, "Geological Education in the United States during the Late Nineteenth Century" (Ph.D. diss., Ohio State University, 1974).

3. John Durand, *The Life and Times of A. B. Durand* (1894; reprint, New York: Da Capo Press, 1970), 194–95.

4. John Ruskin, *The Letters of John Ruskin, 1827–1869*, in *The Works of John Ruskin*, ed. E. T. Cook and Alexander Wedderburn (London: G. Allen, 1903–12), 36:115.

5. Carol T. Christ, *The Finer Optic: The Aesthetics of Particularity in Victorian Poetry* (New Haven, Conn., and London: Yale University Press, 1975), 13.

6. On attitudes toward subjectivity/objectivity in the late nineteenth and early twentieth centuries, see Lorraine Daston and Peter Galison, "The Image of Objectivity," *Representations* 40 (Fall 1992): 81–129; Jonathan Crary, *Techniques of the Observer: On Vision and Modernity in the Nineteenth Century* (Cambridge, Mass.: MIT Press, an October Book, 1990); Christ, *Finer Optic*.

7. Daston and Galison, "Image of Objectivity," 81.

8. Ibid.

9. Charles Rosen and Henri Zerner, *Romanticism and Realism* (1984), quoted in Daston and Galison, "Image of Objectivity," 120.

10. Georgiana Burne-Jones, *Memorials of Edward Burne-Jones*, 2 vols. (London, 1904), 2:261, quoted in Allen Staley, *The Pre-Raphaelite Landscape* (Oxford: Clarendon Press, 1973), 95.

11. Christ, *Finer Optic*, 3.

Selected Bibliography

MANUSCRIPTS

Louis Agassiz Material. Houghton Library, Harvard University, Cambridge, Massachusetts.

Frederic Church Library and Papers. Olana State Historic Site, Hudson, New York.

Frederic Church Papers. Archives of American Art, Smithsonian Institution, Washington, D.C.

Thomas Cole Papers. Detroit Institute of Arts, Detroit, Michigan.

Thomas Cole Papers. New York State Library, Albany.

Asher Durand Papers. New York Public Library, Manuscript Division.

Sanford Gifford Papers. Typescripts in the Archives of American Art, Smithsonian Institution, Washington, D.C.

William Stanley Haseltine Papers. Archives of American Art, Smithsonian Institution, Washington, D.C.

William Stanley Haseltine Class Records. Harvard University Archives, Cambridge, Massachusetts.

Gordon Hendricks Papers. Archives of American Art, Smithsonian Institution, Washington, D.C.

John F. Kensett Papers. Archives of American Art, Smithsonian Institution, Washington, D.C.

Milch Gallery Papers. Archives of American Art, Smithsonian Institution, Washington, D.C.

Thomas Moran Papers. East Hampton Free Library, East Hampton, New York.

Thomas Moran Papers. Huntington Library and Art Gallery, San Marino, California.

Thomas Moran Papers. Thomas Gilcrease Institute of American History and Art, Tulsa, Oklahoma.

John Muir Papers. Huntington Library and Art Gallery, San Marino, California.

William Trost Richards Papers. Archives of American Art, Smithsonian Institution, Washington, D.C.

"Russell Smith Memoirs," Smith Family Papers. Archives of American Art, Smithsonian Institution, Washington, D.C.

OTHER WORKS CITED

Adams, Henry. *The Education of Henry Adams: An Autobiography.* 1906. Reprint edition. Boston: Houghton Mifflin, 1918.

Adamson, Jeremy Elwell. *Niagara: Two Centuries of Changing Attitudes, 1697–1901.* Exh. cat. Washington, D.C.: Corcoran Gallery of Art, 1985.

Agassiz, Louis. *Contributions to the Natural History of the United States.* Boston: Little, Brown and Co., 1857–62.

——. *Étude sur les Glaciers.* Neuchatel: Jent et Gassmann, 1840.

Agassiz, Louis. *Geological Sketches.* Boston: Fields, Osgood, and Co., 1866.

——. "The Ice Period in America." *Atlantic Monthly* 14 (July 1864): 89–93.

——. *Principles of Zoology.* Boston: Gould, Kendall, and Lincoln, 1848.

Alison, Archibald. *Essay on the Nature and Principles of Taste.* 3rd ed. London: Longman, 1812.

Anderson, Nancy K., and Linda S. Ferber, *Albert Bierstadt: Art and Enterprise.* Brooklyn Museum in association with Hudson Hills Press, New York, 1990.

——. "The Kiss of Enterprise: The Western Landscape as Symbol and Resource." In *The West as America: Reinterpreting Images of the Frontier, 1820–1920,* ed. William H. Truettner. Washington, D.C.: Smithsonian Institution Press, 1991.

——, et al. *Thomas Moran.* Exh. cat. Washington, D.C.: National Gallery of Art, 1997.

Antczak, Frederick J. *Thought and Character: The Rhetoric of Democratic Education.* Ames: Iowa State University Press, 1985.

Avery, Kevin. *Church's Great Picture: The Heart of the Andes.* New York: Metropolitan Museum of Art, 1993.

——. "*The Heart of the Andes* Exhibited: Frederic E. Church's Window on the Equatorial World." *American Art Journal* 18 (1986): 52–72.

——. "Whaling Voyage Round the World: Russell and Purrington's Moving Panorama and Herman Melville's 'Mighty Book.'" *American Art Journal* 22 (1990): 50–78.

Baatz, Simon. "'Squinting at Silliman': Scientific Periodicals in the Early American Republic, 1810–1833," *Isis* 82 (June 1991): 223–44.

Baigel, Matthew. *Thomas Cole.* New York: Watson Guptill, 1981.

Barber, Lynn. *The Heyday of Natural History, 1820–1870.* London: Jonathan Cape, 1980.

Bartlett, Richard A. *Great Surveys of the American West.* Norman: University of Oklahoma Press, 1962.

Bassford, Amy O., ed. *Home Thoughts from Afar: The Letters of Thomas Moran to Mary Nimmo Moran.* East Hampton, N.Y.: East Hampton Free Library, 1967.

Beaux, Cecilia. *Background with Figures.* Boston: Houghton Mifflin, 1930.

Bedell, Rebecca. "The Anatomy of Nature: Geology and American Landscape Painting, 1825–1875." Ph.D. diss., Yale University, 1989.

——. "Thomas Cole and the Fashionable Science." In *Art and Science in America: Issues of Representation,* ed. Amy R. W. Meyers. San Marino, Calif.: Huntington Library, 1998.

——. "Haseltine, Agassiz, and the Rocks at Nahant." *Nineteenth Century* 14, no. 1 (1994): 3–9.

Belanger, Pamela J. *Inventing Acadia: Artists and Tourists at Mount Desert.* Exh. cat. Rockland, Maine: Farnsworth Art Museum, 1999.

Bender, Thomas. *New York Intellect.* New York: Knopf, 1987.

——. "The Rural Cemetery Movement: Urban Travail and the Appeal of Nature." *New England Quarterly* 47 (June 1974): 196–211.

Bendiner, Kenneth. "John Brett's 'The Glacier of Rosenlaui,'" *Art Journal* 44 (Fall 1984): 241–48.

Bennewitz, Kathleen Motes. "John F. Kensett at Beverly, Massachusetts." *American Art Journal* 21, no. 4 (1989): 46–65.

Bode, Carl. *The American Lyceum: Town Meeting of the Mind.* New York: Oxford University Press, 1956.

Boekenkamp, Richard Paul. "Geological Education in the United States during the Late Nineteenth Century." Ph.D. diss., Ohio State University, 1974.

Boller, Paul F. *American Transcendentalism, 1830–1860: An Intellectual Inquiry.* New York: G. P. Putnam's, 1974.

Brigham, David R. *Public Culture in the Early Republic: Peale's Museum and Its Audience.* Washington, D.C.: Smithsonian Institution Press, 1995.

Brooke, John Hedley. "The Natural Theology of the Geologists: Some Theological Strata." In *Images of the Earth,* ed. L. J. Jordanova and Roy S. Porter. *Boston Society for the History of Science Monographs,* vol. 1 (1979): 39–64.

Brown, Chandos Michael. *Benjamin Silliman: A Life in the Young Republic.* Princeton, N.J.: Princeton University Press, 1989.

Brown, Dona. *Inventing New England: Regional Tourism in the Nineteenth Century.* Washington, D.C.: Smithsonian Institution Press, 1995.

Bryant, William Cullen, ed. *Picturesque America.* 2 vols. New York: D. Appleton, 1872–74.

Carr, Gerald. *Frederic Edwin Church: The Icebergs.* Exh. cat. Dallas Museum of Fine Arts, 1980.

Carver, John. *Sketches of New England.* New York: E. French, 1842.

Casteras, Susan P., et al. *John Ruskin and the Victorian Eye.* New York: Harry N. Abrams, 1993.

Childs, Elizabeth C. "Time's Profile: John Wesley Powell, Art, and Geology at the Grand Canyon." *American Art* 10 (Spring 1996): 7–33.

Christ, Carol T. *The Finer Optic: The Aesthetic of Particularity in Victorian Poetry.* New Haven, Conn., and London: Yale University Press, 1975.

Cikovsky, Nicolai Jr. "'The Ravages of the Axe': The Meaning of the Tree Stump in Nineteenth-Century American Art." *Art Bulletin* 61 (December 1979): 611–26.

Clark, Carol. *Thomas Moran: Watercolors of the American West.* Austin: University of Texas Press for the Amon Carter Museum of Western Art, 1980.

Cole, Thomas. "Essay on American Scenery." 1836. In John W. McCoubrey, *American Art 1700–1960: Sources and Documents,* 98–109. Englewood Cliffs, N.J.: Prentice-Hall, 1965.

Comstock, J. L. *Outlines of Geology.* Hartford: D. F. Robinson and Co., 1834.

Cook, Clarence. *Art and Artists of Our Time.* 3 vols. New York: Selmar Hess, 1888.

Crary, Jonathan. *The Techniques of the Observer: Vision and Modernity in the Nineteenth Century.* Cambridge, Mass.: MIT Press, an October book, 1990.

Cremin, Lawrence A. *American Education: The National Experience, 1783–1876.* New York: Harper and Row, 1980.

Cross, Barbara M. *Horace Bushnell: Minister to a Changing America.* Chicago: University of Chicago Press, 1958.

Curtis, George William. *Lotus-Eating: A Summer Book.* 1852. New York: Harper and Brothers, 1874.

Cuyler, Theodore L. "A Sabbath on the Catskills." In *The Scenery of the Catskill Mountains.* New York: D. Fanshaw, 1864.

Daniels, George H. *American Science in the Age of Jackson.* New York: Columbia University Press, 1968.

Daston, Lorraine, and Peter Galison, "The Image of Objectivity." *Representations* 40 (Fall 1992): 81–129.

Dean, Dennis R. "The Influence of Geology on American Thought and Literature." In *Two Hundred Years of Geology in America: Proceedings of the New Hampshire Bicentennial Conference on the History of Geology,* ed. Cecil J. Schneer. Hanover, N.H.: University of New England Press, 1979.

D'Emilio, Sandra, and Suzan Campbell. *Visions and Visionaries: The Art and Artists of the Sante Fe Railway.* Salt Lake City: Gibbs Smith, 1991.

Dickason, David Howard. *The Daring Young Men: The Story of the American Pre-Raphaelites.* Bloomington: Indiana University Press, 1953.

Dix, John. *A Hand-book of Newport and Rhode Island.* Newport: C. E. Hammett Jr., 1852.

Downing, Andrew Jackson. *Rural Essays.* New York: R. Worthington, 1881.

——. *A Treatise on the Theory and Practice of Landscape Gardening.* New York: Putnam, 1849.

Driscoll, John Paul, and John K. Howat. *John Frederick Kensett: An American Master.* Exh. cat. Worcester, Mass.: Worcester Art Museum, 1985.

Durand, John. *The Life and Times of A. B. Durand.* 1894. Reprint, New York: Da Capo Press, 1970.

Dwight, Theodore. *The Northern Traveller and Northern Tour.* 5th ed. New York: Goodrich and Wiley, 1834.

Featherstonhaugh, G. W. *Geological Report of an Examination of the Elevated Country between the Missouri and Red Rivers.* Washington, D.C.: Gales and Seaton, 1835.

Ferber, Linda S., and William H. Gerdts. *The New Path: Ruskin and the American Pre-Raphaelites.* Exh. cat. Brooklyn Museum, 1985.

Ferber, Linda S. "William Trost Richards (1833–1905): American Landscape and Marine Painter." Ph.D. diss., Columbia University, 1980.

Figuier, Louis. *The World before the Deluge.* Trans. from the 4th French ed. London: Chapman and Hall, 1865.

Foshay, Ella M. "Luman Reed, A New York Patron of American Art." *The Magazine Antiques* 138 (November 1990): 1074–85.

——. *Mr. Luman Reed's Picture Gallery.* New York: Harry N. Abrams, 1990.

——. *Reflections of Nature: Flowers in American Art.* Exh. cat. New York: Alfred A. Knopf, in assoc. with the Whitney Museum of American Art, 1984.

Fox, Dixon Ryan. *The Decline of the Aristocracy in the Politics of New York.* New York: Columbia University, 1919.

Frederickson, George M. *The Inner Civil War.* New York: Harper & Row, 1965.

Fryxell, Fritiof, ed. *Thomas Moran: Explorer in Search of Beauty.* East Hampton, N.Y.: East Hampton Free Library, 1958.

Gillispie, Charles Coulton. *Genesis and Geology.* Cambridge, Mass.: Harvard University Press, 1951.

Goetzmann, William H. *Exploration and Empire.* New York: W. W. Norton, 1966.

Gould, Stephen J. *Time's Arrow, Time's Cycle: Myth and Metaphor in the Discovery of Geological Time.* Cambridge, Mass.: Harvard University Press, 1987.

Greene, John C. "Protestantism, Science, and American Enterprise: Benjamin Silliman's Moral Universe." In *Benjamin Silliman and his Circle,* ed. Leonard G. Wilson. New York: Science History Publications, 1979.

Greene, Mott T. *Geology in the Nineteenth Century: Changing Views of a Changing World.* Ithaca, N.Y.: Cornell University Press, 1982.

Gully, Anthony Lacy. "Sermons in Stone: Ruskin and Geology." In *John Ruskin and the Victorian Eye,* Susan P. Casteras et al. New York: Harry N. Abrams, 1993.

Hales, Peter B. *William Henry Jackson and the Transformation of the American Landscape.* Philadelphia: Temple University Press, 1988.

Haley, Bruce. *The Healthy Body and Victorian Culture.* Cambridge, Mass.: Harvard University Press, 1978.

Hallam, A. *Great Geological Controversies.* New York: Oxford University Press, 1983.

Haltman, Kenneth. "The Poetics of Geologic Reverie: Figures of Source and Origin in Samuel Seymour's Landscapes of the Rocky Mountains." In *Art and Science in America: Issues of Representation,* ed. Amy R. W. Meyers. San Marino, Calif.: Huntington Library, 1998.

Harris, Neil. *Cultural Excursions.* Chicago: Chicago University Press, 1990.

——. *Humbug: The Art of P. T. Barnum.* Chicago: Chicago University Press, 1973. Reprint, Chicago: University of Chicago Press, 1981.

Harvey, Eleanor Jones. *The Painted Sketch: American Impressions from Nature, 1830–1880.* Exh. cat. Dallas Museum of Art in assoc. with Harry N. Abrams, 1998.

Hawkins, Kenneth Blair. "The Therapeutic Landscape: Nature, Architecture, and Mind in Nineteenth-Century America." Ph.D. diss., University of Rochester, 1991.

Hayden, Ferdinand V. *Sun Pictures of Rocky Mountain Scenery.* New York: Julius Bien, 1870.

——. "The Wonders of the West — II: More about the Yellowstone," *Scribner's Monthly* 3, no. 4 (February 1872): 388–96.

——. *The Yellowstone National Park, and the Mountain Regions of Portions of Idaho, Nevada, Colorado and Utah.* Boston: L. Prang, 1876.

Hewison, Robert. *John Ruskin and the Argument of the Eye.* Princeton, N.J.: Princeton University Press, 1976.

Hitchcock, Edward. *Sketch of the Scenery of Massachusetts with Plates from the Geological Report of Professor Hitchcock.* Northampton, Mass.: J. H. Butler, 1842.

Holmes, Oliver Wendell. *The Autocrat at the Breakfast Table.* Boston: Houghton Mifflin, 1858.

Homer, James Lloyd. *Nahant, & Other Places on the North-Shore.* Boston: W. Chadwick, 1848.

Hovenkamp, Herbert. *Science and Religion in America, 1800–1860.* Philadelphia: University of Pennsylvania Press, 1978.

Howat, John K. *John Frederick Kensett, 1816–1872.* Exh. cat. New York: Metropolitan Museum of Art, 1968.

Howe, Julia Ward. *Reminiscences: 1819–1899.* Boston: Houghton Mifflin, 1899.

Humboldt, Alexander von. *Aspects of Nature in Different Lands and Climates.* Trans. Mrs. Sabine. London: Longman, 1849.

——. *Cosmos: A Sketch of a Physical Description of the Universe.* 5 vols. Trans. E. C. Otté. London: Henry G. Bohn, 1849–52.

——. *Personal Narrative of Travels to the Equinoctal Regions.* Trans. Helen Williams. Philadelphia: M. Carey, 1815.

Huntington, David C. "Church and Luminism: Light for America's Elect." In *American Light*, ed. John Wilmerding. Exh. cat. Washington, D.C.: National Gallery of Art, 1980.

——. "Frederic Edwin Church, 1826–1900: Painter of the Adamic New World Myth." Ph.D. diss., Yale University, 1960.

——. *The Landscapes of Frederic Edwin Church.* New York: G. Braziller, 1966.

Jackson, William Henry. *Descriptive Catalogue of the Photographs of the U.S. Geological Survey of the Territories, for the Years 1869 to 1873, inclusive.* Washington, D.C.: Government Printing Office, 1874.

Jackson, William Henry, in collaboration with Howard R. Driggs. *The Pioneer Photographer: Rocky Mountain Adventures with a Camera.* Yonkers-on-Hudson, N.Y.: World Book Co., 1929.

Jaher, Frederick Cople. *The Urban Establishment: Upper Strata in Boston, New York, Charleston, Chicago, and Los Angeles.* Urbana: University of Illinois Press, 1982.

Jarves, James Jackson. *The Art Idea*, 1864. Reprint edited by Benjamin Rowland Jr. Cambridge: Harvard University Press, 1960.

Judson, Isabella Field. *Cyrus W. Field: His Life and Work.* New York: Harper & Bros., 1896.

Keeney, Elizabeth B. *The Botanizers: Amateur Scientists in Nineteenth-Century America.* Chapel Hill: University of North Carolina Press, 1992.

Kelly, Franklin W. *American Paintings of the Nineteenth Century, Part I.* The Collection of the National Gallery of Art Systematic Catalogue Series. New York: Oxford University Press, 1996.

——. *Frederic Church and the National Landscape.* Washington, D.C.: Smithsonian Institution Press, 1988.

——. "Myth, Allegory, and Science: Thomas Cole's Paintings of Mount Etna." *Arts in Virginia* 23 (1983): 2–17.

Kelly, Franklin W., and Gerald L. Carr. *The Early Landscapes of Frederic Edwin Church, 1845–1854.* Fort Worth, Tex.: Amon Carter Museum, 1987.

——, et al. *Frederic Edwin Church.* Exh. cat. Washington, D.C.: National Gallery of Art, 1989.

Keyes, Donald D. *The White Mountains: Place and Perception.* Exh. cat. Durham: University Art Galleries, University of New Hampshire, 1980.

King, Clarence. *Mountaineering in the Sierra Nevada.* 4th ed. Boston: James R. Osgood, 1874.

——. *Systematic Geology.* Washington, D.C.: Government Printing Office, 1878. With chromolithographs after paintings by Gilbert Munger and photographs by Timothy O'Sullivan.

Kinsey, Joni. *Thomas Moran and the Surveying of the American West.* Washington, D.C.: Smithsonian Institution Press, 1992.

Kirchhoff, Frederick. "A Science against Sciences." In *Nature and the Victorian Imagination*, U. C. Knoepflmacher and G. B. Tennyson, eds. Berkeley and Los Angeles: University of California Press, 1977.

Klonk, Charlotte. *Science and the Perception of Nature.* New Haven, Conn., and London: Yale University Press, 1996.

Knoepflmacher, U. C., and G. B. Tennyson, eds. *Nature and the Victorian Imagination.* Berkeley and Los Angeles: University of California Press, 1977.

Kohl, Lawrence Frederick. *The Politics of Individualism.* New York: Oxford University Press, 1989.

Kohlstedt, Sally Gregory. "Parlors, Primers, and Public Schooling: Education for Science in Nineteenth-Century America." *Isis* 81 (1990): 425–45.

——. "Curiosities and Cabinets: Natural History Museums and Education on the Antebellum Campus." *Isis* 79 (1988): 405–26.

LaBudde, Kenneth James. "The Mind of Thomas Cole," Ph.D. diss., University of Minnesota, 1954.

Laudan, Rachel. *From Mineralogy to Geology: The Foundations of a Science, 1650–1830.* Chicago: University of Chicago Press, 1987.

Lawall, David. *Asher B. Durand: A Documentary Catalogue of the Narrative and Landscape Paintings.* New York: Garland Publishing, 1978.

———. *Asher Brown Durand: His Art and Art Theory in Relation to his Times.* New York: Garland Publishing, 1977.

Leslie, Charles Robert. *Memoirs of the Life of John Constable.* London: J. M. Dent, 1911.

Lewis, Alonzo. *Picture of Nahant.* Lynn, Mass.: J. B. Tolman, 1845.

Lewis, R.W.B. *The American Adam: Innocence, Tragedy, and Tradition in the Nineteenth Century.* Chicago: University of Chicago Press, 1955.

Linden-Ward, Blanche. *Silent City on a Hill: Landscapes of Memory and Boston's Mount Auburn Cemetery.* Columbus: Ohio State University Press, 1989.

Lodge, Henry Cabot. *An Historical Address.* Nahant, Mass.: Town of Nahant, 1904.

Lowenthal, David. *The Past is a Foreign Country.* London: Cambridge University Press, 1985.

Ludlow, Fitz Hugh. *The Heart of the Continent.* New York: Hurd & Houghton, 1870.

Lurie, Edward. *Louis Agassiz: A Life in Science.* Chicago: University of Chicago Press, 1960.

Lyell, Charles. *Lyell's Lectures on Geology: Eight Lectures on Geology Delivered at the Broadway Tabernacle in the City of New York.* New York: Greeley & McGrath, Tribune Office, 1842.

———. *Principles of Geology.* 3 vols. New York: D. Appleton, 1859. First published in London, 1830–33.

———. *Travels in North America in the Years 1841–2.* New York: Wiley and Putnam, 1845.

Mabee, Carleton. *The American Leonardo: A Life of Samuel F. B. Morse.* New York: Alfred A. Knopf, 1943.

Mantell, Gideon Algernon. *Thoughts on a Pebble; or a First Lesson in Geology.* 7th ed. London: printed for the author by Reeve Bros., 1846.

Manthorne, Katherine. *Creation and Renewal: Views of Cotopaxi.* Exh. cat. Washington, D.C.: National Museum of American Art, 1985.

Marcou, Jules. *Life, Letters, and Works of Louis Agassiz.* New York: MacMillan and Co., 1896.

McAllister, Ethel M. *Amos Eaton: Scientist and Educator.* Philadelphia: University of Pennsylvania Press, 1941.

McClellan, B. Edward, and William J. Reese, eds. *The Social History of Education.* Chicago: University of Illinois Press, 1988.

McNulty, J. Bard, ed. *The Correspondence of Thomas Cole and Daniel Wadsworth.* Hartford: Connecticut Historical Society, 1983.

Merrill, George P. *The First One Hundred Years of American Geology.* New Haven, Conn., and London: Yale University Press, 1924.

Merrill, Lynn L. *The Romance of Victorian Natural History.* New York: Oxford University Press, 1989.

Metcalf, Samuel L. "The Interest and Importance of Scientific Geology as a Subject for Study," *Knickerbocker* 3 (April 1834): 225–35.

Meyers, Amy R. W., ed. *Art and Science in America: Issues of Representation.* San Marino, Calif.: Huntington Library, 1998.

Miller, Angela. *The Empire of the Eye: Landscape Representation and American Cultural Politics, 1825–1875.* Ithaca, N.Y.: Cornell University Press, 1993.

———. "Spaces as Destiny: the Panorama Vogue in Mid-Nineteenth-Century America." 3: 739–44. In *World Art: Themes of Unity in Diversity,* ed. Irving Lavin. 3 vols. University Park, Penn.: University of Pittsburgh Press, 1989.

———. "Thomas Cole and Jacksonian America: The Course of Empire as Political Allegory." *Prospects* 14 (1989): 65–92.

Miller, David C., ed. *American Iconology.* New Haven, Conn., and London: Yale University Press, 1993.

Miller, Douglas T. *Jacksonian Aristocracy.* New York: Oxford University Press, 1967.

Miller, Hugh. *The Old Red Sandstone.* Boston: Gould and Lincoln, 1858. First published in London, 1841.

———. *The Testimony of the Rocks.* Boston: Gould and Lincoln, 1858.

Miller, Lillian B. "Charles Willson Peale as History Painter: *The Exhuma-*

tion of the Mastodon." *American Art Journal* 13 (Winter 1981): 47–68.

Mitchell, Timothy F. *Art and Science in German Landscape Painting, 1770–1840.* New York: Oxford University Press, 1993.

Moran, Thomas. "Knowledge a Prime Requisite in Art," *Brush and Pencil* 12, no. 1 (April 1903): 14–16.

Morand, Anne R., Joni Kinsey, and Mary Panzer. *Splendors of the American West: Thomas Moran's Art of the Grand Canyon of the Yellowstone.* Exh. cat. Birmingham, Ala.: Birmingham Museum of Art, 1990.

Morse, Edward Lind. *Samuel F. B. Morse: His Letters and Journals.* Boston: Houghton Mifflin, 1914.

Myers, Kenneth. *The Catskills: Painters, Writers, and Tourists in the Mountains, 1820–1895.* Yonkers, N.Y.: Hudson River Museum of Westchester, 1987.

——. "On the Cultural Construction of Landscape Experience." In *American Iconology,* ed. David C. Miller. New Haven, Conn., and London: Yale University Press, 1993.

Nahant: A Collection from Sundry Sources of Some Noteworthy Descriptions of the Town. Lynn, Mass.: John MacFarlane, 1899.

Nevins, Allan, ed. *Diary of Philip Hone.* New York: Dodd, Mead and Co., 1936.

Noble, Louis Legrand. *After Icebergs with a Painter.* New York: D. Appleton, 1861.

——. *The Life and Works of Thomas Cole.* 1853. Reprint edition. Cambridge, Mass.: Harvard University Press, 1964.

Novak, Barbara. *Nature and Culture: American Landscape and Painting, 1825–1875.* New York: Oxford University Press, 1980; rev. ed. 1996.

Oakes, William. *Scenery of the White Mountains.* Boston: Crosby and Nichols, 1848.

Ostrom, John H. "Mr. Peale's Missing Mastodon." *Discovery* 17 (1983–84): 3–9.

Paradis, James, and Thomas Postlewait, eds. *Victorian Science and Victorian Values: Literary Perspectives.* New Brunswick, N.J.: Rutgers University Press, 1985.

Parry, Ellwood C., "Acts of God, Acts of Man: Geological Ideas and the Imaginary Landscapes of Thomas Cole." In *Two Hundred Years of Geology in America: Proceedings of the New Hampshire Conference on the History of Geology,* ed. Cecil J. Schneer. Hanover, N.H.: University Press of New England, 1979: 53–71.

——. *The Art of Thomas Cole: Ambition and Imagination.* Newark: University of Delaware Press, 1988.

——. "Landscape Theater in America." *American Art Journal* 59 (1971): 52–61.

——. "Recent Discoveries in the Art of Thomas Cole." *Antiques* 120 (November 1981): 1156–65.

——. "Thomas Cole's Ideas for Mr. Reed's Doors." *American Art Journal* 12 (Summer 1980): 33–45.

Paterson, Stanley C., and Carl G. Seaburg. *Nahant on the Rocks.* Nahant, Mass.: Nahant Historical Society, 1991.

Pessen, Edward. *Riches, Class, and Power Before the Civil War.* Lexington, Mass.: D. C. Heath, 1973.

Plowden, Helen Haseltine. *William Stanley Haseltine, Sea and Landscape Painter.* London: Frederick Muller, 1947.

Pointon, Marcia. "Geology and Landscape Painting in Nineteenth-Century England." In *Images of the Earth,* eds. L. J. Jordanova and Roy S. Porter. *Boston Society for the History of Science Monographs,* vol. 1 (1979): 39–64.

Powell, Earl A. III. "Thomas Cole and the American Landscape Tradition: Associationism." *Arts Magazine* 52 (April 1978): 113–17.

——. "Thomas Cole and the American Landscape Tradition: The Naturalist Controversy." *Arts Magazine* 52 (February 1978): 114–23.

——. "Thomas Cole and the American Landscape Tradition: The Picturesque." *Arts Magazine* 52 (March 1978): 110–17.

Purchase, Eric. *Out of Nowhere: Disaster and Tourism in the White Mountains.* Baltimore: Johns Hopkins University Press, 1999.

Quick, Michael. *American Portraiture in the Grand Manner: 1720–1920.* Exh. cat. Los Angeles County Museum of Art, 1981.

Reingold, Nathan. *Science in American Society: A Documentary History.*

New York: Hill and Wang, 1964.

Reynolds, Joshua. *Discourses on Art.* Ed. Robert R. Wark. New Haven, Conn., and London: Yale University Press, 1975.

Ringe, Donald A. "William Cullen Bryant and the Science of Geology." *American Literature* 26 (January 1955): 507–14.

Rockwell, Charles. *The Catskill Mountains and the Region Around.* New York: Taintor Bros., 1867.

Rosenberg, John. *The Darkening Glass: A Portrait of Ruskin's Genius.* New York: Columbia University Press, 1961.

Rudwick, Martin. "The Emergence of a Visual Language for Geological Science, 1760–1840." *History of Science* 14 (1976): 149–95.

———. *Scenes from Deep Time: Early Pictorial Representations of the Prehistoric World.* Chicago: University of Chicago Press, 1992.

Ruskin, John. *Deucalion and other Stories in Rocks and Stones,* vol. 26, *The Works of John Ruskin,* ed. E. T. Cook and Alexander Wedderburn. London: G. Allen, 1903–12.

———. *Elements of Drawing,* vol. 15, *The Works of John Ruskin,* ed. E. T. Cook and Alexander Wedderburn. London: G. Allen, 1903–12.

———. *The Letters of John Ruskin, 1827–1869,* vol. 36, *The Works of John Ruskin,* ed. E. T. Cook and Alexander Wedderburn. London: G. Allen, 1903–12.

———. *Modern Painters,* 5 vols., vols. 3–7 in *The Works of John Ruskin,* ed. E. T. Cook and Alexander Wedderburn. London: G. Allen, 1903–12.

Schuyler, David. *Apostle of Taste: Andrew Jackson Downing, 1815–1852.* Baltimore: Johns Hopkins University Press, 1996.

Schweber, S. S. "Scientists as Intellectuals: The Early Victorians." In *Victorian Science and Victorian Values: Literary Perspectives,* ed. James Paradis and Thomas Postlewait. New Brunswick, N.J.: Rutgers University Press, 1985.

Sears, John. *Sacred Places: American Tourist Attractions in the Nineteenth Century.* New York: Oxford University Press, 1989.

Sellers, Charles Coleman. *Charles Willson Peale: The Early Life (1741–1790).* Philadelphia: The American Philosophical Society, 1947.

———. *Mr. Peale's Museum.* New York: W. W. Norton, 1980.

Sellers, Charles Grier. *The Market Revolution: Jacksonian America, 1815–1846.* New York: Oxford University Press, 1991.

Sheldon, George W. *American Painters.* New York: D. Appleton, 1879.

Shepard, Paul, Jr. "Paintings of the New England Landscape: A Scientist Looks at their Geomorphology." *College Art Journal* 17 (Fall 1957): 30–42.

Silliman, Benjamin. *Outline of the Course of Geological Lectures Given in Yale College.* New Haven, Conn., 1820.

———. *Remarks Made on a Short Tour between Hartford and Quebec in the Autumn of 1819.* New Haven, Conn.: S. Converse, 1824.

Simpson, Marc, et al. *Expressions of Place: The Art of William Stanley Haseltine.* Exh. cat. The Fine Arts Museums of San Francisco, 1992.

Simpson, Pamela H. *So Beautiful an Arch: Images of the Natural Bridge, 1787–1890.* Exh. cat. Lexington, Va.: Washington and Lee University, 1982.

Stafford, Barbara Maria. *Artful Science: Enlightenment, Entertainment and the Eclipse of Visual Education.* Cambridge, Mass.: MIT Press, 1994.

———. *Voyage into Substance: Art, Science, Nature and the Illustrated Travel Account, 1760–1840.* Cambridge, Mass.: MIT Press, 1984.

Staley, Allen. *The Pre-Raphaelite Landscape.* Oxford: Clarendon Press, 1973.

Stannard, David, ed. *Death in America.* Philadelphia: University of Pennsylvania Press, 1975.

Starr King, Thomas. *The White Hills: Their Legends, Landscape, and Poetry.* Boston: Crosby & Nichols, 1862. First published 1859.

Stein, Roger B. "Charles Willson Peale's Expressive Design: *The Artist in His Museum,*" In *New Perspectives on Charles Willson Peale,* ed. Lillian B. Miller and David C. Ward. Pittsburgh: University of Pittsburgh Press for the Smithsonian Institution, 1991.

———. *John Ruskin and Aesthetic Thought in America, 1840–1900.* Cambridge, Mass.: Harvard University Press, 1967.

Stillman, William James. *The Autobiography of a Journalist.* 2 vols. Boston: Houghton, Mifflin, 1901.

Story, Ronald. *The Forging of an Aristocracy: Harvard and the Boston Upper Class, 1800–1870.* Middletown, Conn.: Wesleyan University Press, 1980.

[Sturgis, Russell?]. "Fine Arts: The Kensett Relics." *The Nation* 16 (20 March 1873): 204.

Sullivan, Mark. "John F. Kensett, American Landscape Painter." Ph.D. diss., Bryn Mawr College, 1981.

Sweeney, J. Gray. *American Painting at the Tweed Museum of Art and Glensheen, the University of Minnesota, Duluth.* Duluth: Tweed Museum of Art, 1982.

———. "The Artist-Explorers of the American West, 1860–1880." Ph.D. diss., Indiana University, 1975.

Sweetser, Moses Foster, ed. *The White Mountains: A Handbook for Travellers,* 9th ed. Boston: Ticknor & Co., 1888.

Toulmin, Stephen, and June Goodfield. *The Discovery of Time.* Chicago: University of Chicago Press, 1965.

Trenton, Patricia, and Peter Hassrick. *The Rocky Mountains.* Norman: University of Oklahoma Press, 1983.

Truettner, William H. "The Genesis of Frederic Edwin Church's *Aurora Borealis.*" *Art Quarterly* 31 (Autumn 1968): 267–83.

———. "'Scenes of Majesty and Enduring Interest': Thomas Moran Goes West." *Art Bulletin* 58 (1976): 241–59.

———, and Alan Wallach. *Thomas Cole: Landscape into History.* New Haven, Conn.: Yale University Press and National Museum of American Art, Smithsonian Institution, Washington, D.C., 1994.

Trump, Richard Shafer. "Life and Works of Albert Bierstadt." Ph.D. diss., Ohio State University, 1963.

Tuckerman, Henry T. *Book of the Artists: American Artist Life.* New York: G. P. Putnam, 1867.

Tymn, Marshall, ed. *Thomas Cole: The Collected Essays and Prose Sketches.* St. Paul, Minn.: John Colet Press, 1980.

Wagner, Virginia. "Geological Time in Nineteenth-Century Landscape Paintings." *Winterthur Portfolio* 24 (Summer/Autumn 1989): 153–64.

———. "The Idea of Geology in American Landscape Painting, 1825–1875." Ph.D. diss., University of Delaware, 1987.

———. "John Ruskin and Artistical Geology in America." *Winterthur Portfolio* 23 (Summer/Autumn 1988): 151–67.

Wallach, Alan. "Cole, Byron, and the Course of Empire." *Art Bulletin* 50 (December 1968): 375–79.

———. "Thomas Cole and the Aristocracy." *Arts Magazine* 56 (November 1981): 94–106.

Walter, Cornelia W. *Mount Auburn Illustrated.* New York, 1847.

Weekley, Carolyn. *The Kingdoms of Edward Hicks.* Williamsburg, Va.: Colonial Williamsburg Foundation, 1999.

Weiss, Ila. *Poetic Landscape: The Art and Experience of Sanford R. Gifford.* Newark: University of Delaware Press, 1987.

Welter, Rush. *American Writings on Popular Education: The Nineteenth Century.* New York: Bobbs-Merrill, 1971.

Whitney, J. D. *The Yosemite Book.* New York: Julius Bien, 1868.

Wilkins, Thurman. *Thomas Moran: Artist of the Mountains.* Norman: University of Oklahoma Press, 1966.

Wilmerding, John, ed. *American Light: The Luminist Movement, 1850–1875.* Exh. cat. Washington, D.C.: National Gallery of Art, 1980.

Wilson, Leonard G., ed. *Benjamin Silliman and His Circle.* New York: Science History Publications, 1979.

Winthrop, Theodore. *A Companion to The Heart of the Andes.* New York: D. Appleton, 1859.

Index

Photography Credits

The Art Museum, Princeton University, Princeton, New Jersey (fig. 26)
Autry Museum of Western Heritage, Los Angeles (fig. 73)
Collection Bayly Art Museum, University of Virginia, Charlottesville (fig. 38)
Collection of the Bronck Museum of the Greene County Historical Society, Coxsackie, New York (fig. 5)
Brooklyn Museum of Art (fig. 58)
The Century Association, New York, photo Geoffrey Clements (fig. 52)
© The Cleveland Museum of Art, 2000 (fig. 10)
Photograph © Davis Museum and Cultural Center, Wellesley College, Wellesley, Massachusetts, photo David Stansbury (fig. 45)
Photograph © 1994 The Detroit Institute of Arts (figs. 6, 7, 15); © 1985 (fig. 41)
Courtesy of the Fogg Art Museum, Harvard University Art Museums, Cambridge, Massachusetts, © President and Fellows of Harvard College, Harvard University, photo Katya Kallsens (fig. 68)
Collection of Jo Ann and Julian Ganz Jr. (fig. 57)
Reproduced by permission of The Huntington Library, San Marino, California (fig. 47)
Maier Museum of Art, Randolph-Macon Women's College, Lynchburg, Virginia (fig. 9)
Maryland Historical Society, Baltimore (fig. 1)
Mead Art Museum, Amherst College, Amherst, Massachusetts, photo Stephen Petegorsky (figs. 39, 54, 55)
All rights reserved, The Metropolitan Museum of Art, New York (fig. 29); © 1979 (fig. 40); © 1992 (fig. 48)
Munson-Williams-Proctor Arts Institute, Utica, New York (fig. 12)
Museum of Comparative Zoology, Harvard University, Cambridge, Massachusetts, photo © President and Fellows of Harvard College (fig. 62)
Courtesy, Museum of Fine Arts, Boston. Reproduced with permission. © 2000 Museum of Fine Arts, Boston. All Rights Reserved. (figs. 11, 66)
© 2000 Board of Trustees, National Gallery of Art, Washington, D.C. (figs. 25, 33)
National Park Service, Yellowstone National Park (figs. 67, 69, 70)
© Collection of The New-York Historical Society (figs. 18, 19, 21, 22, 23, 30, 31, 43, 56)
New York State Historical Association, Cooperstown (fig. 13)
Courtesy of the Pennsylvania Academy of the Fine Arts, Philadelphia (figs. 3, 27)
Reynolda House, Museum of American Art, Winston-Salem, North Carolina, photo Jackson Smith (fig. 32)
The Saint Louis Art Museum (fig. 53)
Smithsonian American Art Museum, Washington, D.C. (figs. 16, 71, 72)
Courtesy of the Society for the Preservation of New England Antiquities, Boston (fig. 61); photo Baldwin Coolidge (fig. 63); photo C. H. Newell (fig. 60)
Courtesy of Terra Museum of American Art, Chicago (fig. 59)
Wadsworth Atheneum, Hartford, Connecticut (figs. 17, 44)
The Warner Collection of Gulf States Paper Corporation, Tuscaloosa, Alabama (fig. 8)
Andrew M. K. Warren (figs. 14, 34, 35, 36)
The Washington County Museum of Fine Arts, Hagerstown, Maryland (fig. 65)
Yale University Art Gallery, New Haven, Connecticut (figs. 4, 28)

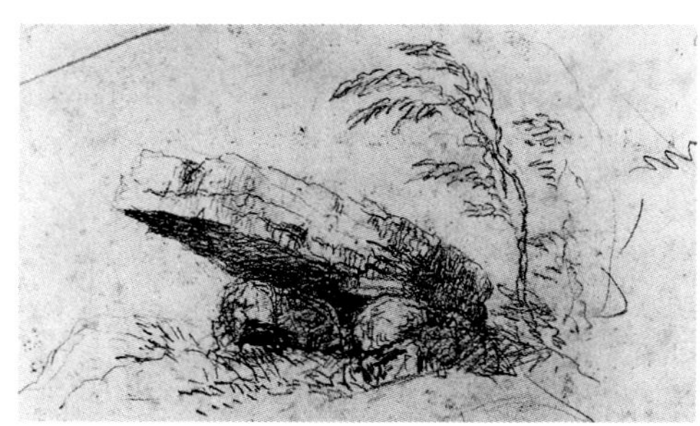

DESIGNED BY SUSAN MARSH

COMPOSED IN FILOSOFIA

BY DUKE & COMPANY, DEVON, PENNSYLVANIA

SEPARATIONS BY BRIGHT ARTS, HONG KONG

PRINTED ON 157GSM NIPPON PAPER MATT ART

PRINTED AND BOUND BY SOUTH CHINA PRINTING, HONG KONG

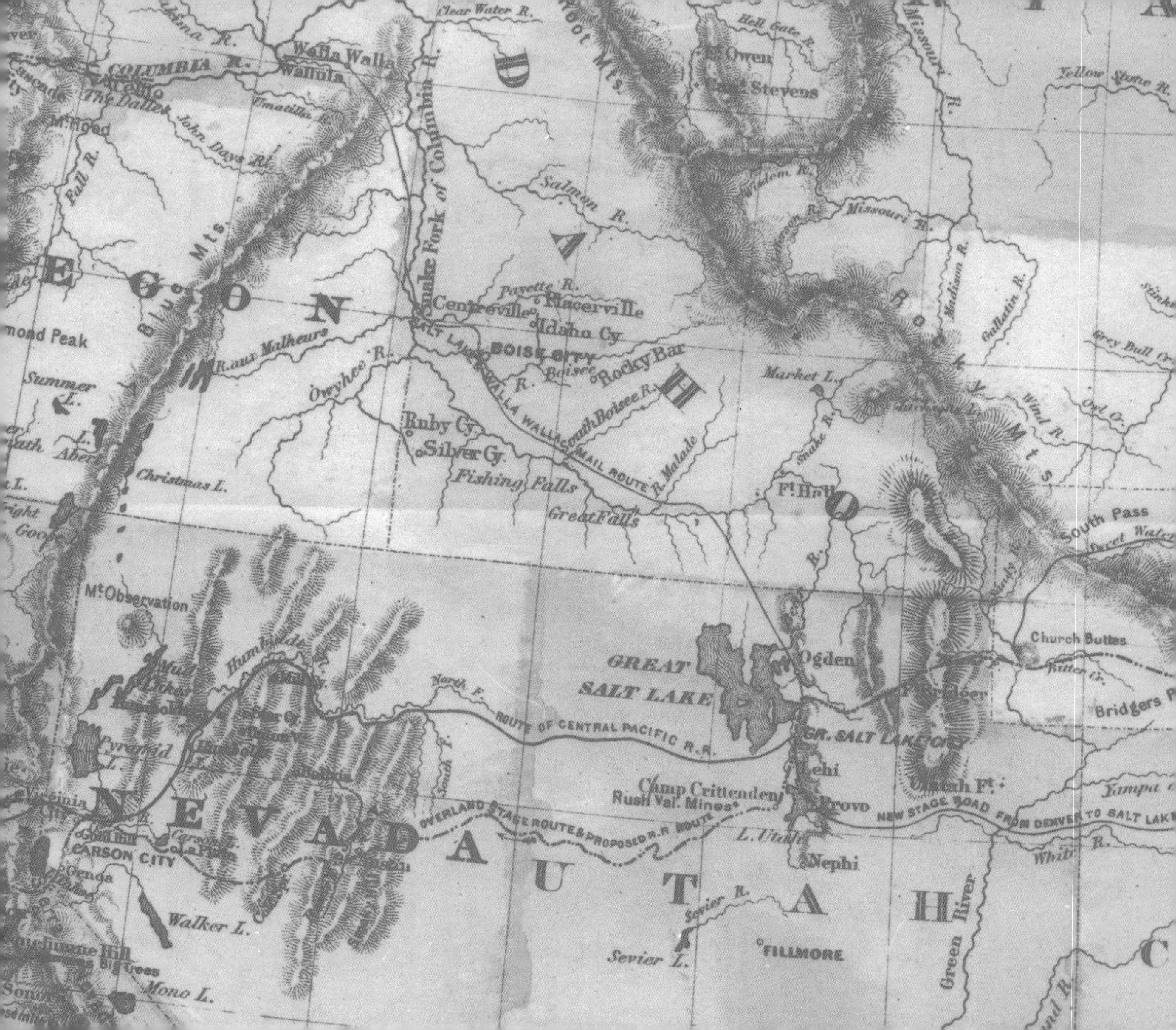

COLUMBIA R.
Walla Walla
Wallula
The Dalles
Mt. Hood
John Days R.
Umatilla R.
Clear Water R.
Hell Gate R.
Missouri R.
Ft. Owen
Cant. Stevens
Yellow Stone R.
Snake Fork of Columbia R.
Salmon R.
Wisdom R.
Missouri R.
Madison R.
Gallatin R.
Fall R.
Blue Mts.
Payette R.
Placerville
Centreville
Idaho Cy.
BOISE CITY
Rocky Bar
R. aux Malheurs
Owyhee R.
Boisee R.
South Boisee R.
Market L.
Grey Bull Cr.
Wind R.
Owl Cr.
Summer L.
Ruby Cy.
Silver Cy.
Fishing Falls
WALLA WALLA MAIL ROUTE
R. Malade
Snake R.
Christmas L.
Ft. Hall
Great Falls
South Pass
Sweet Water
Mt. Observation
ROCKY Mts.
Church Buttes
Bitter Cr.
GREAT SALT LAKE
Ogden
Humboldt R.
North F.
ROUTE OF CENTRAL PACIFIC R.R.
South F.
Bridgers P.
GR. SALT LAKE CITY
Pyramid L.
Lehi
Camp Crittenden
Rush Val. Mines
Provo
Uintah Ft.
Yampa
NEW STAGE ROAD FROM DENVER TO SALT LAKE
NEVADA
OVERLAND STAGE ROUTE & PROPOSED R.R. ROUTE
L. Utah
Nephi
White R.
CARSON CITY
Genoa
Walker L.
Sevier R.
UTAH
Green River
Sevier L.
FILLMORE
Big Trees
Mono L.